Lifelong Learning

Policies, Practices, and Programs

Edited by Michael J. Hatton

Canadian International
Development Agency

AN APEC-HURDIT NETWORK PROJECT

APEC

ASIA PACIFIC ECONOMIC COOPERATION

Association of Association
Canadian   des collèges
Community   communautaires
Colleges   du Canada

APEC Publication # 97-HR-01.5

Published by the School of Media Studies at Humber College
205 Humber College Boulevard, Toronto, Ontario, Canada M9W 5L7

Canadian Cataloguing in Publication Data

Main entry under title:

    Lifelong learning: policies, practices and programs

Includes bibliographical references.
ISBN 0-9682334-0-6

    1. Continuing education. I. Hatton, Michael J. (Michael John), 1948 -
II. Humber College of Applied Arts and Technology. School of Media Studies

LC5215.L497 1977   374   C97-900630-0

APEC publication #97-HR-01.5

This book was published with support from the Canadian International Development Agency. It is based on a project developed through the Association of Canadian Community Colleges, and has been endorsed and supported by the Asia Pacific Economic Cooperation (APEC) Forum's Human Resource Development (HRD) Working Group (WG).

The seal incorporated into the cover design of this book was adapted from Ch'i Pai-shih's seal, translated as, *I shall study as long as I breathe* (see page 172 of T. C. Lai's 1973 volume on Ch'i Pai-shih, published by Swindon). Ch'i Pai-shih was born in 1863, the year of the pig. An artist of extraordinary distinction, his life is the story of one person for whom living, learning and art were indistinguishable.

Cover concept by Melanie Cullimore. Page layout by Matthew Blackett. Editorial support from William Hanna, John Holland, Bethany Lee, James MacDonald, Patricia Meek, Michela Pasquali, and John Steckley. Production supervision by James Cullin. Production management by Peter Perko (Eye Cue Design). The electronic version of this book, designed by Bethany Lee, can be found at: *http://www.apec-hurdit.org*.

The ideas and opinions expressed in this book are those of the authors. They are not intended to represent those of the Asia Pacific Economic Cooperation Forum or its member economies, the Canadian International Development Agency, the organizations where the authors are employed or with whom the authors associate, or any other association, society or corporation whether mentioned or not in this book.

Printed in Canada on recycled paper.

Table of Contents

Preface	**v**
Acronyms	**vii**
Half a Revolution: A Brief Survey of Lifelong Learning in New Zealand *by Peter J. B. Methven and Jens J. Hansen*	**2**
HRD in a Multicultural Workplace: The Need For Lifelong Learning *by Motoyo Ogisu-Kamiya*	**18**
Lifelong Learning: The Whole DAMN Cycle — A Singapore Perspective *by Daphne Yuen Pan*	**34**
Advancing Lifelong Learning through Adult Education Policy in Chinese Taipei *by Cheng-Yen Wang*	**54**
Articulation and Transfer: Critical Contributions to Lifelong Learning *by Frederick C. Kintzer*	**68**
Trends in Hong Kong University Management: Towards a Lifelong Learning Paradigm *by Sandra Liu*	**84**
Lifelong Learning in a Developed and a Developing Economy *by Charles Beaupré*	**98**
An Empirical Framework for Implementing Lifelong Learning Systems *by Law Song Seng and Low Sock Hwee*	**112**
Lifelong Learning and Vision 2020 in Malaysia *by Yip Kai Leong*	**128**
Lifelong Learning and Basic Literacy: Adult Literacy Education in Chinese Taipei *by Ching-jung Ho*	**140**
Schools as Centres of Lifelong Learning for All *by Judith Chapman and David Aspin*	**154**
Lifelong Learning in the United States and Hong Kong: Before 1997 and After *by Albert H. Yee and Joseph Y. S. Cheng*	**168**
Lifelong Learning: An Instrument for Improving School Education in Japan? *by Yukiko Sawano*	**186**

Lifelong Learning in Hong Kong   202
by Grace O. M. Lee

Lifelong Learning and Cultural Identity: Canada's Native People   216
by Brian Rice and John Steckley

Non-formal Education in the Philippines: A Fundamental Step Towards Lifelong Learning   230
by Ma. Celeste T. Gonzales and Ma. Concepicon V. Pijano

Distance Education: A Key Strategy for Lifelong Learning in Chinese Taipei   242
by Judy Huang

Prior Learning Assessment: U.S. Experience Facilitating Lifelong Learning   256
by Carolyn M. Mann

Thoughts on a Regional Approach for Lifelong Learning   266
by Jiro Yoshio

Contribution of SMP Terbuka Toward Lifelong Learning in Indonesia   280
by Arief S. Sadiman and Rafael Rahardjo

Two Wheels for Lifelong Learning in Korea: Credit Banking & Multimedia Technology   292
by Min Sun Pak

Lifelong Learning, Workforce Development and Economic Success   302
by Alice Lee

From Supplemental Education to Lifelong Learning in Chinese Taipei   316
by Chuan Lee

Recent Developments in Japan's Lifelong Learning Society   328
by Atsushi Makino

Lifelong Learning in the People's Republic of China   346
by Huiping Wu and Qilian Ye

A Pure Theory of Lifelong Learning   360
by Michael J. Hatton

Preface

This book is one of the consequences of a broader project rooted in a thematic interest of the Asia Pacific Economic Cooperation (APEC) Forum's Human Resource Development (HRD) Working Group (WG). That project had as its overarching goal the development of dialogue pertinent to lifelong learning. The project included: (a) the development of an Asia Pacific database of organizations and individuals with specific interests in lifelong learning issues; (b) meetings, discussions and an international conference germane to lifelong learning; and (c) the publication of this book of papers which explores lifelong learning policies, practices and programs within the region.

Established in 1989, APEC is a policy-oriented organization that discusses economic and trade issues of interest to its 18 members. APEC's objectives include: sustaining economic growth within the region; enhancing gains resulting from increasing economic interdependence; developing and strengthening an open multilateral trading system; and reducing the barriers to trade in goods, services and investment among member economies and within the region. Critical to APEC is the notion that its most important purpose is to increase the quality of life for the people within the region, people being both the assets and the beneficiaries. Lifelong learning has attracted interest within the APEC agenda in that it is seen as a critical mechanism for fostering employment and supporting economic development.

APEC's current membership is diverse, though all member economies border on the Pacific. Included are Australia, Brunei, Canada, Chile, People's Republic of China, Hong Kong, Indonesia, Japan, Korea, Malaysia, Mexico, New Zealand, Papua New Guinea, the Philippines, Singapore, Chinese Taipei, Thailand and the United States of America. APEC economies have a combined GNP in excess of US$13 trillion, and represent more than 50% of world trade in merchandise, expected to rise to more than 70% within the next three years.

Within the past few years, the term lifelong learning has been described in different ways, and examined from various perspectives with a multiplicity of goals in mind. This book follows that tradition. However, as a starting point for reading and discussion, lifelong learning may be described inclusively as learning that occurs in or is related to formal educational and training institutions, including work-related on-the-job and off-the-job training, as well as broader learning within the community and in the home. Lifelong learning takes place throughout the lifespan.

Current issues associated with lifelong learning are many and varied. These issues include assessment of the foundations or platforms for lifelong learning; facilitating transitions between learning institutions and work; re-tooling or upgrading workforce skills; increasing participation rates in learning programs; particularly for women, the poor, and marginalized groups; the use of new technologies and new types of institutions to broaden learning opportunities; and the roles and responsibilities of government, publicly supported education and training institutions, the private sector, families, and the learners themselves with regard to developing, financing and participating in vocationally related and non-vocationally related lifelong learning programming.

The 34 authors who contributed the 26 papers in this volume are an eclectic group, something akin to the subject itself. They include scholars, researchers and practitioners, and were sifted from a group of more than 200 potential contributors. The authors reflect a variety of perspectives on what the issues are and how these should be addressed. In short, they are as distinct as the economies about which they write. Readers are cautioned that, within this text, analysis is often broad and conjectural in nature, the dominant purpose being to stimulate and encourage debate and discussion. The confidence to offer candid critique and commentary on the subject has been fundamental to the project.

The purpose of this book is to serve as a resource and, more importantly, to encourage and focus discussions that explore next steps for developing project work that within APEC will further the goals of identifying, examining, advancing and implementing activities related to lifelong learning. Within this context, it is important to recognize that developing the motivation for continuous learning within the population is a crucial end. Beyond that, APEC members must create structures that support the development of and access to learning opportunities throughout the lifespan (or remove structures that deter learning, including restrictive trade and mobility practices). What is needed are short term action plans, but with a long term perspective and framework.

Also needed is sensitivity to cultural heritage and stages of economic development. There is no single platform or plan that will suit all APEC member economies, just as there is no formal or informal learning program that suits all learners. However, the advantages to sharing ideas and perspectives through a forum such as that created by this book and the associated meetings include forging consensus with respect to action plans, helping to accelerate the implementation of policies and best practices, contributing to institutional capacity building, and creating network externalities — the benefits associated with an increased number of members contributing ideas and opinions on a given subject.

Learning throughout the lifespan is currently available for many of the most privileged in APEC member societies. What is needed is for all economies to ensure the widest possible access to learning opportunities.

Michael J. Hatton,
June 15, 1997

Acronyms

AAACE	American Association for Adult and Continuing Education
ABEP	Adult Basic Education Programs (Chinese Taipei)
ACCC	Association of Canadian Community Colleges
ACD	Advisory Committee on Diversification (Hong Kong)
ACE	American Council on Education
ACSC	Association of Christian Schools and Colleges (Philippines)
ACT	American College Testing Services
ACTS	Adult Cooperative Training Scheme (Singapore)
AEP	Accreditation Equivalency Program (Philippines)
APEC	Asia Pacific Economic Cooperaton (Forum)
ASEAN	Association of South East Asian Nations
ANTEP	Association for Non-Traditional Education in the Philippines
BEST	Basic Education for Skills Training (Singapore)
BNFE	Bureau of Non-Formal Education (Philippines)
CAEL	Council for Adult and Experiential Learning (U.S.A.)
CAEL	Cooperative Assessment of Experiential Learning (U.S.A.)
CBE	Competency-Based Education
CDAC	Chinese Development Assistance Council (Singapore)
CE	Continuing Education
CEAP	Catholic Educational Association of the Philippines
CET	Continuing Education and Training (Singapore)
CEU	Continuing Education Unit (U.S.A.)
CFE	Colleges of Further Education (Great Britian)
CHED	Commission on Higher Education (Philippines)
CLL	College of Lifelong Learning (U.S.A.)
CNC	Computer-aided Numerical Control
CoC	Certificate of Competency (Singapore)
COJTC	Certified On-the-Job Training Centre (Singapore)
CORT	Cognitive Research Trust (Singapore)
CPEP	College Proficiency Examination Program (U.S.A.)
COMETT	Community in Education and Training for Technology (U.S.A.)
DECS	Department of Education, Culture and Sports (Philippines)
DELSILIFE	Development of a Learning System for the Improvement of Life (Philippines)

EEC	European Economic Community
EFA	Education For All (Philippines)
ETS	Educational Testing Services (U.S.A.)
ERASMUS	European Community Action Scheme for Mobility of University Students
GCE	General Certificate of Education
HRD	Human Resource Development (both a generic term and also the acronym for one of APEC's Working Groups)
HEI	Higher Education Institute (Hong Kong)
HTML	Hypertext Markup Language
HURDIT	Human Resource Development in Industrial Technology (a Network within the APEC HRD Working Group)
IKIP	Institutes of Teachers' Education and Training (Indonesia)
ILO	International Labour Organization
IMD	International Management Development
INNOTECH	Regional Centre for Educational Innovation and Technology
ITC	Industrial Technician Certificate (Singapore)
ITE	Institute of Technical Education (Singapore)
IT	Information Technology
ITI	Information Technology Institute (Singapore)
LLDS	Lifelong Learning-Oriented Middle Stage Adult Education Development Scheme (Chinese Taipei)
MMT/Ls	Multimedia Teaching and Learning Resources
MOE	Ministry of Education (Chinese Taipei and Singapore)
MOHA	Ministry of Home Affairs (Indonesia)
MOI	Ministry of Information (Indonesia)
MORA	Ministry of Religious Affairs (Indonesia)
MOST	Modular Skills Training program (Singapore).
MSC	Multimedia Super Corridor (Malaysia)
NGO	Non-Governmental Organization
NCB	National Computer Board (Singapore)
NKIT	National Kaohsiung Institute of Technology (Chinese Taipei)
NMYC	National Manpower and Youth Council (Philippines)
NSTB	National Science and Technology Board (Singapore)
NTC	National Technical Certificate (Singapore)
NTUC	National Trades Union Congress (Singapore)
NUS	National University of Singapore
ODA	Overseas Development Assistance
OECD	Organization for Economic Cooperation and Development
OLI	Open Learning Institute (Hong Kong)
OJT	On-the-Job Training
PAASCU	Philippine Accrediting Association of Schools, Colleges and Universities
PEPT	Philippines Educational Placement Test
PLA	Prior Learning Assessment

PONSI	Program on Noncollegiate-Sponsored Instruction (U.S.A.)
PQLI	Physical Quality of Life Index
PRC	People's Republic of China
PRISNANFE	Private Institutions and Schools National Association in Non-Formal Education (Philippines)
REAP	Rural Education Activities Programs (New Zealand)
REDP	Regents External Degree Program (U.S.A.)
RRI	Radio Republik Indonesia
SDF	Skills Development Fund (Singapore)
SDL	Self-Directed Learning (Malaysia)
SEAMEO	South East Asian Ministers of Education Organization
SEP	Supplementary Education Programs for the Stages of Fundamental Schooling (Grade 1 through Grade 9) (Chinese Taipei)
SINDA	Singapore Indians Association
SIPA	Science-Based Industrial Park (Chinese Taipei)
SMEs	Small- and Medium-sized Enterprises
SMILE	Students' Multimedia Integrated Learning Environment (Singapore)
SUNY	State University of New York
TAD	Technology and Applications Development (Canada)
TESDA	Technical Education and Skills Development Authority (Philippines)
TIME	Training Initiative for Mature Employees (Singapore)
TIMSS	Third International Mathematics and Science Study
TQC	Total Quality Control (Japan)
TVRI	Telvisi Republik Indonesia
UCLA	University of California at Los Angeles
UGC	University Grants Committee (Hong Kong)
UP	University of the Philippines
UPGC	University and Polytechnics Grants Committee (Hong Kong)
UNESCO	United Nations Educational, Scientific and Cultural Organization
UPOU	University of the Philippines Open University
VITB	Vocational Industrial Training Board (Singapore)
VRML	Virtual Reality Markup Language
WCC	Whole Construction of Community (Chinese Taipei)
WEA	Workers' Educational Association (Australia, Great Britian, New Zealand)
WISE	Worker Improvement through Secondary Education (Singapore)

Lifelong Learning

Peter J. B. Methven

and Jens J. Hansen

Peter Methven holds an Honours Degree in Economics from the London School of Economics. His career has been eclectic, including employment in accounting, secondary school teaching, community education organizing, polytechnic management, computer programming and government policy analysis. Currently, he is manager of the Qualifications Evaluation Service, a component within the New Zealand Qualifications Authority. In this role, he has written and edited key documents pertaining to New Zealand's qualifications reforms as well as a host of government policy papers on education-related topics. His leisure time interests include fine wine, good food, concert music, golf, and crime and fantasy fiction.

Jens J. Hansen holds a Ph.D. in Adult Learning from the University of New England in Armidale, Australia. As an educator, sociologist and distance education specialist, he has worked in community and adult education, and has a special passion for rural education and the use of simple technologies as they can be applied to adult learning. Currently, Dr. Hansen teaches research methodologies at The Open Polytechnic of New Zealand. His own research focuses on the identification, evaluation and application of tele-learning, and on strategies for the establishment of tele-cottages. A strong family person, his avocations include fine wine and good food (often with Peter and his partner), as well as building and badminton.

Half a Revolution:
A Brief Survey of Lifelong Learning in New Zealand

by Peter J. B. Methven and Jens J. Hansen

This paper examines lifelong learning both generally and in relation to education and training reforms in New Zealand. It is argued that, while a lifelong learning philosophy may arise spontaneously within any culture, its effective implementation is almost certainly influenced as much by the nature of the culture itself and by the educational infrastructure that the culture supports, as by its intrinsic merits. Examples are drawn from both the New Zealand experience and from international developments. It is noted that the transformation of a traditional structure into a framework for lifelong learning has the potential to create counter-productive tensions between educational stakeholders that, in the absence of a supportive culture and infrastructure, undermine the benefits that might otherwise emerge. Although such tensions may be considered an inevitable outcome of developing a national lifelong learning culture, and may cause temporary dislocations of process within education and training, it is suggested that a national climate of flexible entry and active participation in lifelong learning is a significant foundation for economic well-being. It becomes necessary, therefore, for stakeholders to foster and develop both a learning culture as well as associated systems and processes that provide individuals with equitable access to learning opportunities throughout their lives. Without doubt, the role of government in facilitating such development is pivotal.

The growth of the APEC member economies and the opening of those economies to freer trade and investment through the adoption of open regionalism has imposed changing human resource requirements demanding dynamic policy responses in terms of education and training at basic, vocational and professional levels. (Braddock 1996, p. 1)

INTRODUCTION

Education and training systems are generated in concordance with the value systems and contextual infrastructures of societies.[1] Educational values are generally, although not always, congruent to the values held and promoted by the encom-

---

[1] In the context of this paper *education* will be understood to subsume *training*. This expedient acknowledges the extensive debate surrounding these terms, and the traditional academic-vocational divide.

passing culture. The educational infrastructure, closely interconnected with the social and economic infrastructure, is that web of legislation, funding, institutions, training, curriculum, assessment regimes, and qualifications systems that supports or inhibits educational activities.

An education system, therefore, is at once a proactive and responsive entity within society that influences, and is influenced by, society's other dynamics. It operates amid a web of "cardinal" (super-ordinate or explicit) tensions (for example, government policies of academic accountability and audit versus the idea of academic freedom) and "manifold" (subordinate or implicit) tensions (market forces versus individual learning needs, for instance).[2] These too are variables within the dynamic.

Many economies have education systems rooted in an apparently European cultural tradition. Their characteristics are that:

- children up to the age of adolescence acquire basic knowledge and skills at a primary school, usually local;

- a selection process at the end of primary education is used to determine individual placement in a particular type of secondary school;

- adolescents continue their learning, often in a larger and more distant secondary school, initially following programs of broad general studies but with increasing specialisation as they advance to senior secondary school;

- a further selection process at the end of secondary education determines placement in one of several possible types of tertiary institution;

- tertiary institutions are overtly divided between those providing academic learning and those providing vocational learning;

- at all levels, norm-referenced (ranking) tests and examinations form the prime evidence from which achievement and progress is assessed;

- and control of the education system is vested in a Ministry or Department of Education.

The traditional education system celebrates academic excellence. Its structure facilitates the identification and deployment of scholarly achievers. It was, and remains, time-based and teacher-centred, with programs arranged by academic year, term or semester. On exit, graduates, whether holders of a school leaving certificate or of an advanced degree, are typically considered to have been *educated for life* in whatever field of employment (including academia) they have qualified. Under the traditional regime, the business of the teacher is to confer knowledge. Concomitantly, the business of the learner is to absorb what is taught. The traditional system has been, and still is in the minds of many educationists, a *front-end* preparation for future employment.

---

[2] English (1995) has adopted "cardinal" and "manifold" tensions as the central theme in his explanation of cross-cultural trade negotiations.

Such systems tend to be inert, orderly, bureaucratic, and resistant to change. They typically satisfy the perceived needs of societies in which the pace of social and technological change is modest and employment for life in a single occupation is perceived as the norm (Innis, 1986; Meecham, 1987). Such conservatism may, it should be noted, result in educationists becoming sheltered in progressive isolation from society: autonomy can become insularity, tradition a straitjacket, and structural self-transformation a mechanism for apparent innovation without real change.

Clearly, the inherent weakness of a system in which it is assumed that one can be *educated for life* is that life itself changes. This has never been more evident than in the latter half of this century. Such populist writers as McLuhan (1964), Bell (1974), and Toffler (1980) have adopted as their major theme the frenetic pace and consequences of cultural acceleration. Their original insights have become truisms over time, not merely from the effect of the scientific-technological revolution, which has itself been exponential, but equally from interwoven social, political and economic transformation.

If individuals, organisations, and economies are to maintain control over, rather than be controlled by, their ever-changing social and economic environment, they must first understand it. This can be achieved only by actively building on the reservoir of human knowledge and skills through the acquisition of new knowledge and skills, as they arise and as they are needed. Hence, importance is being given increasingly to continuing professional education, 'just-in-time' recurrent training, and adult education programs (Marsick, 1987, 1988; Marsick and Watkins, 1990; Brennan, 1990).

Such considerations have revived, and to a large extent transformed, the concept of *lifelong learning*. In its beginnings, and under other names, it was perceived as an instrument of social change and an augmentor of economic advancement. Initially, in the form of *mechanics' institutes* or *mutual improvement societies,* and later in the guise of *adult, continuing* or *community education,* lifelong learning was originally a working class movement whose purpose was the intellectual, economic and political betterment of those who might otherwise remain an ill-paid, badly-housed, poorly-educated reservoir of cheap labour and occasional cannon-fodder. Lifelong learning's extension, in the first half of the century, was interwoven with the rise of socialism in its various forms, trade unionism, and the embryonic welfare state. Its intention initially was magnanimously liberal (Jarvis, 1987; Merriam and Caffarella, 1991).

In Brazil, Freire (1972) employed basic education and literacy programs in a radical sense for the *conscientizacion* of the masses so that the populace could become *politicised,* and hence influential within the society. Coombs and Ahmed (1974) and Schramm (1977) describe similar development strategies that have been employed in Asia.

From the mid-century on, the lifelong learning movement has survived (albeit, frequently undernourished) against a background of world-wide economic fluctuation. Consequently, enthusiasm and support for adult education have been cyclical in most Western countries, with successive governments alternating policies of relative liberalism and relative authoritarianism. Much of the original idealism associated with the idea of lifelong learning now appears to have evaporated, and seems to have been replaced by an economic agenda (although what is really needed may be a human resource development agenda).

Lifelong learning policies, structures and practices articulate into learning ideologies that implicitly or explicitly can be embedded into a range of adult education philosophies (Merriam and Caffarella, 1991). Underlying many of these is the (virtually self-evident) truth that knowledge and its applications are fluid: that is, they change continuously, so that much learning becomes outdated even as it is achieved. Consequently, societies need to create educational opportunities that are accessible to all individuals at all times in their lives so that new learning needs are able to be met whenever and wherever they arise. Ideally, learners themselves are able to identify those needs or, if they cannot, they are at least able to obtain guidance as to how their needs might be validly assessed and reliably met. A principal concern of the lifelong learning 'teacher', whose role is more that of a facilitator, is to see that learning needs are identified and provided for.

Lifelong learning systems are characterised by:

- individualised learning, directed by negotiation between the teacher and the learner;

- flexibility of programs, so that learning can occur at times and places that suit the learner;

- an absence of selection processes, enabling learners to proceed at a pace and in a direction that meets their individual needs;

- a blurring of barriers between different types of institutions and the learning workplace, so that credit from one is honoured by all;

- and governance of the learning process by individuals and communities of interest.

A lifelong learning culture is flexible, creative, and responsive. It satisfies the needs of societies in which the pace of social and technological change is accelerating and within which a succession of disparate occupations is becoming the norm for those in employment.

In many economies, the post-school learning sector, though inherently vibrant, tends to languish when denied external support. In Australia, for example, the lifelong learning movement has been equated with a Cinderella that needs constantly to be rescued from the ashes (Senate Standing Committee on Employment, 1991). In New Zealand, Hansen (1972),[3] Harré Hindmarsh (1992), and Harré Hindmarsh, Bell, Addison, Gunn and McGray (1993) have made explicit the decline of this sector when government funding is removed.

---

[3]Hansen surveyed all secondary schools within the province of Auckland and found that, after the withdrawal of government subsidies, the number of non-vocational classes fell by 29% (i.e. from 468 in 1972 to 332 in 1973). At the same time, the number of vocational classes grew by 12.5%.

THE NEW ZEALAND CONTEXT

The success or failure of a learning culture rests on two important pre-conditions. It must allow *access* to those with learning needs, and provide *opportunities* for those needs to be met. Neither is of utility without the other. In the highly competitive market economies that are developing currently, there are few to whom educational access is inconsequential, although it may, for political or economic reasons, be withheld. Even where access is unrestricted, the infrastructure underpinning learning opportunities may be deficient. This is well illustrated by the development of post-school learning in New Zealand.

With its brief history, geographical isolation and small population, New Zealand is a society in which change can occur quickly, and cause and effect remain relatively easy to disentangle. In the late nineteenth century, from a foundation in middle-class English and Scottish values, New Zealand rapidly established a universal education system funded by the state. As in its Old World model, the path to professional life lay through the universities and was essentially elitist. Primary and secondary schooling acted as a filter for the scholarly. Those who failed to clear an approved succession of academic hurdles, or for whom the marginal utility of an extra family wage exceeded that of further learning, concluded their formal education at the point at which they fell or withdrew.

Access to post-school learning was restricted, at this stage of the country's history, to an intellectual and economic elite. A further minority became tradespeople through apprenticeship programs, while the majority became labourers by default. Educational opportunities were limited, as a consequence, to academic or work-based preparation for the trades and professions.

The real beginnings of lifelong learning in New Zealand, in the sense of providing on-demand access and opportunity throughout adult life, stemmed from the formation in 1914-15 of Workers' Educational Associations (WEAs) in the nation's five main settlements of Auckland, Wellington, Christchurch, Dunedin, and Invercargill. They emerged as a result of cooperation between trade unions and the four regional colleges of the University of New Zealand, which was in turn inspired by 'missionary' visits from Australian and British WEAs. Government funding of the WEA national council (channeled, according to the conventions of the day, through the universities) began in 1920, and a National Council for Adult Education was established by statute eighteen years later.

Many distinguished political figures, including the Hon. Peter Fraser, the Minister of Education who piloted a far-reaching Education Act of 1938, laid the foundations for their careers in WEA classrooms. The underlying motivation was often to 'better oneself' through education and consequent economic and social advancement. It is worth noting, however, that although the WEA of the time offered an *alternative means of entry* to the established system, it was not, of itself, a genuine alternative. The educational culture remained essentially unchanged. Except for a marginal widening of access for the most able, secondary school qualifications (*matriculation*) remained the accepted (front-end) precursor to entry into higher education. Moreover, such education remained the sole mode of preparation for a professional career, and final entry into a higher occupation was contingent upon the aspirant having successfully completed successive stages of academic preparation.

In the post-war period, little changed beyond a more liberal allocation of state funding. Evening classes at secondary schools attracted increasing numbers of adults, as did the emerging technical institutes, whose main purpose was the training of apprentice tradespeople and technicians. Non-mainstream adult learning, however, was largely confined to 'second-chance' school qualifications and hobby classes. The 'community education' contribution of university extension departments of the time tended to focus on the visits of itinerant academics to distant communities, where they lectured on the arcane, picturesque, and only occasionally relevant. ("Byzantine influences on Renaissance architecture" is an example, quoted to one of the authors by a rural activist of the 1950s.) Access had widened to an extent, but opportunities for learning had not. This was not lost on such seminal New Zealand education writers of the day as Garrett (1984) and Shallcrass (1987) who, like their predecessors of the 1920s, applauded the social and economic merits of a comprehensive lifelong learning culture.

From the mid-1970s, an increasingly vocal community education movement began lobbying for meaningful adult education, championing this process as an agent of social improvement. Clients of the sector included the unemployed and occupationally redundant, the physically and mentally handicapped, cultural minorities, and women, for whom access to learning was an unacknowledged need. The assumption that adult education could serve as a vehicle for social change seemed to spawn a logic that the greater the amount of adult education provided, the greater would be the consequent social change. (The proposition is clearly brittle, given that such variables as appropriateness and quality are equally pivotal.) As a result, the range of education and training opportunities offered by the technical institutes and semi-voluntary community education services expanded rapidly.

It was unfortunate that this positive shift in the prevailing educational culture coincided with an economic downturn and a reflexive tightening of government fiscal policy that progressively undermined the supportive infrastructure. The conservative politicians of the day derided publicly, and somewhat disingenuously, the prospect of providing state funding for 'pottery classes and sewing circles'.

Nonetheless, the government did, because of pressure from strong rural interests and (it was claimed) for electoral advantage, establish thirteen Rural Education Activities Programmes (REAPs). These were staffed by professional educators covering the full spectrum from early childhood to adult learning (Hansen 1983, 1987; Nash, 1983). The level to which each area was resourced appeared to be a corollary of the degree to which that area was electorally vulnerable. It is clear, however, that access to and opportunities for learning in rural areas did, as a result, proliferate.

At the same time, state funding to other community and adult learning agencies was drastically reduced. The REAPs remained because they were protected by strong rural lobby groups and by the susceptibility to electoral change of the voting areas within which they had been established. Further, during the 1980s, REAPs assumed a *de facto* leadership of the adult education movement and were the strongest supporters of the National Association of Community and Continuing

Education. By contrast, less protected organisations had their funding reduced or rescinded. The WEA's was halved. The National Council for Adult Education, instituted by the 1938 Act, was disestablished. The culture of lifelong learning, barely initiated in New Zealand, was again marginalised, surviving with much voluntary effort but scant official support over the next decade. The state education sector, meanwhile, maintained credentialism in time-honoured fashion by turning out ever-increasing numbers of regulation certificate, diploma and degree holders. Those outside the traditional systems continued to agitate for improved access and opportunity.

The harsh economic climate of the late 1980s precipitated a series of Treasury-inspired educational reforms whose effects are still being absorbed. Its outlines, ironically, are in a report titled *Learning for Life* (New Zealand Government, 1989). Nonetheless, for the first time the state accepted the paradigm that learning is lifelong and, perhaps naively, that it is a stimulus to economic development.[4] The policies outlined in *Learning for Life*, and those subsequently refined from them (Methven, Goddard and Thompson, 1994), include:

- the replacement of traditional qualifications with qualifications based upon standards established by stakeholders, including government, employers, teaching institutions, workers' associations, and learners – more or less in that order;

- seamless education – that is, lifelong education and training obtainable across a range of learning environments, including the workplace, and of comparable validity for credit and certification;

- an industry training strategy that includes training entitlements for the unemployed, and for traditionally disadvantaged groups;

- and student support through allowances and loans.

It should be emphasised that, although some acknowledgment of social and equity goals was made in *Learning for Life* (New Zealand Government, 1989) and in concurrent reports on education, the agenda of government and business was, from then on, driven mainly by economic imperatives, with free-market orthodoxy as the underpinning philosophy. For these stakeholders, at least, it appears that quality of life has become synonymous with competitive advantage.

As a consequence of the report's recommendations, the central and regional offices of New Zealand's Department of Education were disestablished. In their place appeared a policy Ministry, a qualifications authority, an education and training support agency whose role has evolved to focus on coordination of industry training, an education review office with inspectorial functions in the school sector, and a career advisory service. (A number of 'consumer protection' agencies in the education sector – for example, a Parents' Advocacy Council – sank without trace within months of the relevant legislation's enactment.) Governance of state institu-

---

[4]There is a school of thought that attributes economic advancement entirely to scientific-technological progression, a debate in which the authors offer no opinion. They hold the position that education is at least a component of economic survival, whatever its role as a catalyst.

tions was devolved to school boards of trustees and tertiary councils. The growth and registration of private training establishments were encouraged. The foundations for a new education and training culture were laid, but under a regime of free market forces rather than the libertarianism of the post-war period. From 1984, when the first reformist government was elected, to the present, the reforms have been pursued with an almost religious fervour by successive administrations.

THE QUALIFICATIONS FRAMEWORK

Central to the establishment of the new education culture is the National Qualifications Framework (Methven et al., 1994). This replaces a plethora of disparate credentials, course-based and institution-centred in the traditional pattern, administered by fifty-three separate examining boards and agencies. The Framework is built upon the assessment *standard*, a short statement of the desired outcomes for a discrete learning area.[5] Sets of such standards articulate into complete *qualifications*. Being neither content- nor time-specific, standards can be used as the basis for a wide range of education and training programs, both institution and work based. Each is assigned a *level* within an eight-tier structure, and a *credit* value reflecting its 'size' in terms of learning effort. Over a five year period, standards have been developed for most of New Zealand's major occupational areas and are beginning to extend to general subjects at senior secondary school level. They have been resisted by the universities, on the grounds that the outcomes of metacognitive learning are too complex to define with the particularity that standards are understood to demand, and that assessment standards frequently become articulated as units of curriculum, which clearly they should not.

New Zealand's example is being paralleled or followed by a number of other countries. Australia has created a national vocational standards framework and is proceeding with a national qualifications framework. South Africa has set up the South African Qualifications Authority (SAQA) based on the New Zealand model. Britain's standards-based Scottish National Certificate and National Vocational Qualifications are well established, and the Welsh (education) Office has a standards-based framework. The USA is beginning to implement National Skills Standards. In each of these examples, a need has been perceived for competence-based assessment standards, particularly in vocational areas, to replace and transcend competitive (group-referenced) qualifications of the past.

The creation of a framework of standards-based assessment makes possible the development of a seamless education and training culture in which credit can be earned in a variety of formal, occupational, and community settings. In theory, such credit can be transferred readily from one learning environment to another, and accumulated across several such environments until a qualification is completed: for example, a qualification may be started at school, continued in a workplace training program, and completed at a tertiary institution. Lifelong learning opportunities are enhanced accordingly, since occasions for earning credit are not limited to specific

---

[5]Unit standards, later *registered standards,* in New Zealand, *NVQs* in the United Kingdom, *competency standards* in Australia.

programs at specific institutions. It is important to note that, in practice, institutions continue to raise barriers to credit transfer, usually (it appears to the external observer) to preserve market advantage.

The process of implementing the Qualifications Framework is incomplete at the time of writing. Nonetheless:

- nearly 100,000 New Zealand learners are 'hooked-on' to the Qualifications Framework, including 50% of senior secondary students and nearly 20,000 Maori, previously considered an educationally disadvantaged group[6];

- a total of 652 teaching institutions, including 82% of secondary schools, are accredited to deliver programs leading to Framework credit;

- and 22 industry training organisations are accredited to register assessors in the workplace (New Zealand Qualifications Authority statistics).

As Fullan (1993) has observed, however, nowhere is resistance to change more evident than in education. The way teachers are trained, the way learning institutions are organised, the way the educational hierarchy operates, and the way that education is treated by political decision makers, all work to create a sub-culture preconditioned to defence of the *status quo*. This is happening in New Zealand, with a concerted effort by traditional institutions to overturn or stand aside from the reforms (New Zealand Vice Chancellors' Committee, 1994; Hall, 1994), strongly supported by those in business (Irwin, 1994) and in government (see, for example, New Zealand Treasury briefing papers to incoming governments, 1984 to 1993) who are opposed on philosophical grounds to state involvement in the provision of social services.

Consequently, although opportunities in education beyond junior secondary school have broadened as a result of the reforms, many educationists cling to the course-based institution-centred programs of the past: in short, to be ruled by habit and tradition. In this they are abetted by a devolution towards institutional autonomy and by a system of state funding that is directed towards the subsidy of courses rather than outputs, and time-on-task rather than learning achievements. Thus, the inherent resistance of the educational establishment and the wholly disparate influence of free-market influences combine to resist the opportunities the new culture was intended to provide.

It could be postulated that empowerment of learners through government funding or employer support might have provided a counter-balance to the dead hand of conservatism. Neither eventuated. A relatively generous regime of state-subsidised tuition fees and learner support has been eroded by the whittling away of institutional *per capita* funding, a substitution of commercial loans for student allowances, and limits to eligibility for means-tested government assistance. The increasing financial burden on learners has been exacerbated further by structural unemployment leading to fewer part-time and short-term vacation jobs. Eligibility for such govern-

---

[6]Given that the Maori, New Zealand's indigenous people, form approximately 10% of the total population, the 20% Maori take-up of Framework programmes is significant.

ment funding as is available is allocated largely to traditional courses in secondary and tertiary institutions. This includes NZ$393.5 million for polytechnics, NZ$46.5 million for teachers' colleges and NZ$608.5 million for universities in 1995/96 (New Zealand Treasury, 1996). The capacity of learners, therefore, to influence through 'consumer power' a greater flexibility in the education and training infrastructure has been repressed.

Employers are key stakeholders in the education and training culture, but this is, despite some inspiring examples to the contrary, a role tardily acknowledged. Nonetheless, employers' organisations in, for example, Britain, the United States, Japan and Australasia, are increasingly involved in the promotion and implementation of training programs at national and local levels. In some countries (Sweden, Japan and Australia, among others) trades unions also assume a leadership role in education and training, because they view ongoing training as a means of improving the economic standing of their members. In other economies, such as New Zealand, trades unions have ceased to be educational providers, after governmental support for union-driven education was first eroded and then altogether removed. The advent of the Qualifications Framework in New Zealand has created some enthusiasm in industry training circles for new forms of occupational preparation, and this has been buttressed by state funding that in 1995/96 included NZ$47 million for industry training and NZ$191 million for pre-employment training (New Zealand Treasury, 1996). However, overall support from industry remains uneven.

The successful establishment of a lifelong learning culture in New Zealand is restrained by a number of tensions, therefore, between:

• free market principles and the public good;

• reformist aims and sectoral conservatism;

• public accountability and academic freedom;

• and national education and training standards and autonomous education and training delivery.

Despite this, the new wave of standards-based learning has probably reached critical mass, and there are few involved in the field of industrial training, for example, who need to be convinced of its merits. Whether the system that is being established is more profit-driven than people-driven remains a moot point that social scientists (and the education sector) should continue to debate. The obstacles that remain – opposition within the educational establishment, inequities implicit in increased private funding and indebtedness of learners, efforts by lobby groups to have traditional qualifications put on an equal footing with standards-based qualifications, among others – should dissolve with time, if the new structure has the merits claimed by its adherents.

LESSONS LEARNED

New Zealand's educational reforms appear to have created their own paradox, in promoting standards while permitting non-compliance, advocating access and opportunity while offering little in the way of real incentives to either. The prevailing political and economic culture, under the influence of monetarist principles, has become adamantly market-oriented in philosophy and practice, the latter reinforced by regulation (termed *de-regulation* in official circles). Successive governments have adopted or been persuaded into free-market policies that conflict with the growth of a coordinated human resource development strategy.

The lesson the reforms deliver is that half a revolution is not enough. To create access without opportunity, or opportunity without access, is a failure of policy. Corrective activity by the government (or by a powerful proxy within society – for example, industry) to support the acquisition of marketable knowledge and skills for all members, first, of the work force and, second, of society in general, will invariably be necessary. This creates a paradox for proponents of the free market, in that the behaviour required to ensure its success, at least in the upskilling and maintenance of a proficient work force, is seen at best as interventionist and at worst as coercive. Neo-classical purists, therefore, appear to be advocating latently dysfunctional strategies, which will not only influence the delivery of essential learning to society, but will also deprive them indefinitely of the work force competencies they need for economic survival.

A pragmatic solution for most economies perhaps lies in the nurturing of large-scale education and training partnerships between the state, employers, workers' associations, and communities. Such structures will vary naturally from economy to economy, according to intrinsic cultural, political and economic preferences. Strategies for the resourcing and implementation of lifelong learning initiatives will, consequently, be equally divergent. It is inevitable, however, that those economies continuing to cherish learning cultures and infrastructures inappropriate to the demands of a global market will thereby limit educational access and opportunities for significant groups within their work forces and general population. The downstream effects may be slow to emerge but will be inescapably damaging. For lack of a flexibly trained and responsive working population, they will struggle to maintain a position in the world economy.

The future ... belongs to societies that organise themselves for learning. What we know and can do holds the key to economic progress, just as command of natural resources once did. Everything depends on what firms can learn from and teach to their customers and suppliers, on what countries can learn from one another, on what workers can learn from each other and the work they do, on the learning environments that families provide, and, of course, on what we learn in school. More than ever before, nations that want high incomes and full employment must develop policies that emphasise the acquisition of knowledge and skills by everyone, not just a select few. The prize will go to those countries that are organised as national learning systems, and where all institutions are organised to learn and act on what they learn.

Marshall and Tucker (1992, p. xiii)

REFERENCES

Bell, D. (1974). *The Coming of post industrial society*. London: Heinemann.

Braddock, R. (1996). *Collaborative labour market policy studies for the APEC region*. Sydney: Asia Pacific Research Institute.

Brennan, B. (1990). Mandatory or voluntary continuing professional education: Is there really an option for professional association? *Proceedings of Continuing Professional Education Conference* (pp. 109-117). Auckland: Centre for Continuing Education, University of Auckland.

Coombs, P. H. & Ahmed, M. (1974). *Attacking rural poverty: How nonformal education can help*. Baltimore: John Hopkins University Press.

English, A. W. (1995). *The double headed arrow: Australian managers in the business context of Asia*. Unpublished doctoral dissertation, University of New England, Armidale.

Freire, Paulo (1972). *Pedagogy of the oppressed*. United Kingdom: Sheed and Ward.

Fullan, M. (1993). *Change forces: Probing the depths of educational reform*. United Kingdom: Falmer Press.

Garrett, D. (Ed.). (1984). *Garrett on education*. Wellington: Tutor Training Unit for New Zealand Technical Institutes.

Hall, C. (1994). *Obstacles to the integration of university qualifications and courses into the National Qualifications Framework*. Wellington: Victoria University of Wellington.

Hansen, J. J. (1972). *The withdrawal of funding and the decline of hobby classes in the Auckland region*. Auckland: Community Activities Section, Auckland Regional Authority.

Hansen, J. J. (1983). Assessing rural education needs. *New Zealand Journal of Adult Learning, 15*, 39-52.

Hansen, J. J. (1987). Introducing a teleconferencing network to the most remote region of New Zealand. *Australian Journal of Educational Technology, 3*(2), 151- 172.

Harré Hindmarsh, J. (1992). Community and continuing education in 1992: Trends and issues. In H. Manson (Ed.), *New Zealand Annual Review of Education* (pp. 179-204). Wellington: Victoria University of Wellington.

Harré Hindmarsh, J., Bell, A., Addison, A., Gunn, C., & McGray, D. (1993). Community and continuing education in 1993. Who is deciding? Who is benefiting? In H. Manson (Ed.), *New Zealand Annual Review of Education* (pp. 285-318). Wellington: Victoria University of Wellington.

Innis, H. A. (1986). *Empire & communications.* Victoria, British Columbia: Press Porcépic.

Irwin, M. (1994). *Curriculum, assessment and qualifications: An evaluation of current reforms.* Wellington: New Zealand Business Round Table for the New Zealand Education Forum.

Jarvis, P. (Ed.). (1987). *Twentieth century thinkers in adult education.* London: Croom Helm.

Marshall, R. & Tucker, M. (1992). *Thinking for a living: Education and the wealth of nations.* New York: Basic Books.

Marsick, V. J. (Ed.). (1987). *Learning in the workplace.* London: Croom Helm.

Marsick, V. J. (Ed.). (1988). *Enhancing staff development in diverse settings.* San Francisco: Jossey-Bass.

Marsick, V. J., & Watkins, K. E. (1990). *Informal and incidental learning in the workplace.* London: Routledge.

McLuhan, M. (1964). *Understanding media: The extensions of man.* London: Sphere Books Ltd.

Meacham, D. (1987). Keep your distance. Educational technology: Bandwagon or hearse; Telematics or masturbatics! (As cited in Hansen, 1987, pp. 170-171) *Australia South Pacific External Studies Association.*

Merriam, S. B., & R. S. Caffarella (1991). *Learning in adulthood.* San Francisco: Jossey Bass.

Methven, P., Goddard, P., & Thompson, T. (1994). *The National Qualifications Framework: Issues.* Wellington: New Zealand Qualifications Authority.

Nash, R. (1983). *Schools can't make jobs.* Palmerston North: Dunmore Press.

New Zealand Government (1989). *Learning for life: Education and training beyond the age of fifteen* and *Learning for life: Two.* Wellington: Government Printing Office.

NZ Treasury (1996). *Estimates of appropriations for the government of New Zealand.* Wellington: New Zealand Treasury.

New Zealand Vice Chancellors' Committee. (1994). *The National Qualifications Framework and the universities.* Wellington: New Zealand Vice Chancellors' Committee.

OECD. (1995). *Education at a glance.* Paris: Author.

Schramm, W. (1977). *Big media, little media: Tools & technologies for instruction.* Beverly Hills: Sage.

Senate Standing Committee on Employment, Education and Training. (1991). *Come in, Cinderella: The emergence of adult and community education*. Canberra: Senate Publications Unit.

Shallcrass, J. (1987). *He Tangata – it is the people*. (Report of the Interim Advisory Group on Non-formal Education.) Wellington: Government Printing Office.

Toffler, A. (1980). *The Third Wave*. New York: Morrow.

Motoyo Ogisu-Kamiya

Motoyo Ogisu-Kamiya holds a Master of Social Science degree from Meji Gakuin Graduate School (Japan) and a Ph.D. from the University of Toronto (Canada). Currently, she is Corporate Secretary and Senior Manager, Head Office Administration & Human Resources at Marubeni Canada Ltd. Dr. Kamiya worked in the non-governmental and governmental sectors, as well as academia, prior to moving into the private sector. Outside the office, Dr. Kamiya especially enjoys travelling and reading.

HRD in a Multicultural Workplace: The Need For Lifelong Learning

by Motoyo Ogisu-Kamiya

This paper describes and discusses issues pertinent to lifelong learning in a multicultural workplace, specifically, a subsidiary of a Japanese multinational firm operating in Canada. Several new initiatives for assessing learning potential as well as promoting general learning activities are described, as are issues related to the contrasting learning experiences and cultural issues of Japanese and Canadian staff. With the increasingly global nature of business, coupled with rapid technological change and escalating competition, the need for staff to engage in lifelong learning activities is unprecedented. Firms that incorporate activities which promote lifelong learning, as well as firms that understand and respond to learning issues brought about by the multicultural interface, will enhance their competitive position in the year 2000 and beyond. Given the free trade agenda of APEC member economies, the lessons and opportunities offered in this paper are particularly relevant.

INTRODUCTION

The investigation of and reflection on issues pertinent to learning and education are hardly new phenomena. Confucius, Buddha and Socrates explored learning issues long before the term lifelong learning came into vogue. Nonetheless, what is critical and important today is the realization that learning needs not only continue throughout the lifespan, but also that the rapid rate of change and the increasingly global nature of our lives predicates a need for successful lifelong learning as well as the successful management of this learning. In fact, our very survival may depend on this (see Thomas, 1991).

In an age characterized by fast-paced technological change and movement towards a global economy, an age where research, application and production can be transferred almost anywhere in the world, quickly and smoothly, there is an enormous competitive advantage associated with a workplace that incorporates a vision, strategy and structure to make human resource development (HRD) a continuous process. Of late, there has been unprecedented discussion on HRD in the workplace. Yet, in most of the private sector, the customary focus is on training - a one-way transfer of pre-defined skills and knowledge - rather than on broader, more complex, individualized, continuous, and self-directed lifelong learning.

This paper describes and scrutinises a private sector experience, specifically referencing cultural issues as they influence the HRD interface. The context is a Japanese multinational firm in the non-manufacturing sector, more precisely in the international trade business. (A more detailed picture of the company emerges later in the paper.)

In its most simplistic form, learning is a complex phenomenon with diverse dimensions. A multinational, multicultural workplace incorporates a host of supplementary factors, and it is not practical to attempt to extract and examine all that influence HRD and the learning context. However, two initiatives have been launched in the workplace under discussion, and these are examined in some detail. The first is an experimental learning program which was introduced in order to respond to emerging and pressing learning needs within the organization; the second is an examination of cultural issues as they relate to learning in the workplace.

This paper is a brief report drawn from observations and insights gleaned for the most part through first-hand experience. It is exploratory in nature, and has as its goal the development of a new vision for lifelong learning in a multicultural workplace as well as the development of practical strategies gleaned from what is very much a preliminary appraisal.

Following this introductory section, which continues by defining the way in which terminology is used, this paper describes the specific workplace under discussion. In turn, this is followed by two major sections: (1) learning in the workplace, which describes experimental assessment and learning programs; and (2) culture, which examines Japanese staff, Canadian staff, and the interface between the two. The paper concludes with recommendations and general observations specific to lifelong learning in the workplace.

The term "lifelong learning", though perhaps relatively new, has managed to attract considerable conceptual and theoretical attention, and at least a modicum of confusion. Related terms, such as "lifelong education", "adult education", and "recurrent education" are often used interchangeably. However, an in-depth discussion on conceptual and definitional issues is beyond the scope of this paper (for discussion and clarification see, for example, Candy and Crebert, 1991; Thomas, 1991). In this paper, lifelong learning" is "the process by which an adult continues to acquire, in a conscious manner, formal or informal education throughout his or her life span, either to maintain and improve vocational viability or for personal development" (Shafritz, Koeppe & Soper, 1988, p.273).

"Lifelong" implies a framework encompassing the entire lifespan including childhood, though discussion of lifelong learning tends to focus on activities taking place in adulthood. Often, "learning" and "education", in broad contexts, are used interchangeably, and may be defined as "the process of acquiring new knowledge and skills through both formal and informal exposure to information, ideas and experiences. "Education", in a narrower context, may be defined as "systematic planned instruction that takes place in school" (Shafritz, Koeppe & Soper, 1988, p. 164).

Lifelong learning may focus on two areas which in industrialized societies have tended to become increasingly distinct and separate. The first of these is career and vocational learning, at the upper-end sometimes described as professional development. The second relates to life-enrichment or personal growth. The distinction is somewhat artificial and likely misguided given that the two are so closely related. Further, as some writers predict the imminent arrival of a "jobless" society, this distinction will need to be reconsidered (see Bridges, 1994; Rifkin, 1995). Regardless, within the context of this paper, the focus will be on work-related learning.

Training is "a planned and systematic sequence of instruction under competent supervision, designed to impact predetermined skills, knowledge or abilities ... " (Shafritz, Koeppe & Soper, 1988, p.478). The central characteristics of training are based on the dual assumptions of a predictable environment and expected outcomes. In the private sector, training issues still predominate. However, at a time when the business environment is experiencing striking change and an unpredictable future, the relevance of training based on traditional and narrow assumptions requires reconsideration.

THE ORGANIZATION

As one of the largest international trade companies in the world, the organization discussed in this paper spans the globe with more than 150 offices and an annual trading volume of more than US$150 billion. Its activities include import, export, offshore trade as well as finance and investment. The diversified business activities reflect the fast-changing and complex business environment, characterised in recent years by a global economy which has intensified the speed and complexity of all transactions. The organization must be prepared to cope on a daily basis with operating in different time zones, a variety of languages, and different cultural contexts.

The Canadian operation, a fully owned subsidiary of the parent company, has been in Canada for more than thirty-five years. Compared with the parent company, the Canadian operation is relatively small, with an annual transaction volume of around CD$2 billion and a workforce of about 60. Recently, it has been reorganizing in order to respond to changes in the business environment.

There are three key factors affecting the employee training environment. These include the complex nature of international trade, the distinctive characteristics associated with a multinational company, and the need for reorganizing and restructuring within the Canadian operation. Taken together, these factors, especially the need for reorganizing and restructuring, have necessitated a new organizational vision and a new generation of internationally oriented staff. At the operational level, this has prompted the company to specifically examine learning initiatives and learning capacities as they relate to current and potential staff members.

The company is strongly influenced and characterized by traditional Japanese corporate culture and organizational structure. In fact, the North American concept of human resource development is very new to the company. Previously, the Canadian operation was viewed vaguely as a simple extension of the Tokyo Head Office. There were few specific, prescribed frameworks for structuring human resource development initiatives, and Canadian staff were seen to be and treated as "helpers." The notion of managing the Canadian operation as a distinct entity was limited. This approach is common with many Japanese overseas operations in the non-manufacturing sector.

As noted earlier, dramatic environmental change including the increasingly competitive environment has brought with it the need for a new generation of staff, and this was and continues to be a major force driving the reorganization of the Canadian operation. In response to this pressing need, the company identified three distinct learning focuses as having special potential for positive influence. The first involved assessing the capacity of and initiative for learning of all job applicants during the recruitment process, the second focused on learning issues specific to newly hired staff, and the third dealt with learning issues related to the existing staff.

LEARNING IN THE WORKPLACE

Following is a summary description of three experimental programs. The emphasis in these programs has been on initiating workable and practical programs that can be implemented within the context of organizational constraints that include limited human resource capacity and the very heavy, traditional Japanese heritage at the heart of the organization. Each of the programs was formulated by experimentally adapting a proactive learning approach and each was gradually implemented over the course of a few years. (Knowles describes proactive learning as including required conditions and skills. Required conditions include institutional support for learning from mistakes, high value for self-direction, commitment to learning as a developmental process, and collaborative relationships with colleagues. Required skills include the abilities to accept responsibility for learning, experiment with new behaviour, and use data for self-diagnosis for self-improvement - see Knowles, 1973, pp. 178-179).

Learning Assessment During Recruitment

During the recruitment process, several learning issues have been addressed. Included are assessment of the applicants' learning attributes and learning styles, their track record for participation in continuous learning activities, and their learning initiative as displayed during the application process. Recently, a small-scale survey on these issues as they linked to job applicants was conducted. The overall survey findings noted that very few job applicants are clearly and sufficiently communicating their learning issues during the job application process. For example, learning style and learning track record were for the most part poorly communicated by the applicants, and learning initiative during the application process was observed among just a small fraction of them (See Ogisu-Kamiya, 1996).

These findings indicate that most job seekers are not receiving guidance on learning issues as these relate to the job application process specifically or overall career development in a more general sense. Aside from fragmented suggestions received from various sources, job applicants are in large part left to "figure things out for themselves." Even common learning-related suggestions, such as "research the company and industry prior to applying for a job", were demonstrated by a very small percentage of the applicants. The urgency of addressing this gap between the needs of job seekers and the availability of services and resources seems to be greater than ever given the sweeping changes affecting the workplace:

- an increasing number of employers have started to focus on "learning" in order to ensure their workforce is able to remain current with the fast changing business environment (one recent survey found that "willingness to learn" was ranked by the employers as the second most important attribute of job applicants - see Mossop Cornelissen & Associates, 1995);

- dramatically changing workplaces in North America are characterized by re-organization, restructuring, and down-sizing, which necessitates that all workers, regardless of their current employment status, take charge of their professional lives more than ever, including responsibility for learning within the context of their career development.

Orientation Program and Guided Self-directed Learning Project

For all newly hired staff, an individually tailored orientation program is prepared. The program has two components. First are generic sessions which, for example, include an overall introduction to the company, its computer system, and the office procedures. Second are department-specific session which are directly related to the new staff members' responsibilities. In addition, guidance with regard to the self-directed learning project described below is included. The involvement of managerial and non-managerial staff in the planning and implementation of these sessions is intended to be part of the learning program for that group.

As well as the orientation program, new staff are required to complete a guided, self-directed learning project. Each must define and research a specific topic pertaining to either the industry broadly, the company's operation and activities more specifically, or products in which the individual has a special interest. The staff member is required to produce a written report within a three-month probation period. The main thrust of this learning project is to facilitate new staff to develop a learning focus from the very beginning of the employment period. It is also expected that this experience will act as a catalyst for each employee to continue with broader and more substantive learning experiences after the probation period ends. Aside from one-page guidelines provided at the orientation session, the framework of the project has been kept open-ended in order to suit each new staff member's ability and comfort level.

These reports show widely differing levels of quality and quantity, with final drafts ranging from vaguely structured 3-4 page essays to an in-depth research paper of about 100 pages. The differences derive mostly from two inter-related factors: the open-ended framework of the learning initiative assumed by each staff member creates the potential for considerable variety; and new staff have a broad spectrum of skills and abilities that far exceeded tentative assessment and assumptions made during the hiring process.

It has become evident that the project is a useful tool to assess skills, abilities and calibre (level of initiative) of new staff. That information can be used subsequently as a benchmark for facilitation of individualized learning activities throughout their career paths. So far, the development of newly hired staff after completing the research project has been encouraging. For the most part they have shown a tendency to continue to take the initiative for learning throughout the ensuing professional development program.

Professional Development Program

The third element in the HRD initiative focuses on learning programs for existing staff. Included are two elements: first are full company-sponsored programs, and second are company-supported self-directed development initiatives. With regard to the company-sponsored programs, computer training as well as some training initiatives of general interest are offered. In terms of the self-directed scheme, the process of learning is emphasized as well as the content of learning. At the outset, a staff member who intends to undertake a learning project is required to produce a written learning proposal. With the involvement of the supervisor, identification of learning needs and the reconciliation of these with corporate objectives are completed. Upon completion of the proposed project, the staff member produces a report. Given the small scale of the Canadian operation and its limited internal resources, emphasis has been placed on external rather than internal learning opportunities. Courses in international trade and business communications are strongly supported as are other job-related courses.

It took considerable time for this professional development program to be initiated. One of management's key concerns was the clear identification of the benefits which the company could reasonably be expected to secure. As well, Japanese management was influenced by the Japanese-style tenured employment, or lack thereof in Canada. In Japan, up until recently, employment practices emphasized hiring new graduates and keeping them for life. In this context, a company is able to invest heavily in on-the-job training and education without fear that employees will leave (Johnson, 1988). In the Canadian context, this is not so clear. In fact, staff turnover within a fluid labour market is often mentioned as one of the major contributing factors for relatively modest in-house training in North America. Nonetheless, the recognition of pressing training needs has superseded the above concerns.

Since its inception in late 1993, the program has grown considerably. Under the full-company sponsorship scheme, a series of extensive computer training activities have been implemented. With regard to the self-directed scheme, an increasing number of staff utilize it for their learning projects. A wide variety of courses have been offered, with the most popular being international trade, Japanese language training, and accounting and finance coursework. As a spin-off, informal learning partnerships are emerging in the workplace. Examples include staff members who take the same course or subject and study together, and staff with advanced knowledge in a certain subject area helping others who are taking courses at basic or intermediate levels.

An in-depth examination of the outcome of these initiatives has yet to be completed. Nonetheless, preliminary reflection indicates that by consciously addressing learning issues through the implementation of relevant and focused programs, the personal learning initiatives of the staff have been stimulated to new levels. Also, directing the learning activities of newly hired staff from the outset has proved to be effective for seeding the first notions of an ongoing learning ethic. In effect, a desire for learning has been sparked in the workplace. Most importantly, however, for the full development of these programs in the years to come, a strong and ongoing organizational commitment is needed.

CULTURE

As well as the assessment and professional development initiatives described earlier, there has been a pressing need within the organization for an exploratory inquiry to examine how learning issues are influenced by the cultural context. In part this results from the fact that the firm is a complex, multinational, multicultural workplace, an environment which poses learning challenges in a different and highly complex context. This inquiry was exploratory in nature.

The human resource composition within the Canadian operation is a combination of two distinct groups: Japanese expatriates and Canadian staff. The expatriates from Japan are mostly key management personnel, each of whom serves for an average term of five years. This group is strongly influenced by Tokyo Head Office rules and hierarchy. They are in Canada for a relatively short period of time, and will almost certainly return to Tokyo upon completion of their assignments. Canadian staff members are hired locally and their appointments and functions are bound solely by the framework of the Canadian operation, though their work extends beyond Canadian boundaries.

For both of these groups, this paper addresses cultural responses to learning experiences, as well as perceived gaps between learning needs and learning capacity and initiative. The interface between the two groups is also addressed. Because the expatriates are dominant within the organization, greater emphasis is placed on this group. While acknowledging a range of individual differences, the paper assumes that it is possible to make general observations about the characteristics of each group and contrast their differing cultural contexts and learning potential.

Japanese Staff

Hall's (1986) conceptual framework is helpful in addressing cultural experiences as these relate to learning as well as some of the interface issues. Hall differentiates between "high context culture" and "low context culture", noting that in a high context environment, such as the Japanese culture, the norms, values and traditions strongly interrelate in order to create an environment where subtle meanings and messages are clear. Most information is stored in the memory of individuals, and as a result very little of it needs to be transferred on an ongoing basis. In effect, the rules and roles are known, the game is well delineated, and everyone who grew up learning the game knows how to play without a great deal of explanation or discussion. Conversely, in a low context environment, such as Canadian culture, far less can be taken for granted and therefore a great deal of day-to-day information must be transmitted. In the definitive low context environment, everybody is told everything in detail.

As a group, the Japanese expatriates are highly homogeneous. All are males ranging from their mid-thirties to more than fifty years of age, all are university graduates, and the company has been their only employer throughout their working lives. For the younger ones, Canada is the first overseas post, while for older expatriates this may be the second or third overseas posting.

During the course of the posting, most expatriates have demonstrated few and relatively weak learning initiatives. For the most part expatriates display a strong tendency to cling to a reactive learning approach, characterized by Knowles (1973) as the ability to retain information, to listen uncritically, to record information, and to predict evaluation criteria. The required conditions for reactive learning include a willingness to be dependent, a strong respect for authority, a solid commitment to learning as a means to an end (for example, credentials), and a competitive relationship with peers.

The Japanese school system is well known for reactive learning, where the focus is on teaching students how to be taught rather than teaching them how to learn. This tendency is exacerbated by highly competitive university entrance exams, for which reactive learning skills are extremely effective. Even at the university level, except for some optional senior level seminar courses, the primary emphasis on reactive learning remains. Learning is typically perceived as the means to an end, namely, earning a degree. The Japanese expatriates have evidenced reactive learning skills by successfully earning credentials from respected universities which almost automatically are the basis for securing a positions in a major established company.

During the period when the expatriate group was hired, lifelong employment was the norm. They were, and still are, expected to be "company men," unwaveringly loyal and responsive to the firm's needs. As a result, most of their core, work-related value orientation comes from the company. Interestingly enough, corporate culture requires and organizationally reinforces the reactive learning characteristics noted earlier: being dependent, respecting authority, committing to learning for succession, and competing with peers. The expatriates' approach to reactive learning has been further reinforced through internal training programs. Ueda (1990) noted that these programs or systems are organized to serve the requirements of corporations rather than the interests of individual employees/learners. By the time the expatriates were assigned to overseas posts, reactive learning had become a deeply entrenched and largely unconscious behavioral pattern. Now, in a fast paced, changing environment, this pattern appears to be a major obstacle.

Hedberg (1981) describes a process of learning, unlearning (discarding previously learned responses) and relearning (obtaining new responses and mental maps), a model which might help break the patterns associated with reactive learning. However, the experience expatriates have with reactive learning, including the positive rewards they have enjoyed and the investments they have made, make change difficult. In this setting, the acquisition of a proactive learning approach based on Hedberg's model or others is improbable.

Additional attributes of the Japanese educational system are worth noting (see Thomas's framework for management of learning in different cultures, 1991). First, the Japanese educational system emphasizes the needs of young learners, and second, learning needs associated with achieving entry into the educational system, and university in particular, are stressed. In both these cases, the learning needs of adults are in large part neglected, though some recent initiatives to mitigate this situation have been reported (Maehira, 1994). Further, Japanese society quite clearly distinguishes between the traditionally recognized stages of life: the learning stage (prior to early adulthood), and the working stage (after graduation from post-secondary institutions). For the most part, it is assumed that all learning takes place in the first stage. Conventionally, learning during adulthood, over and above in-house training, is viewed as an exception rather than the norm.

For the expatriate group, attained social status is another factor that mitigates against broader participation in lifelong learning activities. As male graduates from elite universities, they are for the most part automatically accorded high status as "elite company men" in a major corporation. Social recognition is guaranteed for life, and it is logical for them to support the system that has contributed to their success rather than assume the risks inherent in a new approach.

Regardless of the cultural constraints, overseas assignments require considerably more learning and adaptation on the part of expatriates. Far from the Tokyo Head Office, expatriates must assume a wider range of responsibilities with far less support and supervision. Expatriates must develop effective work relations with the host country staff, all of whom bring different cultural experiences to the workplace. Also, they must adapt to a range of new circumstances including the host country's socio-economic environment, language, and customs. Given the reactive nature of their approach to learning, the capacity and initiative displayed by expatriates is unlikely to respond as effectively to this daunting list of learning needs as might be wished. Overseas assignments require venturing beyond the traditional structure and learning to adapt to new conditions. It is a major obstacle for the expatriates to expand their own learning context, and for the most part they appear to be mentally confined by a reactive learning style and, as a result, lifelong learning potential remains for the most part untapped.

Internationally-oriented management skills is an area where the development of expertise is particularly lacking among the expatriate staff, and there appear to be at least two critical factors associated with this. First, there is the Japanese tendency to assume "management" is a matter of "common sense." This perspective gives rise to the view that "management" can be done just using "common sense," and therefore it can be left mostly to the discretion of the individual. This response may work in an environment comprised of Japanese management and Japanese workers, where both groups share the same assumptions and high cultural context. However, it is not nearly as effective in a cross-cultural environment where members of two cultures operate within radically different sets of assumptions.

The second factor relates to the Head Office environment back in Japan where feudalistic "class" distinctions and strong hierarchical qualities are tightly maintained. In this environment, the need for a variety of strong management skills is marginal. However, outside this environment internationally-oriented management expertise is demanded as the company struggles to operate in a multicultural context and compete around the globe. It has yet to be fully appreciated that the management skills of expatriate staff carry profound cultural constraints. So far, in the non-manufacturing sector, the universality of their skills has proven to be limited.

Canadian Staff

The Canadian staff are characterized first and foremost by their diversity. They include both males and females, ranging in age from twenty to over sixty. Included are a variety of ethnic groups, the majority being of Japanese and Asian background. Some have served the company for more than thirty years, while others are newly hired. Those who work at the management level are predominantly male, Japanese in origin, older, and have a record of long service.

Canadian staff are products of a variety of educational systems, both in Canada and abroad, with terminal education ranging from high school attainment through graduate school. For the most part their work experience includes more than one employer, often spanning several sectors of the economy in Canada and abroad.

By contrast with the expatriate group, the capacity for and approach to learning of the Canadian staff is more flexible and demonstrates greater individual variation. In many instances, younger and newer Canadian staff members have demonstrated the most initiative for new learning. This observation became more noticeable after the professional development programs described earlier in this paper were implemented. Conversely, limited receptiveness and initiative in learning among older, long service staff members has been noted. One of the major contributing factors to this tendency is thought to be the Canadian operation's long practice of providing a job for life and pay based on seniority, or more succinctly described by Johnson (1988) as living wages graduated by age.

Canadian staff who had earlier emigrated to Canada appear to adjust more readily to new learning experiences and the high context environment than those born in Canada. Survival following arrival in this new country had likely necessitated the acquisition of fresh skills and knowledge, and the replication of this learning behaviour is apparently not difficult. In particular, those who have fluency in a second language (not necessarily Japanese) demonstrate more understanding of the somewhat mixed cultural context than do unilingual staff. From a strategic planning perspective, this has been an important discovery. International trade is cross-cultural and cross-border by definition, and the company's workplace is and will continue to be multicultural. Hiring staff who fit and work more easily in this context has strong and immediate benefits.

In Canada, the educational system is primarily a reactive one, though to a lesser extent than is the case in Japan. As suggested earlier in this paper, the reactive approach is poor preparation for lifelong learning (see also Knowles, 1973; Shuttleworth, 1993).

Observation of the Canadian experience suggests that the distinction between learning as a youth and learning as an adult is becoming progressively less marked. More adults are learning in ways that are similar to the learning they experienced as youths. In fact, learning at both these stages has begun to extend in a variety of directions that more directly reflect labour market needs. There is an escalating demand for adult education and training due to such factors as high unemployment, a fluid labour market, and limitations on in-house training. Nowadays, for many adults, participation in lifelong learning directly and significantly influences their economic well-being. As a result, within Canada the cycle of learning, unlearning and relearning is increasingly common and may well occur several times during a person's lifetime.

Within the environment of the company under discussion, considerable learning needs are imposed directly and indirectly on Canadian staff. As described, the firm is a large, complex corporation with diverse global operations dominated everywhere and in every fashion by the Japanese management style. The requirements are particularly demanding for newer and younger Canadian staff members. Even if these workers generally exhibit a higher level of initiative, flexibility and receptiveness in their approaches to learning, fulfilling these requirements is a substantial challenge. Those who are unfamiliar with the high-context Japanese culture are at a disadvantage, and language continues to be a key barrier as most written documentation is in Japanese. As a result, employees who lack proficiency in the Japanese language are effectively locked out of what is arguably the most consequential communications channel. For older Canadian workers, saturated learning capacity and levels of initiative are not in keeping with the learning demands imposed by the fast changing business environment and technological revolution.

The area of management skills and the development of such skills is another example where corporate needs are not being fully met. In the past, locally hired staff, viewed primarily as "helpers," were not expected to have management skills per se. As a result, the hiring process de-emphasized these. Additionally, a watered down version of the "management is common sense" notion described earlier appears to be conveyed by the Japanese administration to the Canadian staff. As a result, even in cases where managerial titles have been given to local staff, usually based on gender and length of service, the skills are not well developed and the expectation for management proficiency remains unarticulated.

Interface - Japanese and Canadian Staff

While the two previous sub-sections of the paper highlighted the capacity, initiative, and orientation towards lifelong learning for the Japanese expatriates and the Canadian staff, this section examines the interface by means of two salient examples.

One of the intersections where fundamental multicultural interface issues surface on a day-to-day basis within the company is in the giving and receiving of instructions between Japanese expatriates and the Canadian staff. High-context Japanese managers automatically expect Japanese speaking Canadian staff to share the same cultural perspective. In other words, the Japanese expect them to understand direction without going into detail or allowing them to pose questions. This is not a reasonable assumption. Even if Japanese speaking Canadian staff are Japanese by origin and do in fact speak the language, the extent to which they can be effective within a high-context environment differs considerably. depending in part on the level of their immersion in the low context culture.

At the same time, high-context Japanese managers often appear reluctant or uncomfortable giving instruction in any great detail to non-Japanese Canadian staff. To provide instructive detail is, quite simply, not a cultural norm to begin with, and doing so in English poses an additional challenge. It is generally held that high-context people constantly experience discomfort in a low-context environment. In fact, Hall (1986, p. 162) suggests that "high context individuals operating in low context

cultures constantly feel put down as shifts in the level of context are metacommu-
nications which indicate shifts in relationship." On the other side, Canadian staff are
often puzzled and frustrated by the lack of clear and detailed direction. As a result,
Canadian staff tend to develop their own terms of reference or, in some cases, a
sense of mistrust.

The second example of the interface issue relates to the regular changes that take
place at the senior levels in the company. As Japanese managers are cycled in and
cycled out of Canada, consistency and continuity get lost. As a result, there is limited organizational accumulation of knowledge and skills, especially as these relate to
management styles and expectations. This is exacerbated by the fact that, without a
uniform and articulated management approach that is understood by Canadian staff,
there is a range of individual differences among Japanese managers, and hence a
lack of predictability with regard to management expectations. For Canadian staff, it
takes time and effort to adjust to the regular changes in management personnel.
Canadian staff who have stayed with the company for an extended period of time
have learned a variety of coping styles, typically coupled with varying degrees of res-
ignation.

RECOMMENDATIONS & CONCLUSIONS

Lifelong learning in general and cultural interface issues in particular have yet to
achieve preferential status within workplace agendas. As a result, few studies have
been completed and little has been written about this area. Following are several
recommendations based on this preliminary investigation.

In order to fully incorporate a lifelong learning approach within a corporate
human resources development plan, several dimensions need to be addressed. To
begin with, learning issues need to be expressly and consciously addressed rather
than relegated to a subordinate role. Second, within a multicultural workplace it is
critical to acknowledge cultural differences in terms of learning styles and educational experiences, and the cultural interface needs to be examined and evaluated.
Third, promotion of a lifelong learning culture, including a proactive learning
approach within the organization, needs to be explicitly endorsed at the corporate
level.

Within the typical workplace setting, two specific strategies are suggested. These
include the development of learning programs and, more broadly, addressing the
human resources infrastructure. With regard to learning programs, organizations need
to explore and evaluate systematic and organized methods for addressing lifelong
learning issues. All the dimensions described in this paper need to be considered in
order to come up with individually-tailored learning-related programs for the workplace. In addition, learning opportunities need to be integrated into as many facets of
human resource practice as possible. This should begin with assessing potential staff
in terms of their learning styles, ability to learn, and willingness to learn. The experience described in this paper suggests that learning assessment programs are easily
adaptable for small- to medium-sized companies, even those firms whose capacities
and resources may be quite limited. In fact, these are the firms which may have the
most to lose by not having effective learning assessment programs.

The development of and support for a learning infrastructure, including the creation of a positive corporate culture and adequate resource allocation, are crucial if workplace lifelong learning is to take place. In this vein, competency within the organization is required in order to facilitate lifelong learning. Strong leadership and an organizational vision, coupled with learning capacity and managerial initiative, must be fostered.

Today's workplace is undergoing drastic change, and multinational and multicultural workplaces present unique challenges and opportunities for human resources development in general and for learning issues in particular. The process of cultivating a lifelong learning ethic can be a fascinating and rewarding learning experience in and of itself for human resource specialists. Beyond that, however, there is no doubt that many corporations, Japanese and others, are at the crossroads. Fresh learning paradigms are required, and this paper has detailed implications for the entire corporate structure. New methods, new models and new commitments are required, and nowhere is this more apparent that in the host of multicultural workplaces located within the Asia-Pacific region.

REFERENCES

Bridges, William (1994). Jobshift - *How to prosper in a workplace without jobs.* New York: Addison Wesley Publishing Co.

Candy, P. & Crebert, R.G. (1991). Lifelong learning: An enduring mandate for higher education. *Higher Education Research and Development 10*(1), 3-15.

Hedberg, B. (1981). How organizations learn and unlearn. *Handbook of organizational design.* (Vol. 1, pp. 3-27). New York: Oxford University Press.

Hall, E.T. (1986). Unstated features of the cultural context of learning. In A. Thomas & E. Polman (Eds.), *Learning and development - A global perspective.* Toronto: OISE Press.

Johnson, C. (1988). Japanese-style management in America. *California Management Review*, Summer, 34-45.

Maehira, Y. (1994). Patterns of lifelong education in Japan. *International Review of Education 40*(3-5), 333-338.

Mossop Cornelissen & Associates. (1995). *What do employers want?* Mossop Cornelissen Report No. 595, Toronto: Author.

Ogisu-Kamiya, M. (1996). Lifelong learning in a new world of work. *NATCON Papers / 1996 Les acts du CONAT - Proceedings of the 22nd National Consultation on Career Development Conference.* Toronto.

Knowles, M. (1973). *The adult learner: A neglected species.* Houston: Gulf Publishing Co.

Rifkin, J. (1995). *The end of work: The decline of the global labor force & the dawn of the post-market era.* New York: G.P. Putman's Sons.

Shafritz, J.M., Koeppe, R.P. & Soper, E.W. (1988). *The facts on file dictionary of education.* New York: Facts on File.

Shuttleworth, D. (1993). *Enterprise learning in action.* New York: Routledge.

Thomas, A. (1991). *Beyond education: A new perspective on society's management of learning.* San Francisco: Jossey-Bass Publishers.

Ueda, Y. (1990). The learning corporation: Japanese experience in occupational training. In J. Muller, Japan. (Ed.) *Education for work, education as work: Canada's changing community colleges.* Toronto: Garamond Press.

Daphne Yuen Pan

Daphne Pan holds degrees from the University of Singapore (B.A.), the University of Surrey (M.Sc.), and York University (M.A. and Ph.D.). She is a Senior Lecturer in the Department of English Language and Literature at the University of Singapore, currently seconded as Director to the university's Centre for Development of Teaching and Learning. Dr. Pan's research interests include the teaching of literature, teaching methods and educational objectives, and "cyber-assisted" learning. She has delivered a wide variety of conference papers including "Education for All: The Singapore Experience" in the Philippines, "Helping Students Learn" in Hong Kong, "Access and Quality in Higher Education" in Brunei, "Assessing Quality in Higher Education" in Finland, and "Faculty Development: The Singapore Experience" in Canada. In her spare time, she enjoys classical music and the cinema.

Lifelong Learning: The Whole DAMN Cycle — A Singapore Perspective

by **Daphne Yuen Pan**

There is growing awareness of the limitations of the traditional 'front-end' education and learning model. With its 'life phase approach' it imposes fairly rigid compartmentalising of learning and working life, and ignores the mutually reinforcing states of being and becoming that characterise, or should characterise, human existence. There is also concern that this inflexible model not only does not maximise human potential but it subverts the capacity and desire for learning and growth. In the effort to correct this, much has been done to put in place lifelong learning systems involving national initiatives and international cooperation. But top-down policy decisions and actions, while undeniably important, are only part of it. This paper reiterates the old Chinese proverb that it takes two hands to clap. Effective and sustained lifelong learning demands both intrinsic and extrinsic inputs. Indeed, it involves the whole DAMN cycle: Desire and Ability to learn on the part of the learner, the Means to support learning, and perceived Needs to prompt all these. As in the learning cycle, the components are equally weighted and linked in an organic sequence that dispenses with fixed starting or ending points.

INTRODUCTION

We are too ready to confuse education with learning.

> (Attributed to a participant at the Centre for Educational Research and Innovation conference on "Learning Beyond Schooling", OECDa, 1995, p. 15.)

Lifelong education has been defined as "a set of organisational, administrative, methodological and procedural measures" (Knapper & Cropley, 1985, p. 18), while lifelong learning describes "the habit of continuously learning throughout life, a mode of behaviour" (Ironside, 1989, p. 15). The former might be said to refer to a set of extrinsic, supply-oriented factors which identify the needs and provide the means, while the latter is intrinsic, demand-oriented and heavily dependent on learner motivation and ability. Obviously, it is important that there be a fine balance of the two in order to generate synergy and productive outcomes.

...rapid change in the nature both of supply and of demand creates the risk that there will not be a good match between them. On the one hand provision of education and training cannot on its own create willing and effective participation; on the other, potential or actual demand of new kinds of provision may go unmet. There is a particular need to avoid an excessively "supply-led" concept of provision — courses and opportunities need to be sensitive to the needs and desires of learners, and not be based simply on new technological possibilities, the ideas of suppliers or their institutional interests.   (OECD, 1995a, p. 11)

By and large, there has been greater concern with the extrinsic rather than the intrinsic, with what is taught rather than how it is learnt. Syllabus and curriculum reviews are fairly commonplace practices and these tend, more often than not, to be prompted by learner-led considerations; Friere's (1972) "pedagogy of the oppressed" is a relatively new proposition. However, educators are increasingly acknowledging the relevance of learning theories and the centrality of the learner in the learning process. At the risk of belabouring the obvious, it is worth restating that in order for learning to occur, there must be the desire and the ability to do so. Only then will meaningful use be made of the "provision of education and training". Holistically, lifelong learning must be predicated on the whole DAMN cycle.

The DAMN Cycle

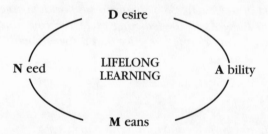

Desire

Why do people learn? Answers include instinct, intellectual needs, and the will to achieve. The desire to learn, then, is an innate tendency and, left to themselves, people will naturally pursue learning unless otherwise conditioned. Regrettably, there are forces at work that blunt or crush this desire. For instance, if learning is made to be a painful experience, then the operation of 'psychological hedonism' — the desire to seek pleasure and avoid pain — will predictably curb interest in learning. The association of "pain" with learning is not uncommon, and may be traceable to the "no pain - no gain" ideology which, fortunately, many now think highly dubious. Suffering may or may not be good for character-building but it certainly does little to perpetuate learning. On the other hand, positive learning experiences develop self confidence and keenness for further learning.

Another de-motivating force has been identified as the shifting of control from the learner to some external authority. If learners have little or no say in what, how, when and why they learn, but are instead forcibly programed to go through the motions in conformity with externally imposed purposes and criteria packaged in ironclad curricular structures and classroom practices, it is also predictable that self-motivation will wither from disuse. Knowles (1984) argues for the andragogical model for the adult learner. This focuses on the learner, including motivation, orientation, readiness to learn and experiences, and there is no reason why this should not be adapted to school pedagogies. More so than with adults, children need to be presented with an attractive and supple learning model, one that is responsive to varied learner needs and reinforces a positive self concept by empowering the learner, thereby nurturing self direction that makes autonomous and continuous learning possible.

Yet another major obstacle is our culture of achievement which rewards success and allows little margin for failure. Ironically, the emphasis on excellence and high performance, because it has engendered a low tolerance for failure, discourages exploration and risk-taking and saps the vitality of the inquiring mind. An educational system heavily underscored by rigid, summative norm-referenced assessment, privileges some at the expense of others, and marginalises the achievement of those on the wrong side of the bell curve. A student who scores 10% is a failure rather than someone who deserves recognition for a 10% success. Little wonder that students soon learn to be more concerned with grades than with learning, more driven to deliver what is wanted than pursue what excites their intellectual curiosity. They begin schooling full of question marks and end with a full stop. George Bernard Shaw remarked wryly that schooling functions as an interruption to education. More fatally, it may go beyond interruption, stifling all interest so that learning is not resumed as a lifelong activity. First and foremost, lifelong learning depends on stimulating the mind, enhancing motivation to learn, and equipping individuals with foundation skills to do so.

Ability

How do people learn? Cognitive psychologists such as Bruner, Ausabel and Piaget stress the learner's consciousness; learning is not merely receiving information, but making sense of it. It is not a 'spectator sport' and students need to be actively engaged in the learning process. Hence, the teaching-learning transaction is essentially dialogic; learning does not automatically occur when the teacher teaches. The logical paradigm shift from teacher-centredness to student-centredness has important implications for instructional theory and strategies. There are obvious limitations to traditional pedagogies which are prescriptive and enforce passive reception.

If children grow up considering knowledge to be something that is merely handed down by teachers, for reasons that are somewhat obscure to the student, they are far less likely to continue learning in adult life than if learning is seen as a voluntary voyage of discovery.   (OECD, 1995a, p. 16)

To effect such epistemological and paradigm shifts requires a change in the traditional balance of power where authority is vested in the teacher. Students have to be enabled to participate in and take responsibility for their learning. Teachers have to be aware of the needs, interests and backgrounds of students, and serve not simply as content specialists but most importantly as facilitators who give support and encouragement, listen to learners, and provide access to relevant tools and resources. To facilitate learning, a conducive learning environment is needed. This involves various aspects of the teaching/learning process, including curricula, instructional modes, and assessment procedures.

For independent, lifelong learning, students for their part need to develop an inquiring mind that will prompt them to question and search, as well as higher order process skills which will enable them to synthesise, evaluate, adapt and apply the knowledge they acquire. Students must learn to think critically, creatively and independently. They have to be trained to be open-minded, to develop tolerance for the risks of discovery learning, to be able to formulate and re-formulate problems, and to generate creative answers and evaluate them critically and imaginatively. Most important, they have to learn to learn so that they can continue to learn if they are to respond intelligently to the exponentially increasing knowledge in our rapidly changing world. As Carl Rogers noted (Entwistle & Hounsell, p. 155),

The most socially useful learning in the modern world is the learning of the process of learning; a continuing openness to experience and incorporation into oneself of the process of change.

Ultimately, to function effectively in a fast-paced environment individuals require more than conventional intelligence — *practical intelligence* and *emotional intelligence* are additional dimensions that have been much highlighted in recent years.

Means

A well designed infrastructure supports the growth of a vigorous learning society. Putting in place such an infrastructure is substantially a public-sector commitment, though there are other, albeit smaller, players. Community groups and professional organisations have, to some extent, been providing lifelong education on a more informal basis. Increasingly, too, employers see that it is in their interest to participate in the provision of lifelong learning opportunities so as to maintain a high quality workforce.

By and large, however, the government's role is central and it is twofold: policy-making and resource provision. Policies must be context-specific and agenda-dependent, and variations are to be expected across geographical and political borders. Nevertheless, there are some common denominators, one of which is the creation of a well articulated learning system. For a start, educational institutions need to become more 'open', more 'flexible' and more 'learner-friendly'; the currently predominant monolithic and chronological 'life phase' approach will not easily accommodate self-directed and lifelong learning. Ideal would be a model that provides access to learning any time, and in any place.

As might be expected, this would be a model of considerable sophistication where balancing a desirable level of flexibility with a practicable degree of structure and quality assurance would be critical. Administrators and academics will need to think long and hard, then work together to develop and refine a system that is appropriate for particular institutions. Alternative pedagogies/andragogies might be investigated to make alternative delivery modes, such as distance, individualised, and resource-based delivery, not only efficient but also effective.

Models will vary in degrees of complexity but, basically, there are components which might, for convenience, be loosely described as hardware and software. The hardware denotes the delivery system, including the facilities and technology. These are quantifiable, expensive and high profile, and have generally attracted most attention. There have been rapid developments within the past decade in the range of media, including broadcast transmission via satellite/cable, electronic networks, dedicated networks on the information superhighway to provide Internet-based and Web-based resources, tele/video conferencing, interactive multimedia, and CD-Rom. But, the warning sounded in the introduction to this paper must be borne in mind:

...courses and opportunities need to be sensitive to the needs and desires of learners, and not be based simply on new technological possibilities, the ideas of suppliers.... (OECD, 1995a, p. 11)

The 'software' is just as important, if not more so, and includes a variety of resources: the instructional materials and its presentation/presenter. Promoting lifelong learning is not merely thrusting information at learners. Attention needs to stay sharply focused on the deployment of methodologies that will facilitate learning, and help students evolve strategies for their own learning. Learning theories derived from cognitive psychology — for instance, the suggestion that knowledge is best received when offered in some coherent and hierarchical sequence (Ausabel, 1960; Gagne, 1970) — have great import for educators.

Teachers must keep in mind that for true mastery, learning must be active and meaningful, and learner preferences and expectations must be recognized and incorporated into the process. Because learners differ and because they learn in different ways (Pask, 1976; Marton & Salijo, 1976), methods and materials must be adapted to different cognitive processes. In an age where knowledge proliferates and is easily available, the teacher's task is not just to supply it; the value-added function consists of enabling students to construct meaning and to continue to process information on a lifelong basis. Hence, however advanced the technology, it is inadequate without the human input required to design and develop an intelligent instructional package.

Re-orientating curriculum and course design will also be necessary. With interdisciplinary approaches gaining currency, exposure to broad-based education and cross-curricular skills is logical. And as the primary goal is no longer information transfer, the concern should no longer be to pack the curriculum with as much content as possible. Research has confirmed what might be logically inferred: excessive material will allow little opportunity for reflection and encourage surface-level learning (see Marton & Salijo, 1976). Certainly, some disciplines are more fact- and skill-based than others, and in these students may justifiably be required to have certain core competencies and be familiar with a basic corpus. There is no convincing argument, however, for students to commit it to memory since technology has made information so readily accessible.

All this, in turn, has implications for assessment: tests and examinations should not focus on recall; rather questions should be designed to demand critical thinking and intelligent application. Increasing learner control over assessment through such means as self evaluation and peer evaluation will also help to reconceptualise roles and demystify examinations. Further, there are implications for the way courses are designed. For instance, while the teacher-dominated lecture mode may be efficient for information transmission, it may be less so for stimulating reflective learning. More appropriate alternatives need to be exploited.

Need

That it is imperative to make concerted efforts to promote lifelong learning hardly needs to be argued. What was a radical proposal in the sixties has become an accepted fact. The rapid changes of the past decades — globalisation, the shrinking world, the shift to the service economy and market demands for adaptability to new conditions and products, redundancy of unskilled labour — clearly signal that the challenges ahead will be extremely exciting and the pace even more dynamic.

With the accelerated growth and obsolescence of information, it is essential that people have the skills that will enable them to continue to learn throughout their lives. It has been suggested that university degrees have a limited shelf life and that they should be re-validated periodically. Among others, the Organisation for Economic Cooperation and Development (OECD) has emphasised the need for the provision of continuing professional education for highly-qualified personnel (OECD, 1995b).

In effect, the needs of the 21st century demand a shift to 'recurrent education': the "lifelong process consisting of discontinuous, periodic participation in educational programs aimed at gradually dissolving the blocks of compulsory education and working life" (Candy & Crebert, 1991, p. 6). No longer is lifelong learning a textbook concept; it has become a necessity, with social, economic and political ramifications. The shrinking world, the breaking down of boundaries, the interplay of market demands and the operation of a more global economy all mean that, in education, as in other spheres of life, cooperative effort among nations — and especially those of the APEC community — is a priority.

LIFELONG LEARNING: A SINGAPORE PERSPECTIVE

The DAMN cycle is a useful paradigm for understanding and appreciating the lifelong learning framework not only in a region but also in a nation.

Desire

Much has been said about the Asian cultural bias with its high regard for authority and education and the consequent influence on learning. Within the traditional master-apprentice relationship, the learner is socialised into passivity and authority-dependency. In a society such as Singapore, which is built on meritocracy, Darwinian natural selection manifests itself in a rather ruthless educational system of essentially one-try learning, streaming on the basis of examination scores which may or may not accommodate individual aptitude and interest, and great pressure to perform on and to demand. Formal educational qualifications loom large and certification by examination is crucial. A profile of the Singaporean student tends to show these characteristics: passive, reward-driven, highly but largely extrinsically motivated, with success in examinations rather than cognitive drive being the major motivational force. These students tend to be surface-level processors who are selective about what is learnt, concentrating their efforts on what is within the syllabus and examinable (see Wee & Huan 1991; Chang, 1994). They are unwilling to take risks or engage in discovery and independent learning.

It has also been pointed out that this relentless pressure "often makes school—and studying—a monumental pain....The worst part may be that [students] become permanently turned off learning" (Nurturing Excellence, 1997). What can be done to redress this? Measures include clarification of educational aims/objectives, re-formulation of assessment procedures, and re-definition of incentives. Most fundamental, learning must be presented as an enjoyable experience. Students should be stimulated and be provided with learning milieus that encourage them to explore and stretch their cognitive and affective boundaries. The curriculum should be challenging in the real sense of the word, not merely as a euphemism for stultifying pressure.

That the issue is being addressed is confirmed in a statement by Education minister, Lee Yock Suan (see Leong, 1996, p. 17): "my vision is that every child maximises his potential, acquires sound values and good discipline...." He proposes that this be achieved by modifying the examination system (introducing open book examinations and putting more emphasis on continual assessment and project work), trimming the school curriculum, and through greater use of information technology in the classroom. These initiatives reflect a shift in focus from teaching content to promoting learning. If the schools succeed in nurturing the desire to learn, students will bring this mindset into tertiary education where it can be reinforced so that they will continue learning throughout their lives.

Ability

Last year, more than 800 students from the top five junior colleges in Singapore scored four distinctions each at the GCE A Level examinations and in the premier Raffles Junior College. More than one in three students obtained straight A's. Even Oriental modesty will not prevent the claim that this is impressive. Undoubtedly, Singaporean students are very able, and hardworking; but questions remain. "Do more A's mean brighter students?" (see Nirmala & Mathi, 1996, p. 2). This question has been sporadically raised and, increasingly, the view is being offered that they are "just more exam-smart". The students themselves say, "You can mug your way to an A as very few questions need analysis." If this is the case, then students are only being sensible when they focus on high scores rather than the unrewarding activity of thinking.

Their addiction seems to be an adaptive strategy, a form of learnt helplessness practised for expedience. However, they have been stereotyped as rote-learners. The opinion of one don, that undergraduates have "to be taught to think" and "lecturers still had to play nursemaid to the students" (Nirmala, 1995, p. 24), is by no means exclusive. Regardless, the following student response is illuminating:

> *Such criticisms distress not because they are untrue — though like all generalisations they have limited validity — but because they are unjust in not taking into account the circumstances and realities within which the Singaporean student has to operate. May I venture to present the student's case? ... This species is not without intellectual curiosity; it does think and would probably do so more publicly if the impression received were not that such an activity is uncalled for, if not unseemly.* (Lim, 1995)

This seems to be borne out in the recent TIMSS (Third International Mathematics and Science Study) survey which found that not only did Asian students secure the highest mathematics scores among 41 of the world's most developed nations, they achieved this because they were able to think through and apply underlying concepts (Nirmala, 1996, p. 1). That said, the fact remains that, in the words of one student (Yap, 1988, p. 5):

> *[There is a] huge expenditure of time on revision, practice and tuition....What a student learns and knows becomes less important than how well he does in an examination....It is easy, under such pressure, to succumb to the 'mugging' techniques so effectively employed by thousands of predecessors....(and) lose sight of the aim of real education.*

Hence the decision at the National University of Singapore (NUS) to provide some induction to tertiary education through a structured program that will ensure undergraduates have the necessary study skills to become more effective learners equipped to deal with the additional and rigorous demands of higher education. The Faculty of Arts & Social Sciences has introduced a credit-earning Faculty Enrichment Module for all first year students, and students in other Faculties are offered the University Foundation Module, a smaller-scale, self-study guide. More important is orienting the students' mindsets so they become reflective and self-directed learners. Speaking at a recent convocation ceremony, NUS's Vice Chancellor Lim (1996) noted that what NUS seeks to produce are graduates with "an enquiring and analytical mind, capable of lifelong independent learning...able to cope with the information explosion and many other rapid changes...."

It is disturbing to note in the 1993 National University of Singapore / Nanyang Technological University graduate survey, merely "a handful (5%) [felt] that they had been helped to develop critical thinking and acquire analytical skills". If this is so, there is a need for vigilance in ensuring the attainment of higher-order skills and the achievement of longer-reach goals because higher education, especially, must serve more than the functionalist end of training manpower. Indeed, it should stimulate intellectual curiosity, and train individuals to think independently, reflect critically and make sound judgments. Implicit in this capacity for introspection and reflexivity is the recognition that all claims to knowledge may be subject to further and higher level investigation (see Popper, 1975; Lakatos, 1977; Habermas, 1978; Wittgenstein, 1978; Lawson and Appignanesi, 1989) and awareness that learning is not finite but open-ended. It must be communicated to students that learning does not stop with formal schooling but has to be a lifelong habit.

Means

Various strategies have been implemented to heighten such awareness and to help learners acquire the lifelong habit.The Ministry of Education (MOE), for instance, has launched CORT (Cognitive Research Trust), a thinking skills program, and actively promoted the teaching of thinking skills.

At NUS the implications of more student-centred approaches have been variously translated. Since 1994, most of the faculties have moved to a modular system in order to exploit a more flexible academic structure which allows for some self-pacing in learning. Apart from periodically reviewing and revising the curricula to ensure relevance and currency, there is also the move to make it 'lean and mean'.At a press interview Vice Chancellor Lim indicated that the curriculum reduction may be as much as 30% to encourage "less book-learning, more self-study" (NUS will cut, 1996, p. 3). More generally, Lim (1996) pointed out that,

> *Transmission of knowledge per se...will recede in importance as multimedia and information technology become alternative effective purveyors of knowledge.... (We aim to) train our students to independently acquire knowledge with the help of information technology.This we propose will be done by trimming the amount of knowledge to be transmitted ... down to fundamentals and principles, emphasising practical application while more time and attention can be devoted to exercises that train students in independent and self-directed learning such as projects, research, field work and open-ended experiments in the laboratories.*

Learner-centred approaches, such as the use of projects and field work, are attracting increasing attention, and these are directly responsive to 'client' needs. In a multi-disciplinary research project on educational objectives and teaching methods at NUS, findings have indicated that teachers and students alike felt that project work, tutorials, and assignments are most productive for the development of analytical and critical thinking, practical application and independent learning skills (Pan, Betts & Liow, 1991). NUS strongly subscribes to the belief that "a personalized approach to teaching is essential if we are to upgrade the quality of education" (Small Group Teaching, 1986), and places great emphasis on small group work, both in regular courses as well as in special programs such as the 'Talent Development Programme' where students work very closely with personal mentors.Assessment procedures and instruments have also undergone revision. Examination questions are designed to test for understanding and thoughtful responses rather than recall and repetition. Continuous assessment has been emphasized, and reflects 20% - 100% of the final course grade. Alternatives to the traditional three hour final examination are also being actively explored, with open book examinations being one of them. The past decade has seen marked interest in modifying and extending the repertoire of instructional skills and methodologies. Such innovations make heavy demands on students, teachers and administrators, but they are imperative for significant changes and improvements in learning. They are also demanding in terms of resources, especially where investment in hardware is involved.

Recent years have seen increased and dynamic activity with regard to plugging education into the IT (Information Technology) world. With its increasing accessibility and robustness, IT has become a feasible and attractive tool for broad use in education. In Singapore, the government has provided leadership in setting directions and in furnishing the resources. The MOE is spending $1.5M (Singaporean) to equip schools with computers. Through agencies such as the National Science and Technology Board (NSTB) and National Computer Board (NCB), the MOE has set in motion a number of projects. By 1997, the 'Accelerating the use of IT in Primary Schools' project will provide these schools with multi-media computers to ensure that all pupils will be computer literate. As well, this project will enable more effective teaching/learning. Five secondary schools are currently piloting the 'Teachers and Students Workbench'. This is an IT2000 flagship project undertaken by the Information Technology Institute (ITI) for the Ministry of Education. It will provide a complete and integrated teaching and learning environment with access to a rich depository of multimedia courseware and electronic library. Teaching laboratories equipped with networked work stations support this resource-based and collaborative learning which, reportedly, is enthusiastically received by its pioneer users.

Noteworthy is the concern for creating a holistic approach which embraces not only the hardware, such as power/physical infrastructure, technology integration, and content security, but also pedagogy and teacher development. Also noteworthy are the efforts to create access points in public areas and provide on-line and digital multimedia content through liaison with various content publishers and developers. Such out-of-school access will encourage the habit of independent discovery learning. As Gan Boon San (1996, p. 8), Deputy Director of the Education Cluster at the National Computer Board, stated: "we want to leverage on the power of Information Technology..., not just for formal education but also for life-long learning."

At the National University of Singapore there is a high-level IT steering committee that actively promotes university-wide use of IT in teaching/learning. All staff are equipped with individual work stations and there are a number of student PC clusters with multimedia capability throughout the campus. These are linked to the NUS intranet as well as the Internet. Media for teaching and learning within this networked community include: lecture-on-demand video server, Web-based course notes, electronic discussion groups, and multimedia and CD-Rom packages. Video-conferencing has been in use for some years and desktop video-conferencing facilities are expected to be readily available very soon. These initiatives involve not only infrastructure and hardware provisions but also careful attention to the 'software' side, including support for relevant research and intensifying education development and manpower training though the NUS Centre for Development of Teaching & Learning. The goal is to empower students to become more efficient learners who are then able to manage their own learning as a lifelong venture.

NUS has also created the Office for Continuing Education which has assumed the responsibilities of the previous Department of Extramural Studies. This new office seeks to strengthen the university-community interface and coordinate the diverse extension programs mounted by different academic departments on campus. Other Singaporean 'service providers' — participants in continuing education and training — consist of government ministries, statutory boards, voluntary agencies, commercial enterprises and professional associations. Specific examples include the following:

- the Singapore Open University Degree Programme, which was established in 1993 in order to allow working adults to read for a university degree on a part-time basis, and which is expected to register more than 6000 students by 2002;

- the Institute of Technical Education (ITE), which provides a range of post-compulsory education options related to pre-employment workforce training, and apprenticeship training for school-leavers as well as in-employment upgrading programs for workers;

- the Singapore Productivity and Standards Board, which provides structured on-the-job (OJT) training related to the OJT 2000 Plan;

- the Singapore Professional Centre, founded with a grant from the Commonwealth Foundation, and which now has 31 member associations with a total membership of more than 12000 professionals;

- Singapore Cable Vision and its education channel which broadcasts with input from the National University of Singapore, Nanyang Technological University, and the Ministry of Health;

- other non-governmental organizations such as the Chinese Development Assistance Council (CDAC), Singapore Indians Association (SINDA), and Mendaki (Malay Community organization), which offer a range of remedial and enrichment programs.

Need

Delivering the Ruth Wong Memorial Lecture in Singapore in 1987, Malcolm Skilbeck (1987, pp. 10 & 17) clearly enunciated that

> ...a sophisticated and well-resourced education system is probably the best socially adaptive mechanism or instrument we have for enabling us as a world-wide society to cope with...pressures and changes....We are for the first time I think coming to grips with the reality of lifelong...education....

There is clear endorsement of this view in Singapore; education is a key item on its socio-political agenda. As a small country with limited human and other resources, education is essential for social cohesion as well as economic health, and continuing education will ensure the ongoing development of a highly skilled workforce which will sustain Singapore's growth rate and viability.

Maximising human potential through on-going training is among the "3 pillars" underpinning Singapore's success in the twenty-first century.

Growth means change. We will not become better off just by doing the same jobs in the same businesses ... we have to learn new skills and absorb new technologies.... . Older workers need constant retraining if they are not to stagnate, or worse become redundant... . Singaporeans have the drive to upgrade themselves and are tireless in the pursuit of excellence. Let us give them the opportunity to do so. (Goh Chok Tong, 1988)

The Ministry of Education (1996) has described and underscored the expertise required of graduates in the twenty-first century. Included are knowledge, skills and values.

Knowledge foundation and attitude
Sufficient fundamental knowledge in the chosen area or discipline which facilitates continual upgrading, and further specialisation and acquisition of multi-disciplinary skills; a proactive mindset and competencies to seek, process and apply information; and a positive attitude towards life-long independent learning.

Generic and critical thinking skills
A high level of generic skills consisting of communication (listening, speaking and writing), teamworking, networking and interpersonal skills; and critical thinking capacity, required for real-life problem solving, consisting of analytical, creative, innovative and systems thinking skills.

Values and social responsibility
A strong sense of social responsibility, a high degree of moral integrity and sensitivity in handling cultural diversity.

The National University of Singapore, as the oldest and most prominent university in the country, is highly responsive to the call for producing such graduates, and recently reiterated its commitment to "enhance NUS as a centre for quality education" (NUS, 1996, p. 12). Various strategies have been identified, including strengthening the teaching-research link, creating knowledge and technology, optimising the use of IT, forging partnerships with public and private-sector organisations, spearheading a responsive continuing education program, and providing quality service to the community. Clearly, NUS shares the vision that continuing education is essential to sustained growth: "the ability to anticipate, to adapt to, and to capitalise on changes in the international environment is, of course, the key for us to stay competitive as a nation" (Lim, 1996).

In addition to academic and professional development, there is a growing need for personal enrichment learning opportunities. This is a discernible ideological shift: the changing society is reflected in changing expectations including the perception of education as not only for bread-and-butter but also for personal enrichment. Skilbeck (1987, p. 18) has pointed out that continuing education must cater to the masses, and it must include "life enhancing values" and "personal and citizenship education". In fact, Singapore recognised this need some decades ago. The People's Association was formed as a community development agency in 1960, catering mainly to lower income groups through its 28 community centres throughout the island. Today it has grown to 115 considerably upgraded centres which offer courses, talks, workshops, seminars, and exhibitions covering a range of arts, leisure, educational, cultural and sports activities.

POLICY, PRACTICE, PROBLEMS AND POTENTIAL

Implications for policy-makers are self evident. Defining the policies, institutionalizing the practices, resolving the problems, and taking advantage of the potential is the challenge.

Policy

As borders come down, governments are having to change how they function [in order] to cope with the increasingly international dimension of policy issues. (Washington, 1996, p. 24)

Regional Cooperation

In the APEC community, the problems arising from the political, economic and social pluralities are real and sizeable, but, fortunately, there are ameliorating factors such as sound leadership and technological growth. Regional cooperation is necessary to prevent counter-productive and wasteful efforts. This is as true in education as in other domains. Policies that support regional cooperation will benefit all.

A Systems Approach

The need for a systems approach, within the context of regional cooperation, is transparent. As Duguet (1996, p. 4) describes, "system-wide changes are necessary to ensure the quality and coherence of provision, to avoid inefficient use of resources and to take full advantage of advances in pedagogy and in information technology."

A global approach to participation is more likely to yield useable blue-prints. Though cynics may argue that too many players often foul up the game, the counter — and arguably stronger — argument is that inputs from many and the sharing of experiences provide a broader knowledge base which will produce more informed decisions. Complementarity and the avoidance of discrepancies in provisions across member countries, for instance, are more probable than if individual countries chartered their own courses. The same need for coordination exists at the national level. Intranational dialogue and coordination among various participating providers of formal/informal education is, again evidently, a sensible strategy.

Practice

In terms of practice, consideration needs to be given to the micro, or intranational, context, and the macro, or international, context.

Micro/intranational Level

Lifelong learning must be orchestrated vertically and laterally. Provisions need to be made for the vertical stages of learning, at different phases in a person's development and for learning throughout life. Just as important, however, is the monitoring of the lateral inputs by different agencies which contribute to and support lifelong learning at any one stage. Included are formal and non-formal schools, professional associations, and private enterprises. Coherent links between education, training and work will support seamless movement between the three, thereby promoting lifelong development.

Macro/international Level

Within the APEC community, synergistic cooperation can be practised in various ways. Included are sharing of information through conferences, workshops and joint research initiatives, providing support and financial aid, and working and lobbying for common causes. Though there are application challenges when working across cultures, there are enough common denominators for general principles to be shared and value obtained.

Problems

Problems need to be addressed, directly and practically. Some are international in flavour, but many are and remain national or domestic in nature.

Parochialism

While collegiality is recognised as a good idea it is — as Ghandi reportedly answered when asked to comment on Western civilisation — as yet largely an idea. Historical and other differences have resulted in the evolution of different educational systems and infrastructures. This does not serve lifelong learning. Especially in a world of growing mobility, individuals need to be able to plug into any learning system, wherever they may happen to be physically located, and at whatever stage in their lives they happen to be. Some standardisation of educational structures, curriculum and practices is therefore desirable.

The issue of internationalisation is being raised with increasing urgency, and it is being examined in more searching and thorough-going ways. Particularly in the professional disciplines, the issue of internationalisation of curriculum has made itself felt. It is no longer adequate to have student exchanges only for specialised international programs. For knowledge and skills to be transferable, and for learning to continue across geographical boundaries, there must be systems which work together.

Bench-marking

Assessment of lifelong learning is even more problematic than is assessment within the traditional and more controlled learning environment. With the diversity of providers and programs, how are standards to be measured? Equitable and sensitive mechanisms have to be developed for measuring skills and competencies which are acquired not only through formal but also non-formal learning.

Since lifelong learning emphasises learning as a continuous process, it mitigates, at least ideologically, against traditional summative assessment. In fact, standard definitions of success and failure no longer apply, and assessment as a selection or ranking instrument is unbecoming. How then might learners and their progress be assessed? One suggestion is to introduce individual profiles of achievement. However, the problem then is that assessment becomes much more human resource intensive, and there is a potential for loss of comparable standards. Another suggestion is to have internal certification of achievement coupled with benchmarking fixed to externally and nationally set standards. The hazard here is that this may result in learners taking the line of least resistance, tending not to put themselves to the rigour of being accredited. As with all attempts at balancing the carrot and the stick, this issue requires careful thought and consideration.

Economic Implications

The adoption of recurrent education has major economic implications. For example, it will greatly alter the nature of the labour market and its operations. For the employer it has financial and other serious implications for human resource deployment and training. On the other hand, the economics of an up-to-date and highly trained workforce balance against training and deployment costs.

Who Pays?

Financing lifelong learning is a large undertaking. Is it to be borne by the public sector? By the employers? Or by the individuals? Government and non-governmental bodies will probably be involved, but to what extent? Employers will be involved if it can be profitably rationalised. Rightly, the individuals who stand to gain the most by sustained self-enhancement should be persuaded to bear the bulk, or at least a substantial part, of the cost. Whether individuals are able to afford this, and how they might be helped to do so, are pertinent questions to raise and address.

Balancing Supply and Demand

As mentioned earlier, the current environment is one where lifelong education is more supply-led than demand-driven, the result being that one half of the DAMN cycle outweighs the other.

> *Perhaps policy makers have tended to neglect learning activity unconnected to identifiable educational "supply"....Yet the dividing line between "supplied" education and learning designed by the learners themselves is becoming more blurred, as technologies [which] can allow learners to chart their own course through well-designed study packages proliferate. Policy*

makers are now starting to realise the importance of considering a wide range of learning activities if they are to devise effective strategies for creating "learning societies". (OECD, 1995a, p. 15)

Any imbalance needs to be corrected.

Establishing Common Platforms

IT will be a key element in popularising lifelong learning. One technical difficulty encountered in exploiting new technologies is the inconsistency in policies regarding the hardware and software. Another obstacle is differing languages, and variation in levels of competency in the more common languages. As a result, computer-based learning materials may not enjoy as wide a market as might be desired for optimisation of effort and resources.

Potential

All the issues, opportunities, policies, practices and problems should be examined only within the context of potential. Lifelong learning and APEC, when combined, have enormous potential for individual members and the forum.

Demand and Clientele

The APEC community is a significant force and many see it as, arguably, the most important trade grouping in the world.

[It] brings together three major economies in the world — Japan, China and the U.S. — within a collegial and cooperative framework. APEC members share enough common interests... (Lee, 1996)

With the Pacific Rim being a high growth area, the region enjoys a degree of vibrancy which augurs well for its undertakings. This is all the more so when the undertaking is one whose importance is as universally acknowledged as is the case with lifelong learning. APEC's success in the economic arena must be understood to rest, now and in the future, with the development of education, and lifelong learning in particular. The literacy rate within APEC is generally high, and demand for education continues to grow. In Singapore, for instance, over the past five years the percentage of the population receiving an upper secondary education has increased from 11% to 16%, while 7% as compared with 4% are now receiving university education (Leong & Leow, 1996, p. 37). This is, of course, just the front end of the tidal wave of non-formal, re-training, informal, on-the-job, leisure, upgrading and other learning activities that are demanded in increasing quantities, in a variety of delivery modes, and in many different places for all persons.

Historical and Cultural Advantage

Traditionally, Asian countries have a learning culture that instills discipline, diligence and dedication. The rigorous demands of a highly competitive society produce students who are quick to grasp the essentials. The challenge for policy makers and educators is to create incentives for investing in lifelong learning. Once those are clearly established, learners will quickly learn to do the necessary.

Another factor working to our advantage might be "the tradition of centralised control that [Singapore has] and that all the Australian states systems have had throughout the whole of their history" (Skilbeck, 1987, p. 18). In this regard, policy-makers are therefore invested with a great deal of influence, and decisions can generally be quickly and efficiently implemented. Non-Asian economies, and those which do not have centralized decision making capacity in terms of educational systems, may be, perhaps even seriously, disadvantaged.

Partnership Capability

With political and economic barriers being lowered, there is much greater opportunity for trans-border partnerships within the region. The rapid growth of IT and the development of the information superhighway, which transcends spatial divisions, give cause for optimism, at least within the region.

Clearly, there is tremendous potential for knowledge, skill and technology transfer. What is crucial — here as with other consortiums, and as in APEC's agenda for free trade — is cooperation and coordination.

> *A strategy for life-long learning involves many participants and requires a rethinking of roles and responsibilities. A field that is already complex becomes all the more so because of the variety of the contents, media, methods and settings of learning, as well as the involvement of a large number of institutions and individuals.... In an increasingly interdependent world, individual choices as well as collective policy decisions must draw on information, research, evaluation and analyses that go beyond national frontiers.* (Duguet, 1996, p. 5)

Ignoring the need for research, commitment, careful consideration and direction will likely produce systemic clashes that frustrate our efforts and waste our energies in a quite different and unproductive DAMN cycle. The opportunity is upon us, but it is we who must seize it.

REFERENCES

Ausabel, D. P. (1960). Use of advance organizers in the learning and retention of meaningful material. *Journal of Educational Psychology*, *51*, 267-272.

Candy, P. C. & Crebert, R. G. (1991). Lifelong learning: An enduring mandate for higher education. *Higher Education Research and Development*, *10*(1), 3-17.

Chang, A. (1994, October 21-22). *Rapport or compliance*. Paper presented at the Seminar on Excellence in Science Teaching, Singapore, National University of Singapore.

Duguet, P. (1995, June/July). Education: Face-to-face or distance? *The OECD Observer*, 194.

Entwistle, N., & Hounsell, D. (1971). *How students learn*. Lancaster: University of Lancaster.

Friere, P. (1972). *Pedagogy of the oppressed*. Harmondsworth: Penguin.

Gagne, R. M. (1970). *The conditions of learning*. New York: Holt, Rinehart and Winston.

Gan, B. S. (1996, April/May). Building a learning nation with IT. *IT Focus*, *8*.

Goh Chok Tong. (1988, February 25). Agenda for action: Towards a better, more secure future. *Straits Times*, p. 10.

Habermas, J. (1978). *Knowledge and human interests*. London: Heinemann.

Ironside, D. J. (1989). Concepts and definitions. In C. J. Titmus (Ed.), *World year book of education*. London: Kogan Page.

Knapper C. K. & Cropley A. J. (1985). *Lifelong learning and higher education*. London: Croom Helm.

Knowles, M. and Associates. (1984). *Andragogy in action*. San Francisco and London: Jossey-Bass Publishers.

Lakatos, I. & Musgrave A. (Eds.). (1977). *Criticism and the growth of scientific knowledge*. Cambridge: Cambridge University Press.

Lawson, H. & Appignannesi, L. (Eds.). (1989). *Dismantling truth: Reality in the post-modern world*. London: Weidenfeld and Nicolson.

Lee H. L. (1996, October). APEC: Breaking down barriers. *Asia Inc.* *5*(10).

Lim, L. (1995). *Letter to the Minister*. (Winning entry submitted to the Oxbridge Society Letter Writing competition, Singapore - available from personal archives of author or archives of the Oxbridge Society.)

Lim, P. (1996, August 27). *Convocation address*. Singapore: National University of Singapore.

Leong, C. C. (1996, December 29). My vision for year 2000. *Straits Times*, p. 17.

Leong, C. T. & Leow, J. (1997, January 8). Median income and education level up. *Straits Times*, p. 37.

Marton, F. & Saljo, R. (1976). On quantitative differences in learning: Outcome and process. *British Journal of Educational Psychology* 46(1).

Ministry of Education. (1996). *MOE strategic planning exercise, working group 6: University education*. Singapore: Author.

Nirmala, M. (1995, March 31). Undergraduates being taught to think and write. *Straits Times*, p. 24.

Nirmala, M. (1966, November 21). Singapore students top maths and science survey. *Straits Times*, p. 1.

Nirmala, M. & Mathi, B. (1996, March 31). Do more A's mean brighter students? *Sunday Times*, p 2.

NUS. (1996, August). *National University of Singapore: Strategic directions for the 21st century.* Singapore: National University of Singapore.

NUS will cut syllabi to allow for more creativity. (1996, August 28). *Straits Times*, p. 3.

Nurturing excellence must combine best of both east and west. (1977, January 3). *Straits Times*, p. 41.

OECD. (1995a). *Learning beyond schooling: New forms of supply and new demands*. Paris: Centre for Educational Research and Innovation.

OECD. (1995b). *Continuing professional education of highly qualified personnel*. Paris: Author.

Pan, D., Betts, M. Liow, S. (1991). *The effectiveness of different teaching methods at NUS: A campus wide survey* (Multi-disciplinary research project RP 910097). Singapore: National University of Singapore.

Pask, G. (1976). Styles and strategies of learning. *British Journal of Educational Psychology, 46*, 128-148.

Popper, K. R. (1975). *Objective knowledge: An evolutionary approach*. Oxford: Oxford University Press.

Registrar's Office. (1986, February 8). *Small Group Teaching*. Singapore: National University of Singapore.

Skilbeck, M. (1987, August 28). *Education and the changing economic and industrial order: An international perspective*. Ruth Wong Memorial Lecture at the National University of Singapore.

Washington, S. (1996, April/May). Globalisation and governance. *The OECD Observer, 199.*

Wee, T. S. & Huan, C. H. (1991, November). *Physics students' perception of teaching and learning*. Proceedings of the Seminar on Teaching Science at the Tertiary Level, Singapore, National University of Singapore.

Wittgenstein, L (1978). *Philosophical investigations*. Oxford: Blackwell.

Yap, Y. C. (1988, April 31). Letter to a Minister. *Straits Times*, p. 5.

Cheng-Yen Wang

Cheng-Yen Wang earned his first Ph.D. in education at National Chengchi University in Taipei. Currently, he is working on a second doctorate at the University of London's Institute of Education. In 1994, Dr. Wang joined the faculty of the Graduate Institute of Adult Education, established at the National Kaohsiung Normal University, where he serves as the Chair of the Institute and Director of the Research Center for Adult Education. With specific research interests in community education, distance education, and adult education policy and administration, he has published more than fifty papers in English and Chinese. Dr. Wang enjoys classical music, art and film, and spends time playing lawn tennis.

Advancing Lifelong Learning through Adult Education Policy in Chinese Taipei

by Cheng-Yen Wang

Lifelong learning has had a brief but already interesting chronology in Chinese Taipei; now it is poised for a period of major development. Adult education, which is positioned to be the major foundation for the development of lifelong learning in Chinese Taipei, is a key element in this educational development. This paper describes and analyzes the two main policy packages in Chinese Taipei which have shaped and are continuing to shape adult education, and at the same time describes how lifelong learning is expected to flower from the second of these. The paper also makes recommendations for enriching adult education policy-making, a key influence for lifelong learning practice. These ideas and recommendations may be useful for other APEC member economies, particularly those economies which are in the process of strengthening their educational policy-making capability and developing their adult education and lifelong learning programming.

INTRODUCTION

Lifelong learning, defined as learning throughout the lifespan, is a concept which is familiar to most Chinese. In fact, many well-known Chinese proverbs have encouraged lifelong learning for thousands of years. The most familiar are: "to learn as long as to live" and "learning has no boundaries." The notions implied in these two proverbs incorporate a variety of lifelong learning related terms such as lifetime learning, life-wide learning, and lifespan learning. The central theme, of course, is that learning must continue as long as a person lives. These Chinese proverbs, however, did not have significant modern educational and psychological import until the arrival of adult education. Since then, the proverbs have paved the way for developing adult education and lifelong learning in modern Chinese Taipei. Most of Chinese Taipei's people are familiar with these proverbs, and they can be employed as a starting point to understand lifelong learning and adult education.

During the past half decade in Chinese Taipei, programs which extend an individual's learning opportunities throughout the lifespan have had an excellent opportunity to grow. However, prior to that time, and in comparison with most developed economies, Chinese Taipei's adult education programming was conducted mostly in non-formal settings and styles, and the term, adult education, was not familiar to the public. Currently, formal adult education is offered mainly through distance education institutes and supplementary schools which are attached to secondary and primary schools.

In order to stimulate adult education, Chinese Taipei formulated the "Develop and Improve Adult Education Five Year Scheme" (Five Year Scheme), employing it from 1992 through to June, 1996. It was then followed by a new scheme called the "Lifelong Learning-Oriented Middle Stage Adult Education Development Scheme" (LLDS). It was as a result of the Five Year Scheme that adult education policy and practices began to be taken seriously and grow systematically within Chinese Taipei. With regard to community-based adult education, a strong contribution came from President Lee Tein-Hui when he stressed the importance of cultivating community consciousness, expanding community culture, and promoting the idea of "commonality of life". President Lee's emphasis on community inspired the policy, "The Whole Construction of Community" (WCC), implemented by the Council for Cultural Affairs. These policies gave adult education, which has been the mother of lifelong learning in Chinese Taipei, the opportunity to develop both in stature and effectiveness.

Official policies act as guidelines for administration. Successful policies steer and direct the administration, and result in change. Policies within Chinese Taipei that relate to adult education and lifelong learning have detailed prescriptive expectations as well as descriptive phenomenon. In the next few pages, this paper analyzes ways in which adult education policies may be used to establish a successful and permanent foundation for lifelong learning within the Chinese Taipei context. This analysis may be helpful for policy makers in other APEC economies, especially those who are involved with adult education programs that are evolving into lifelong learning practices.

A CHANGING SOCIETY

Society in Chinese Taipei has been changing quite dramatically. This change, which has taken place in a relatively short period of time, has been called "The Quiet Revolution". Revolution implies rapid change, and this pace has been witnessed in the political, economic, social, and educational dimensions of life.

Political Dimension

After revoking Martial Law in 1986, politics in Chinese Taipei changed perceptibly. Shifts included the liberation of political organisations, the wide availability of newspapers and other publications, and direct election of the Executive. Some expected reforms are yet to come, including amendments to the Constitution.

Also during this period, new political parties were organized. The three main political parties, the Kaomintom (KMT), the Democratic Progressive Party (DPP) and the New Party (NP), have enlarged the democratic process of policy formation, thereby reflecting different demands from various groups. For example, the DPP emphasizes the grassroots culture which has indirectly facilitated the growth of adult education. Political shifts are fundamental to other changes, including educational reform, as each of the three political parties develop and expand policy agendas.

Economic Dimension

During the past decade, Chinese Taipei has faced increasing economic pressure as it competes in global markets. Since the 1970s, Chinese Taipei has enjoyed a dynamic economic history, earning itself the well-deserved title of "Little Tiger". Low-skill manufacturing has, however, during the past few years gradually moved in significant measure to other developing economies, including the new Little Tigers such as Thailand, Malaysia, Indonesia, and the Philippines. As a result, Chinese Taipei's current economic development lags slightly behind the three older Tigers, Singapore, Hong Kong, and South Korea. Many economic indicators have demonstrated this trend.

In this context, Chinese Taipei's economic competitiveness has declined from 11th in the world in 1992 to 18th in 1996 (Wu, 1996). In spite of this drop, Chinese Taipei has had an average economic growth rate of 6.34% during this same period, a rate higher than most developed economies (Chinese Statistical Association, 1996). Lower rankings have led to some degree of pessimism, and it is thought that Chinese Taipei's economic development must be enhanced, especially if it is to compete successfully with other newly developing economies. In this climate of economic aggressiveness, adult education and lifelong learning are viewed as critical instruments for enhancing economic development through workforce upgrading, including professional education.

Social Dimension

Chinese Taipei society has developed into a postmodern era (Jarvis, 1996). In this context, there are more diverse needs arising from a variety of sources. With advances in medical science and an increase in living standards, the life expectancy of people in Chinese Taipei is now 75 years of age (Ministry of the Interior, 1996). As of 1994, people over the age of 65 constituted more than 7% of the population, making Chinese Taipei an aging society according to the United Nations standards. Additionally, more people are retiring before the official age of 65, and this aging population is demanding more opportunities to learn. Before 1968, when the government extended compulsory education from six to nine years, women had comparatively fewer opportunities to gain an education. This group, now entering middle age, encompasses a high percentage of the illiterate population, and remedial programs are demanded.

These changes have reduced the supply and increased the cost of labour. As a result, employers may, under certain conditions, hire foreign workers. Currently, there are approximately 200,000 foreign workers registered in Chinese Taipei, most of whom come from south east Asia including the Philippines and Thailand. The growing number of foreign workers has increased the importance of adult basic education, particularly with regard to the need for language instruction.

Educational Dimension

In Chinese Taipei, and elsewhere in the world, education is a valued commodity. However, there have been recent developments which suggest the possibility for change. Most significantly, the unemployment rate for that portion of the population holding a bachelor's degree and above is higher in Chinese Taipei than is the unemployment rate for those with a lower level of education. Specifically, in February of 1996, the average unemployment rate in Chinese Taipei was 2.1%, while the unemployment rate for those with a bachelor's degree and above was 2.56%. At the same time, the unemployment rate for those holding no more than senior high school certificates was 2.23%, and the unemployment rate for those with only secondary school certificates, or less, was 1.78% (see Directorate-General of Budget, Accounting and Statistics, 1996).

The suggestion that higher education may result in a greater likelihood for unemployment has potentially affected the overall view of higher education in Chinese Taipei. Most young adults now focus on getting a good job as their number one priority. A popular route is in-service education coupled with entry into the labour market as soon as possible. This is then followed by technical updating or part-time enrolment in professional education. In this environment, demand for recurrent education is growing.

Adding to the changes in Chinese Taipei education, starting next fiscal year (1997), each national college and university is responsible for raising 20% of its budget. In order to achieve this target, institutions have been developing extension education activities and expanding extramural education. In the recent past, only private colleges and universities were interested in extension education, now the field is expected to expand greatly, particularly at the higher levels.

Figure 1: Major Influence Resources on AE Policy-making

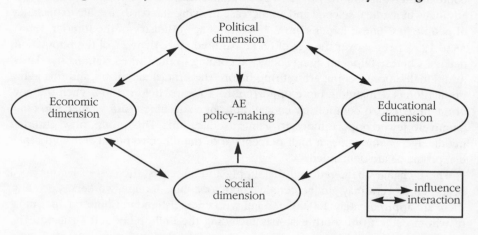

The Combined Context

As Figure 1 demonstrates, the political, economic, social, and educational contexts, both separately and together, affect adult education and the potential for a lifelong learning system in Chinese Taipei. Given their influence, they represent important indicators in so far as evaluating policy directions and program outcomes.

A major weakness in the field of adult education within Chinese Taipei is directly the result of little or no productive collaboration between providers, particularly in the mix of statutory, voluntary, and professional institutions. At present, institutions which offer adult education activities are facilitated by the government departments of Education and Social Administration. However, during the last five years many local governments began establishing another variety of educational institution aimed at older learners. These have not, however, filled the gap nor operated in a fashion which draws the field together in order to make a coordinated whole. Some argue that the shortage of professional adult education institutions, operating in a fashion similar to American community colleges, is a fundamental barrier for developing adult education in Chinese Taipei. Resolving this issue is a central concern if adult education is to flower into an integrated system of lifelong learning. On an optimistic note, the government, the academic world, and the public have identified this weakness and discussions are occurring with regard to how institutions should be established and coordinated. These discussions were reflected in part within the Five Year Scheme and the LLDS.

GOVERNMENT'S ADULT EDUCATION POLICIES

The Five Year Scheme was the first planned adult education policy directive in Chinese Taipei. As discussed earlier, prior to 1992, adult education within Chinese Taipei was in its infancy. It was the Five Year Scheme that laid the foundation for an exacting analysis which has the potential to grow into a mature and stable system of adult education practices, and then into a lifelong learning system. In this section of the paper, the Five Year Scheme and the LLDS are discussed in detail. In addition, though the WCC is for the most part a cultural policy, its influence on education will be discussed. It is important to develop this discussion with the understanding that these three schemes are national policies.

Five Year Scheme

The Five Year Scheme was conducted from July 1992 through June 1996 (Ministry of Education, 1991). Since the Five Year Scheme was the first systematic policy package for adult education, it reviewed, in depth, past practices as these related to adult education. With a budget exceeding US$132 million, the goal of the scheme was to give adult education in Chinese Taipei a new life (Ministry of Education, 1991). In terms of the overall education budget, this was a large project, suggesting that the government was very serious about promoting, developing and improving adult education in Chinese Taipei.

The ten domains of the scheme included the following: a) researching and assessing adult education; b) enacting the Adult Education Act and ratifying the Supplementary Laws; c) establishing adult education institutes and enhancing equipment, facilities, and staff; d) coordinating the relevant government departments, schools, social education institutions, research institutions, public and private enterprises, foundations, and professional associations which offer adult education;

e) cultivating adult educators by providing in-service education in order to improve teaching methods; f) developing and improving curriculum and learning materials; g) planning the use of television, broadcasting, newspapers, books, and magazines for adult education; h) enhancing the promotion of adult education; i) reinforcing adult education for disadvantaged groups within the population; and j) evaluating the effectiveness of adult education.

A major needs assessment and the establishment of professional institutions were the key directions in the Five Year Scheme. In order to evaluate demand, and use this as the basis for program development, the government commissioned a number of research studies from adult education specialists. These were conducted in different counties and cities throughout Chinese Taipei in order to look for variations and realize a comprehensive overview. Ten research projects were completed, and the results did reveal some differences in local demand. However, it was the shortage of professional adult education institutions that was found to be the major weakness throughout Chinese Taipei.

To date, four research centres and two graduate institutes respond to the demand for professional adult education — not nearly enough. Discussions continue with regard to what sorts of institutions and structures would be most helpful in order to enhance the current structure. Community colleges, which could be created from Social Education Institutes, provide one practical possibility. In addition, the two metropolises, Taipei and Kaohsiung, plan to establish open universities in order to provide lifelong learning opportunities for their citizens. Given the lack of professional institutions, and the fact that adult education programming is offered by so many sectors, the need to coordinate activities was also stressed in the scheme.

During the Five Year Scheme, the government played a major role in developing and improving adult education. Significant contributions from the Five Year Scheme included the generous funding, the universal needs assessment, the development of institutes within universities, and the marketing of adult education. During the scheme and after, adult education has been developing, albeit gradually, and a solid foundation has been established. Weaknesses at this stage include the speed at which programming is being developed — not fast enough — and the fact that many of the principles of adult education have yet to be incorporated into the programming.

Lifelong Learning Oriented Middle Stage Adult Education Development Scheme

The LLDS began in July 1996, and is intended to replace the Five Year Scheme. Whereas the Five Year Scheme can be viewed as the foundation for adult education and lifelong learning in Chinese Taipei, the LLDS focuses more on programming and implementation. The focus of the LLDS is the unravelling of the essence of adult education in order to bring forth the flower of lifelong learning. LLDS identifies lifelong learning as the aim of adult education in this second stage.

In terms of the domains, the similarities between the LLDS and the Five Year Scheme are obvious. The ten domains of the LLDS (Ministry of Education, 1996) include the following: a) continuing the program of the Five Year Scheme; b) enacting relevant legislation to establish an adult education system; c) creating new adult education institutions; d) establishing a system for employing and cultivating adult education professionals; e) encouraging current institutions to offer adult education programming, and coordinating and integrating these efforts; f) enhancing curricula, programming and teaching methods; g) linking media resources and the community in order to develop adult education; h) promoting lifelong learning and building the information networks for learning; i) developing lifelong learning for disadvantaged adults; and j) conducting research and evaluation. With the exception of the explicit inclusion of and emphasis on lifelong learning, the domains are quite similar to those in the Five Year Scheme. Domain "g" is particularly significant. It advocates the promotion of community adult learning activities through the incorporation of strategies such as organising study circles under the support and guidance of local schools. This is the first domain to employ concrete strategies for programming.

At this writing, the LLDS is scheduled to be in effect for almost another five years. Its budget comes from the Ministry of Education, but is not as large as was the case with the Five Year Scheme. This could become its chief shortcoming. Optimistically, however, the explicit development and incorporation of lifelong learning is encouraging. Clearly, the definitive goal is the creation of a learning society imbued with a comprehensive and integrated lifelong learning system.

The Whole Construction of Community

In essence, the WCC is a cultural policy package not an educational one. However, it is closely related to adult education, and has important contributions to make to this cause. As the Vice-Chair of the Council for Cultural Affairs, Dr. Chen Chi-Nan said, "The purpose of the WCC is to set up a systematic learning society and a learning community" (Chen, 1996). Given this mandate, it is easy to see the relationship to the Five Year Scheme and the LLDS. As many researchers have noted, adult education can assist in the construction of an educative community or learning society (Brookfield, 1983; Fasheh, 1995; Knowles, 1980). The WCC has a slogan: "Culturalisation of industry and industrialisation of culture".

With the full support of President Lee, and coupled with good timing, the WCC has aroused the public's consciousness of community through diverse activities. From 1994 onward, WCC has been a popular term. Currently, it enjoys a high level of popularity and can be reasonably described as a social movement in present day Chinese Taipei.

The WCC has paid attention to the possible contributions of primary and secondary schools to the community, but lacks a professional perspective and expertise with regard to adult education. From the WCC viewpoint, local schools can participate in community construction through a variety of approaches (Architecture and City-Country Research and Development Foundation of Taiwan University, 1995): a) by assisting the community to develop a community culture; b) by establishing grassroots education in the schools; c) by cooperating with and supporting community development projects; d) by increasing the involvement of parents' associations; and e) by providing resources for community activities. These approaches for involving schools in community construction are a starting point, but the overall potential is yet to be developed. And although some of the key people, such as Dr. Chen, understand the significance of adult education, the WCC's contribution to adult education is likely to remain limited. In part this is because the WCC lacks knowledge of adult education and lifelong learning opportunities and potential. What is needed is for the WCC to draw more attention to adult education programming. This will not only advantage WCC goals, but will also advance the development of adult education. There will be a win-win effect for adult education, lifelong learning, and the WCC.

IMPROVING ADULT EDUCATION THROUGH POLICY FORMATION

Adult education policy-making directly influences the implementation and administration of programming, and in this regard is critical for the contextual development of lifelong learning. Thus, what adult education and lifelong learning will be, is very dependent on the nature of policy-making at this stage of educational reform. It is for this reason that Clyne (1993) notes adult education policy as the central task of public policy. Naturally, therefore, the public's interest in this will be correspondingly high. The two prime policy packages, the Five Year Scheme and LLDS in Chinese Taipei, are basically aimed at raising the standards of adult education and then lifelong learning. These two policy packages represent the precursor for a systematic approach to lifelong learning. By closely analyzing the needs that arise from various applications, and projecting future directions, educational authorities in Chinese Taipei's central government can adjust adult education policy-making in order to ensure it applies to the broader and more integrated context of lifelong learning. This approach could also be used by other APEC economies. However, the following elements should be considered.

Bridging the Gap Between Policy and Practice

Policy is created from past practice and is refined with a view towards implementation in the current context. How to effectively link policy with current practice and build from that point forward is the major challenge for policy makers. To satisfy demand in the world of adult education, policy makers have to bridge the gap between policy and practice by being consistent and realistic. One useful approach for bridging this gap is to develop a precise and universal needs assessment tool. The focus of needs assessment should not only be to determine present demands, but also to reveal future trends. Horizontal and longitudinal analyses are required.

After reviewing the results of the Five Year Scheme, the LLDS needs to put forth a more concerted effort for assessing the direction in which adult education is moving. Although needs assessment was one of the domains of both schemes, but by no means a prominent one, it is a necessity. In fact, when the Five Year Scheme was finished, a multiple-dimensional needs assessment should have been undertaken prior to beginning the LLDS.

The success of any needs assessment depends for the most part on a bottom-up procedure instead of the more common top-down approach. Specifically, with regard to adult education and lifelong learning, a grassroots examination is required, and this should incorporate a field study approach conducted in the context of the community. In this way, the needs assessment can bridge the gap and provide for the development of realistic and viable linkages between policy and practice.

Increasing Multiple Participation in Policy-making

Multiple participation in adult education policy-making is a common characteristic, as is diversity in terms of providers. Government and non-government sectors, as well as profit and not-for-profit organisations, serve adult education. When developing adult education policy, policy makers need to listen to the different voices. Beyond participants and providers, adult education policy links to other government departments, including social, labour, culture and communications. This demands multiple participation.

The formation of the Five Year Scheme and the LLDS was commissioned by the Ministry of Education in conjunction with committees composed of various academics from different fields. Although the committees did invite opinions from different groups when schemes were being developed, the interaction between committees and outsiders was insufficient. In fact, the committees did not gather enough cogent material from the real world to draw practical conclusions that will lead to the most effective and efficient policy. Multiple participation can help resolve this sort of problem by gathering data from all sectors.

Balancing Descriptive and Prescriptive Demands

The development of adult education encompasses practical and ideal dimensions to meet both descriptive and prescriptive demands. If adult education policy merely meets the descriptive demands, it cannot reflect the needs of the future. In contrast, if adult education policy only stresses future needs, it will enlarge the gap between policy and practice and hinder the process of implementation. Therefore, as Brookfield (1983) has shown, adult education has different paradigms to meet the different needs.

Balancing the descriptive and prescriptive demands is difficult for policy makers.

Figure 2: The Distribution of AE Policy-making

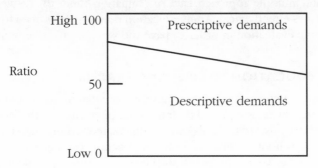

Development of AE

Data collection through multiple participation is mostly descriptive, so policy makers must supplement this by considering future developments and theoretical analyses. Balancing descriptive and prescriptive needs in adult education policy is not a matter of weighing each equally. Distribution must reflect developmental and immediate, theoretical and practical, and present and future needs. A suitable approach for adult education policy makers is to divide the distribution of bilateral demands into different stages based on the development of adult education. As shown in Figure 2, when adult education is in its infancy, policy makers can place more emphasis on policy that meets descriptive demands and encourages motivation. As programming grows and prospers, prescriptive policy will increase in ratio until descriptive and prescriptive demands are roughly balanced.

Improving Evaluation

Ongoing, multiple evaluation is a key strategy for improving the quality of adult education policy. The chief purpose of evaluation is to ensure improvement continues and is consistent. To achieve this, adult education policy makers must conduct evaluations not only at the end of the policy implementation period, but also at the beginning and throughout the process. In other words, adult education policy must include formative and summative evaluation. The former is useful during the process, and the latter at the end.

Multiple evaluation implies that adult education policy requires inter-departmental and intra-departmental evaluation. In terms of Chinese Taipei's adult education policy, evaluation is not only carried out by the Ministry of Education, but also by other government departments, private organisations, and even the public. As well as evaluators from the Ministry of Education, there are others from outside the Ministry who bring a variety of perspectives. In general, insiders are apt to have blind points about their own activities, while outsiders often have more objective observations.

Evaluation of development and research was one of the domains in the Five Year Scheme and the LLDS. However, in actual practice, it is difficult to locate examples of multiple evaluation in these policy packages. There was some inter-departmental evaluation in the Ministry of Education, but it appears to have lacked a continuing, systematic, and multiple approach. Lack of evaluation blinds the results, and this negatively influences effectiveness. Adult education policy makers need to entrench continuing multiple evaluation in order to pave the way for effective policy formation.

FROM ADULT EDUCATION TO LIFELONG LEARNING

The period during which adult education has the potential to affect and influence individuals occupies the largest part of their lives. For most citizens, this occurs from about the age of 18 onwards. Those who immediately enter higher education extend their "youth" schooling for a few years, but become candidates for adult education shortly thereafter. Given the increasing lifespans of the population in Chinese Taipei, there is an ever-growing need and demand for adult education opportunities, in both the formal and non-formal sectors.

A Learning Society

The creation of a fully developed and completely integrated learning society in Chinese Taipei is the goal described as lifelong learning. This vision of the learning society, as Hutchins (1968) concluded, is one of fulfillment. It is a world community, civilised and humane. Jarvis (1995, p. 40) described this learning society as needing to be acknowledged, learner-based, having no access barriers, and providing multifaceted, lifelong opportunities. It is a society organised in such a manner that all learning opportunities are available to everyone on a full- or part-time basis. Thus, a true learning society is one where the right to learn is protected, and everyone can continue learning for whatever reasons they choose, by various means, with abundant resources and complete flexibility.

Given Chinese Taipei's need to compete in the global marketplace, the establishment of a learning society is quite clearly an important tactic. The Council of Educational Reform and Consultancy, created two years ago with the intention of developing a comprehensive examination of the total education system, has recommended focusing on the creation of a lifelong learning society. The Council for Cultural Affairs has also called for the restoration of an old concept, the "Society of bookishness". Cultivating local leaders who will establish study circles in the communities is a first step towards implementation. However, as Van der Zee (1991) has pointed out, there is a growing regional and perhaps even world-wide consensus that all reform in education should focus on the goal of creating a learning society.

Other Economies and Lifelong Learning

International trends with regard to lifelong learning are also increasingly obvious and common. For example, 1996 was the European Year of Lifelong Learning, a measure designed to highlight awareness and the importance of learning through the lifespan. A variety of activities in the 12 member European Union helped to target a learning society as a central goal. Objectives for the year included: a) encouraging acquisition of new knowledge; b) bringing schools and the business sectors closer together; c) combatting exclusion from education; d) promoting proficiency in three community languages; and e) treating capital investment and investment in training on an equal basis (Cresson, 1996, p. 217).

The American Association for Adult and Continuing Education (AAACE) also has a lifelong learning vision. Recently, it emphasized that "all communities will have access to Lifelong Learning facilities where adults can plan career objectives and receive counselling and educational services as needed" (AAACE, 1996, p. 23). AAACE also stressed the importance of adult education and lifelong learning for the United States in the coming century.

As is the case in Chinese Taipei, most APEC economies, particularly in East and Southeast Asia, have pent-up demand for lifelong learning, not only to support continuing economic growth but also for resolving social and cultural issues. Lifelong learning needs to be on government policy agendas, and perhaps even at the top of the list. This need is amplified by the fact that other areas in the world are stressing the importance of lifelong learning, and pressing it into practice. APEC member economies, particularly those in Asia, cannot hesitate to follow the global example. Although economic performance for many APEC economies in Asia is excellent, there are fundamental problems which could threaten economic security. Included are the relatively late development of high technology and advanced manufacturing techniques, illiteracy, the widening gap between the rich and the poor, and increasing social and psychological problems resulting from rapid changes taking place in society. Although lifelong learning is not the only instrument for addressing these problems, it is one of the major strategies for achieving prolonged social stability and economic growth in APEC economies. Thus, it is time for APEC economies to enhance lifelong learning not only to create significant domestic benefits but also to build for economic success in the increasingly competitive global market.

SUMMARY AND CONCLUSION

In the experience of Chinese Taipei, the multiple contexts of the political, economic, social, and educational dimensions provide a strong foundation for understanding the development of adult education and lifelong learning policy and practices. Policy packages such as the Five Year Scheme and the LLDS have to some degree responded to the demands initiated by different sectors of Chinese Taipei society, but there is still much work to do.

Policy development is critically important, and it must be a focus for the government and all other stakeholders. Adult education and lifelong learning policy must be reviewed continuously and extensively in order to maximize potential. This paper has analyzed the background and contexts for developing and improving adult education in Chinese Taipei, extensively reviewed two policy packages which have influenced adult education during the past five years, and explored relevant cultural policy. Following this analysis, the paper identified four strategies to strengthen adult education, with specific regard to policy-making.

Given that adult education is the major element in the development of an integrated system of lifelong learning, it must be supported by sound, rational and productive policies. Adult education policy-making, therefore, is central to fulfilling the promise of lifelong learning, and the strategies developed in this paper may be used to stimulate other APEC members as they advance the deployment of lifelong learning in their own economies.

REFERENCES

AAACE. (1996). Visions. Visions. Visions. *Adult Learning*, 7(3), 23.

Architecture and City-Country Research and Development Foundation of Taiwan University. (1995). *Manual for the whole construction of community.* Taipei: Author.

Brookfield, S. (1983). Community adult education: A conceptual analysis. *Adult Education Quarterly*, 33(3), 154-160.

Chen, Chi-Nan. (1996). The Whole Construction of Community is the opportunity to reconstruct Taiwan's soul. *U-Com, 3, 4.*

Chinese Statistical Association. (1996). *Newsletter of the Chinese Statistical Association,* 7(5), 39.

Clyne, P. (1993). Adult education in Europe: Structure and organisation. *Adults Learning*, 4(7), 176-177.

Cresson, E. (1996). The European year of lifelong learning. *Adults Learning*, 7(9), 215-218.

Directorate-General of Budget, Accounting and Statistics. (1996). *Monthly bulletin of manpower statistics, Taiwan area, 269.* Taipei: Author.

Fasheh, M. J. (1995). The reading campaign experience within Palestinian society: Innovative strategies for learning and building community. *Harvard Educational Review, 65*(1), 66-92.

Hutchins, R. M. (1968). *The learning society.* New York: The New American Library.

Jarvis, P. (1995). *Adult and continuing education: Theory and practice.* (2nd ed.). London: Routledge.

Jarvis, P. (1996). *The public's recognition of lifelong learning.* Paper presented at the Conference of Community Adult Education, April 25-26, National Kaohsiung Normal University, Kaohsiung.

Knowles, M. S. (1980). *The modern practice of adult education: From pedagogy to andragogy.* Englewood Cliffs, New Jersey: Cambridge Adult Education.

Ministry of Education. (1991). *Outlines of "Develop and Improve Adult Education Five Year Scheme".* Taipei: Author.

Ministry of Education. (1996). *Lifelong learning-oriented Middle Stage Adult Education Scheme.* Taipei: Author.

Ministry of the Interior. (1996). *Taiwan-Fukien Demography Quarterly, 22*(2), 12-23.

Van der Zee, H. (1991). The learning society. *International Journal of Lifelong Education, 10*(3), 213-230.

Wu, Yi-Jing. (1996). The grade of Taiwan's economic competitiveness. *Common Wealth, 182,* 46-50.

Frederick C. Kintzer

Frederick C. Kintzer holds a B.A. from the University of Washington and an M.A. and Ed.D. from Stanford University. He joined the University of California at Los Angeles (UCLA) faculty in 1960, following two community college presidencies. For five years he served as the Vice Chair of the UCLA Department of Education, and is now Professor Emeritus of Higher Education at UCLA. Professor Kintzer has written widely and extensively on education, including five books and more than 130 monographs and articles. In addition, he has served as a consultant and lecturer in various countries, including two international conferences in Paris, at the University of Hiroshima, Japan, at the National Cheng Kung University, Tainan, Chinese Taipei, and at Ben Gurion University, Israel. As the recipient of two Fulbright Scholar Awards, he served as an education advisor to the governments of Sri Lanka and Kenya. At home, he enjoys a daily swim in the municipal pool near his house in San Luis Obispo, California.

Articulation and Transfer:
Critical Contributions to
Lifelong Learning

by Frederick C. Kintzer

Strong systems and mechanisms for articulation and transfer are central to the full and complete development of lifelong learning. In many APEC economies, as well as others, there are a growing number of short-cycle institutions - educational organizations that have proven to be fundamental in their support for and development of articulation and transfer processes. As well as transfer credits for formal learning, there is a growing need for accrediting non-formal and experiential education. A variety of approaches have been developed in this regard, the most enduring have been documented by Willingham and Whitaker. Although the future is difficult to predict, it is likely that short-cycle institutions will continually modify courses for the growing numbers of adult re-entry students, industry will become increasingly involved in the delivery of post-secondary education credits, and technology will expedite non-traditional and non-sponsored education. Together, these influences will greatly affect the development and delivery of lifelong learning.

INTRODUCTION

As recognized in a growing number of economies, opportunities for the interchange of credits, courses and articulation services between secondary-level schools and post-secondary colleges and universities directly and positively enhance opportunities for lifelong learning. A potential influence in much of the world, the benefits of the articulation and transfer phenomenon are well documented in the United States and in parts of Canada.

This paper will identify and explain what is meant by articulation, transfer and lifelong learning, then address questions that include the following: What is the role of short-cycle institutions in the articulation and transfer process? Who is served by effective articulation and transfer processes? How can experiential learning be evaluated for credentialing purposes? What suggestions for implementation can be offered to policy makers and practitioners? What does the future suggest for articulation and transfer? All these questions are addressed within the broader context of lifelong learning.

DEFINITIONS

Articulation is the totality of processes and relationships involved in the systematic movement of students vertically and laterally throughout formal and informal education systems. A variety of services to prospective and current students is included, such as, advisement at the secondary level, matriculation considerations while still attending secondary school, assessment of prior learning, placement in college classes, counselling following higher education enrolment, housing, and job placement. *Transfer* - the mechanics of credit, course, and curriculum exchange - is one of the articulation processes. Included are recognition of and credit for learning that includes experiential as well other activities not specifically taken for credit. Cooperative relationships and a student centred focus are essential if the entire operation is to succeed, along with the willingness of politicians and educators alike to support policy decisions favouring students. (See Kintzer, 1976, for discussions of these definitions.)

Some definitions of lifelong learning emerged in the United States during the early 1970s, as the adult part-time learner became a major concern of many of the heretofore traditional universities. While not always motivated by altruistic concerns, universities quickly organized programs specifically for adults outside the main stream of the post-secondary environment. In 1973, the U.S. Commission on Nontraditional Study published a philosophical comment which led to further refinement, at least within the U.S., of the term. Perspectives such as: "more an attitude than a system," "puts the student first and the institution second," "encourages diversity of individual opportunity rather than uniform prescription," and "de-emphasizes time, space, and even course requirements [as well as credits]" became recognized as characteristics of lifelong learning (see the Commission on Nontraditional Study, 1973, p. xv).

The Commission's perspectives, promoted in several publications, led to a definition that was adopted by the General Council of UNESCO in 1976. It placed the learner at the centre of the learning society.

The term 'lifelong education and learning' denotes an overall scheme aimed both at restructuring the existing education system and at developing the entire educational potential outside the education system; in such a scheme men and women are the agents of their own education. (UNESCO, 1976, p. 2)

Later defining descriptions of lifelong learning processes included the provision of credit for experiential learning, and the rapidly growing non-credit programs offered in formal classrooms and laboratories as well as in non-formal settings were translated into policies and operational strategies of articulation and transfer. The development of continuing education units (CEUs) added flexibility and variation to lifelong learning. As a result, academic credits for professional upgrading could be earned, or even required, and non-academic activities, documented at any point in life, could be systematically translated into degree or certificate credits.

These more recent concepts strengthen the theme of this paper, that effective articulation and transfer contributes greatly to the global development of lifelong learning opportunities and potential. Further, an immediate effect resulting from the institutionalization of articulation and transfer, and a goal of educators and politicians alike, is to narrow the opportunity gap between educational "haves" and "have-nots".

SHORT-CYCLE HIGHER EDUCATION

The exchange of credits and courses for entry into advanced or higher education is now found, at least in policy form, in 30 to 40 nations where postcompulsory, postsecondary institutions known as "short-cycle colleges" have been created. These institutions link "lower" and "higher" education in both academic and non-academic fields. Variously named "junior college," "community college," "polytechnic," "regional college," "institute of technology," "fachhochschule," "higher school," "uppersecondary," these institutions have non-university characteristics. Included are (1) an emphasis on work preparation, (2) an emphasis on teaching rather than pure research, (3) a high percentage of faculty employed part-time in industry, (4) a high percentage of part-time students, (5) an administrative structure similar to that found in secondary schools, and (6) lower costs per student and, hence, less expensive for governments to create and maintain.

Some short-cycle institutions have as one goal to develop formal and informal arrangements for exchanging credits, primarily academic credits, leading to the first tertiary degree - the baccalaureate. But in only a few countries has this objective been implemented on a broad scale. The potential for furthering lifelong learning, particularly through formal linkages, is increasingly recognized, but translating policy into uniform procedures on a national scale is only slowly emerging, and only in a few nations have short-cycle colleges and training institutions been fully integrated and accepted for articulation purposes.

On the optimistic side, interest in developing a uniform system of course and credit exchange throughout postcompulsory education is moving ahead quite dramatically in several countries in widely separate geographic locations. In Great Britain, events in the last half decade have been remarkable, following two decades of planning. Established in 1969, the British Open University has offered an option - an alternate route to higher education - to thousands of adults. Similar experiences resulted from the open-entry matriculation system for non-advanced courses in the Colleges of Further Education (CFE). Now, under The Education Reform Act of 1988, operational changes have occurred, first expressed in policy heavily debated and in consultation with educators primarily from the United States and Canada. The CFEs and Sixth-Form Colleges were removed from the control of local authorities and have been re-born as free-standing corporations. It is anticipated that the accent on greater attention to aims, objectives, and achievement will encourage "in-country" cooperative efforts and collaborations with American colleges. (See Graystone, 1994, for details.)

Among Pacific Rim economies, Chinese Taipei has aggressively created formal linkages, especially between five-year junior colleges and regional teachers' colleges. Substantial emphasis is given to computer technology in all types of short-cycle colleges, and entrance exams often are required as well as later exams for university admission. Exam preparation for work certificates is a major function, and in larger institutions, such as the National Kaohsiung Institute of Technology (NKIT), non-credit programs directly support lifelong learning potential. Chinese Taipei also fosters a wide range of technical training programs delivered by industry, with or without institutional collaborations.

In Japan, considerable research has been published on the potential of such linkages particularly by professors in the Research Institute for Higher Education at Hiroshima University. However, a nationwide policy has yet to appear. In addition, short-cycle colleges in Canada, the U.S. and Pacific Rim nations are developing a host of joint projects and partnerships in support of lifelong learning potential (Hatton, 1995).

Developments in another APEC economy, Singapore, exemplify departures from traditional principles of degree-giving. In the area of industry/institution collaborative training, applied projects, sometimes called "capstone" courses, integrate learning co-hosted by Singaporean polytechnics and private sector corporations. In a similar vein, Singapore's Precision Engineering Institute (PEI) uses a variety of cooperative projects with industry to fuel the human resource needs of the precision tooling industry. The school becomes the factory, and the needs of industry are considered central to all training (see Hatton, 1995, pp. 147-166).

Though not an APEC economy, the case of Argentina is worth considering for the way in which it exemplifies the expansion of short-cycle higher education. For decades, post-secondary "non-universities" offered higher studies in technical training, teacher training, and the arts. However, in 1993 the Federal Education Act forced dramatic changes, shifting elementary and secondary education from the central government to the provincial governments, and supporting the development of non-universities named *colegios universitarios* by the Argentine National Congress. These post-secondary institutions are beginning to offer two- and three-year transferable academic programs, as well as vocational technical training. More importantly, all are required to have a linkage with at least one Argentinean university. Five university colleges were opened by October 1995, and several have assumed the community college label. Decentralization and deregulation are key concepts in this strategy (Holcombe and Greene, 1996). The "collegiate function" or the "collegiate connection" are expressions currently used to describe the linkage concept. However, the more comprehensive terms, "articulation and transfer", are favoured in this paper (see Cohen and Brawer, 1987, for a thorough discussion and evaluation of the "collegiate function").

Several qualities of short-cycle institutions are persuasive factors supporting the notion that these colleges are viable and highly important linkages supporting the growth of articulation/transfer and, hence, lifelong learning. Wherever found, they sponsor occupational education and, increasingly, academic and continuing education opportunities. Other assets include: flexibility and comparative ease of program development under practitioner-oriented professionals, convenience of location, scheduling more in tune with adult needs, a flattened administrative profile suited for more rapid decision making, and a less expensive corporate unit for state or national governments to maintain. Private short-cycle colleges, however, are more costly to students than public institutions.

Some universities are changing, becoming more international and competitive, and moving closer to the societies they profess to serve. "Superuniversity" is a European term applied to universities which offer systematized and routine credit exchange. Programs initiated through the European Economic Community (EEC), including COMETT - Community in Education and Training for Technology, and ERASMUS - European Community Action Scheme for Mobility of University Students, have been designed as multinational credit exchange systems. These reflect, at least in part, recognition within the ECC of the critical relationship between education and economic development. At the same time, applied policy initiatives are increasingly based on principles fundamental to a new age of higher education, one where equalizing opportunities for access and accreditation, repairing outmoded curricula, and introducing new delivery systems are fundamental.

Extending and deepening the acceptance and integration of short-cycle higher education should be of paramount concern for all APEC economies. Entrenched systems and old-style, powerful, degree granting institutions remain the greatest barrier. Recent events in Australia, Argentina, Chinese Taipei, England, Mexico, and Singapore mark increasing dialogue among educators, legislators, industrialists, and community leaders. The United States, through public and private agencies including consortia of colleges and universities, is very active in national dialogues. Generally, principles are being translated into action policies, and while the results are not as yet perfected, community colleges and other short cycle institutions are springing up in a host of countries. All this suggests a promising future for articulated short-cycle higher education worldwide.

THE STUDENTS

From the beginning of the junior college movement in the United States, the performance and persistence of students transferring vertically through state systems has been monitored and evaluated. Generally, results of this evaluation have been very positive. Community and junior colleges are also active as entrepreneurial partners in the horizontal transfer of students, marked by lateral movement within postsecondary institutions or systems and often marked by direct relationships within industry. Again, evaluation has suggested very positive results.

Specialists studying the articulation and transfer phenomenon have identified a typology of at least a dozen varieties of transfer students in the United States. A few examples follow:

- regulars (vertical and horizontal transfer), including intercollege/interuniversity and intrastate;

- stopouts (those who leave for a time);

- dropdowns (those who return to two-year colleges, following at least some university attendance, usually with the goal of improving grades or qualifying for further study);

- double reverse transfers (those who make a second application to a senior institution after returning to the community college);

• and vocational-technical majors (some of whom might have started in the academic track).

As pressure mounts for continuous (lifelong) education, it is reasonable to believe that other economies will be confronted with similar types of transfer aspirants, *each of whom has specific needs*. Stopouts, for example, represent a rapidly growing adult group whose needs vary according to skill base, state of the economy, stage of life, family issues, and so on. This group is often most heavily involved in non-credit continuing education, but will quickly look for credit when their economic interests interrelate with accreditation. To require duplication in learning, as compared with providing effective articulation, is unproductive and costly.

Other types of transfer students competing for accommodation in the U.S. system include those who are transferring credits from work experience or from the military and other quasi-educational and non-academic courses, the poorly prepared, the underserved, and finally, those who are physically or psychologically disadvantaged. Added to these complex and overlapping types are the international transfer students for whom only cursory attention is generally shown and even then only because for many institutions they represent a significant revenue stream. As a result, commercial "credit-counters" in the U.S. are reaping a financial harvest as institutional and accrediting agency policy lags. Most significant is the fact that this typology will expand greatly as educational opportunities increase for those who are currently not served by post-compulsory opportunities.

TYPES OF INTRAINSTITUTIONAL AGREEMENTS

Junior colleges initially appeared in the U.S. midwest as extensions of high schools, then spread westward to California under the same auspices. Formal transfer and articulation arrangements were negotiated first in regions where the number of applicants demanded action, and particularly in California where the University of California supported the notion of developing formal relationships with junior colleges. The following typology and discussion of the four interrelated classifications of transfer and articulation agreements should be helpful to policy makers who are presently studying potential strategies that support the exchange of credits between non-universities and universities for continuous uninterrupted formal education.

Formal and Legally Based Guidelines and Policies. Legal or quasi-legal articulation status is based on legal code, education statutes, or a state-sanctioned master plan. In this context, general or liberal education is virtually always recognized as "transfer tender". Emphasis is placed on completion of a two-year college associate degree prior to transfer eligibility. Approximately eight U.S. states fall in this category, including Florida ("Formal Agreement Plan") and Illinois ("Legally-based Plan").

Special Statewide Agreements on Vocational-Technical Credit Transfer. In this example, vocational-technical credits and courses are transferred in blocks toward baccalaureate degrees. This is most reliable and easiest to achieve where major universities in a state or region offer first-level degrees in vocational subjects to their own students. At least five states have or have had special financial grants that give particular attention to vocational-technical credit transfer, including Michigan

("Mandated Policies for Community Colleges and Universities") and North Carolina ("Health Articulation Project"). As well, and as one would suspect, all these examples have well developed academic credit/course transfer.

State System Policies. In this instance, policies are usually concentrated on the transfer process, and less on articulation services. A high degree of state control is exerted. Approximately 25 states are involved, including New Jersey ("Full-Faith-and-Credit Policy") and Oklahoma ("Statewide Higher Education System Plan").

Voluntary Agreements Among Systems or Individual Institutions. Characterized chiefly by their voluntary nature, processes and arrangements are informal and cooperatively negotiated often through faculty disciplines, and almost always with comparatively little state control. Approximately 20 states follow this approach, including Washington ("Intercollege Relations Commission,") and California ("Intersegmental Articulation Committee Action"). (See Kintzer and Wattenbarger, 1985, for detailed explanation and discussion.)

CREDIT FOR EXPERIENTIAL LEARNING

Learning acquired from a broad spectrum of non-academic and non-technical experiences is the most difficult and complex to express in policy, to establish procedures for, and to negotiate an articulation/transfer compact. Two types of evaluation for non-traditional credit attract broad interest. The first and most common, credit by examination - the "easy way" to measure learning progress - has dominated the world scene. By way of example, qualifying throughout the British Commonwealth of Nations by means of highly formal and rigid examinations has for decades been widely accepted as the most practical system in this context. The second type, credit awarded for experiences that are not supervised by a college or university, is comparatively rare.

Background

In the early 1960s, the Regents of the State University of New York (SUNY) launched the College Proficiency Examination Program (CPEP) as the nation's first statewide credit-by-examination program. Most of the tests in this program, which are available in a variety of academic disciplines and technologies, are part of the Regents External Degree Program (REDP). Thousands of credits based on these standardized tests have been awarded across the U.S. by colleges and universities. By 1970, entire degrees were being awarded by the Regents without regard to study method, age, or residence. Foreign countries were regularly represented (Nolan, 1979, pp. 71-75). The Regents External Degree and the Empire State College became, and remain, the nation's largest non-traditional programs.

Special assessment, which involves the validation of non-sponsored experiential education, including oral performance and portfolio examination of artistic, musical, and literary accomplishments, began later in the decade. Individual institutions across the country promulgated these programs, including Empire State College (New York), Ramapo College (New Jersey), Evergreen State College (Washington), Webster College (Missouri), Goddard College (Vermont), and Marylhurst Education Center (Oregon).

The movement that focused on recognizing "experiential learning" or "prior learning," appeared nationally in the early 1970s alongside the creation of the Commission on Nontraditional Study. The Commission, under the sponsorship of the College Entrance Examination Board and the Educational Testing Service, and supported by a grant from the Carnegie Corporation, became the administrative vehicle for prior learning assessment (PLA). In mid-1973, a research unit known as the Cooperative Assessment of Experiential Learning (CAEL) was created for the purpose of further developing the concept, as well as for creating guidelines and principles that could be adapted to local circumstances. This allowed many adult learners to pursue educational objectives and accreditation without having to duplicate experiences through study in formal classrooms. At this stage, it became much easier for post-secondary institutions to develop and implement their own plans for realistically serving adults who for a wide variety of personal reasons, tended to drop in and out of regular school attendance.

Books by Patricia Cross and John Valley, Morris Keeton, Samuel Gould, Peter Meyer, and Miller and Mills were major contributions to the literature of this effort. Warren Willingham's paper, titled *Principles of Good Practice in Assessing Experiential Learning*, was released by CAEL in 1977. It served for more than a decade as the basic document for educators incorporating PLA in overall program planning. Whitaker's book, *Assessing Learning: Standards, Principles, & Procedures* (1989) is now the definitive document describing principles and procedures for assessing experiential learning.

Current Scene

Assessment procedures detailed by Whitaker (1989) require extensive student participation in building portfolios of accomplishments, comprehensive counselling, and intricate faculty evaluation. Portfolio submissions similar to the collection and analysis of creative works in the performing arts, particularly music, are frequently mandated, and external evaluators are often included as members of assessment teams. Some institutions conduct planning seminars for students applying for credits that have been earned experientially.

Institutions dedicated to accrediting experiential learning lean heavily on the continuing activities of CAEL, now named the Council for Adult and Experiential Learning, and the work of the American Council on Education's (ACE) Center for Adult Learning and Educational Credentials. One of the functions of the Center is to determine credit equivalencies for various types of extra-institutional learning - another term also found in the literature on learning attained outside the sponsorship of legally authorized and accredited post-secondary institutions. The ACE Center's three key programs that focus on this issue are: the Military Evaluations Program, the Program on Noncollegiate-Sponsored Instruction (PONSI), and the Credit by Examination Program, where individuals bank credits earned in industry-sponsored settings. A national external degree program is now being developed.

Prior learning assessment, as mentioned earlier, flourished in single institutions during the 1970s and 1980s, but procedures for exchanging such credits intrainstitutionally were slow to develop. Factors contributing to the difficulty of negotiating exchanges included: (1) the volume of the itinerant post-secondary population, (2) the diversity of the new clientele, (3) the almost limitless potential of experience-based learning, (4) the resistance to change that characterizes most higher education systems, and (5) the expense of creating and maintaining PLA programs.

Nevertheless, the pressure for launching such a program is mounting in many nations. How can governments perfect approaches for assessment of educational accomplishment that will insure accurate and appropriate issuance of certificates, diplomas, and degrees? In fact the creation of government-sponsored non-traditional institutions or centres, such as Everyman's University in Tel Aviv and the Open University in Sri Lanka, suggests that organizations specifically favouring adult learners can be developed and are in place in many geographically-distant countries, and that these institutions can serve as models for other economies. In particular, distance education institutions, such as the Open Learning Agency on Canada's west coast, may, perhaps, be the solution for the all too common situation where traditional higher education systems have failed to entrench a learner-centred service perspective.

Special reference should be made regarding educational reorganization in Japan. The formal system of higher education includes two segments: universities (long-cycle) and junior colleges, technical colleges, and special training schools (short-cycle colleges). Similarly, the non-formal system, specializing in adult education, is divided into two segments: grand schools, universities of the air, and specialized technical schools; and junior colleges, correspondence education, and college preparatory schools sponsored by short-cycle institutions. For a variety of reasons, potential for extending lifelong learning, including credit systems, is rooted in the first grouping of non-formal institutions (Abe, 1989). It will be interesting and instructive to see how this develops.

J.W. Peltason, former President of the American Council of Education (ACE), must have been speaking to governments around the world when he reminded us that "the post-secondary community [in the United States] needs to move forward in modifying the present credit and credential system to accommodate learning attained in a variety of settings and under a variety of sponsorships, and at the same time to maintain academic standards" (Miller and Mills, 1978, p. xii). At this time, nearly two decades after Peltason's comments, techniques for planning and assessing experiential or prior learning are valid and indeed reliable. Most can be used quite reliably by other economies.

IMPLEMENTATION

In this section of the paper observations and suggestions are offered to practitioners and policy makers. First, attention will be given to planning and assessing experiential or prior learning, and second to building national higher education systems for the new century.

Planning and Assessing

The Planning Stage and the Need for Broad Involvement. When developing policies and systems for recognizing experiential or prior learning, it is critical to involve all constituents who will be affected by success or failure - educators, politicians, business and industry, as well as students, for whom policy changes are being sought. This notion may appear self evident; however, full involvement in the haste of planning is not always observed.

Involving "doubters" in the process can bring striking and immediate success. Such was the case when in the mid-1970s, credit transfer was under negotiation in Norway between the newly opened regional or district college system and the university system. A prominent university professor who had expressed misgivings was asked to chair the planning council, and as a result success came faster. A similar situation occurred in the U.S. state of Arizona when representatives of the entire education community, secondary and higher education representatives, were creating a statewide transfer guidebook. The university leader, representing one of the more difficult disciplines to deal with, agreed to chair the committee. This placed the university in a leadership role, and prospects for agreement were enhanced. It's worth noting that in both cases the requirement for a credit transfer system had been mandated.

Assessment Details. The first step in assessing prior learning experience is the *documentation* stage, and it focuses on the collection and preparation of evidence to support claims for credit. It is recommended that the applicant be compelled to assume responsibility for this stage. However, as mentioned earlier, portfolio seminars sponsored by institutions can be very helpful in steering students along the right path and for clarifying expectations and obligations. Credit is awarded only for what is determined to be college-level learning with the appropriate balance of theory and practice, as determined by faculty.

The next step, *identification*, is where the faculty review the portfolio presented by the applicant in order to identify potentially creditable learning. As noted earlier, the learning must be college-level as determined by the faculty.

The third step, *articulation*, is a joint activity where the faculty member along with the student identify the amount and type of credit being considered in relation to the academic, personal, and professional goals as outlined by the applicant. One of the major challenges associated with this stage is evaluating the relevancy of the specified learning applicable to the regular academic program.

Steps four and five, *measurement and evaluation*, are faculty responsibilities, first to identify the level of competence achieved and then to determine credit equivalencies.

The final step, *transcription*, is an administrative process whereby an appropriate record is prepared. These often differ from standard record keeping procedures since transcriptions of PLA and experiential learning often include brief explanations of the learning (see Whitaker, 1989, for detailed insights).

Building National Higher Education Systems

The re-development of higher education to enhance and support lifelong learning suggests a model that includes: (1) the development of concept statements; (2) the issuance of general guidelines; (3) the testing of policies; and (4) the implementation of well defined regulations and procedures. A close look at recent changes taking place in Hungary and the Czech and Slovak Federal Republics details a model which can be instructive for many APEC economies.

Prior to the passage of legislation in 1991 and 1992, these economies issued exhaustive concept statements that included the historiography of higher education coupled with descriptive lists and detailed characteristics associated with the current system. These included the lack of access, the need to extend services to larger sectors of the populations, the lack of curricular practicality, and too much centralization and regulation. General guidelines of beliefs or goals were also included or, in some cases, appended. These were based on educational theory and societal characteristics.

Next, policy statements identified specific approaches to the issues and problems raised in the original concept papers. What should the new institutions be like? How should the projected non-university system differ from the universities? How should these two systems relate to compulsory education?

Procedures and regulations are currently under preparation, and these will establish the rules/directions for implementing policies, going so far as to include a day-to-day decision making schedule. While the four levels of planning are not as uniform nor as exacting as the model may suggest, all the elements are found in the broad application.

In a developmental context, the U.S. Fullbright Scholar Awards, and particularly the senior research scholar program, has been a useful tool for many nations throughout the world to investigate higher education including articulation and transfer. Many economies are eligible to obtain research scholars and, through joint financial support, analyze specific issues, systems and approaches to higher education. In this context, external observers are often able to document, validate and make recommendations that may be problematic for in-country experts. Clearly, articulation and transfer fall in this category.

Lifelong learning materials service centres are being developed in some, usually large and well endowed, universities. These are cooperative ventures incorporating the talents of faculty, behavioral scientists, learning specialists, and media and information agents. A variety of courses and course materials are packaged, the primary goal being to create a diverse series of high quality learning materials employing various educational technologies and delivery systems. These are then made available to students in order to "top up" or fill gaps that in turn support the notion of learner-driven and easily accessible, seamless lifelong learning systems. Although relatively little research has been completed in this area, activities such as these are intuitively strong when all the potential benefits are considered.

A very visible and highly successful lifelong learning organization is found in New Hampshire, U.S.A., where 25 years ago the Trustees of the state university system established the School of Continuing Studies. This grew and evolved, and is now the College of Lifelong Learning (CLL) composed of a network of 10 regional centres. Utilizing the resources of the entire university system, this Concord-based college enrols approximately 7,000 adult learners in some 50 locations. Four undergraduate degree programs are available, along with credit for prior learning, self-designed courses and non-credit courses. The possibilities are endless.

THE FUTURE

Prognosticating is risky in an arena as dynamic as articulation and transfer. However, the following trends can be an aid to forecasting as well as a guide for policy considerations.

There will be increased emphasis on the modification of transfer courses by short-cycle and senior colleges/universities to attract and accommodate re-entry adults, the less prepared and less talented, and international applicants, especially, in the U.S., immigrant foreign students.

There will be explosive growth in educational and training programs sponsored by industry with or without the permission or cooperation of the higher education system and often in competition with traditional systems, particularly those that continue to offer educational opportunities solely according to institutional imperatives.

There will be increased use of technology to foster and expedite sponsored and non-sponsored experiential learning and other experimental efforts, as well as to track the results of these activities.

The lingering second place reputation of short-cycle institutions may continue to attract inadequate funding for these institutions, the ones most likely to support lifelong learning activities, programs and policies.

Providing learning experiences the world over is a recurrent obligation. Education cannot be a one-time chance; there must be a lifetime of opportunities. As economies increasingly come to accept and believe in the economic benefits of a lifelong learning culture, policies must be developed and implemented that support institutions which have been demonstrably most able to support the phenomena. That is the biggest challenge facing politicians and policy makers.

By definition, the terms, articulation and transfer connote unpredictability because they identify complex processes that are affected by the attitudes of both planners and implementers. However, there appears to be sufficient evidence to predict a very optimistic future.

REFERENCES

Abe, Y. (Ed.). (1989, March). Nonuniversity sector of higher education in Japan. *R.I.H.E. International Publication Series No. 3.* Hiroshima, Japan: Hiroshima University Research Institute for Higher Education.

Cohen, A. M., & Brawer, F. B. (1987). *The collegiate function of community colleges.* San Francisco: Jossey-Bass.

Commission on Nontraditional Study. (1973). *Diversity by design.* San Francisco: Jossey-Bass.

Coordination Office for Higher Education. (1991). *Concept for higher education development in Hungary.* Budapest: Coordination Office for Higher Education.

Cross, P. K., Valley, J. R., & Associates. (1974). *Planning nontraditional programs.* San Francisco: Jossey-Bass.

Gould, S. B. (1970). *Today's academic condition.* New York: McGraw Hill.

Graystone, John. (1994, Spring). British educational reforms: Quality, accountability, expansion, and efficiency. *Trustee Quarterly*, 6-9, 14.

Harach, L., Kotasek, J., & Hendrichova, J. (1992, January). *Higher education in the Czech and Slovak Federal Republic (CSFR).* Prague-Bratislava: Czech and Slovak Federal Republic.

Hatton, M. (Ed.). (1995). *Exemplary training models in industrial technology.* Ottawa: Association of Canadian Community Colleges.

Holcombe, W., & Greene, W. (1996, February/March). Florida community colleges Argentina project. *Community College Journal* 66(4), 35-37, 42.

Keeton, M.T., & Associates. (1977). *Experiential learning: Rationale, characteristics, and assessment.* San Francisco: Jossey-Bass.

Kintzer, F. C. (1976). *Articulation and transfer.* (Topical paper number 59). (ERIC Document Reproduction Service No. ED 130746)

Kintzer, F. C., (1979). Problems in awarding and transferring experiential learning credits. *New Directions for Experiential Learning*, 4, 37-46.

Kintzer, F. C., & Wattenbarger, J. L. (1985). *The articulation/transfer phenomenon: patterns and directions.* Washington, DC: American Association of Community and Junior Colleges.

Mayer, P. (1975). *Awarding college credit for non-college learning.* San Francisco: Jossey-Bass.

Miller, J. W., & Mills, O. (1978). *Credentialing educational accomplishment.* Washington, DC: American Council on Education.

Nolan, D. J. (1979). State leadership in experiential learning: The New York experience. *New Directions for Experiential Learning*, 71-77.

UNESCO. (1976, October-November). *Recommendations on the development of adult education*. (Recommendations adopted at General Conference, Nairobi, Kenya, October-November, 1976). Paris: UNESCO.

Whitaker, U. (1989). *Assessing learning: Standards, principles, & procedures*. Philadelphia: Council for Adult and Experiential Learning.

Willingham, W. W. (1977). *Principles of good practice in assessing experiential learning*. Columbia, MD: Cooperative Assessment of Experiential Learning.

Sandra Liu

Prior to joining the Department of Marketing at Hong Kong Baptist University as Assistant Professor, Sandra Liu worked in the pharmaceutical industry. Her focus within that industry included clinical research, sales and marketing in the United States, Chinese Taipei and other Asia Pacific economies. She is a council member of the Hong Kong Institute of Marketing and takes charge of collaboration with the Asia Pacific Marketing Federation for the Institute. Professor Liu's research interests centre on strategy and marketing management, and she is currently completing a Ph.D. in Higher Education at the University of London. When not involved with her research, writing and other scholarly pursuits, Sandra works with the youth at her church.

Trends in Hong Kong University Management:

Towards a Lifelong Learning Paradigm

by Sandra Liu

To survive in a rapidly changing environment marked by decreased financial support from the government and increased competition within the university sector, institutions of higher education in Hong Kong must become more entrepreneurial and customer focused. The alternative, to remain elitist, removed from and blind to market forces, is a prescription for isolation and, eventually, obsolescence. Institutions that identify market forces, seek out competitive advantages, and respond to customer needs will join the lifelong learning paradigm - the archetype for all education and training in the future. This paper proposes a model that examines the relationships between the users and suppliers of higher education, and a perspective for appreciating the need for a new university dynamic that supports substantive change. The goal is for universities to be pivotal players in the lifelong learning context, while the reward is institutional survival.

INTRODUCTION

An education system may be viewed from a macro perspective "as adapting to social requirements and responding to the demands of society not of individuals" (Archer, 1984, p.2). It has also been described as having the function of contributing to the economic, political, and other legitimate needs of the State in order to support and preserve the process, context, and legitimacy of the capital accumulation process and its continued expansion (Dale, 1989). As higher education institutions produce graduates for the labour market, in turn contributing to social and economic development, one could argue that the changes in higher education systems witnessed during recent decades flow from this context. Clearly, the evolution of higher education systems in East Asia, in response to the dynamic forces generated by burgeoning economies, is linked to the increased demand for higher learning. In the new order of things the traditional model of "finishing schools" has been challenged by the more typically American "service station" notion of a university for recurrent education users (Duke, 1992).

Contemporary universities (both old and newly designated ones) have more functions to fulfil than was once the case. In Hong Kong, for instance, changes resulting from new mass education policies have forced elite universities, such as the University of Hong Kong, to become part of an integrated higher education system, despite the Hong Kong Funding Council's previous efforts to segregate them by granting more privileged treatment. They are no longer separated, at least operationally or functionally, from the "diversities and pluralities of outside society" (Lovatt, 1987, p. 30; Niblett, 1974), as much as they used to be or as much as they would like to be. In essence, rapid change driven by societal needs, including government pressures and market forces, is affecting the fundamental organization and operation of universities in Hong Kong and elsewhere in East Asia.

EVOLUTION OF HIGHER EDUCATION IN HONG KONG

The purpose of higher education in Hong Kong is to respond to labour force demands in order to support smooth social and economic growth in the territory. Industry exerts its force via the government, which in turn regulates directions and operations of institutions by means of the funding mechanism. As a result of its rapid socioeconomic development and its importance as an international financial and business centre, Hong Kong has witnessed massive, increasing demand for professional level human resource expertise since the 1980s. In October of 1989, the government announced plans for the rapid expansion of higher education in the 1990s. Since then the number of universities has increased from two to seven, and each university has a growing student body drawn from the adult population, particularly in the continuing education area. Universities are under pressure to re-evaluate their internal operations as well as to position themselves strategically in this competitive and ever more complex community of higher learning.

In October of 1996, the University Grants Committee (UGC) of Hong Kong announced a cut in its 1998-2001 three-year higher education budget. As a result, universities in Hong Kong will now be compelled to develop entrepreneurial activities and attitudes, operational efficiencies and effective management strategies as a result of the explicit and directive funding mechanisms. Universities are expected to be high quality and cost-effective institutions providing for the advancement of knowledge, the pursuit of scholarship, and, at a more pragmatic level, the education of students in terms of their vocational careers both now and in the future. As a result, the universities play a key and vital role in responding to market forces, thereby facilitating the social and economic development of the territory. It is also important to note that the student population has expanded from the traditional 18-22 year age group to include many more mature students (mostly part-time) from all walks of life, most of whom have personal and specific goals related to career advancement or self development. With these pressures, academic institutions are being forced to become more customer oriented, responding to both the funding council, which wields the stick of deciding which seats to purchase, and to the changing demands of students and employers.

As July 1997 looms on the horizon, Hong Kong's role in overall Chinese economic development becomes more pertinent and both government and industry have expressed concern over the evolution of the educational system. The University and Polytechnics Grants Committee (UPGC) in its Interim Report (1993, back cover) noted that it will "encourage and reward excellence in each of the institution's activities, including teaching, research, and other scholarly activity in accordance with its specified role and mission." Although there were no explicit guidelines regarding how scholarly activities are being evaluated and rewarded in terms of funding, the signal is clear that higher education institutions need to develop new orientations on their own initiative in order to survive in an increasingly competitive higher education community. In fact, unless the universities become a major provider within the developing lifelong learning culture, they run the risk of becoming marginalized and isolated. No longer can Hong Kong universities, even the most senior among them, afford to operate without concern for the major changes occurring in society and the higher education community specifically within Hong Kong.

While the government is proposing decentralization of accountability down to the cost centres within each institution, the monitoring of performance and allocation of resources have actually become more centralized at the institutional level. Universities as a whole enjoy more autonomy in determining their own destinies, and, in turn, this requires university leaders to apply closer examination and evaluation of performance at the department and program levels. Further, rather than relying on traditional development models, universities are being encouraged to decentralize elements of their decision making hierarchy by allowing academics to develop new programs based on environmental scanning and situational analyses in accordance with their expertise. This will allow each institution to capitalize on its unique competitive advantages, and ultimately these same institutions will evolve differently while responding to specific needs and niches, the result being a more diverse set of institutions. Visionary administrators are being called upon to rekindle, revitalize and bring new methods and creative approaches to the universities' traditional responsibility for producing educated citizens by providing forums for liberal thinking and supporting the quest for knowledge and truth. This transformation in the perceived role of higher education and university management demands a new paradigm, one that allows evolving university institutions to reconsider their position within the community, the relationship they have with their students, and their role in the lifelong learning paradigm.

A TAXONOMY FOR MANAGING A CONTEMPORARY UNIVERSITY

Higher education around the world has experienced rapid growth, particularly in South East Asia. At the same time, strong pressures include increasing costs and cutbacks from traditional funding sources. In spite of these, educational institutions have become large enterprises, often with thousands of employees, huge physical plants, and diverse missions. Increasingly, universities are compelled to consider market oriented, business strategies, at least in terms of student recruitment and fund-raising activities (Wheale, 19991; Conway, Mackay & Yorke, 1994). Other scholars in the field of higher education marketing have gone further, stressing the importance for these institutions to be responsive to market demands and more specifically to actively pursue strategies that create high levels of customer satisfaction (Doyle, 1976). With regard to market demands, it is important to consider that marketing includes educating and motivating prospects' (potential clients) latent needs, or marketing a set of institutional expectations in the direction of the prospects (Litten, 1980). In effect, although universities are service providers, they also have significant responsibilities for providing leadership and direction within the field of higher education, including the setting of standards relating to qualifications, research and scholarship.

As universities grapple to develop distinctive and marketable identities, a taxonomy representing the relationship between suppliers and users becomes a useful device; a choice construct for higher education and for integrating both mainstream higher education and lifelong learning in institutional strategic planning (see Figure 1). Different from Kerr's (1982) idea of a multiversity which integrates several communities with varying missions and objectives along a continuum, this taxonomy attempts to integrate the communities of the undergraduate, the graduate, the professional schools, and so forth, in order to formulate an institutional mission and direction. The implication is that the strategic objective for each quadrant would vary according to the relationship between the user and the supplier.

Figure 1: A Taxonomy of Supplier/User Relationships in Higher Education
Supplier specified

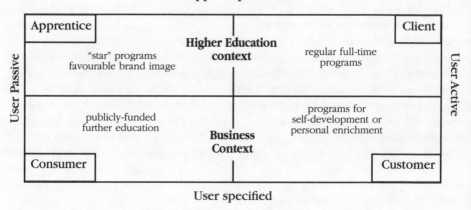

User specified

A traditional mainstream full-time post-secondary educational institution targets mainly 18-22 year old high school graduates. These students may be categorized as either "Apprentices" or "Clients" depending on their bargaining power. A student's academic record and the demands of the particular program that the student is interested in are the main leverages. In general, "star" programs, or institutions with distinguished reputations, are positioned within the upper left-hand quadrant. Programs and institutions in this quadrant are highly selective when screening their "Apprentices". Faculty members representing departments in these institutions are given greater autonomy when developing courses and/or academic programs. By comparison, institutions having only programs that compete for the same student groups are positioned in the "Client" quadrant. The interaction between institutions in this quadrant, and their students, is primarily one of competition in an effort to attract the best qualified "prospects". These two "supplier-specified" quadrants function in the context of traditional higher education; however, their success is inextricably linked with the level of service, and hence positioning, they provide. The marketing framework for the organization therefore shifts from external to one that is internal, and includes internal marketing as well as post-purchase customer services, as is the case in business.

Socioeconomic opportunities and advancements related to education and training have, within recent decades, prompted increasing demand for lifelong learning opportunities as these relate to university training. Innovative institutions have sought ways to widen access for mature students, most of whom are interested in part-time programs. This shifts the transaction to the "user-specified" lower quadrants within the matrix, an environment which more closely resembles the pure business context. The model makes a distinction between "Consumers" who enrol in publicly funded programs and "Customers" who personally pay the full costs of the educational product. Many programs offered in Continuing Education are planned and designed solely on the basis of market demand. Administratively, these are self-sufficient. In the lower right-hand side of the quadrant, students are true "Customers", paying the full costs of the educational product and in a position of relative strength in so far as determining whether or not to buy the program. Factors influencing the purchase decision may include perceived relevancy as well as the quality of the program and its delivery characteristics. In the lower left-hand side of the quadrant students enrol in publicly supported programs that incorporate flexible modes of learning (evening, weekends and so forth) with the ultimate goal of attaining formal certification. As noted earlier, these students, once enroled, are described as "Consumers". Institutions offering these programs, which include the M.B.A. and M.Phil. degree programs, are increasingly providing additional educational opportunities and services to students in order to compete with other institutions offering similar programs. The goal is to recruit the best qualified students. Also in this quadrant are students from open learning institutions, which are, in general, subsidized by government funding. As the allocation of resources to higher education institutions in Hong Kong is becoming more centralized, both at the regulatory level and institutional levels, the relationship between the user and the supplier tends to become more complex. The concurrent issue of need versus the ability to pay makes it important for universities to view the Funding Council and research councils as part of the customer mix.

INSTITUTIONAL ENTREPRENEURSHIP FOR UNIVERSITY MANAGEMENT

As universities struggle to adapt to the changes in higher education, including more stringent control by the Funding Council and increasing competition from within the higher education community, many are increasingly compelled to develop and deliver a set of services which gives them a niche or competitive edge in the marketplace. In turn, the various elements of their "educational products" are influenced by: a) faculty members' active involvement in the curricular design process and in research projects as driven by their understanding of the competitive market, b) selective student participation, both as clients and products, and c) the quality and type of services developed and delivered by administration and support staff. This is a collegial model where academic operations, including curricular design, course/program planning and research endeavours, are initiated and to a certain extent controlled by individual faculties.This model facilitates "corporate venturing" (see Figure 2), or what others have referred to as intrapreneurship (see Jones & Butler, 1992; Wonders & Gyure, 1991), and is identified primarily with individual entrepreneurship in the institution. In effect, academic staff in the new order are expected to capitalize on market trends, research opportunities and their own expertise to develop new courses and program.

Figure 2: Layers of Institutional Entrepreneurship*
for Higher Education Institutions

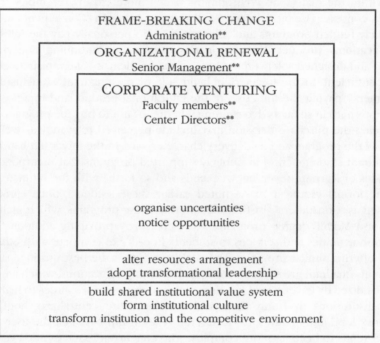

> FRAME-BREAKING CHANGE
> Administration**
>
> ORGANIZATIONAL RENEWAL
> Senior Management**
>
> CORPORATE VENTURING
> Faculty members**
> Center Directors**
>
> organise uncertainties
> notice opportunities
>
> alter resources arrangement
> adopt transformational leadership
>
> build shared institutional value system
> form institutional culture
> transform institution and the competitive environment

* Three types of corporate entrepreneurship according to the Stopford and Baden-Fullen (1994) framework.
** Major players for outer layers include the ones in the inner layer.

Moreover, the recent trends of increasing regulatory and institutional control (for example by evaluating performance indicators for funding purposes), along with greater public accountability as it relates to higher education, have further encouraged the process of corporate venturing and entrepreneurship among faculty members. Many Hong Kong institutions have research centres headed by faculty members that are designed for external research and/or consultancy projects. Although the professional bureaucratic structure (see Mintzberg, 1979) existing in higher education institutions is arguably an inflexible structure for innovation (see Maassen and Potman, 1990), the university multi-divisional structure does have value in ensuring strong functional control and supervision, and is appropriate for raising visibility with regard to individual performance and accountability.

Organizational renewal describes the "expansive notion of a complete business altering its resource pattern to achieve better and sustainable overall economic performance" (Jones and Butler, 1992, p. 522). In the higher education institutional context, sustainable renewal requires greater involvement and more creative leadership from senior management. Also, Kogan (1995) suggests an appropriate differentiation and connection between bureaucratic levels when institutions are faced with changes in the tasks and the relative power of academics and administrators. This is even more important in light of the recent changes in the higher education environment and the reduced funding from traditional sources. Senior management should, therefore, be treated as separate from the basic administrative structure because of their distinctive responsibilities and authority. Senior management, depending on the organizational structure of individual institutions, includes at least the Vice Chancellor, Pro Vice Chancellors, Academic Deans, Registrar, and Financial Comptroller. These administrators sit on all committees that are vital for policy making and strategy formulation, including the Senate, Council, and Steering Committee or Senior Executive Committee.

As regulatory and institutional controls are becoming more exacting due to changes in governmental funding policies, the terms of reference for senior managers have become similar to those of managers in the traditional bureaucratic model. Senior management controls resources and functions as a gate-keeper in terms of interpreting the funding policies and, in turn, formulates strategies and directions for the institution. This business-like, manager-oriented organization should underpin the drive for inculcating effective intrapreneurship. Coexistence of the bureaucratic and collegial models in universities, however, tends to create tension between senior management and faculty members. In order for institutional renewal to survive the developmental period, it is important for senior managers to acquire transformational leadership skills, characterized by a long-term perspective, and to view intra- and extra-organizational factors from a holistic orientation (Dubinsky, Yammarino, Jolson & Spangler, 1995). Leaders of this sort know how to develop a vision of what the organization can be (often being entrepreneurs themselves), are able to mobilize the organization to accept change and become more productive, and can institutionalize changes that will last over time. Alternatively, and differing from this traditional individual-centred view of leadership, Bensimon and Neumann (1993) suggest that leadership in universities should be considered as a collective, where interactivity is the most important element. They view the senior management team as a culture which stresses processes - including ways of coming together, growing together, working together, and also coming apart - rather than stressing the product.

When senior management embraces "frame-breaking change" for the institution in an effort to find and deploy new combinations of resources as a means for developing positional leadership among rival institutions, tensions may arise between the senior management and the general administrative staff who, in a broad sense, see their responsibility as one of safeguarding standards, governmental policies and institutional regulations in order to ensure continuity of institutional operations and preserve existing systems. The internal marketing process then becomes critical at the operational level for building a shared institutional value system based on senior management's vision and, eventually, of forming a fully developed, intrapreneurial, institutional culture. Part of this will involve devising appropriate management techniques, personnel policies, internal training policies, and planning and control procedures. In addition, a marketing plan and a marketing control system are essential in order for institutions to operate with greater focus and to utilize resources more effectively. Overall, the role of senior management in terms of effectively re-orienting the institution to participate in the lifelong learning paradigm is fundamental.

POLICY IMPLICATIONS

The Hong Kong Government founded the first university in the territory in 1911 with the specific purpose of establishing a university of "Western learning", not only for the Colony, but also for the Empire (Mellor, 1980). The Chinese University of Hong Kong was founded in 1956 and then, following the example of the British University Grants Committee, the Government established the University Grants Committee (UGC) in 1965 (later to become the University and Polytechnics Grant Committee, and then to revert again to the University Grants Committee in 1994) to provide advice regarding the budget for higher education and the allocation of funds among the institutions by means of three-year block grants. However, it wasn't until the publication of the 1978 White Paper that the government became actively and directly involved in developing higher education in Hong Kong. In 1979, the government appointed the Advisory Committee on Diversification (ACD) to evaluate the higher education system. The findings of this Committee highlighted the insufficient production of highly-skilled professionally trained personnel, particularly in technical fields, that would be required to meet both student and labour market demands. The Committee recommended that technical institutes be given greater flexibility to respond to the needs of industry and that Hong Kong's human resource base be upgraded through the systematic development of part-time adult learning opportunities. This was the first time that the traditional university sector had been directly linked through policy applications with the fledgling notion of lifelong learning. Although extramural education had been instituted in universities since the late 1950s, it had always been a second class addition well isolated from mainstream university education.

As a response to expected competition from universities in Southern China after July 1997, the University and Polytechnic Grants Committee believes that higher education institutions in Hong Kong must "incorporate centres of excellence having local, regional and international functions. They should provide very high quality bilingual manpower for both Hong Kong and the mainland and should act as points of reference, particularly in Business and Social Studies and in innovative science and technology, for development in Southern China and more widely" (1993, p.7). Further, the Committee argued that the government should urgently formulate policies to facilitate these processes. Although there have not been explicit policy guidelines on the holistic development of higher learning, the same policy paper stipulates the importance of each university being able to develop new orientations or specializations based on its own initiatives. Assuming this takes place, and it is difficult to imagine what forces would prevent it from occurring, what will develop sooner rather than later, impelled for the most part by market forces, will be a market-influenced and institutionally-shaped system of universities and university products within a larger lifelong learning system.

The taxonomy described earlier in this paper permits universities to evaluate their academic programs and target markets in order to strategically plan their evaluation and respond to competitive forces within the scope of labour market developments. Recent behaviour exhibited by the University of Hong Kong and others illustrates how the universities are responding within this framework of forces. Since the 1994 transition of polytechnics and colleges to university status, the traditional universities in Hong Kong, and the Hong Kong University in particular, have encountered greater competition for research funds. In addition, the University and Polytechnics Grants Committee has since 1994 devolved the authority for academic planning to the institutional level. It subsidizes universities with HK$50,000 per student, and expects institutions to balance their budgets with other revenue generating activities. The University of Hong Kong, as a result, has been compelled to become more market-oriented in the planning and delivery of its academic programs. As the contemporary higher education market is becoming more focused on broad lifelong learning opportunities, there are stronger market demands for in-service educational programs, and the University has breached the divide between the traditional liberal and the vocational faculties by replacing the Department of Extramural Studies (DES) with a new School of Professional and Continuing Education (SPACE). This permitted the University to expand its activities in the developing areas of part-time, adult higher education by creating closer links to the "main stream" university faculties. For example, a Bachelor of Science in Nursing Studies is now offered by SPACE in collaboration with the Faculty of Medicine. This program targets local in-service nurses with the objective of further developing their professional competencies and skills within the context of the Hong Kong health care system.

In another example, the City University of Hong Kong now offers a Master's of Manufacturing Engineering and Management degree, and has gone so far as to change the name of the Manufacturing and Engineering Department to the Manufacturing Engineering and Engineering Management Department. This is in direct response to the rapid economic restructuring taking place in Hong Kong, and the need for engineering graduates to have management expertise for the work many of them do in the Peoples' Republic of China. In 1997-98, the department began offering a similar degree at the bachelor's level. In addition, the Faculty of Science at the University of Hong Kong has launched a Computational Mathematics and Operations Research theme focusing on the practical aspects of transportation, construction, production management, foreign exchange, investment and the service sectors. It draws on interdisciplinary contributions from the departments of Statistics, Management and Computer Science. These programs and others are in direct response to market demands for human resource expertise that combines technical and management proficiencies.

Although many newly-designated universities claim to position themselves strategically as teaching universities, much of their planning and strategy is in fact aimed at obtaining public research funding. They have, as a result, had to work very hard at improving their research record within a short time span. These institutions are caught in a dilemma. On the one hand, if they don't concentrate on strengthening their research capabilities, they won't get research funding. On the other hand, if they dedicate themselves to research activities, they will send confusing signals to the marketplace and may compromise their competitive advantage in teaching and vocational training. Established universities clearly face increased competition for research funds as the newly-designated universities now compete in this sector. An additional constraint relates to the fact that public funding for higher education will continue to contract in Hong Kong for the three-year period, 1998-2001. As a result, all the universities are looking for opportunities to generate income through the development of new training programs, often in collaboration with industry. The proposed framework of institutional entrepreneurship described above provides a holistic approach for understanding and examining these activities. By necessity and design, higher education is joining the lifelong learning paradigm.

The bureaucratic collegium of academic operations, resulting from the recent trend of increasing regulatory and institutional control, facilitates intrapreneurship. This, in turn, will develop into an organizational renewal, and eventually form frame-breaking changes. Each stage is dominated by one type of entrepreneurship and encompasses earlier ones, similar to expanding concentric circles of activity. Each circle requires time to build the entrepreneurial based activities and to allow systems and attitudes to evolve and change in fundamental ways. When strategically planning for the future in a volatile and transient environment like that found in Hong Kong, institutions need to go beyond conventional annual budgetary planning. A beginning may involve encouraging intrapreneurship among academic staff. Beyond that, institutional renewal and eventual frame-breaking changes require leadership which is able to embrace and integrate positional and strategic marketing, to develop a vision of what the institution can be, to mobilize the institution to accept change and become productive, and to institutionalize changes in order to create a new university culture. Most importantly, universities must realize that they need to actively become part of the broad lifelong learning paradigm, one that educates and re-tools the population in anticipation of a rapidly evolving society and economy.

REFERENCES

Archer, M. S. (1984). *Social origins of educational systems.* London: SAGE.

Bensimon, E. M. & Neumann, A. (1993). *Redesigning collegiate leadership: Teams and teamwork in higher education.* Baltimore, MD: The John Hopkins University Press.

Conway, T., Mackay, S., & Yorke, D. (1994). Strategic planning in higher education: Who are the customers? *International Journal of Educational Management* 8(6), 29-36.

Dale, R. (1989). *The state and education policy.* Milton Keynes: Open University Press.

Doyle, P. (1976, January). *Marketing and the responsive university.* Inaugural Lecture delivered at University of Bradford, England.

Dubinsky, A. J., Yammarino, F. J., Jolson, M. A. & Spangler, W. D. (1995, Spring). Transformational leadership: An initial investigation in sales management. *Journal of Personal Selling and Sales Management XV*(2), 17-29.

Duke, C. (1992). *The learning university: Towards a new paradigm?* Buckingham: SRHE and Open University Press.

Jones, G. R. & Butler, J. E. (1992). Managing internal corporate entrepreneurship: An agency theory perspective. *Journal of Management 18*(4), 733-749.

Kogan, M. (1995, November). *Conditions favouring academic productivity.* Paper presented at the IMHE Seminar on Human Resources and Staff Development, Hong Kong Baptist University, Hong Kong.

Litten, L. H. (1980). Marketing higher education: Benefits and risks for the American academic system. *Journal of Higher Education 51*(1), 40-59.

Lovatt, W. D. (1987). Tertiary education in Hong Kong: Can we learn from the English experience? In Hong Kong Baptist College Student Union (Ed.), *Overview of post-secondary education in Hong Kong* (pp. 29-32). Hong Kong: King-Lin Publishing Company.

Kerr, C. (1982). *The uses of the university* (3rd ed.). Cambridge: Harvard University Press.

Maassen, P. A. M. & Potman, H. P. (1990). Strategic decision making in higher education: An analysis of the new planning system in Dutch higher education. *Higher Education 20*, 393-410.

Mellor, B. (1980). *The University of Hong Kong: An informal history* (Vol. 1). Hong Kong: Hong Kong University Press.

Mintzberg, H. (1979). *The structuring of organizations.* Englewood Cliffs: Prentice Hall.

Niblett, W. R. (1974). *Universities between two worlds*. London: University of London Press.

Stopford, J. M. & Baden-Fuller, C. W. F. (1994). Creating corporate entrepreneurship. *Strategic Management Journal 15*, 521-536.

University and Polytechnic Grants Committee (UPGC) of Hong Kong. (1993). *Higher education 1991-2001: An interim report*. Hong Kong: Author.

Wheale, J. (1991). *Generating income for educational institutions: A business planning approach*. London: Kogan Page.

Wonder, T. J. & Gyure, J. F. (1991). Opportunistic marketing in higher education. In T. J. Hayes (Ed.), *New strategies in higher education marketing* (pp. 1 - 16). Binghamton, NY: The Haworth Press.

Charles Beaupré

Charles Beaupré holds degrees from Montreal's McGill University in East Asian Studies (B.A.) and Educational Psychology (Ph.D.). Currently, he is an Assistant Professor at Saint Mary's University in Nova Scotia, Canada, where he teaches languages and lectures on East Asian culture. In addition to lifelong learning, Dr. Beaupré's research focuses on education for indigenous populations in Asia. He enjoys writing fiction for children and is presently preparing a book of children's stories which will be illustrated by his wife.

Lifelong Learning in a Developed and a Developing Economy

by Charles Beaupré

Lifelong learning, and the ideologies and foundations on which it rests, are strongly influenced by culture, as well as political and economic developments. This paper, by comparing the evolution of lifelong learning in Chinese Taipei and Vietnam, describes factors in the cultural, political and economic makeup that are influencing approaches and attitudes towards lifelong learning. For example, in Chinese Taipei the combination of political ideology and Confucian principles has meshed with the powerful economic development of the past twenty-five years to create a strong and well developed platform for lifelong learning. Vietnam, on the other hand, is focusing by necessity on its ongoing transformation from a centralized agrarian-based economy to a market driven system. Educational policies and practices, including those that support the lifelong learning context, are quite naturally influenced by this. Irrespective of the developing and developed economy distinction, there is an important philosophical predisposition towards learning in general that lends popular support for lifelong learning.

INTRODUCTION

This paper examines lifelong learning phenomena in Chinese Taipei and Vietnam.[1] Presented as a cross-cultural comparative analysis, the paper considers past and present lifelong learning issues in both economies, and makes projections for the future. In addition to reviewing a range of secondary sources, the paper includes data collected from informal, on-site interviews conducted in Taipei and Hanoi. In both instances, 50 subjects were purposefully chosen from a representative cross section of adult learners participating in secondary-level supplementary education programs. In Chinese Taipei the group of adult learners was attending English language classes at a Municipal Cultural Center in Yong-ho, a suburb of Taipei. In Vietnam the adult learners were attending a language arts class in the evening at a high school located in the Tran Xuan Soan district. All interviewees were middle-aged and older. In Chinese Taipei 27 men and 23 women were interviewed. All of

---

[1]Vietnam is not a member of APEC. However, it has applied for membership and the majority of its international trade is with APEC members. The value of this paper, from APEC and Asia Pacific perspectives, rests in large part on the "more developed" vs. "less developed" economy comparison.

these respondents were high school graduates and several had attended college. In Vietnam 21 men and 29 women were interviewed. Of these, only 16 had finished a secondary level education. The paper concludes by identifying developments in both these economies that are broadly instructive for lifelong learning educators and policy makers in all Asia Pacific economies. It identifies a philosophical predisposition, embodied in Confucian ethics, that overcomes at least some economic barriers (or lack of administrative initiative) in pursuing lifelong learning interests. The implications of a greying population are considered within the context of older adults acting as key educational resources in Chinese Taipei.

CHINESE TAIPEI

In the earlier part of this century, Sun Yat-sen, a principal figure in turn-of-the-century Chinese history, expounded his views on education. Essentially, these were comprised of his political philosophy, merged with basic Confucian virtues, and formulated as the Three Principles of the People (*San Min Chu I*): People's Rule (nationalism), People's Authority (democracy), and People's Livelihood (sometimes described as socialism) (see Meyer, 1988). At the time they were presented, Sun's principles of education were meant to apply quite broadly; however, various struggles intervened, and this was not to be. These principles have, however, influenced education policies in Chinese Taipei, and an acknowledgement of them supports a better appreciation of the overall social and educational developmental context.

Lifelong Learning – Recent Past

Earlier in this century, as Chinese Taipei's educational system was being established, Chiang Kai-shek and others elaborated on Sun Yat-sen ideological principles, adapting them to developing doctrines. In 1953, Chiang published his political views on education in *Supplementary Statements on Education and Recreation and the Principle of Livelihood*. This became a source for guiding principles or the *raison d'être* influencing much of the educational philosophy and structure in Chinese Taipei. According to Chiang, the people of Chinese Taipei should observe basic virtues of loyalty, filial piety and righteousness in order to become citizens "who love [Chinese Taipei] more than their own lives" (Chiang, 1959, p.276). Thus, the spirit of education, including education for adults, came to be enveloped in loyalty. During the 1950s, and for various reasons, Chinese Taipei policy makers worked hard to present the economy as a principal conservator of Chinese civilization. Educational authorities responded to Chiang's directive of promoting 'cultural fidelity' by merging broad ideologies with traditional Chinese values, that is, those embodied in Confucianism (Lucas, 1982; Meyer, 1988; Taylor, 1988)[2].

Thus, in terms of ideology, education in Chinese Taipei came to feature a mixture of political doctrine and Confucian humanism. Given the conservative outlook of

---

[2]Essentially, Confucianism is a moral system that fosters a universal 'inner-world morality' (Hall & Ames, 1987). At the heart of Confucianism is the notion of *ren*, or love, human kindness, and virtue. Of all the Confucian virtues, filial piety has been traditionally regarded as the most outstanding manifestation of *ren*. According to Confucius, filial piety serves as the fundamental ethical principle guiding the *five traditional relationships*: that between father and son, elder and younger siblings, husband and wife, friend and friend, and ruler and subject (Tan, 1990).

the administration, the interpretation of Confucian morality focused primarily on the maintenance of social order. In everyday terms this was achieved through the expansion of the individual's social duty, beginning with the family, extending to the community, and culminating in the society as a whole. Given the orthodox interpretation of this Confucian social doctrine, more liberal interpretations of the role of education were largely ignored.

Following the guidelines set by the central authorities, the task of establishing a national curriculum for all educational programs in Chinese Taipei was given to the Ministry of Education (MOE). The MOE in turn created the departments of elementary education, secondary education, higher education, physical education, technological and vocational education, social education, and general affairs.[3] Depending on their nature, lifelong learning activities fell either under supplementary vocational education or under the rubric of social education. During the ensuing decades lifelong learning remained relegated to the functional vocational track or to (traditional) socio-cultural activities. This basic division continues to this day.

Lifelong Learning – Present

Typically, vocational training is offered through public and private vocational schools, focusing on seven major areas: agricultural, industrial, commercial, opera and arts, home economics, health and nursing, and marine products (Ministry of Education, 1990). However, these conventional schools do not easily integrate teaching methods and techniques that draw upon workers' previous experiences, thereby limiting the transfer of knowledge from one working situation to another. For older adult learners, this has been a major impediment in linking concepts and practices taught in a vocational class with their own professional abilities. In response to this shortcoming in the public vocational education system, private enterprises have developed more innovative training programs focusing on effective skill recycling of older employees. Many such enterprises have taken seriously the concept of continuous learning, critical thinking, and problem solving as an integral part of in-service training (Pucel & Lyau, 1995; Yuen, 1993). They have come to appreciate the long-term benefits of empowering employees with the concept of continuous improvement. It is important to note, however, that the unemployed and other marginal groups do not have access to these opportunities, a situation typical in most economies, both developed and developing.

As for social education, programs are for the most part designed to raise adult learners' cultural and educational levels. Typical social education programs include Mandarin Language usage (the official language of Chinese Taipei), family education, fine arts, physical education, and vocational skills. Cultural and educational activities are provided in a wide variety of forms such as elementary, secondary and college nonformal and informal programs, social education centres, agricultural extension services, labour organizations, and cultural organizations, such as museums, parks, art galleries, cultural centres and libraries (Epstein, 1988; C. J. Lin, 1983; Ministry of

---

[3] The formal educational structure emulates the American model, that is, a 6-3-3-4 structure. This includes six years of primary level instruction, three at the junior high school level, three more at the high school level, and four years of university.

Education, R.O.C, 1990). Again, it is worth noting that marginal groups, including the illiterate, have little or no useful access to this programming.

To this day education authorities continue to view social education as a means of cultivating appropriate ideas and behaviour compatible with building a modern economy. Consequently social education remains purposefully integrated with economic development, social reconstruction, and cultural renaissance.

Lifelong Learning – Future

Although the social education system has remained essentially the same for the past four decades, recent socio-political developments are spurring educational officials to make certain adjustments to the program. Ironically, the ideological impetus for many of these changes stems from the thoughts of Sun Yat-sen and Confucius, and both have important implications for the future of lifelong learning in Chinese Taipei.

When we read the *Three Principles of the People*, we discover that it contains many progressive notions, celebrating many contemporary concepts such as international brotherhood, pacifism, human rights, and others. Among these concepts we find that the most progressive ideas are embedded mainly within two of Sun Yat-sen's principles: democracy and the people's livelihood. Interestingly, these two pillars of Sun's ideology can be interpreted as having direct bearing on lifelong learning. First let us examine the principle of participatory democracy.

The process of democratization has greatly transformed the socio-political scene in Chinese Taipei over the past decade. Given the pervasive nature of this process, perhaps it was to be expected that the world of education would be influenced as well, including adult education and perspectives on lifelong learning. These changes were observed in responses to the interviews completed in Taipei. Asked whether they were satisfied with present lifelong learning opportunities, the majority of the respondents (37 out of 50) indicated that the administration should give them better, more comprehensive educational services. Asked for the reasons behind this view, many respondents cited their basic rights as citizens. One respondent phrased it in the following manner, as Chinese Taipei "has become a democracy (*min-chu-hua*), everyone, young and old, should enjoy worthwhile educational activities". Responses of this type suggest that adult education has taken on socio-political dimensions, closely linked with democratic principles.[4] In other words, it would appear that for today's adult learners, the administration has a *duty* to provide quality educational opportunities. This attitude of expectation differs from the past, when adult learners were regarded as passive recipients of education services bestowed by the government. In coming years it is highly probable that the trend for greater administrative accountability with regards to lifelong learning will become more evident.

The other notion, that of livelihood, is clarified as follows: "Education and culture shall aim at the development among the citizens of ... morality, good physique, sci-

---

[4]Several subjects were quite informed about the promotion of lifelong learning in the international community, making specific references to the concept of lifelong education as promulgated by the United Nations Educational, Scientific and Cultural Organization (UNESCO).

entific knowledge, and the ability to earn a living" (quoted in C. J. Lin, 1983, p.112). In view of the rapidly changing professional standards required of today's human resources in Chinese Taipei, many adults are finding themselves unable to earn a living, as they are unqualified to compete in the job market (Yuen, 1993). Although some of their needs are being met by the vocational education system, according to data from the interviews many adult learners under this system feel that the content and teaching methods overemphasize trade training at the expense of a broader context of lifelong learning, one that would address changing personal, psychological, and social situations. A large number, 23, specifically mentioned their right to adequate professional training *framed within a lifelong learning context*.

A third factor, ideologically linked with the socio-political promotion of lifelong learning in Chinese Taipei, is Confucian morality. According to Confucius, the deference accorded one's elders stems mainly from their being learned and wise individuals. From the Confucian viewpoint, the role of "benevolent intellectual" is not taken lightly. In order to live up to this image, most adults adhere to the age-old Confucian maxim that one should study as long as one lives. Given the general acceptance of Confucian attitudes toward the application of learning throughout one's life, many adult lifelong learners are motivated to engage in educational activities from this viewpoint, that is, as a moral responsibility (see Chang, 1990). In this regard the adult subjects interviewed were nearly unanimous; in pursuing lifelong learning they were acting in accordance with the moral precepts of Confucius. Interestingly, many subjects perceived a mutual moral contract between themselves and the government, in the sense that, if they were willing to engage in lifelong learning, the administration has the moral obligation to provide them with satisfactory lifelong learning opportunities.

Public support for the wider socio-cultural implications of lifelong learning has not gone unnoticed by Chinese Taipei's administration. Over the last few years the MOE has increased its subsidies to cultural organizations offering lifelong learning programs to adults (Yuen, 1993). In addition to cultural organizations, the educational media, presented mainly in the form of radio and television programming, has quickly become an important means of promoting lifelong learning. High quality mass media programs, covering a diverse range of topics, such as foreign language courses, culinary skills, meditation and self-healing, workshops, fine arts, physical education, etc., have been well received by lifelong learners (Chang, 1990; H. P. Lin 1995).

This is an encouraging trend, for the learning needs of older adults will become an increasingly urgent concern in Chinese Taipei. As with most industrialized societies, Chinese Taipei's population is aging. The Council for Economic Development Planning (cited in Yang, 1992) has estimated the elderly population age 65 and over will represent 8.7% of the total population by 2011, as compared to 2.4% in 1956, and the administration intends to mobilize much of this vast resource of retired older adults. However, well-planned utilization of this human capital will require a social support system that includes a host of integrated, wide ranging lifelong learning opportunities. More specifically, an increasing number of people over the age of 65 will need practical programs such as occupational guidance and job training as well as comprehensive socio-cultural enhancement programs to enrich their personal lives. Furthermore, whether on a voluntary basis or as part of an elderly employment program, older members of the society may be used to provide instruction for younger generations. Fortunately, Confucian values have rendered Chinese Taipei psychologically predisposed to make good use of learning models within the lifelong learning paradigm that celebrates older members of the society as valuable transmitters of knowledge and wisdom to younger generations. This is very different from what may be observed in other economies, and western society in particular, and much could be learned from this model by policy makers in a host of APEC economies.

VIETNAM

The Republic of Vietnam, as it exists today, was established in June, 1976. This followed a long period of struggle and conflict, as well as division between north and south. During the French colonial period (1867-1945), Vietnam remained largely underdeveloped and educationally backward. French rule had ensured that only a minority of "loyal" Vietnamese received formal training and education under a system that emphasized individualism and academic specialization. During this era the rate of illiteracy exceeded 90% for those 12 through 50 years of age.

Lifelong Learning – Past

In 1945, when the Viet Minh administration was formed in Hanoi, one of its first major educational policies was to initiate a campaign to eliminate illiteracy. This continued even during periods of conflict, so that by the late 1950s more than 90% of the population under Communist jurisdiction was literate. In 1975, when the economy was reunified, another literacy campaign was launched. By 1978 authorities claimed that the eradication of illiteracy in the adult population of Vietnam had been achieved.

In conjunction with the effort to eliminate illiteracy, Vietnam's leaders felt the need to reform the economy's education system to reflect more closely socialist values as well as inculcate greater political consciousness in the people. They attempted to achieve this by combining study and productive work, theory and practice. These goals translated into educational programs aimed at increasing the levels of schooling and improving the working skills of the population. This effort resulted in the creation of an education and training system divided into four sectors: preschool, general (consisting of a nine-year basic cycle plus a three-year secondary cycle), vocational/technical education, and higher education. The general sector was also given the mandate of administering "complementary education", designed to provide lifelong learning opportunities for adults.

Lifelong Learning – Present

The nonformal complementary education system was created alongside the formal system to provide corresponding education and in-service vocational training for adults on a full- or part-time basis. Complementary education is delivered primarily in the form of post-literacy programs to allow adults to complete their basic or secondary education. Post-literacy learning materials vary according to whether the delivery takes place in a rural or urban setting. For those learners in rural areas, the materials focus on conventional agricultural training, such as horticulture and animal raising. In urban settings, literacy follow-up materials converge on more contemporary competencies, such as industry- or enterprise-related technical skills, monetary management, or scientific or technological knowledge. Curriculum objectives are grouped according to three levels, ranging from the consolidation of reading and writing skills up to preparation for post-secondary studies. Many curriculum objectives have been specifically designed to meet the needs of young or middle-aged learners. The latter group receives simplified and more practical instruction, the rationale being that these learners are busy with their full-time work.

Although the complementary education system has been praised for its contribution to the attainment of literacy and universalization of first-level education, it may be critiqued for lack of follow-up programs in terms of specific courses, especially in science and technology. As well, the system may favour target groups of elite, male cadres and state employees to the disadvantage of common workers, ethnic members, and women. A third comment, particularly relevant to lifelong learning, is that the system does not easily accommodate target populations above the middle-age range, and teaching methods are inappropriately similar to those utilized in formal educational settings, stressing lectures, drills, testing, and so forth. Finally, complementary education is hampered by financial restrictions, a chronic shortage of materials and instructors, and limited efforts to experiment with novel pedagogical approaches or innovative teaching materials (Le Son, 1986; Nguyen, 1994).

Lifelong Learning – Future

In view of the shortcomings, administrators have introduced corrective measures for complementary education. For example, they are trying to diversify the curriculum so as to meet a broader spectrum of educational needs within the different categories of adult learners. Educational authorities are more willing to accept the assistance of NGO education specialists in order to develop syllabi and pedagogical approaches more suitable for older learners, namely, nonformal and informal educational approaches. Officials have also become more supportive towards the implementation of technological advances in education, including distance education based on audio and video mediums. At the forefront of this latest thrust are the Vietnamese People's Open Universities, presently one in Hanoi and another in Ho Chi Minh City, that produce programming which supports a lifelong learning context. As a result of these efforts, complementary education curricula is becoming richer and more stimulating. This augurs well for the future.

Whatever its shortcomings, complementary education will likely continue to be the main thrust at providing post-literacy and lifelong learning opportunities for the adult population. Programming is becoming more flexible in order to meet the educational needs of a wider range of target groups in terms of age and profession, and governmental efforts to promote lifelong learning seem to have a great deal of support from the adult learners themselves. Informal interviews conducted with adult learners in Hanoi revealed much enthusiasm for lifelong learning, with all respondents stating that lifelong learning is both an obligation and a right. Interestingly, many of them explained their views on lifelong learning in terms of the teachings of Ho Chi Minh and Confucius. For example, several subjects paraphrased Ho Chi Minh: "learning is like a book with no final page", and "learning is as if there were no final rung to a ladder". Others readily referred to Confucius: "Confucius taught us that education is for everyone, it discriminates against no one", and "Confucius insisted that everybody should be given the same opportunity in education".

The juxtaposition of Ho Chi Minh and Confucius is not coincidental if one remembers that Vietnamese culture, including education, was greatly influenced by the Chinese. Evidently, Confucian educational philosophy has had a lasting impact on Vietnam, despite the recess during times of friction. In this sense, typical attitudes among Vietnamese adult learners towards lifelong learning are not unlike those of their Chinese Taipei counterparts. In other words, there appears to be little distinction *in this context* between learners in the developing economy of Vietnam and the more developed economy of Chinese Taipei. One point of distinction, however, is the socio-political perspective on lifelong learning in the two economies. Vietnam has experienced considerable change in the past decade. These reforms have included changes designed to attract more foreign investment, and this process of economic liberalization has led to calls for reform in other spheres, including the educational system (Sloper & Le Thac, 1995). For the most part, however, criticism tends to be expressed by individuals, and there is little public commentary on any educational matters, including those relating to lifelong learning. This was confirmed through interviews in Hanoi where the prevailing attitude of respondents towards lifelong learning issues could be appropriately described as one of acquiescence. In Chinese Taipei, by comparison, respondents had little hesitation in openly expressing opinions.

CONCLUSION

The histories of Chinese Taipei and Vietnam diverge on many fundamental points in terms of social, political, and economic growth. These have important implications for the respective groups of adult lifelong learners. First, demographically, Vietnam's population is far from facing a greying problem. Approximately 40% of the total population is less than twenty years old (Europa World Book, 1995), and so the collective voice of those 65 years of age and over will not be heard as loudly as is the case in Chinese Taipei.

Secondly, the human resource needs of Chinese Taipei reflect a technologically advanced industrialized free-market economic power, while in Vietnam the focus is on reforming an agrarian-based centralized economy towards a market-oriented system. Accordingly lifelong learning concerns in Chinese Taipei, as a model for more developed economies, converge on: (1) providing adequate professional training to older individuals whose skills need to meet post-industrial occupational demands, and (2) providing opportunities for older adult lifelong learners to satisfy their more holistic educational needs, enabling them to become more fulfilled intellectuals. Vietnam, out of necessity, and in the context of the developing economy framework, concentrates lifelong learning activities on: (1) training a relatively young labour force in technological and industrial fields that support the fledgling market-oriented economy, and (2) providing learning opportunities to older more experienced learners in areas that can guide economic development, such as fiscal management, entrepreneurship, investment, trade, and so forth. In other words, in the developing economy context, there is greater emphasis on vocational and economic training.

Over the last two decades Chinese Taipei's economic performance has earned the respect of the international community. In line with its "economic miracle", Chinese Taipei's political system has undergone a steady process of democratization. Combined, these developments have affected the promotion, implementation and outcomes associated with lifelong learning. The steadily aging population and the redefinition of the elderly within the society has presented challenges and worked to shape the general outlook on lifelong learning. As we approach the next millennium, Chinese Taipei is in the enviable position of having one of the best educated populations in the world, a solid social/vocational education infrastructure to build upon, and a relatively high degree of consensus regarding the desirability of enhancing lifelong learning. All of this suggests that Chinese Taipei may become an international model for lifelong learning, at least with regard to the more developed economy context.

Vietnam, as a developing economy comparison, is faced with tremendous challenges for the delivery of basic and adequate social services, including basic education. The prospects for achieving human and economic potentials associated with lifelong learning are influenced, and perhaps frustrated, to at least some degree, by a vastly different context and stage of economic development. Nonetheless Vietnam does exhibit characteristics that will support the need for and the effective development of lifelong learning, including a vigorous labour force, a strong work/study belief system, a solid basic education system, and an ethic that prizes learning.

Despite great differences in circumstances that affect lifelong learning, it is instructive to note that educational authorities in both Chinese Taipei and Vietnam have the political will to fund research in lifelong learning, addressing such key issues as the memory capacity of adults for learning, the optimum division of time for work, study and lifelong learning activities, and socio-affective factors that influence learning motivation. For Chinese Taipei and Vietnam, this is a clear indication that lifelong learning is becoming a more central concern in both economies.

There are important patterns and issues in these developed and developing economies that are instructive for other Asia Pacific economies. For example, in both economies Confucian tradition serves as an important philosophical predisposition to pursue lifelong learning, especially in non-vocational areas. Although most of the adult learners interviewed hoped for greater governmental support (most notably in Chinese Taipei), many respondents indicated that they had nonetheless previously engaged in self-generated lifelong learning activities, relating mainly to cultural enrichment or foreign language learning. The fact that this response pattern was found in both economies would suggest that there is an underlying Confucian learning ethic, coming primarily from the people, fostering in them a predisposition that overcomes at least some economic barriers.[5] Some scholars would even argue that the Confucian learning ethic goes beyond mundane moral consideration, that there often is a mystical dimension ascribed to this process—one that ultimately leads to spiritual enlightenment.[6]

It may be reasonable to assume that adult learners living in Asia Pacific economies influenced by a Confucian mental culture can benefit from non-vocational lifelong learning programs that highlight self-study and cultivation of the mind. If anything, adult learners with relatively lower per capita incomes can get more out of lifelong learning syllabi that emphasize self-instruction as an alternative to 'systematized' lifelong learning programs. Such being the case, government educational policy makers should focus on *channeling* the motivational factors behind adult learners' lifelong educational activities rather than preoccupying themselves with *fostering* such a willingness. Moreover, if the cases of Chinese Taipei and Vietnam can be extrapolated, education authorities in many Asia Pacific economies could highlight more readily celebrated national figures, compatible with the Confucian viewpoint, to further champion the cause of popular lifelong learning.

In economies where a pervasive Confucian educational element is absent, namely occidental economies such as the United States and Canada, educational authorities need to give greater thought to the philosophical implications of the spirit of lifelong learning. Perhaps it would be possible to use classical intellectual figures drawn from Western traditions, for instance Plato or Aristotle, as focal points to promulgate more effectively a spirit for lifelong learning.

Finally, it is worth considering the implications of a greying population on economies within the APEC community. The case of Chinese Taipei can serve as an apt illustration of the potential to tap into the vast wealth of human resources found in the 'older adult' section of the population, many of whom can serve as key educational resources providing indispensable cultural knowledge tempered with hands-on experience to younger generations. Naturally, lifelong learning syllabi featuring mature instructors should not view learning activities as unidirectional, rather the learning process should accentuate the bilateral nature of lifelong learning experiences between generations. There are some members of the APEC community who do not have to deal with such demographic issues at this stage of economic development, but as this phenomenon manifests itself most clearly in the more developed economies, it would be sagacious for all policy makers to regard this challenge as inevitable.

---

[5]It is important to remember that Confucius taught that edification sprang from the will for self-improvement. There are numerous Confucian morality tales that recount how individuals, later to become prominent historical figures, surmounted much adversity in order to educate themselves.

[6]Historically Confucian doctrine often intermixed with other metaphysical interpretations of intellectual maturation, namely Buddhism, connecting the 'spirit' of Confucian learning with the Buddhist pursuit of nirvana (Hall & Ames, 1987).

REFERENCES

Chang, F.T.J. (1990). *A study of technological and vocational education in the Republic of China: Some concepts and their implementation.* Paper presented at the annual meeting of the International Vocational Education and Training Association. Cincinnati, Ohio. (ERIC Document Reproduction Service No. ED 326 668)

Chiang, K.S. (1959). *National fecundity, social welfare and education.* (Supplements to Sun Yat-sen's Lectures on the Principle of People's Livelihood.) (S.F. Chen, Trans). Taipei, Taiwan: China Publishing.

Epstein, I. (1988). Taiwan. In T.S. Kurian (Ed.), *World Education Encyclopedia.* New York: Facts on File.

Europa world book. (1995). London: Europa Publications.

Hall, D.L., & Ames, R.T. (1987). *Thinking through Confucius.* Albany, NY: State University of New York Press.

Le Son (1986). Learning strategies for literacy follow-up and complementary education in the context of lifelong education in Vietnam. In R.H. Dave (Ed.), *Learning strategies for post-literacy and continuing education in China, India, Indonesia, Nepal, Thailand and Vietnam.* Hamburg, Germany: United Nations Educational, Scientific, and Cultural Organization. (ERIC Document Reproduction Service No. ED 324 501)

Lin, C.J. (1983). The Republic of China (Taiwan). In R.M. Thomas & T.N. Postlethwaite (Eds.), *Schooling in East Asia: Forces of change.* New York: Pergamon Press.

Lin, H.P. (1995). *A new English teaching design for adult Taiwanese learners.* Wisconsin: Department of Educational Psychology, University of Wisconsin-Madison. (ERIC Document Reproduction Service No. ED 385 119)

Lucas, C.J. (1982). The politics of national development and education in Taiwan. *Comparative Politics, 14*(2), 211-225.

Meyer, J.E. (1988). Moral education in Taiwan. *Comparative Education Review, 32*(1), 20-38.

Ministry of Education, R.O.C. (1990). *Educational statistics of the Republic of China.* Taipei, Taiwan.

Nguyen, D. (1994). *The development of technical and vocational education for Vietnam — A case study for quality improvement.* Melbourne, Australia: Royal Melbourne Institution of Technology. (ERIC Document Reproduction Service No. ED 391 032)

Pucel, D. & Lyau, N.M. (1995). *An organization's economic return on training investment.* Paper presented at the World Conference of the International Federation of Training and Development Organizations. Sept. 11-14, 1995.

Helsinki, Finland. (ERIC Document Reproduction Service No. ED 391 003)

Sloper, D. & Le Thac, C. (1995). *Higher education in Vietnam: Change and response*. Singapore: Institute of Southeast Asian Studies.

Tan, T.W. (1990). Some Confucian insight and moral education. *Journal of Moral Education, 19*(1), 33-37.

Taylor, M.J. (1988). Conference Report: Moral education East and West—tradition and innovation. *Moral Education Forum, 13*(2), 4-9.

Vavrek, B. (1995). *Rural and small libraries: Providers of lifelong learning*. Paper presented at the conference Public Libraries and Community-Based Education: Making the Connection for Life Long Learning. Washington, DC: National Institute on Post-secondary Education, Libraries, and Lifelong Learning. (ERIC Document Reproduction Service No. ED 385 254)

Yang, J. (1992). The aging: A great potential human resource of Taiwan. *International Review of Education. 38*(4), 427-446.

Yuen, S. (1993). *Vocational education and training plays an important role in Taiwan's economic miracle*. Paper presented at the joint meeting of the International Vocational Education and Training Association and the America Vocational Association. December 4, 1993. Nashville, TN. (ERIC Document Reproduction Service No. ED 363 795)

Law Song Seng

and Low Sock Hwee

Law Song Seng received his B.Eng. from the University of Auckland and his M.S. and Ph.D. degrees in mechanical and production engineering from the University of Wisconsin. Currently, Dr. Law is the Director and C.E.O. of the Institute of Technical Education in Singapore. He has been honoured by the government and industry for his contributions to vocational and technical training in Singapore. Dr. Law enjoys golfing and karaoke singing.

Low Sock Hwee graduated from the National University of Singapore (B.B.A.). At the Institute of Technical Education, she manages part-time training programs for adult learners. In her free time, she reads about garden flowers, and puts the tropical climate to the test with seasonal flower seeds. She also enjoys the outdoors, and has scaled Mt. Kinabalu, the highest peak in southeast Asia.

An Empirical Framework for Implementing Lifelong Learning Systems

by Law Song Seng and Low Sock Hwee

Among governments, economic advisors and policy makers, there has been much recent debate and discussion with regard to lifelong learning. However, beyond the rhetoric, there is a need to translate interest into effective systems of learning. This paper proposes an empirical framework of value to policy makers and practitioners who are interested in the development and implementation of lifelong learning systems. The foundation for this framework is based on a literature search into factors that affect the provision of learning opportunities for adults. Two broad groups of factors were identified: namely, characteristics which influence the changing environment and characteristics that motivate adults as learners. Through this process, ten key strategies were identified, grouped and integrated into the proposed framework. The framework has been empirically validated against experience with three successfully run national worker education and training programs. Four of the ten key strategies, specifically, active tripartite partnership, affordability, accessibility and accreditation, were extensively applied across the programs. Although the extent of applicability with regard to the other strategies varies, all ten are viewed as important conditions for implementing effective learning systems. Further research will be necessary to test the sufficiency of these conditions and transferability of experience among different countries.

INTRODUCTION[1]

Lifelong learning, in its broadest sense, is the continuation of any and all forms of learning throughout one's life. It encompasses adult education, vocational skills acquisition and other less formal activities that contribute to the social well-being and personal development of an individual. However, increasingly, lifelong learning is viewed as an essential capability in a people, workforce and society in order to compete successfully in a global economy. This recognition has not only generated much interest in economic groupings like the Organisation for Economic Cooperation and Development (OECD) and the Asia Pacific Economic Cooperation (APEC) Forum, but has also encouraged discussions among governments and policy

[1]The authors are grateful to H. C. Tan, Y. B. Aw, C. M. Chia, C. S. Chor and J. Ho for their valuable contributions towards the preparation of this paper.

makers. The consequence is a proliferation of research, innovative programs and ideas on lifelong learning in recent years throughout Europe, North America and the East.

Beyond these debates and initiatives is the need to translate interest into effective systems of learning. The provision of lifelong learning programs does not always elicit spontaneous response from the targeted population. Studies have, for example, shown that the lower the initial education, the less likely the learner will be to continue to learn in adult life (Titmus, 1989). Ironically, the less qualified are the ones most in need of upgrading in the face of social, economic and technological changes. To date, authors on lifelong learning have mainly focused on strategic policies and concepts of lifelong learning. There is no single unified framework which can be used to facilitate, motivate and reward adult lifelong learners. Such a guide will be valuable to policy makers and practitioners who are interested in the operational thrusts of providing lifelong learning programs.

This paper proposes such a framework for implementing lifelong learning systems. It is based on a literature search and validation against the experience of a national training institution, the Institute of Technical Education (ITE) in Singapore.

A PROPOSED FRAMEWORK

Theoretical Foundation

The foundation for this framework was derived from a literature search into factors that broadly affect the provision of learning opportunities for adults. Two groups of factors were identified. The first relates to the influence of the changing environment on the provision of learning opportunities (Coombs, 1985; Gelpi, 1979). The second focuses on the characteristics of adults, recognizing that others who have extensively examined the subject of adult education invariably emphasize these characteristics as having a significant influence on the learning process (Courtney, 1992; A. Rogers, 1986; J. Rogers, 1989; Titmus, 1989). An effective lifelong learning system for adult learners must respond not only to the dynamic environment but also to the motivational factors.

Environmental Factors

One of the most notable features of the modern age is the accelerated pace of change and the resultant influence on political, socioeconomic and demographic trends. Technological advancement has a significant influence on transforming the workplace, occupational profiles and job skills. In the post cold war era, international political conflict has given way to economic competition and market liberalization. This has led to a demand for a more educated and better trained workforce in keeping with the needs of industrialisation. Hence, the demand for more open and democratic systems of learning for all (Ireland, 1979). As countries move up the economic ladder, there will be greater demands on individuals not only to learn and re-learn, but also to achieve higher skill levels and qualifications. Therefore, it is government's responsibility to ensure that education can be acquired by all (Garelli, 1996). Business corporations, in which individuals invest their time, energy and resources, must also continuously adapt and respond so as to stay relevant within the external environment.

In addition, there is a clear demographic trend towards increased life expectancy for the world's population. This means that workers are expected to remain in the labour market for a longer time. There is also the problem of a greater number of more highly skilled young people displacing less skilled older people as competition for jobs grows more fierce. These factors will have significant influence on lifelong learning systems in that learning opportunities will have to be constantly reviewed to meet the changing needs of an aging population.

Characteristics of Adult Learners

As well as environmental factors, an effective lifelong learning framework must consider the learning characteristics of adults. The majority of adult learners, whatever their situation or stage of development, are likely to exhibit characteristics that distinguish them from younger students in full-time schools (Uden, 1993). Generally, adults as learners:

- are likely to have a wealth of experience which needs to be taken into account when planning programs;

- are more likely to participate intermittently in learning programs due to work and family commitments, and as a result need training achievements formally recognised in smaller elements or increments;

- are constrained in terms of where and when they study by work and family commitments, which means that learning programs targeted at adults need to be available at convenient times and locations, and via appropriately flexible modes of study;

- are often influenced by earlier negative experiences with the education system and as a consequence need to be persuaded back into learning, which, in turn, requires appropriate teaching strategies and specific approaches to the planning, marketing and delivery of courses;

- participate voluntarily, and approach the learning environment in order to satisfy specific needs or goals. (Hoale in his 1961 classic, *The Inquiring Mind*, identified three main orientations for learning - also see Rogers, 1986. Some adult learners are *goal-oriented*, and they approach the learning environment in order to achieve a specific objective such as a certificate or promotion. A second group is described as *activity-oriented*, and they participate for social or personal growth needs. The third group is described as *learning-oriented*, and their motivation is based on knowledge or skill for its own sake.)

The first four characteristics can be interpreted as extrinsic factors that either facilitate or inhibit learning. But the last characteristic is intrinsically driven. The implications for the lifelong learning system are two-fold. First, it must incorporate features that *facilitate and reward learning* so that dissonance associated with learning is removed. However, these features do not in themselves make learning satisfying. Second, there must be features to *motivate the adult learner's goals* so as to increase readiness to learn (A. Rogers, 1986). This latter factor is particularly challenging. It may require a behavioural change on the part of the adult learner where learning in itself becomes a motivator so that the learning becomes satisfying (McClelland, 1985).

Identifying Strategies for a Lifelong Learning Framework

Preliminary findings on environmental and motivational factors led to a further lit-

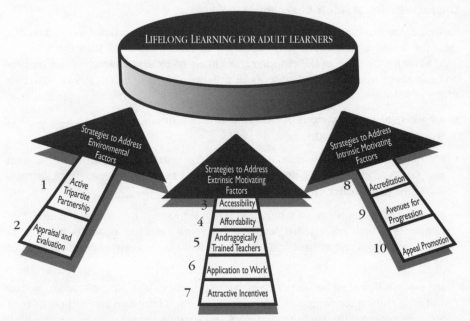

Figure 1: An Empirical Framework for Implementing Lifelong Learning Systems

erature search focusing on strategies and good practices, whether simply advocated or actually in practice, which characterize successful learning programs. Ten key strategies were identified, grouped and integrated into the proposed framework as illustrated in Figure 1.

The first set of strategies seeks to maximise support from the environment. The second set reflects the extrinsic motivating factors faced by adult learners. The third set addresses the intrinsic factors that can increase the self motivation of adults to learn and to continue learning.

Strategies To Address Environmental Factors

Two strategies ensure that a lifelong learning system is interactive with and draws on the vast resources within its environment.

Strategy 1 : Active Tripartite Partnership

An effective lifelong learning system is not an end but a means to an end. The beneficiaries of such a system include individual learners, businesses and the society as a whole. The system is a means to enhance the competitive edge of an economy and it must be clear that the government, employers and trade unions are all stakeholders in the system. An OECD (1996) publication titled *Lifelong Learning for All* stressed the importance of this tripartite partnership involving government, employers and unions as active providers of education and training.

There is increasing agreement that government needs to assume a significant role in coordinating the provision of lifelong learning. Government should disseminate information and provide guidance on available options. It is also the responsibility of government to establish the appropriate framework conditions and incentive systems for lifelong learning. At the same time, Longworth & Davies (1996) argue that employers have a role to create an environment and conditions to facilitate lifelong learning among adult learners. Trade unions also stimulate lifelong learning through initiating joint training programs with business (Uden, 1993).

In a study of vocational education in five developed countries, Cantor (1989, pp. 157-158) concluded that "a successful system of vocational training ... is likely to be one which recognises and promotes a 'dual mandate', namely the education and vocational training of the individual both in his own interest and for that of the economy". For this to occur, the government and employers must assume direct responsibilities for the provision of learning opportunities.

Strategy 2 : Appraisal and Evaluation

For a lifelong learning system to remain relevant and effective in an environment marked by rapid social, economic and technological change, it must be subjected to regular appraisal and evaluation. A performance review must not be an end in itself, or merely a check on current progress. It must challenge the development of new areas and work towards new levels of achievement. By seeking continual improvement, investment in human resources can be maximised.

Today, learning audits, in which companies carry out surveys into past experiences of learning and analyze the future learning needs of employees, are being tested in Europe (Longworth & Davies, 1996). The results of these surveys can lead to greater satisfaction of learning needs.

Strategies to Address Extrinsic Motivating Factors

The following five strategies address motivating factors. By removing external barriers to learning and providing suitable encouragement, these strategies increase the adult learner's ability and willingness to respond.

Strategy 3 : Accessibility

Timing, location and physical accessibility of training opportunities are all factors which affect adult participation in learning activities (Uden, 1993). When the provision of learning opportunities is made more flexible, the barriers to learning are removed and this may be the crucial external motivating factor which encourages participation among many adult learners.

Flexible training schedules, modular curricula structures, work-based learning and open and distance learning are examples that promote accessibility.

Strategy 4 : Affordability

Research into industrialised economies has shown that when the updating of knowledge, skills and competencies is not possible, individuals face increased risk of low earnings, high unemployment and even marginalisation (OECD, 1996). In other words, the likelihood of unemployment and lower average earnings is highest among the least qualified — the ones most in need of opportunities for lifelong learning.

Therefore, financial support to pursue lifelong learning opportunities is imperative. This need is greatest for basic education and occupational skills training in order to ensure that there are no financial barriers for those whose need is greatest.

Strategy 5 : Andragogically Trained Teachers

OECD Ministers acknowledge that the quality of education depends mainly on the skill, experience and motivation of teachers and trainers (Longworth & Davies, 1996). The challenge for teachers of adult learners is greater since adult learners bring with them an accumulation of experiences and expectations. One consequence is that trainers involved in the provision of education and training for adults need to be equipped with skills appropriate for this clientele (Uden, 1993). This will help to ease the transition from work to classroom, particularly for adult learners who have negative recollections of past learning experiences or those who have been out of the formal education system for a long period of time.

Strategy 6 : Application to Work

Motivation to learn will increase when adults comprehend the benefits of education. Adult learners are eager to learn when they see education as a solution to their problems and when they are able to apply the learning in their daily lives (Reizen, 1996). Therefore, adult learners' needs must be directly reflected in the curriculum. Increasingly, training programs are tailored to be concurrent with work, thereby supporting the work-related needs of learners. Relevance to work has the joint advantages of increasing motivation and promoting improved performance on the job (Murphy, 1996). The emphasis on linking learning to settings in which adults feel competent and knowledgeable also helps adult learners to develop positive feelings about learning (Titmus, 1989).

Strategy 7 : Attractive Incentives

The provision of financial incentives acts as an external motivator, attracting adult learners to engage in lifelong learning opportunities. Ball (Longworth & Davies, 1996) recommended that financial incentives should be systematically developed for increased participation. Not all rewards need be financial, however. Book vouchers and time-off from work can also be used to enhance participation.

Strategies to Address Intrinsic Motivating Factors

Three strategies are proposed which may be used to motivate adult learners to participate in lifelong learning by capitalising on intrinsic motives and thereby propelling them to action. These strategies will also make learning more satisfying in the process, and they are internalised in that they are driven by the adult learner's inner needs for recognition, growth and self development (J. Rogers, 1989).

Strategy 8 : Accreditation

Adult learners are results-oriented, and accreditation of training is important to them (Kuo, 1981). The desire to learn will be greater if achievements are recognised. As such, any person with a particular skill should be able to have it evaluated and validated regardless of how it was acquired (Arbault, 1996).

Various initiatives have been launched in order to improve the marketability of educational programs. For example, New Zealand has established a single national framework for the recognition of school, vocational and higher academic qualifications. Germany has attempted to put qualifications for part-time vocational studies on an equal footing with those for general education. Canada has established a system for the recognition of prior learning (OECD, 1996). These steps enhance the recognition of skills and competencies, and in doing so act as a motivator in support of lifelong learning.

Strategy 9 : Avenues for Progression

To facilitate the adult learner's need for growth and self-development, paths for continuous learning throughout the entire life span must be available. In fact, this is the first and most obvious principle of lifelong learning. Vertical integration, where learning at one stage serves as a preparation for the next, is critical (Knapper & Cropley, 1985).

In this light, it is important for accreditation to be portable and transferable. Otherwise, various forms of accreditation will not facilitate linkages between learning stages (Titmus, 1989). The European Union, for example, is considering the notion of a European Personal Skills Card. This, if adopted, will allow for the transfer of qualifications and competencies between Member States, and between workplace and educational institutions.

Strategy 10 : Appeal Promotion

J. Rogers (1989) argued that the more obvious the need and purpose for learning, the greater the motivation will be to learn. Adult learners need to be persuaded, and they must be convinced that the benefits derived from attending a training program outweigh the opportunity costs.

Learning must not be offered on a take-it or leave-it basis. On the contrary, marketing and packaging must make learning an opportunity that cannot be refused. Marketing and promotion must also be widespread and have sufficient penetration to ensure that information is effectively conveyed to the target groups.

VALIDATING THE LIFELONG LEARNING FRAMEWORK

Having identified the ten key strategies as significant characteristics of lifelong learning systems, the validity of the proposed framework was empirically tested using three ITE national training programs.

ITE is an integral part of Singapore's education and training system. As a post-secondary technical institution, its primary function is to provide vocational and technical training for school leavers who have received ten years of general education. A second primary function of ITE is to provide worker education and training opportunities for working adults through a comprehensive system of Continuing Education and Training (CET) programs. The CET programs are broadly grouped as Worker Education, Skills Training, and Industry-Based Training. Each category of programming meets different training needs of workers in Singapore.

Worker Education programs allow adults to continue their academic education up to secondary levels. These include the Basic Education for Skills Training (BEST), Worker Improvement through Secondary Education (WISE), and Continuing Education (CE) programs. Skills Training programs provide opportunities for adults to learn new skills or update current skills. The first of these programs offered was the Modular Skills Training (MOST) program. Over the years, ITE has introduced additional Skills Training programs, including the Training Initiative for Mature Employees (TIME) and Adult Cooperative Training Scheme (ACTS), each targeted at different groups of adult workers. ITE launched its latest initiative, the Certified On-the-Job Training Centre (COJTC) System, an Industry-Based Training program, two years ago in order to expand training opportunities in the workplace.

Two of ITE's pioneer CET programs, BEST and MOST, along with the more recently introduced COJTC System, were used for empirical validation of the proposed framework. Table 1 summarizes these results.

BEST

BEST was launched in 1983 as a national program to provide workers with a basic education so that they could upgrade their skills and keep pace with changes in the industry. BEST offers 4 modules each in English and mathematics up to the Primary Six level (see Vocational Industrial Training Board, 1983, 1986).

Tripartism has been a key strategy underlying much of the success of BEST. Various government bodies, the National Trades Union Congress (NTUC) representing the unions, and employers were involved in the development of BEST, and a tripartite advisory council was formed to oversee the implementation. This ensured that the needs of workers and industry were fully reflected in the program. At the same time, this approach encouraged joint ownership as well as active support for and participation in the program.

Under the direction of the advisory council, the teaching materials and instructional aids for BEST were developed and have been revised and updated several times. Surveys are conducted periodically to obtain feedback from participants, instructors and employers. The last survey, conducted in 1992, showed that 90% of the graduates found BEST to be effective in upgrading their English communication skills and competency in mathematics (VITB, 1992).

The accessibility of BEST is another important characteristic. The strategy was to extend the program through an extensive network of training centres involving not only the educational institutions but also the unions and companies. This nation

Table 1: Validating the Lifelong Learning Framework

	BEST	MOST	COJTC
Environmental Factors			
Active Tripartite Partnership	★★★	★★★	★★★
Appraisal and Evaluation	★★★	★★	★
Extrinsic Motivating Factors			
Accessibility	★★★	★★★	★★★
Affordability	★★★	★★★	★★★
Andragogically Trained Teachers	★★	★★	★★
Application to Work	★★★	★★	★★★
Attractive Incentives	★	★	★
Intrinsic Motivating Factors			
Accreditation	★★★	★★★	★★★
Avenues for Progression	★★★	★★★	★★
Appeal Promotion	★★★	★★	★★

Key
Applied to a large extent	★★★
Applied to some extent	★★
Applied to a small extent	★

wide network of 132 company in-house centres, 35 NTUC centres, 4 ITE institutes and 8 school centres ensures that training is within easy access for all workers. And there are other motivating features. An open door policy was adopted to encourage participation, and training is conducted in modules so that results can be seen within a period of 20 weeks. The two intakes each year provide adults with more frequent choices of training opportunities. Flexible scheduling — evenings, weekdays and weekends — helps meet the needs of working adults. Many workers at company centres attend the program during working hours.

The course fee is kept affordable, a strategy advocated in the lifelong learning framework. This is especially important as workers who need basic education generally come from the lower income group. BEST is nationally funded by the Skills Development Fund (SDF). Participants pay a nominal fee of $15 (Singapore) per module, a token sum to encourage ownership for learning. In addition, community self-help groups provide training subsidies and incentive awards for those who need financial assistance, and companies receive capital and training grants to set up training centres and conduct BEST. Workers attending BEST classes at company centres generally do not pay fees.

The learning needs of adults were a prime consideration during the development of this program. The materials were produced by specialists in adult learning who ensured that the curricula are oriented towards the work situation and the interests and experience of the target group. Teachers are trained to manage an adult learning environment. The first batch of 240 BEST program teachers were trained by instructors from the Alberta Vocational Centre in Edmonton, Canada. Today, all newly recruited teachers must undergo a five day Teachers' Training Course that includes andragogy skills.

Accreditation of Training scores highly as another lifelong learning motivating strategy. BEST participants are awarded a nationally recognised module certificate upon passing the prescribed tests, and the pass rate has averaged 84%. With certification, participants may continue to upgrade through WISE, CE or other Skills Training programs.

Various promotional strategies are employed to publicize BEST. The easy to recognise acronym has been very effective in this regard. A team of officers promotes CET programs to employers and workers across all industrial sectors, and advertisements in major newspapers precede each intake in order to generate awareness. The NTUC has been an active partner in the promotion and conduct of BEST, and there are frequent reminders and exhortation in the media which encourage workers to accept lifelong learning as a way of life ("Asian Workers...", 1996).

BEST was launched in 1983 for a target group of some 225,000 workers who lacked a primary-level qualification in English and mathematics. Today, BEST, in its 14th year of implementation, has reached over 207,000 workers. The demand for the program remains strong with about 20,000 training places taken up every year.

MOST

The MOST program was launched in 1987 to upgrade the skills of the workforce and enhance Singapore's global competitiveness. Under MOST, workers can choose from a wide range of part-time courses leading to the National Technical Certificate (NTC) and Certificate of Competency (CoC) national skills qualifications. Each NTC course has four self-contained modules which lead to employable skills, while the CoC course has two modules.

Although MOST is primarily government-driven by ITE, the element of tripartism is still strong. The courses which follow the established national skills standards are developed in consultation with industry so that training will be relevant to the workplace. Industry representatives sit on training advisory committees in the various trades to review the curriculum at regular intervals. Surveys are also taken periodically to obtain feedback from employers. The NTUC has long been a staunch supporter of worker education and training. Employers too have shown support for MOST, sponsoring more than 30% of the participants.

MOST has a highly accessible training infrastructure. The courses are offered at nine ITE Institutes island-wide. In addition, 56 approved training providers set up by companies, commercial training organisations and private schools also conduct training in selected courses. ITE has deliberately set minimal entry requirements based on education or work experience, and participants are free to choose modules relevant to their needs. In view of the different providers, training can be tailored to suit the schedules of workers.

In line with the principle of affordability, the cost of training is subsidised at a rate of 80%. Fees for MOST courses vary between $90 and $130 (Singapore) per module depending on the level of training. In addition, study incentives are extended by the NTUC and community self-help groups to participants who need financial assistance, and employers who sponsor their workers for training may claim up to 80% reimbursement of fees from SDF.

Accreditation of Training is another feature that corresponds with the framework. As with BEST, participants receive a certificate upon successful completion of each module. A participant who has been awarded 4 module certificates in the same trade is deemed to have attained full certification. Employers readily accept the certification for recruitment as it is an integral part of the national system. The average pass rate for MOST programming is 85%. This reflects the effectiveness of the learning process. The majority of the teachers are qualified ITE instructors. Instructors from industry must be pedagogically qualified.

The strategies used for promoting MOST are similar to those used with BEST. Like BEST, the acronym, MOST, has become a household name in Singapore. Opportunities to continue learning after MOST are readily available. A MOST participant may progress to a higher level of training at the NTC Grade 2 and the Industrial Technician Certificate (ITC) levels.

In a 1990 survey of MOST participants, more than 90% of the respondents indicated that they had benefited from the courses (VITB, 1990). The benefits that received the highest ratings were (a) an increase in knowledge and skills in the area of work and (b) an increase in willingness to continue to learn and improve. These findings, coupled with a demand for some 15,000 training places annually, support the continuing popularity of MOST.

COJTC

In 1994, ITE introduced a new certification system to certify and recognise companies with good on-the-job training (OJT). The COJTC System encourages employers to implement quality OJT programs, and upgrade the skills of their workers as a continuous learning process. OJT is a flexible and cost-effective way of training workers, a practice very much entrenched in Japanese and German companies.

In the COJTC System, employers assume the main responsibility for training their workers. The role of ITE is to promote, audit and certify companies as OJT centres. Once authorised, companies are free to conduct OJT and award OJT certificates to workers. ITE also works closely with the NTUC in promoting the COJTC System to companies.

Companies whose OJT systems meet the basic requirements stipulated by ITE are registered as COJTCs. An important requirement of a COJTC is the commitment to provide systematic training, including proper planning, job analysis and scheduling. Instructors assigned to conduct OJT must have attended a recognised Coaching Skills course. As training is directly focused on job needs, results are more explicit and workers and employers are better motivated. Companies are also given an incentive of $3 per trainee-hour by the SDF to help offset the cost of training.

The principle of accessibility is one of the strongest features of a COJTC. Conducted on-the-job during working hours, training is literally available at the doorstep. Qualified OJT instructors provide the coaching, and no fees are involved. The OJT certificate is recognised for entry into MOST courses.

Started with 14 companies in 1994, the scheme now has over 300 COJTCs, providing some 40,000 training places annually. The national target is to certify 500 companies by the year 2000.

ANALYSIS AND LIMITATIONS

Table 1 shows that four of the key strategies have been extensively applied across the programs. *Active tripartite partnership* is particularly notable. All three programs are government-driven, but union support is strong and explicit. And employers are taking on a more active and direct role in the training of their workers, especially with the introduction of the COJTC System. Another significant feature is the role of the government in ensuring that the programs are *affordable* through ITE and the SDF. Also evident is the very comprehensive and integrated CET system, demonstrating that *accessibility* and *accreditation* are key strategies. All training, from basic education to OJT and technical skills, is recognised and leads to national certification.

BEST, MOST and the COJTC are examples of well-established national worker education and training programs, part of an overall strategy for lifelong learning. They continue to attract the support of employers and the participation of workers. On the strength of the success of these three programs, it may be concluded that the ten key strategies are important conditions for an effective framework supporting the implementation of lifelong learning systems. The extent of applicability of each strategy, however, varies across programs. More research will further test the sufficiency of these strategies.

There are potential limitations. The experience of one country in implementing the framework may not be directly applicable to another. In the validation exercise, the emphasis placed on particular strategies reflects the underlying philosophy and culture in implementing lifelong learning programs. Given a different set of social and economic conditions, the relative importance of each strategy to the success of a program may vary. In some countries there are centralized approaches for governing continuing vocational training, whereas in other countries control is at the regional level. All these differences will have implications for implementing lifelong learning programs. Hence, it would be valuable to further test the proposed framework against the experiences of other countries.

Ultimately, lifelong learning is not about learning, but more about learning how to learn. But effective programs must be created to facilitate the first step in the process. The lifelong learning framework presented here is a good reference point for policy makers and practitioners who are responsible for creating effective lifelong learning systems.

REFERENCES

Arbault, F. (1996). The European skills validation and accreditation project. *Le Magazine*, 5, 11. Luxembourg: The European Commission.

Asian workers must accept lifelong learning. (1996, June 5). *The Straits Times*, p. 25.

Cantor, L. (1989). *Vocational education and training in the developed world: A comparative study*. London: Routledge.

Coombs, P. H. (1985). *The world crisis in education: The view from the eighties*. New York: Oxford University Press.

Courtney, S. (1992). *Why adults learn*. London: Routledge.

Garelli, S. (1996). What is world competitiveness. *The World Competitiveness Yearbook*. Lausanne, Switzerland: International Institute for Management.

Gelpi, E. (1979). *A future for lifelong education 1*. Manchester: University of Manchester, Department of Adult and Higher Education.

Hoale, C. O. (1961). *The inquiring mind: A study of the adult who continues to learn*. Madison: University of Wisconsin Press.

Ireland, T. (1979). *Gelpi's view of lifelong education*. Manchester: University of Manchester, Department of Adult and Higher Education.

Knapper, C. K., & Cropley, A. J. (1985). *Lifelong learning and higher education* (2nd ed.). London: Kogan Page.

Kuo, E. (1981). *Life-long education and social development in Singapore: A country review*. Singapore: National University of Singapore, Department of Sociology.

Longworth, N., & Davies, W. K. (1996). *Lifelong learning*. London: Kogan Page.

McClelland, D. C. (1985). *Human motivation*. Illinois: Scott, Foresman and Company.

Murphy, G. (1996, May/June). Employment & training. *Adult Learning I*, 22-31. Washington: American Association for Adult and Continuing Education.

Organisation for Economic Co-operation and Development. (1996). *Lifelong learning for all*. Paris: OECD.

Riezen, K. Van. (1996). Non-formal education and community development: Improving the quality. *Convergence, XXIX*(1), 82-93.

Rogers, A. (1986). *Teaching adults*. Philadelphia: Open University Press.

Rogers, J. (1989). *Adults learning* (3rd ed.). Philadelphia: Open University Press.

Titmus, C. J. (1989). *Lifelong education for adults : An international handbook*. Oxford: Pergamon Press.

Uden, T. (1993, March). *The learning imperative*. Leicester: National Institute of

Adult Continuing Education.

Vocational Industrial Training Board. (1983). *Report on the pilot scheme of the BEST programme*. Singapore: Author.

Vocational Industrial Training Board. (1986). *Report of the project committee on the post-BEST programme*. Singapore: Author.

Vocational Industrial Training Board. (1990). *Survey on the effectiveness of the MOST scheme*. Singapore: Author.

Vocational Industrial Training Board. (1992). *Survey on the effectiveness of the basic education for skills training (BEST) programme by Forbes Management Consultants*. Singapore: Author.

Yip Kai Leong

Yip Kai Leong holds a B.A. from Universiti Sains Malaysia / University of Science Malaysia and a Certificate in Training and Development from the Institute of Personnel Development, United Kingdom. Currently, he is Assistant Manager for Training Support Services in the Centre for Training and Technology Development of Institut Kejuruteraan Teknologi Tenaga Nasional (IKATAN). He is married with four children, two boys and two girls. In his free time he raises tropical fish, jogs, swims and cooks for the family.

Lifelong Learning and Vision 2020 in Malaysia

by Yip Kai Leong

Most APEC economies share a common goal: namely, how to ensure their educational systems are relevant in times of rapid economic and social change. This challenge has become a preoccupation and a major challenge within Malaysia, in large measure because of its importance in relationship to achieving Vision 2020, the national development plan which has as its focus the creation of a fully developed economy by the year 2020. This paper describes global change and the need for human resource development in Malaysia, the changing nature of education, formal education at the primary and secondary school levels within Malaysia, changes taking place in higher education within Malaysia, and non-formal education in Malaysia. Within this overview, the paper critically analyses various policies and strategies taken by the Malaysian government in what can only be described as a major restructuring of the education system. The paper then argues that the logical extension for these changes is the development of a fully integrated lifelong learning system.

MALAYSIA, CHANGE AND HUMAN RESOURCE DEVELOPMENT

The Government of Malaysia has adopted, as a principal goal, the creation of a fully "developed" economy by the year 2020 (Ahmad Sarji Abdul Hamid, 1993, pp. xiii-xxi). However, the Malaysian model of a developed economy will be different from other developed economies as they exist in the world today. In his paper titled *Malaysia: The Way Forward*, presented to the Malaysian Business Council, Prime Minister Mahathir Mohamad (1992, p. 196) described the development model for Malaysia as follows:

> *Without being a duplicate of any of them, we can still be developed. We would be a developed country in our own mould. Malaysia should not be developed only in the economic sense. It must be a nation that is fully developed along all dimensions: economically, politically, socially, spiritually, psychologically and culturally. By the year 2020, Malaysia can be a united nation, with a confident Malaysian society, infused by strong moral and ethical values, living in a society that is democratic, liberal and tolerant, caring, economically just and equitable, progressive and prosperous and in full possession of an economy that is competitive, dynamic, robust and resilient.*

In the effort to achieve developed country status, one of the strategies undertaken by the government involves the development of the country's most important asset — its human resource base. In order to face the challenges of the twenty-first century, new skills and fresh knowledge, coupled with exemplary attitudes, must be learned and re-learned on an ongoing basis throughout life. This learning will take place both inside and outside the formal education system, and the resulting quality and resourcefulness of the workforce will directly determine the degree to which Malaysia is successful with regard to achieving its economic development goals. In effect, it is understood within Malaysia that the professional workforce will play the pivotal role in so far as demarcating Malaysia's competitive edge with respect to other nations.

Malaysia's economy has been quite literally transformed within the last decade, moving rapidly away from a low-technology, commodity-based environment to one where manufacturing and the services sectors are employing higher and more sophisticated technology. Malaysia must compete through continuous productivity improvements, more value added operations, and enhanced product quality. The competitive advantage associated with cheap and abundant labour will continue to be eroded with the advent of low cost producers. Clearly, education is a critical component of any competitive workforce strategy.

Rapid industrialisation, coupled with a shift towards more capital intensive production, has changed human resources development in Malaysia. Currently, the country is facing a shortage of trained manpower, particularly in the fields of engineering and management. The government, though concerned about rapid industrialisation and concomitant needs, recognizes that the required foundation in science and technology to support this development has yet to be acquired. Foreign expertise is still very much needed for development, as are an array of human resource development policies and programs which will continuously upgrade and improve the education and training system. In this context, there are three important dimensions.

First, there needs to be a stronger focus on strengthening the higher education system as it pertains to the teaching of science and mathematics and the English language, as well as to the broad expansion of vocational and technical education so necessary to cope with developing knowledge and skills requirements. Second, Malaysia needs to master state-of-the-art management techniques and systems through entrepreneurial and management development programs. Third, Malaysia needs to equip its workforce with training in the latest technological and industrial processes. Within this framework, retraining and skills upgrading of the present workforce must be a priority. These three dimensions, when implemented in an integrated fashion, will support the strategies and programs designed to dovetail with the objectives of Vision 2020 (Ahmad Sarji Abdul Hamid, 1993).

One significant measure that has been introduced by the government to increase the supply of skilled workers is the establishment of the Human Resources Development Fund under the "Human Resources Development Act 1992". This fund encourages and facilitates employers in the manufacturing and service sector to increase the pace of retraining and skills upgrading in their workforce, as well as to equip employees with specialised and up-to-date skills as manufacturing processes become increasingly automated and more complex. Recognising the need for large initial outlays in technical human resource development and skills training as well as optimising the utilisation of training facilities in the public sector training institutions, the Ministry of Human Resources and the Ministry of Education have implemented the concept of time-sector privatisation for retraining and skills upgrading.

Malaysia is a developing country with a per capita income of RM9,786 (US$3,914) in 1995 (Economic Planning Unit, 1996, p. 5). The government is aggressively implementing development programs for the eradication of privation, and the incidence of poverty among Malaysians fell from 17% in 1990 to 9% in 1995 (figures rounded to the nearest whole number) (Economic Planning Unit, 1996, p. 71). Many basic needs, including housing, health and education, continue to be addressed by government; however, at the same time, foreign investment and privatisation have created many jobs and considerable wealth. In this environment, the objective for most adults participating in non-formal learning activities is to earn more money through promotion or a job change. This clearly takes precedence over learning for personal development or recreational purposes.

THE CHANGING NATURE OF EDUCATION

The evolution of the world into a global village has gone beyond mere rhetoric. We know that borders are disappearing and the information age is changing the way we work, play and interact with each other. A significant development in one part of the world has an almost instantaneous effect everywhere. The spread of ideas, ideologies, cultures and technologies has no confines in our borderless world, and there is every indication that life in the twenty-first century will be accompanied by an accelerated rate of change. With advances in the fields of science and technology, and the explosive growth in information, we are constantly being reminded that our knowledge and skills, often just acquired, are quickly obsolete. These developments greatly affect human life, and the ability to cope with change has become paramount.

Knowles (1980) identified four forces which he felt are ongoing influencers of effective educational practices. The first of these pertains to the purpose of education. Traditional perspectives argue that the purpose of education, at its most simplistic level, is to produce an educated person. In this context, education is limited in the sense that it has an end. However, in the current era, one marked by an explosion of knowledge, revolution in technology, and social policies that argue for equality of educational opportunity, this traditional purpose of education and the belief in the power of a fixed knowledge set are no longer appropriate. Now, the educational mission is to produce a workforce of competent people who are able to apply knowledge under changing conditions and, more importantly, who are able to continue learning on their own.

The second force is the shift from a focus on teaching to a focus on learning. In the past, emphasis was placed, often with great deliberation and in great detail, on training teachers to be the centre for information and control. The teachers taught and the students learned; if there was no teaching, there was no learning. Now, the focus is on the learning side and emphasis is placed on the students. In this model, learning is student driven, not teacher controlled.

The third force is the concept of lifelong learning as the organising principle for all education, the reason being that, in a world of accelerating change, learning must be a lifelong process, one that extends throughout the lifespan. Formal elementary and secondary schooling, therefore, must be concerned primarily with the development of the skills of inquiry, and adult education must be concerned primarily with the provision of resources and support for self-directed learning.

The fourth force relates to the development of new delivery systems for learning. These enable individuals to continue learning throughout their lives, at a time and place of their own choosing. Flexibility is the key. These new delivery systems include examples and characteristics which have been variously labeled as "non traditional study", "external degrees", "multimedia learning systems", "community education", "learning communities", "learning resource centres", and "learning networks". Thankfully, education is no longer a monopoly business housed within educational institutions and framed by teacher-centred offerings. Resources for learning are everywhere, and the task of learning organizations is to link learners with learning resources.

Education in Malaysia is changing quite rapidly, as described later in this paper, and the forces described by Knowles are alive and well within the country.

FORMAL EDUCATION —
ELEMENTARY AND SECONDARY SCHOOL FOCUS

The provision of "basic education for all" has long been a goal of the Government of Malaysia, and various strategies have been implemented during the past several decades in pursuit of this. Results suggest that this goal has become a reality, and emphasis has shifted from "basic education for all" to a new vision — "quality education for all in the twenty-first century". Malaysia subscribes to the concept of "education for life", that is, the notion that education is not an end in itself, but rather its purpose is to serve life. As our lives undergo change, education must change to be in concert with this. In the past, when Malaysia advocated education for all, emphasis was placed on the basics — reading, writing and arithmetic. It was thought that this approach to learning and education would fulfil the basic needs of life as it was then experienced. Now, as Malaysia prepares for an era of constant and accelerated change, it is clear that basic education alone will not equip people for the challenges and opportunities in the twenty-first century.

By advocating "quality education for all" in the formal school system, it is necessary to include more than basic reading, writing and numeracy skills. There is a need to emphasize the development of critical thinking skills. Life in the twenty-first century promises to be filled with the need for continuous adjustment and development, and change will be unpredictable with few discernible patterns. Therefore, education must prepare learners to cope with change, rather than depend on habitual responses. In effect, education for the future should place less emphasis on acquiring knowledge, which is transient, and focus instead on developing critical thinking skills, which will allow learners to process and respond to change, and even embrace and look forward to it, rather than resist or oppose it.

"Quality education for all" also means we must place greater emphasis on nurturing broad human development than has occurred in the past. In our pursuit of progress and economic advancement, people are increasingly driven by materialistic values. However, high per capita incomes are not necessarily an indicator of the standard of happiness and contentment among people. Quality education needs to address value issues and help people seek satisfaction and balance in their lives.

Also important in this revitalized framework is the need to develop among students an appreciation for and understanding of the rest of the world, including other cultures and value systems. The global village requires peaceful and even respectful co-existence. "Quality education for all" should produce a common curriculum which cultivates in children a sense of trust and love for others. This strong international component in the educational system is required in order to diminish hostility and distrust, while instilling positive thoughts for peace, love and harmony.

Progress has been made in so far as implementing the concept and goals of "quality education for all", and, as a first step, a philosophy in tune with quality education has been developed, including the following mission statement (Wan Mohd. Zahid, 1994, p. xvi).

Education in Malaysia is an on-going effort towards further developing the potential of individuals in a holistic and integrated manner, so as to produce individuals who are intellectually, spiritually, emotionally and physically balanced and harmonious, based on an affirmed belief in and devotion to God. Such an effort is designed to produce Malaysian citizens who are knowledgeable, who possess high moral standards, and who are responsible and capable of achieving a high level of personal well-being as well as being able to contribute to the betterment of the society and the nation at large.

A second step, currently underway, involves the development and acceptance of a clear statement of principles, in the form of a national education policy, to guide thinking with regard to the design of educational programing. This national policy should be pragmatic and useful, not merely decorative. It must form the basis for each and every educational activity and program. All educators, both formal and non-formal, and elementary-focused through higher education, must be committed to the policy and be prepared to translate the goals into actual educational activities. It is important that Malaysians be consciously aware of the fact that education does not occur just in schools, but also in many other formal and non-formal environments.

A third element related to the goal of "quality education for all" in the twenty-first century is the emphasis on integrated education for all levels of schooling. Central to this is the development of a well-rounded individual with physical, intellectual, spiritual and social competencies and qualities. An integrated approach refuses to compartmentalise learning, instead it develops learners through a consolidated approach. An integrated education presumes children study the natural sciences in order to relate to their environment, that they study human sciences so as to forge meaningful relationships with other fellow human beings, and that they study religious sciences and the associated values in order to develop strong moral principles.

In the past, formal education has focused primarily on intellectual development, with little or no emphasis on the aesthetic and moral development of the learners. The Government of Malaysia has now started to emphasise values education as well as religious education as a means to prepare young learners for the challenges of the twenty-first century. The government is committed to a vision of a society that has, at its core, a deep sense of religious consciousness coupled with the highest standards of ethical and moral values, and where the people are industrious, dynamic and dedicated towards advancement and progress.

HIGHER EDUCATION AND TRAINING IN MALAYSIA

Institutions of higher education play a critical role in the development of human resources. In a very general sense they provide opportunities for the academically gifted to study at high levels and advance the world's storehouse of knowledge. At a more pragmatic level, they produce professionals who help meet national human resource needs and requirements. They also act as a home for research facilities and consultancy services. Institutions of higher education include universities, colleges and polytechnics. It has been recognized that there is a need to make radical changes in the system of higher education within Malaysia in order to meet future challenges. In this context, Najib Tun Razak, the Malaysian Education Minister, made the following remarks in his opening speech to the first regional Conference on Higher Education For The 21st Century (Sahibudllah & James, 1996), organised by the Southeast Asia Ministers of Education Organisation (SEAMEO).

[Institutions of higher education] must be willing to adopt or adapt new and revolutionary ideas, strategies, concepts and tools from whatever disciplines to enable them to effect the radical changes or make the quantum leap. To enable us to achieve dramatic improvements to our standard of education, we need to carry out a re-engineering, a fundamental re-thinking and a radical redesigning of our existing educational processes. This should include re-thinking existing structures, procedures and entrenched norms, notions and practices pertaining to education. For this to be possible, it is equally vital for ASEAN countries to re-examine the issue of institutional governance including the distribution of power, authority and influence within the institutions of higher learning and the flexibility to devise new mechanisms for academic and general management. In this context, we need to re-examine the whole question of financing of public universities. So long as they are partially or wholly financed by governments, there is little urgency for them to improve the element of financial accountability.

Radical changes have been planned for the overhaul of the higher education system in Malaysia. Some have already been implemented, while others are yet to come. These changes are in keeping with the government's goal of making Malaysia a regional centre for excellence in education.

With a specific view towards liberalising the education sector, five bills related to higher education were passed by the Malaysian Parliament in 1996. These include the "Education Act", the "Universities and University Colleges (Amendment) Act", the "Private Higher Educational Institutions Act", the "National Council of Higher Education Act" and the "National Accreditation Act". The Education Act, among other things, permits the establishment of branch campuses of foreign universities and the creation of private universities in Malaysia. This will be direct competition for the present nine universities which are publicly owned and state financed.

The raison d'être behind the government's move to permit the establishment of foreign and private universities is to reduce the outflow of about RM2.5 billion (US$1 billion) annually for overseas education. Currently, approximately 60,000 Malaysian students study overseas. The private sector has been called upon by the government to develop higher education as an industry, and to turn Malaysia from consumer status to provider status in this regard. Part of this may involve increasing the number of twinning arrangements that Malaysian institutions have with foreign universities where a part of the program can be completed locally and the remainder done overseas.

The creation of foreign campuses in Malaysia could take longer than originally projected, as the government's first priority is to establish universities associated with national utility and resource companies. Included are the proposed Petronas University (oil and gas), the Telekom University (information technology), and the Tenaga Nasional University (power). Petronas, Telekom and Tenaga Nasional are state charted companies with abundant resources and expertise. Private local universities and branches of foreign universities can only be established in Malaysia through an invitation from the Ministry of Education, and the National Accreditation Act has established an Accreditation Board designed to ensure the quality of private local and foreign universities.

The government posits that by having branches of foreign universities, Malaysia will attract students from other parts of the world to study. The goal is cross cultural mixing and understanding. For example, it is thought that students from Britain will complete part of their studies in Malaysia, and Malaysian students will do the same course in Britain. Both groups will learn beyond their disciplines, and cross cultural understanding will result.

Amendments to the University and University Colleges Act have paved the way for the "corporatisation" of public universities in Malaysia. Universities will have greater autonomy to manage and operate their institutions in a more dynamic and proactive manner. They will have greater flexibility to develop their own revenue sources, increase their capacities for consultancy services and the commercialisation of research findings, and recruit and remunerate teaching staff in a more entrepreneurial fashion. These institutions, however, will continue to be guided by overall government policy direction and objectives.

The government is committed to ensuring that higher education institutions will continue to be accessible by lower income groups and the disadvantaged. This will be championed in part by appropriate financial assistance packages. In the 1997 budget, the government has established an RM100 million (US$40 million) loan fund to assist students who face financial constraints (*Budget Speech*, 1996). And in another move to enhance the higher education environment, the government has stipulated that half of the income received by non-resident lecturers who lecture in approved institutions and organisations in selected disciplines will be exempt from income tax. The government has permitted the entry of foreign lecturers in order to overcome the shortage of experts.

In this overall context of change within higher education, the government has directed state owned universities to expand their existing distance learning and off-campus course initiatives. This is an effort to provide "second chances" for adults who did not acquire degrees through the normal course of study. Entry require-ments for these courses have been lowered to enable those who lack the paper qualifications, but who have the necessary experience, to enrol in these programs.

NON-FORMAL EDUCATION IN MALAYSIA

The term non-formal education, as used in this paper, denotes all forms of education provided to adults or children which are not encompassed within the formal system of elementary, secondary and higher education. In the Malaysian context, this has typically included such diverse programing as agricultural extension and farmer training programs, adult literacy programs, further education, occupational skills training, youth organisations which are training-focused, human resource training, workforce upgrading, cooperatives, and various community programs that provide instruction in health, nutrition, and family planning.

Non-formal education has been part of the Malaysian cultural heritage since time immemorial. Long time examples include instruction on martial arts, or the *silat*, and the teaching of Islamic studies through the hut or *pondok* system of education. Unlike the philosophy and implementation of formal education, non-formal educa-tion in Malaysia is broad, fragmented and has never been supported, evaluated or considered as a single system.

The general idea behind the efforts of the various forms of non-formal education is to improve the social and personal living and occupational capabilities of the pop-ulation. There are limits to what can be taught in the formal school system, hence there should be other and continuing efforts to develop the foundations laid by schools. This is particularly so in the case of vocational or occupational training, and in community development such as home economics, nutrition and health for women's groups. In general, the non-formal system provides continuing education to enable learners in the community to acquire new knowledge, skills and attitudes.

Formal education is organised by established institutions, most often highly bureaucratic in nature, which view teaching and education as their primary mission. Non-formal education in the Malaysian context generally incorporates a much more flexible structure and organisation. Also, non-formal education is not controlled by one agency or ministry, as per formal education and the Ministry of Education, but instead falls under the jurisdiction of various agencies. Some of these are govern-ment agencies while others are voluntary or private in nature. The teaching and learning focus is aided, if not supplanted, by a more problem solving approach, and there is a strong emphasis on meeting individuals' social, vocational and recreational needs as well as objectives related to community development projects. Various methods and media are used for non-formal instruction, and programing is delivered in home, at work, in mosques, at clinics, as well as in formal classes or special institutions.

In terms of flexibility, the non-formal system employs variety in the curriculum, total hours of instruction, time at which programing is delivered, place where programing is delivered, age of students, and class sizes. Non-formal education is not, however, without structure. As well, planning and co-ordination of non-formal education, including research on problems and issues related to this sector, are necessary in order to develop and assess non-formal programing.

A study by Nor Azizah Salleh (1991) identified characteristics which contribute positively and strongly to adult learning in the Malaysian context. Many of these, including the following, are employed in the non-formal learning environment:

- a peaceful social-psychological environment facilitates learning;

- there needs to be two-way communication between teachers and learners, and a willingness to share information by both parties;

- learning is a voluntary process, and teachers must be sincere;

- attitudes are difficult to change, and teachers must be patient;

- learners need and demand respect, and teachers need to be diplomatic as they interact with learners;

- language should always be simple and acceptable to the learners;

- teaching must be interesting, and presentations should employ various methods and techniques;

- knowing the background of the participants will help teachers provide illustrations that are familiar to the learners;

- learners should be given opportunities to share their expertise;

- teachers need to socialise within the community;

- teachers need to update their skills to meet learners' needs.

(It is interesting to note these factors appear to apply equally well to both the formal and non-formal educational context, but have only been adopted in the main by the non-formal side.)

At this stage of development the relationship between the formal and non-formal learning systems can be characterized as complementary but not integrated. This will likely change as the need to have a seamless educational system becomes more apparent.

SUMMARY AND CONCLUSION

The quality of life is heavily influenced by education. The more you have, the better things are, at least generally. The more everybody in the society has, the better life becomes for the economy as a whole. In Malaysia, it is clear that economic development, as stated in Vision 2020, is heavily intertwined with the development and re-development of education, for all.

The forces identified by Knowles (1980) — educating people to direct their own learning, focusing on learning not on teaching, incorporating lifelong learning principles, and applying new delivery methods for supporting the learning environment — should be the basis for education in the twenty-first century. Clearly, these principles are fundamental to Malaysia's plan of "quality education for all". Within this new context, elementary and secondary school education is changing under the influence of "quality education for all". The higher education environment in Malaysia is also undergoing rapid change, including increased private sector competition and encouragement for foreign universities to establish branch campuses. The goal is for Malaysia to become a centre for excellence in learning, and to reduce the number of Malaysians studying overseas. Change is also afoot in the non-formal sector. There is increased emphasis on human resource updating, and the prospects for job advancement and higher wages are creating significant demand from companies and individuals. All these changes are, of course, taking place within a Malaysian context, one which emphasizes the whole development of the individual, including the spiritual component.

Most critically and more important than the individual pieces, however, is the notion that as a whole they will create a system, a lifelong learning system. With effort and design, the opportunities will dovetail, programs will link, and learners will be able to take part in a full range of learning opportunities throughout the lifespan at times and in places which meet their needs. Only then, with a lifelong system that integrates the elementary, secondary, higher and non-formal education sectors, will the learning needs associated with Vision 2020 be met.

REFERENCES

Ahmad Sarji Abdul Hamid. (1993). *Malaysia's vision 2020: Understanding the concept, implications and challenges*. Kuala Lumpur: Pelanduk Publications.

Budget Speech. (1996, October 26). *New Straits Times*, p. 15.

Economic Planning Unit. (1996). *Seventh Malaysia plan 1996-2000*. Kuala Lumpur: Author.

Knowles, M. S. (1980). *The modern practice of adult education: From pedagogy to andragogy*. Englewood Cliffs, NJ: Cambridge Adult Education.

Mahathir Mohomad. (1992). *Malaysia the rising star: Business and investment opportunities and challenges towards 2020*. Kuala Lumpur: Kuala Lumpur Stock Exchange and Malaysian Strategic Consultancy Company.

Nor Azizah Salleh. (1991). *Adult education activities* (Research Project 42/89). Kuala Lumpur: Universiti Kebangsaan Malaysia, Bangi.

Sahibudllah, M. & James, A. (1996, July 10). Najib: Revamp education system in ASEAN. *New Straits Times*, p. 9.

Wan Mohd. Zahid. (1994). Quality education for all: Direction and challenges in the 21st century. In Anicia Alvarez, Myint Swe Khine and Jim Welsh (Eds.), *Proceedings of the international conference on education for all* (Universiti Brunei Darulsalam) (p. xvi). Brunei: Educational Technology Centre, Universiti Brunei Darulsalam.

Ching-jung Ho

Ching-jung Ho received her B.A. in History from the National Taiwan University, and her Ph.D. in Continuing and Vocational Education with a minor in Art History from the University of Wisconsin-Madison. Currently, Dr. Ho is Associate Professor in the Graduate Institute of Adult Education at the National Kaohsiung Normal University of Chinese Taipei. She is dedicated to adult literacy and has published several articles in this field, including *An Examination of Adult Literacy Education in Taiwan Based on an Analysis of the Meaning of Literacy and Literacy Education Issues* (1995) and *A Study of Older Learners' Characteristics in Literacy Programs of Taiwan, R.O.C.* (1996). Dr. Ho is a regular museum goer, appreciates contemporary art in particular, and because of this has chosen to live near an art museum. In addition, she has a green thumb and enjoys her plants each and every day.

Lifelong Learning and Basic Literacy: Adult Literacy Education in Chinese Taipei

by Ching-jung Ho

Lifelong learning is a deliberate process; it must emphasize learners' autonomy and life-wide learning as well as learning throughout the lifespan. This paper argues that a paradigm for understanding and evaluating adult literacy comes directly from within the lifelong learning context. In essence, adult literacy education, as a primary subset of lifelong learning, should emulate the best and strongest characteristics associated with lifelong learning. In Chinese Taipei, with respect to adult literacy programs, this is not the case. Even though the accomplishments of adult literacy programming have been documented, in fact, adult literacy programs are static, conservative, narrowly applied and isolated. The solution is to adopt, through specific strategies, an integrated, flexible, broad-based approach to the development and delivery of adult literacy programming; to, in effect, make it part and parcel, the first plank if you will, of lifelong learning.

INTRODUCTION

Recently, lifelong learning has become an agreeable, almost seductive, goal in Chinese Taipei, advocated, encouraged and endorsed by a host of ministries, government departments, councils and agencies. The Ministry of Education has just proposed a policy titled the "Middle Term Plan for the Development of Adult Education towards Lifelong Learning" (Ministry of Education, 1996), and the Council for Culture Planning and Development, Executive Yuan, has connected lifelong learning with community reform, as an essential means for developing and transforming Chinese Taipei society (Chen, 1996). Even the President, Teng-hui Lee, has incorporated in many of his speeches, directly and indirectly, the importance of building a "learning society".

Rhetoric aside, do our educational policies and practices at all levels reflect the active, dynamic, integrated and seamless principles that are typically associated with the best aspects of lifelong learning? Or are there unfulfilled promises and limitations associated with the actual implementation of lifelong learning in our educational policies and practices? In order to move beyond the slogans and take a serious, reflective and measured view of lifelong learning in Chinese Taipei, this paper addresses the following: (a) How should the concepts associated with lifelong learning be used as the basis for adult literacy education policies and practices in

Chinese Taipei, and (b) what recommendations can be made for the actualization, rather than simple promotion, of a lifelong learning culture within the adult basic education and literacy context.[1]

During the past few years, adult literacy education has been a central concern within the adult education community. In response, the Government developed and implemented a new program titled "Adult Basic Education Program" (ABEP), and at the same time made great efforts to improve the older literacy related program titled "Supplementary Education Program for the Stages of Fundamental Schooling (Grade 1 through Grade 9)" (SEP). Since 1991, enrolment in ABEP has increased dramatically. In 1991 there were 63 ABEP sections offered in 41 schools; however, by the first session of the 1994 school year this had increased to 493 ABEP sections offered in 352 schools (Ministry of Education, 1991a, 1994a). Annually, there are approximately 10,000 ABEP graduates (Ministry of Education, 1993, 1994a). With regard to SEP, growth has also been very fast. In the 1990 school year, 138 elementary schools offered SEP, with a total enrolment of 19,415 students (Ministry of Education, 1991b). By 1993, 292 schools offered SEP, enroling 24,975 students (Ministry of Education, 1994b). Thus, from 1990 to 1993 the number of elementary schools offering SEP grew by 154 or 112%, and an additional 5,560 students enroled, representing an increase of 29%. However, in spite of the additional facilities and the growth in the participation rate, ABEP and SEP drop-out rates continue to be very high and many think the learning materials are too difficult and complicated for all but above average students (Ho, Ho, Tsai & Hsieh, 1995).

To develop an understanding of the key issues and forces at work in this paradigm, and to offer recommendations, requires a broad examination of the adult literacy education polices and practices in Chinese Taipei.   This examination demonstrates broadly how the operational definition of adult literacy education may be understood as a critical basis for lifelong learning policies and practice, or the lack thereof, and specifically how certain changed practices would be beneficially important to the illiterate portion of the population.

LIFELONG LEARNING AND ADULT LITERACY

Learning is a natural lifelong process. However, lifelong learning is more than a simple experiential activity; it comprises deliberate learning and the associated processes that give rise to certain meanings, interpretations and purposes. As Jarvis (1992, pp. 11-12) pointed out, learning is:

> *of the essence of everyday living and of conscious experience; it is the process of transforming that experience into knowledge, skills, attitudes, values, and beliefs. It is about the continuing process of making sense of everyday experience.... Learning is, therefore, a process of giving meaning to, or seeking to understand, life experiences ... [however] ... unless provision is made for learning, the experience of everyday living may be restrictive,*

---

[1]Definitions of adult basic education and adult literacy education are not the same; however, they are used interchangeably in Chinese Taipei. In this article, the term "adult literacy education" encompasses "adult basic education".

and learning may be limited to the primary experiences of life.

More specifically, "deliberate" learning (see Tough, 1971) is a significant component of lifelong learning and, as Knapper & Cropley (1985, p. 20) noted, has a multiplicity of characteristics. For example, deliberate learning is intentional, and learners are aware that they are learning. It has definite and specific goals, and is not directed at vague generalizations such as developing the mind. The goals provide the rationale that motivates the learner, as compared with other factors such as "boredom". Further, the learner intends to retain what has been learned for a significant period of time.

From a broader and more inclusive perspective, Cropley & Knapper (1983, p. 17), describe lifelong learning as lasting for the whole lifetime of the learner; leading to the orderly acquisition, renewal, upgrading or completion of knowledge, skills and attitudes; fostering and depending for its existence on people's increasing ability and motivation to engage in learning, much of the time without dependence upon traditional schools or school-like institutions; and depending on the contribution of all available educational influences including formal, non-formal and informal.

Effective lifelong learners need to be self-directed learners. Knapper and Cropley (1985) describe effective learners as being aware of the relationship between learning and real life, cognizant of the need for learning throughout the lifespan, motivated to learn throughout the lifespan, and in possession of a self-concept supportive of lifelong learning. Specific skills for lifelong learning include the ability to set personal objectives in a realistic way; the ability to apply knowledge already possessed; the ability to evaluate one's own learning; the ability to locate information; the ability to use different learning strategies and learn in different settings; the ability to use learning aids, such as libraries or the media; and the ability to use and interpret materials from different subject areas. Above all, lifelong learning must emphasize learners' autonomy and learning life-wide (a wide breadth of learning, not simply length of learning) as well as throughout the lifespan. These are basic principles for lifelong learning of all stripes, including adult literacy education. The question addressed in the following sections of this paper is to what degree these characteristics and skills are supported in the delivery of one component of the lifelong learning continuum, namely, adult literacy education.

ADULT LITERACY EDUCATION

A review of the literature supports the conclusion that literacy is an abstract term. It changes with time, and has no agreed upon common definition (see Campbell, Kirsch & Kolstad, 1992; Cervero, 1985; Fingeret, 1992; Hunter & Harman, 1979; Imel & Grieve, 1985; Jarvis, 1990; Levine, 1986). According to *An International Dictionary of Adult and Continuing Education*, literacy has at least three common definitions (see Jarvis, 1990, p. 204). For example, the United Nations Educational, Scientific and Cultural Organization (UNESCO) defines a functional literate person as one who has acquired the knowledge and skills in reading and writing which enable that person to engage effectively in all activities in which literacy is normally assumed to be required within that specific culture or group. Other definitions include a reading age level of 9.5 years, or five years of completed schooling.

UNESCO's definition rests on a concept known as "functional literacy", a perspective which was widely adopted in the 1950s and broadly applied through the 1970s. According to this view, the meaning of literacy depends on and changes in accordance with the individual, as well as with the time and place. A synthesis by Hunter and Harman (1979, pp. 7-8) describes functional literacy in the following manner, with an emphasis on the individual perspective:

> *[It is] the possession of skills perceived as necessary by particular persons and groups to fulfil their own self-determined objectives as family and community members, citizens, consumers, job-holders, and members of social, religious, or other associations of their choosing. This includes the ability to obtain information they want and to use that information for their own and others' well-being; the ability to read and write adequately to satisfy the requirements they set for themselves as being important for their own lives; the ability to deal positively with demands made on them by society; and the ability to solve the problems they face in their daily lives.*

Based on the functional literacy noted earlier, obviously, basic literacy benchmarks are being elevated as technology becomes more pervasive and increasingly complex. To a greater and greater degree, literacy is a crucial prerequisite for obtaining information and using basic technology. Without basic literacy, it is increasingly difficult to fulfil goals that form the basis for a comfortable and fulfilling life in a developed economy. In this sense, learning for literacy is the most basic stepping stone in life-wide and lifelong learning.

Literacy is not simply a mechanism for adjustment in order to "fit" or "survive". As Scribner (1984) pointed out, literacy has at least two other principal functions: first, it furnishes power; and second, it contributes to a "state of grace". Literacy as power emphasizes the liberating nature of knowledge. As Freire (1970, p. 205) suggested, literacy "is truly an act of knowing, through which a person is able to look critically at the culture which has shaped him, and to move toward reflection and positive action upon his world." Literacy as a state of grace is perhaps best appreciated and understood as the tendency in many societies to endow literacy with exceptional virtues. Examples can be seen in Chinese sayings such as "beauties are in books", "gold is hidden in books" and "bookish traditions are superior to everything".

The power and grace functions of literacy are not contradictory and, as this researcher (Ho, 1995a, p. 63) has noted, "the kind of education which [Chinese Taipei] presently lacks is how to help individuals with life adjustment and then how to empower them to participate in cultural creation." In this context, learning for literacy becomes a broad lifelong learning endeavour, and particularly so within the functional literacy context where the needs of the individual are continually changing. (In concrete terms, it is interesting to consider how dramatically levels of computer literacy have changed in the past twenty years.)

The purpose of adult literacy education cannot be limited to helping people obtain conventional reading, writing, mathematical, and the somewhat newer addition, computing abilities. Literacy must be a mechanism for empowerment, unleashing creative and inquisitive energy. This means that structures and programming to support adult literacy in Chinese Taipei must be centred on a holistic view of lifelong learning and giving power to people (see Ho, 1995a, p. 63). In effect, the characteristics of effective lifelong learning need to be embedded within literacy education, and the target groups for literacy education need to be defined quite broadly.

ADULT LITERACY – PROGRAMS AND POLICIES

As mentioned earlier, there are two adult literacy programs in Chinese Taipei: SEP and ABEP. The former was established on the basis of the Supplementary Education Act of 1976, and can be traced to the idea of using supplementary education to compensate for the shortage of the provisions of formal education that existed since the late Ching Dynasty (Ke, 1993, p. 491). (The Supplementary Education Act was revised in 1982, yet the basic rationale for SEP has not been changed.) The goals of the Supplementary Education Act are as follows:"to complement citizens' life knowledge [and] raise educational levels; to teach practical skills [and] increase productive competence; [and] to cultivate healthy citizens [and] promote the development of the society" (Ministry of Education, 1976). According to the fourth item of the Act, SEP includes both elementary and junior high school levels, and was established for people who are beyond the fundamental school age of 15 (Ministry of Education, 1976). Elementary SEP is divided into two sub-levels: six months to one year at the Junior Level, and one and one half years to two years at the Senior Level. Graduates from elementary schools' SEP are seen to be equivalent to graduates from elementary schools (Grade 1 through Grade 6). At the junior high school level, the length of SEP is no less than three years, and graduates from this level are equivalent to graduates from junior high schools (Grade 7 through Grade 9) (Ministry of Education, 1976). Graduates from both the elementary school or junior high school level of SEP receive certificates following completion of their studies.

In 1990, statistics showed that there were about 1,340,000 illiterate people in Chinese Taipei (Ministry of Education, 1991c). At that same time, Western notions of "adult basic education" and "functional literacy" as well as adult education had been introduced into Chinese Taipei (Ho, 1996). As a result, the Government started to review policies pertaining to adult literacy education, and it was found that the elementary level SEP, the only adult literacy education program, contained many shortcomings (Ministry of Education, 1991c). For example, with its long history of being subordinate to fundamental education, SEP did not even have its own facilities, including desks and chairs for students. Also, SEP was not large enough to meet the demands for literacy education. As a result of this review, improvements were made to SEP, and as well ABEP was initiated through the Working Project of Adult Education Plan of 1990 and the Hsin-min (New People) Project: A Five-Year Plan of Adult Basic Education of 1991. Officially, ABEP is considered to be equivalent to the Junior Level of the supplementary program of elementary education and is connected to the Senior Level of SEP in elementary schools.

The purpose of adult literacy education in Chinese Taipei is to "cultivate the listening, speaking, reading, writing and numeracy abilities of those who have been unable to attend schools in order to complement their basic life knowledge and skills and raise their educational levels" (Ho, 1996, p. 19). Both SEP and ABEP are offered through elementary schools in the evening and are taught by elementary school teachers. However, SEP is a regular program based on law and funded through local governments, whereas ABEP is project-based, temporary by nature and funded through the Ministry of Education. Accordingly, SEP follows the national curriculum standards and uses the same textbooks which are based on the rationale of fundamental education (Ho, 1995a, p. 61). ABEP does not use these texts, and in fact, because of a lack of textbooks, ABEP teachers are encouraged to prepare some of their own teaching materials. As well, the Ministry of Education provides funds directly to the elementary schools and recruits experts to compose learning materials for ABEP literacy programs. As previously mentioned, concepts associated with functional literacy as well as adult education have been accepted in Chinese Taipei since 1990, and as a result practical aspects have been used as a basis for the development of ABEP learning materials (see Ho, 1996, pp. 19-20).

There are some policy issues associated with these programs. First, literacy education in this context is considered to be a reimbursement device or a form of social welfare directed solely at older adults who were deprived of educational opportunities because of the political and economic fluctuations that occurred in Chinese Taipei during the 1940s. From the explicit policy, one may not see this social welfare rationale. However, since the fundamental school entrance rate is very high, it is widely believed that, if illiterates do exist in this country, they are older adults. This is demonstrated, for example, by the design of a popular television program for illiterates titled "Every Day is Study Day". Its songs and lessons are clearly designed for older adults (Ho et al., 1995). When operationalized, this narrow view of the illiterate population automatically excludes certain segments and sets limits for the function and application of literacy education. Research has identified at least four target groups for basic literacy education, and the targeted group of older adults represents only about one third of this population (Ho, 1995a, 1995b). Other groups include: (a) people who are younger than 50 years of age and who may have participated in fundamental education at one time or another but dropped out before developing basic skills; (b) people who speak and understand partial Mandarin and who would benefit from learning the language to a functional level; and (c) foreign labourers who came to Chinese Taipei after the job market opened during the past few years and who have now temporarily settled here.

A second issue associated with these policies is the fact that basic literacy education is confused with supplementary education, and the result is that neither is able to fulfil its potential. ABEP, with funding from the Ministry of Education, is viewed quite simplistically as an impermanent device to promote adult literacy education under the given shortage of opportunities available through SEP. With no summer classes, the total length of ABEP training is nine months, and students are only allowed legally to enrol once since the program is considered to be the equivalent of the Junior Level of SEP elementary education, which in turn is connected to the Senior Level of SEP in elementary schools. In fact, a survey by Ho et al. (1995)

found that many students returned to the same ABEP classes in subsequent years, expressing a desire for expanded literacy programs of more than one year. They did not enrol in SEP to continue their literacy learning because they did not want the full SEP curriculum, just the Mandarin courses. This situation not only identifies a gap between the continuation of the Senior Level of SEP in elementary schools and ABEP, but also reveals that the older design of SEP does not address the need for basic literacy education.

Originally, SEP had as its main purpose the education of youths who did not complete elementary schooling. The goal was to help them learn basic reading and writing and numeracy skills. As the fundamental schools' entrance rates have increased with each passing year, adults, and more specifically older adults, have become the main target for SEP. SEP's curricula, standards, materials, and teaching approaches, however, were not designed for an older age group, nor do they even touch on fulfilling broader lifelong learning tasks such as preparation for retirement and leisure time activities. With its strong conventional and very formal educational features, SEP is not only unsuitable for adult learners, but may also be unsuitable for the underprepared youth groups. In effect, through SEP, adult literacy education has been implemented as traditional school-based education delivered at least partly in a form contextually designed for young people. This reflects a narrow view of literacy, a narrow pedagogical perspective, and dismissal of the best characteristics of lifelong learning.

Conventional and restrictive practices for adult literacy education are also seen at the level of provision. For example, even though the Ministry of Education has created a policy that encourages institutions in addition to the publicly funded schools to support adult literacy programming, these private institutions are required to cooperate with publicly funded schools in order to get subsidies (Ho et al., 1995). This continues to have a tremendously limiting effect on the provision of adult literacy education and is inconsistent with one of the most basic principles of lifelong learning – providing as many different opportunities for as many people in as many forms and venues as possible.

According to a survey by Ho et al. (1995), there are a number of other key issues associated with the delivery of adult literacy education in Chinese Taipei. For example, most of the teachers delivering adult literacy courses are elementary school teachers. These teachers have little or no training specific to the teaching of adults. For many of them, teaching in adult literacy classes is just an extra job. In addition, the curriculum is far too weighty. It emphasizes a foundation appropriate for learners who plan to spend many years in the formal system of education. The content of SEP avoids a practical approach, stressing instead abstract, enigmatic and even obscure cases. As a result, the attrition rate is as high as 43% (Ho et al., 1995).

As mentioned earlier, for older learners, attending SEP and ABEP is psychological compensation for earlier lost learning opportunities. These learners are very humble in their approach to learning, assuming and accepting the merits of education, learning, and schools with no questions or doubts. Though this view brings a respectful attitude and strong measure of support to the learning environment, it also tends to foster passive learning, a learning style that makes the acquisition of language and mathematical skills difficult. Younger learners, on the other hand, differ in their attitudes and performance. More often, they come to SEP and ABEP for certificates in order to better their lot in life by achieving basic literacy levels and then moving on to other studies.

Even though the policies and programs used to support adult literacy education in Chinese Taipei have drawbacks, accomplishments have been documented. For example, Ho et al. (1995) identified the following as achievements of the current system: (a) it helps selected learners acquire basic Mandarin; (b) it broadens the learners' vision of society and improves attitudes and temperament; (c) it promotes and actually increases grandparent to child and parent to child communications; (d) it increases the quality of leisure time in the learners' lives; (e) it provides learners with a sense of self-satisfaction; and (f) it establishes a bridge between schools and communities. This study also found that some learners view literacy as a means to awaken their interest in self, life, and learning even though that was not the original intention of the policies.

LIMITATIONS OF ADULT LITERACY EDUCATION

The above mentioned programs and practices carry implicit but generally unstated views with regard to the meanings of literacy, learning, education, and lifelong learning as these pertain to the broader society. Inappropriately, literacy classes for the most part focus narrowly and directly on basic speaking, reading, writing, and numeracy skills. Even though the term "functional literacy" has been used in Chinese Taipei for many years, the implications described earlier in the paper are, from a policy and curriculum development perspective, only superficially in evidence if at all. For example, training that deals with some of the practical problems associated with day-to-day living, such as paying bills and completing application forms, are incorporated into literacy curriculum. However, as described by Heath (1986), higher level and, ultimately, more meaningful applications such as social-interaction activities, news-related contexts, memory-supportive frameworks, and substitutes for oral messages are not embedded in adult literacy education. The notion of literacy for empowerment is completely absent, and practitioners still count the number of words that students should learn as the criteria for literacy education. As a result, literacy is isolated from the socio-cultural context. This static view of literacy ensures that it remains apart and separate from the lifelong learning context.

Literacy education in Chinese Taipei is narrowly defined and operationalized as school education or formal education at a primary level. This is documented by the actual policies as well as the learners' needs, attitudes and levels. Although ABEP and SEP do attract learners, they only deal with the small subset who are willing to come to schools and study in a conservative and non-adaptive environment. Unjustifiably, illiterates who are unwilling or unable to survive in the formal school context have no options. This creates what Mezirow, Darkenwald and Knox (1975) referred to as the "creaming effect". The original intention may have been egalitarian, but the effect is quite different.

As previously mentioned, in Chinese Taipei it is common for learning to be associated with the development of a state of grace. Also, people generally link learning most directly to formal education and schooling. These thoughts, in turn, further influence people's attitudes toward adult literacy education. It can also be concluded that adult literacy education is not a broad topical issue, in part because the elementary school entrance rate in Chinese Taipei exceeds 99%. This creates a general perception that there is no serious illiteracy problem and that illiteracy tends to be first and foremost an issue for the least developed economies. It is widely believed that, if illiterates do exist in Chinese Taipei, they are older adults who did not, and perhaps did not find it necessary to, complete their fundamental education in the elementary school system. In fact, as described in this paper, illiteracy in Chinese Taipei is not effectively addressed by the current programs and policies (see Ho, 1995b).

Responding to adult literacy needs through the formal school system mitigates against the development of learner-based lifelong learning tools as described by Knapper and Cropley (1985) and noted earlier in this paper. In Chinese Taipei, schools have a long history of being instruments for controlling knowledge. Examinations, for example, have been institutionalized to the degree that they overpower the educational system, becoming the end instead of the means. In this context, formal schooling stands as the symbol for the official, standardized approach for literacy training and rates. The way literacy is currently taught and institutionalized completely ignores the notion that it can be a tool for participation, power and for the development of fundamental skills – self direction as a key example – that provide the basic sustenance for full and active participation in the lifelong learning process.

CONCLUSIONS AND RECOMMENDATIONS

In order to realize the potential for adult literacy training, and at the same time provide an accommodating and supportive platform for the transition to the full range of lifelong learning opportunities, there needs to be change in the definitions, goals, platforms and policies regarding literacy, learning and lifelong learning in Chinese Taipei.

Learning needs to be viewed as a process whereby meaning and purpose is constructed throughout one's lifetime. Through learning, the depth and breadth of life is enlarged and enhanced, making learning life-wide as well as lifelong. Literacy is the most fundamental tool for awakening individuals' interests in self, life, and learning. True learning for literacy should, as Mezirow (1991) stated, help learners transform their perspectives about life. Thus, literacy and learning should not be confined to basic writing, reading, and calculating skills. Instead, literacy needs to be a vehicle whereby empowerment is the legitimate end. At the same time, learners need to learn how to learn, and they need to become self-directed learners, something that doesn't happen within the current more formal and narrow setting. Also, learners also need to assume responsibility for their own learning.

With regard to policy, it is important to include avenues and opportunities for all groups in need of basic adult literacy programming, including drop-outs, foreign labourers, and older illiterates. Also, different levels, different contexts, and different providers need to be available and drawn into the mix. Adult literacy education must go beyond schools and reach out to communities as well as families. This is particularly important in that it will draw people who have negative attitudes towards schools, and encourage them to attend. Also, it helps break stereotypes about schools, education and the student-teacher relationship, and in turn renews and broadens the public's view of learning. Community-based and family-directed literacy programs are essential, and there is much to learn from English as a Second Language Programming used in the United States and other countries (see Fingeret, 1984; Nickse, 1990). Most importantly, adult literacy students need to become active, self-directed, autonomous learners if they are to continue down the lifelong learning continuum.

In summary, the Ministry of Education needs to achieve a number of objectives. These include: redefining and expanding the role of ABEP; amplifying the SEP functions making the programming delivery and design more flexible; encouraging a host of institutions to provide adult literacy education; re-inventing and emphasizing teacher training programs; developing new approaches for teaching and skill training; revising learning materials, and encouraging studies and experiments to evaluate and enhance teaching methods and materials; and, most importantly, linking adult basic literacy to a wide range of lifelong learning activities and opportunities. This latter point is what will draw adult basic literacy programming out of its narrow and confining shell and into the broader learning context rightfully associated with responsible holistic participation in the society at large. Redefined, restructured and revamped adult basic literacy programming and practices will do much for groups that are currently excluded from the opportunities associated with full participation in a learning society, and in the end the entire community will benefit from increased cohesion and economic potential.

REFERENCES

Campbell, A., Kirsch., & Kolstad, A. (1992). *Assessing literacy: The framework for the National Adult Literacy Survey*. Educational Testing Service and Westat, Inc.

Chen, C. N. (1996). *Lifelong learning and community holistic construction*. [Translated]. Paper presented in Rooted in Communities for Lifelong Learning: Community Adult education Symposium. Kaohsiung: National Kaohsiung Normal University.

Cervero, R. M. (1985). Is a common definition of adult literacy possible? *Adult Education Quarterly, 36*(1), 50-54.

Cropley, A. J. & Knapper, C. K. (1983). Higher education and the promotion of learning. *Studies in Higher Education, 8*(1), 15-21.

Fingeret, H. A. (1984). *Adult literacy education: Current and future directions*. Columbus, Ohio: ERIC Clearinghouse on Adult, Career and Vocational Education. (ERIC Document Reproduction Service No. ED 246 308)

Fingeret, H. A. (1992). *Adult literacy education: Current and future directions*. ERIC Clearinghouse on Adult, Career and Vocational Education, Columbus, Ohio. (ERIC Document Reproduction Service No. ED 354 391)

Freire, P. (1970). The adult literacy process as cultural action for freedom. *Harvard Educational Review, 40*(2), 205-225.

Heath, S. B. (1986). The functions and uses of literacy. In S. de Castell, A. Luke, & K. Egan (Eds.), *Literacy, society, and schooling: A reader* (pp. 15-26). Cambridge, New York: Cambridge University Press.

Ho, C. J. (1995a). An examination of adult literacy education in Taiwan based on an analysis of the meaning of literacy and literacy education related issues. *Kaohsiung Normal University Journal, 6*, 45-68.

Ho, C. J. (1995b). Myths and reflections in adult literacy in Taiwan. [Translated]. *Taiwan Education Review, 535*, 23-28.

Ho, C. J. (1996). Reflections on limitations and moving forward: A study of essential issues in adult literacy education in Taiwan. [Translated]. *Taipei Adult Education Information Centre Quarterly, 12*, 17-22.

Ho, C. J., Ho, J. T., Tsai, P. T., & Hsieh, D. C. (1995). *Planning of adult literacy education based on learners' characteristics*. [Translated]. Kaohsiung: National Kaohsiung Normal University.

Hunter, C. S. J., & Harman, D. (1979). *Adult illiteracy in the United States: A report to the Ford Foundation*. New York: McGraw-Hill.

Imel, S., & Grieve, S. (1985). *Adult literacy education*. Overview. Columbus, Ohio: ERIC Clearinghouse on Adult, Career, and Vocational Education. (ERIC Document Reproduction Service No. ED 259 210)

Jarvis, P. (Ed.). (1990). *An international dictionary of adult education*. London: Routledge.

Jarvis, P. (1992). *Paradoxes of learning: On becoming an individual in society*. San Francisco: Jossey-Bass.

Ke, J. F. (1993). The Supplementary Education Act. In Y. H. Chen (Ed.) *An analysis of main educational laws and regulations in the Republic of China*. (pp. 485-518) [Translated]. Taipei: Wu-nan.

Knapper, C., & Cropley, A. J. (1985). *Lifelong learning and higher education*. London: Croom Helm.

Levine, K. (1986). *The social context of literacy*. London: Routledge & Kegan Paul.

Mezirow, J., Darkenwald, G., & Knox, A. (1975). *Last gamble on education*. Washington, DC: AEA.

Mezirow, J. (1991). *Transformative dimensions of adult learning*. San Francisco: Jossey-Bass.

Ministry of Education (1976). *Supplementary education act*. [Translated]. Taipei: Author.

Ministry of Education (1991a). *Handbook for the subsidized adult basic education programs in the first and second sessions of school year 1991*. [Translated]. Taipei: Author.

Ministry of Education (1991b). *Education statistics of the Republic of China*. Taipei: Author.

Ministry of Education (1991c). *Hsin-min Project: A five-year plan of adult basic education*. [Translated]. Taipei: Author.

Ministry of Education (1993). *The materials for applying the adult basic education program of 1994*. [Translated]. [Unpublished raw data]. Taipei: Author.

Ministry of Education (1994a). *The materials for applying the adult basic education program of 1995*. [Translated]. [Unpublished raw data]. Taipei: Author.

Ministry of Education (1994b). *Education statistics of the Republic of China*. Taipei: Author.

Ministry of Education (1996). *Middle term plan for the development of adult education towards lifelong learning*. [Translated]. Taipei: Author.

Nickse, R. S. (1990). *Family and intergenerational literacy programs. An update of the noises of literacy*. Columbus, Ohio: ERIC Clearinghouse on Adult, Career, and Vocational Education. (ERIC Document Reproduction Service No. ED 327 736)

Scribner, S. (1984). Literacy in three metaphors. *American Journal of Education*, *93*, 6-21.

Tough, A. (1971). *The adult's learning projects*. Toronto: Ontario Institute for Studies in Education.

Judith Chapman

and David Aspin

Judith Chapman is Professor of Education at the University of Western Australia. Prior to taking up that position she was Director of the School of Decision Making and Management Centre in the Faculty of Education at Monash University. Professor Chapman has done extensive work for international agencies such as the OECD, UNESCO and IDP, and has written and edited a number of publications that include *Quality Schooling, The Reconstruction of Education* and *Creating and Managing the Democratic School.* Her interests also include cooking, gardening, reading, and travel.

David Aspin is Professor of Education and former Dean of the Faculty of Education at Monash University. Prior to assuming this position he was Professor of Philosophy at King's College, London. Professor Aspin's publications include *The Arts in Schools* and *Logical Empiricism* and *Post-Empiricism in Educational Discourse.* In addition to his lecturing and writing, he enjoys rowing, rugby, good food, fine wine, and travel.

The following paper draws from material in a forthcoming book by Judith and David titled *The School, Community and Lifelong Learning* to be published by Cassells (London).

Schools as Centres of Lifelong Learning for All

by Judith Chapman and David Aspin

In countries across the Asia Pacific region a multitude of factors is shaping the character of our societies and economies. In this context, member economies of the Asia Pacific Economic Cooperation (APEC) Forum are finding it timely to review their provision of education, to evaluate and reassess the role of schools in their societies, to reconsider relationships between schools, parents, business, commerce, and constituencies in arts and other cultural fields, and to re-conceptualise new roles and functions for educational institutions. Underpinning recommendations made in this paper for the development and direction of schools for tomorrow is the notion of creating "schools as community learning centres". These revitalized institutions would offer a range of lifelong learning opportunities to all members of what are fast becoming learning societies.

THE IMPORTANCE OF LIFELONG LEARNING FOR ALL

A number of Asia Pacific economies have concluded that a lifelong approach to learning should be supported and developed as a key response to some of the major challenges associated with the twenty-first century. Access to education and training for all citizens is seen as an investment in the future, a pre-condition for economic development, social cohesion and a foundation for effective participation in society and personal growth.

The work of international agencies, such as the United Nations Educational, Scientific and Cultural Organization (UNESCO) and the Organization of Economic Cooperation and Development (OECD), the European Parliament, and the Nordic Council of Ministers, has focused on a variety of themes pertinent to lifelong learning which have wide-ranging implications for Asia Pacific economies (see Chapman and Aspin, in press). These include:

- emerging awareness of the importance of the notions of the knowledge economy and the learning society;

- accepting the need for a new philosophy of education and training, with institutions of all kinds – formal and informal, traditional and alternative, public and private – having new roles and responsibilities for learning;

- ensuring that foundations for lifelong learning are in place for all citizens during the compulsory years of schooling;

• promoting articulation between schooling, work, further education and other agencies offering opportunities for learning across the lifespan;

• providing government incentives for individuals, employers, and the range of social partners with a commitment to learning, to invest in lifelong learning;

• ensuring that emphasis on lifelong learning does not reinforce existing patterns of privilege and widen the existing gap between the advantaged and the disadvantaged on the basis of access to education.

THE CONCEPT OF LIFELONG LEARNING

The commitment by governments across the Asia Pacific region to the ideals of lifelong learning will involve the expenditure of substantial amounts of public funds. It is important that these expenditures be undertaken with clear understanding and agreement as to what is being done in the name of the public interest to realize the goal of lifelong learning.

One approach to conceptualising lifelong learning asserts that it is concerned primarily with the promotion of skills and competencies necessary for the development of general capabilities and specific performance in roles and activities that relate directly to economic development. Skills and competencies acquired through programs of lifelong learning, it may be argued, will have a direct bearing on how well workers perform their job responsibilities as well as how well they are able to adapt their general and particular knowledge and competencies to new functions. This economic justification for lifelong learning is dependent upon two prior assumptions: first, that lifelong education is instrumental for and anterior to some more ultimate goal; and second, that the goal of lifelong learning is highly job-related and economic-policy-dependent. This view, as we have seen from recent discussions at OECD (1996), UNESCO (Delors, 1996), the European Parliament (1995) and the Nordic Council of Ministers (1995), has been rejected as presenting a too narrow and limited understanding of the nature, aims and purpose of lifelong education.

A second perspective rests on different assumptions. Instead of lifelong learning being primarily an instrument to achieve an extrinsic goal, education is equally regarded as an intrinsically valuable activity, something that is good in and for itself. Incorporated in this perspective is the belief that those engaging in lifelong education do so not simply in order to arrive at a new place, but "to travel with a different view" (Peters, 1965) - to travel with a qualitatively better, richer and more elevated set of perspectives from which to view the world. There is wide acceptance that people engaging in educational activities are enriched by having their view of the world and their capacity for rational choice continually expanded and transformed by increasing varieties of experiences and cognitive achievements that the lifelong learning experience offers.

This second view has been adopted by a variety of community groups and, in addition to opportunities for lifelong learning through traditional institutions and agencies, there is a growing trend for lifelong learning activities to be offered through a host of non-traditional community initiatives. Lifelong learning conceived of and made available through these channels often offers people the opportunity to update their knowledge and enjoyment of activities they had either long since laid aside or always wanted to do but were previously unable to pursue; to try their hands at activities that they had previously imagined were outside their available time or competence; or to extend their horizons by examining significant cognitive advances of recent times.

This is not to suggest that lifelong learning is an activity restricted or even primarily directed towards those who have passed the age when education in formal or institutional settings has ebbed. In fact, cognitive and skill development can and should continue throughout one's life. This is an indispensable part of one's personal growth and development as well as a foundation for social and economic participation more broadly in society. Individual and community welfare is protected and promoted when communities arrange for lifelong learning activities to be available to the widest range of constituencies through as many channels as possible and in as many forms as are viable. Smethurst (1995, pp. 38-39) describes this well:

Is education a public or a private good? The answer is, neither: it is both. There is some education which is overwhelmingly a public good in that its benefits accrue very widely, to society at large as well as to the individual. Equally there is some education which, while benefiting society, confers overwhelming benefits on the individual learner. But much of education sits annoyingly between these two extremes, leading us, correctly, to want to influence the amount and type of it supplied and demanded, because society has an interest in the outcome, but also to note that it confers benefits on the individual above those societal benefits.

The argument that lifelong education is a public good supports the notion that the availability of educational opportunities throughout the lifespan is a pre-requisite for informed and effective participation in society by all citizens (see Grace, 1994; McLaughlin, 1994; Smethurst, 1995). Similarly, services such as health, housing, welfare, and the legal system, along with education, constitute the infrastructure which people need in order to construct and realise a satisfying and fulfilling life, one that is supportive, inclusive and just.

THREE ELEMENTS IN LIFELONG LEARNING

There is a complex and interdependent relationship between three major elements or outcomes of lifelong learning: education for a more highly skilled workforce; personal development leading to a more rewarding life; and the creation of a stronger and more inclusive society. It is the interplay between these elements that animates lifelong learning and this is in part why lifelong learning is a complex and multifaceted process. The process itself begins in pre-school, continues through compulsory and post-compulsory periods of formal education and training, and is then carried on throughout the remainder of the lifespan. It is actualized through provision of learning experiences and activities in the home, the work-place, universities and colleges, and in other educational, social and cultural agencies, institutions and settings – both formal and informal – within the community.

For the effective development of educational policies and lifelong learning practices in particular within APEC member economies, this triadic emphasis requires a coherent, consistent, coordinated and integrated, multi-faceted approach to learning. Realising a lifelong learning approach for economic progress and development, for personal development and fulfilment, and for social inclusiveness and democratic understanding and activity will not be easily achieved.

The central elements in the triadic nature of lifelong learning are interrelated, and they are fundamental prerequisites for a range of benefits that members of the APEC Forum regard as important goals related to economic, educational and social policies. Subscription to policies for lifelong education will help achieve a variety of policy goals that include building a strong, adaptable and competitive economy, providing a fertile range of opportunities for personal development, and developing a richer social fabric where principles and ideals of social inclusiveness, justice and equity are practised and promoted.

To achieve these goals will require a substantial re-appraisal of the provision, resourcing and goals of education and training, and a major re-orientation towards the concept and value of the idea of "the learning society". Herein lies the major challenge for governments, policy-makers and educators in the Asia Pacific region as they grapple with conceptualising lifelong learning and realising the aim of "lifelong learning for all".

LIFELONG LEARNING AND COMPULSORY SCHOOLING

The concept of lifelong learning and the ends at which it aims will require APEC economies to consider the idea and institutions of compulsory education in a new light. As Hughes (1993, p. 17) points out:

Rather than being a unique period of schooling leading on to vocations or higher education, [compulsory education] is a phase in a lifelong process. That phase however has two key requirements: one is to provide a basis for further learning; the other is to ensure a continuing motivation for it. This may imply a greater organisational flexibility in approach than is the case with current schooling. It certainly implies a need for greater and more constructive student involvement in the planning and conduct of their education.

Ball (1993, p. 2) maintains that, for the purpose of promoting and supporting lifelong learning, compulsory schooling must achieve two goals: the provision of a knowledge base and the development of meta-skills for learning. However, developing these skills, as any teacher, parent or student knows, is not easy. Great difficulties arise when more and more curriculum content is added to the compulsory years of schooling, in part because of the information overload and resulting conceptual confusion. Such an approach also risks diminishing the time and energy available for the mastery of learning and research skills relevant to newer approaches for learning.

Increasingly, the compulsory period of schooling should be regarded as the phase of education in which students are provided with general knowledge for cognitive and affective development and for acquisition of learning skills which will be required for learning throughout the lifespan. More specific knowledge and skills can be taught as needed later in life and in places more suited to their acquisition.

In addition to evaluating curriculum, teaching and learning in the drive towards improving the provision of lifelong learning programs and opportunities, it will be necessary for APEC economies to examine issues related to the governance, management and patterns or relationships within education. Fundamental to this will be the notion of creating schools as "learning organisations".

Schools must model the best characteristics of learning organisations, a type of organizational notion now being accorded strong credence and prominence in many societies. In today's knowledge economy, the ability to learn has an increasingly direct and obvious relationship to economic and personal well being. As a result, if economies in the Asia Pacific region are to achieve the goals and benefits associated with lifelong learning, schools and other educational institutions need to be learning organisations and centres for community learning. Indeed, all constituencies with interests in the work of schools will want to play a role as members of the whole learning community of which they and their schools are a part.

LIFELONG LEARNING AND THE FAMILY

There are important ways in which families can function as a source of support for and a stimulus towards increasing the understanding of the meaning and value of lifelong learning. Campbell (1992, pp. 2-3), for example, has identified a number of family characteristics which encourage learning: a feeling of control over their lives; frequent communication of high expectations to children; a family dream of success for the future; recognition of hard work as a key to success; an active versus sedentary lifestyle; a perception of the family as a mutual support system and problem solving unit; adherence to clearly understood household rules, consistently enforced; and frequent contact with teachers.

The idea of the learning family and its link to lifelong learning has a number of dimensions and possibilities for the school. For example, there are important areas of content and values within the school curriculum which are vital to getting young people "started right". Families will understandably want to have a large say regarding what and how young people learn with regard to human relationships as well as the rights and responsibilities of being a family member. There is much that young people can learn about these issues in surroundings external to the family and the school. However, successful and effective learning in these and other areas is strengthened and encouraged by incorporating the educational opportunities afforded by the obligations and responsibilities of belonging to a family and a community into the life of the school.

One powerful means of encouraging this is through parental involvement in the school's activities. This may necessitate access to courses for parents, often using school facilities and other institutional resources. There are many other ways of involving parents in the whole range of school activities, and schools and other educational institutions can do a great deal to build a sense of community as they function as "centres" for the various constituencies within the "learning community". Parental involvement in the learning environment establishes, between schools, parents and community groups, a sense of partnership in learning activities. In this process, parents must be regarded as equals when evaluating educational experiences and activities for children. Parental goodwill, including active co-operation, is enhanced when parents know how to participate and feel welcomed as full partners in the learning process.

The corollary to all this is that parents need to know more about curriculum innovations and other changes in approaches to teaching and learning. Only then can they support and assist with the learning process. In this regard, there is an increasing need for parents to take courses to familiarise themselves with recent developments in learning theory and new learning technologies. This is where schools can provide considerable support for lifelong learning in the local community. If schools and other learning institutions succeed in encouraging more parents and others involved in the learning activities of the young, the result will be broader acceptance of changes in schooling that result from the increasing emphasis on lifelong learning.

As schools contribute to the growth of new learning opportunities through cooperative activities with the family, there are, from the other side of the partnership, a variety of benefits accruing to the schools. For example, one of the potential benefits of greater parent involvement in the learning process is the links they provide to schools with other community agencies, groups and constituencies.

SCHOOLS AND THE BUSINESS COMMUNITY

Policy-makers, educators and members of the community need also to focus on the relationships between schools and the business, commercial, and industrial communities as well as other professional entities and organisations. The development of these sorts of relationships can have significant and positive influences on, for example, the effective preparation of students for the workforce. Partnerships in these areas create shared goals between educators and employers as well as trade unions and professional associations. In turn, this influences the behaviour, plans and goals of business, industry and commerce. These activities must be developed within the context of joint interests, and can serve as rich sources for broader community development.

Merenda (1989) has drawn attention to the different levels at which partnerships between private sector business and commercial interests and schools operate. These include the following:

- partnerships at the level of policy in which co-operative efforts are developed by businesses, schools, and public officials in order to shape the public and political debate about schools, leading to changes in legislation or governance;

- partnerships that focus on systemic educational improvements, including the identification of needed reforms and the work to bring them about;

- partnerships that focus on management at the school level;

- partnerships in teacher training, in which businesses become involved in teacher and career counselor training and professional development, providing opportunities for professional educators to update, upgrade or maintain skills or to learn about the labour market in the community;

- partnerships in the classroom, where volunteers from business and industry bring private sector or occupational expertise into the classroom.

At this time, unfortunately, such a sophisticated and multifaceted approach to the establishment and deployment of school-business partnerships has not developed in Asia Pacific economies, at least to the extent described by Merenda. The forms that such relationships might take and the ways in which they can be developed for the benefit of those concerned are often poorly conceived. At the moment, industry gives a great deal to education, but this has for the most part been on a voluntary, sporadic and ad hoc basis. A new approach for the development of relationships between schools and industry and the opportunities they offer for mutual advantage needs to be cultivated. Clearly, consultation and communication between all parties is an important element in the creation of new partnerships which are vital for planning a range of lifelong education and training opportunities.

Following are suggestions for specific strategies, ways and means for business and education to co-operate:

- all parties need to develop a common vision and shared purpose for giving expression to positive and productive forms of their partnership, and partnerships between education and business should not merely be concerned with raising money, sponsorships and additional funding;

- students should experience a variety of workplace and extra-curricular activities so as to widen their appreciation for the challenges of the world of work and the demands of industry, business and commerce;

- successful school-business links could include work placement programs, the employment in schools of career counselors with recent experience and knowledge of industry, arranging teacher/industry placements and exchanges, and instituting an "adopt a school" program.

Such activities and relationships provide benefits for all parties and offer lessons for the wider learning community.

ARTS AND CULTURE FOR SCHOOL-COMMUNITY INTERACTION

Schools and other educational institutions can contribute to the cultural and artistic activities and institutions of the broader community, provide insight into and understanding of the ethnic diversity of our multicultural societies, and respond sympathetically to the religious beliefs and practices of different ethnic groupings. In this way schools can increase racial and religious tolerance and improve social harmony.

Cultural and artistic activities can act as foci for community activities and lifelong learning and, in fact, many people are drawn to arts and cultural events in large part for the social interaction and creative activities they provide. It is important, however, that relevant cultural artistic activities be available for all social and ethnic groups regardless of location. Schools can be the neutral venue for cultural and artistic pursuits, thereby promoting wider participation in cultural life and helping to create an integrated community. The arts have the potential to provide meaningful learning experiences for individuals and groups who might otherwise feel marginalised, including those with disabilities, and schools can ensure access for these and other groups.

These programs can be hosted in community/school centres, places where formal and informal learning activities come together. Included would be courses and programs in a wide range of artistic and creative activities, including theatre, music and ethnic presentations. Most schools have the basic infrastructure and resources for this: a hall (often with a proscenium, theatre lighting and amplification), musical instruments or even a music suite, art rooms, a gymnasium with a sprung floor, maybe a dance studio, wheels for pottery and kilns, woodwork and metalwork shops, and other such facilities. Though these resources and facilities may be used primarily for traditional purposes during much of the week, they could be opened up to the community in the evenings and weekends in the interests of lifelong learning for all.

Other ways in which schools can provide opportunities for lifelong learning include bringing artists into the schools or hosting artists in residence programs, holding art exhibitions, and providing studio space for dancers, musicians and theatre troupes who would then perform for the community. Some schools offer "enrichment" programs where the students mix with arts groups, often becoming involved with the productions. Other schools arrange for qualified and artistically/culturally significant people in the local community to act as mentors for the arts and craft activities.

Cultural and artistic activities enhance the quality of life for everyone. They help develop rich sources of enterprise that lead to personal fulfilment, and often develop skills relevant for participating more broadly within the society. Further, in some instances, cultural and artistic exposure develops expertise that has direct workplace applications. The various ways in which the school can serve as a centre for the provision of and access to different forms of life-enhancing non-formal learning for the community are limited only by the range of ideas people bring to the discussion. Clearly, the field of arts and cultural pursuits is heavy with implications for the development of people within the community and the direct involvement of the schools and other community centres.

FORGING PARTNERSHIPS AMONG SCHOOLS AND OTHER LEARNING PROVIDERS

The institutionalization of lifelong learning implies that, while education may start in a formal, compulsory school setting, it will extend far beyond to a variety of other settings, in a range of other institutions, and via a multiplicity of pathways. A host of agencies will offer lifelong learning opportunities: some formal and others informal, some traditional and others more innovative. In effect, lifelong learning subsumes the concept of co-investment.

A constructive lifelong learning system presupposes a series of connections between schools and other institutions all of which provide different educational opportunities. In fact, there are at the present time a wide range of these institutions providing educational services and opportunities in many APEC member economies. Included are universities, colleges, other tertiary education institutions, hospitals, neighbourhood houses, broadcasting corporations, private sector firms and industrial enterprises, trade unions, local councils, councils of adult education, and open universities. Societies are now entering a stage where the separate but complementary and mutually supportive contributions of a range of providers of lifelong learning opportunities are at work in the community. The planning and development of productive relationships between them is a matter of pressing concern.

In these relationships there must be clearly defined and flexibly articulated pathways for effective interaction and connections. These will enable institutions and students to build networks of linkages, and help avoid duplication in the same sector and on the same level. What is needed are integrated offerings between different levels and sectors. A good model is the complex articulations of the climbing-frame, in which people do not simply get to the top by one particular route through a single linear and uninterrupted progression. Instead they may choose to move across, backwards and down, before proceeding along and upwards towards the goal. People wanting to use lifelong learning educational services will need advice and assistance to move to and through different stages. Schools constitute only one element in the framework of educational opportunities, and they need to blend with many other network partners.

To ensure that lifelong learning opportunities are presented through a complex web or multiplicity of pathways, the various institutions need to offer a wide range of interrelated routes and opportunities for learners. These must permit individuality and provide comprehensive coverage. This implies coherence and complementarity within the group of providers, and must certainly be based on consultation and interactivity. This will require coordination and synergy. Such provision, and a wide awareness of both its availability and the ways in which it can be accessed, will enable people to connect with others who have related, though not necessarily the same learning needs. There will emerge a community of learners rather than, as is the case at present, pockets of separate interests and needs.

There is a need, therefore, to dismantle existing obstacles that prevent closer relationships between schools and other educational institutions. This is necessary for the successful coordination of efforts and resources among the community's educating agencies, so that students can move easily from one to the other and so accelerate their progress in learning. There will be a need for some nurturing in the early stages of collaboration if all of the many possibilities among schools and other learning providers are to be realised and capitalised upon. In fostering the ideal of lifelong learning for all, schools, community institutions, government agencies and private sector organizations will find their missions enhanced by espousing and implementing a cooperative approach when providing opportunities for learners, as well as in the establishment of various pathways and channels.

SCHOOLS AS CENTRES FOR THE LEARNING COMMUNITY

If the development of schools as principal centres for "learning for all" is an appropriate and sound method for offering lifelong learning opportunities, one of the first tasks is to link schools and the community more closely. In the past schools have been too compartmentalised, too isolated from the community. In fact, many of them erect barriers to exclude outsiders - an attitude well illustrated by the notices that some schools in the past put on their entrance gates: "Parents stop here".

Not only have the boundaries related to community involvement in the work of schools been territorial, they have also been conceptual. Teachers in some schools have inhibited the development of a diverse range of approaches and pathways for lifelong learning by holding fast to theories which support linear and compartmentalised progress through fixed stages of learning. This is embodied most obviously in the traditional and too often followed linear journey through elementary and secondary schooling.

Another barrier has been epistemological. Schools have focused on compartmentalising knowledge and styles of learning, separating learners in horizontally organised groups according to chronological age. As well, curriculum is often discipline based, and examined only in classrooms that are remote from real life experience and application. Modern thinkers argue that there is no epistemic warrant for such theories, and since the time of Dewey (1938) new theories have called these demarcation lines into question, and laid the basis for a more integrated, problem solving approach.

Given these changing perspectives, schools are now breaking down traditional barriers between the classroom and the learning that can take place outside the school. In the future, the structure and organisation of learning in and outside the classroom will change quite dramatically. Education in the future will provide more multi-skilling and student grouping will reflect a range of ages and language capabilities. Further, there will be increased emphasis on enquiry and experience-based learning. Knowledge and information is available to students not only from books and other resources located within the school but also from computers, the Internet, and a host of other information sources from around the world. As a consequence, one of the largest barriers to flexibility and independence in learning – the timetable as it is now structured – must become less dominating.

If schools are to become centres for the benefit and use of community learners, they will need to be opened up for broader access. This has implications for the responsibilities schools currently have to care for younger learners, and in many cases the explicit expectation placed on schools for creating a safe and separate learning environment. However, it can't be ignored that the physical barriers which schools erect, even if these are in response to a statutory "duty of care", act as obstructions to the aims of lifelong learning and to the many rich sources of interaction that can take place when learning "on the outside" is mixed with "learning on the inside". Achieving a balance between the custodial role of the school and the need to open up the school to greater community involvement will be a major challenge for school leadership.

The heart of this issue is that learning does not take place only in schools. Nowadays we are expanding our list of places and venues that are appropriate for formal, non-formal and informal learning: libraries, cultural and religious centres, through technology, in the home, and in work settings. Given the multiplicity of student needs and choices, and the variety of learning pathways open to them, schools and other learning institutions need to offer more choices through flexible programming, modularization, and other alternative instructional modes.

Schools of tomorrow must cater to modes of learning that give students the greatest access and the most benefit. Educators will use their experience, expertise and professional judgment to decide which approaches best suit the needs of particular learners. This will support the emergence of a recognisable community of learners where "thinking schools" and "thinking people" are linked together in interlocking circles of interest with a commitment to lifelong learning for all. In these schools all citizens will be encouraged and able to learn throughout the lifespan for employment, for broad participation in society, and for personal growth and development.

REFERENCES

Ball, C. (1993). *Lifelong learning and the school curriculum.* Paris: OECD/CERI.

Campbell, D. (1992, April). Parents and schools working for student success. *NASSP Bulletin.* 1-9.

Chapman, J. D. & Aspin, D. N. (in press). *The school, the community and lifelong learning.* London: Cassell.

Delors, J. (1996). *Learning: The treasure within.* Paris: UNESCO.

Dewey, J. (1938). *Experience and education.* New York: Macmillan.

European Parliament. (1995). *Commission of the European communities: Amended proposal for a European year of lifelong learning.* Brussels: European Parliament Publications Office.

Grace, G.R. (1994). Education is a public good: On the need to resist the domination of economic science. In D. Bridges & T. H. McLaughlin (Eds.), *Education and the market place.* London: Falmer.

Hughes, P. (1993). *The curriculum re-defined: Implications from OECD associated projects.* Paris: OECD.

McLaughlin, T. H. (1994). Politics, markets and schools: The central issues. In D. Bridges & T. H. McLaughlin (Eds.), *Education and the market place.* London: Falmer Press.

Merenda, D.W.. (1989, October). Partners in education: An old tradition renamed. *Educational Leadership.* 4-7.

Nordic Council of Ministers. (1995). *The golden riches in the grass: Lifelong learning for all.* Copenhagen: Author.

OECD. (1996). *Making lifelong learning a reality for all.* Paris: Author.

Peters, R. S. (1965). Education as initiation. In R. D. Archambault (Ed.), *Philosophical analysis and education.* London: Routledge & Kegan Paul.

Smethurst, R. (1995). Education: A public or private good? *RSA Journal, CXLIII*(5465), 33-45.

Albert H. Yee

and Joseph Y. S. Cheng

Dr. Albert Yee was Professor and Academic Dean in the United States and East Asia for many years before retiring from teaching in 1995. He edited *East Asian Higher Education: Traditions and Transformations* in 1994. At present Dr. Yee is working on his tenth book, titled *Whither Hong Kong: 1840-1997 and Beyond*. His pursuits include Sino-American history, gardening, and the Western Montana (U.S.) Stanford Alumni Club, which he founded in 1997.

Dr. Joseph Cheng is a Professor and Chair of the Political Science Department at the City University of Hong Kong. He is the founding editor of the *Hong Kong Journal of Social Sciences*. Professor Chen's interests include reading and international travel.

Lifelong Learning in the United States and Hong Kong: Before 1997 and After

by Albert H. Yee and Joseph Y. S. Cheng

This paper examines and compares the development of and support for lifelong learning in Hong Kong and the United States with the framework of certain psychological and sociocultural perspectives. Of specific interest are Erikson's Eight Stages of Life, Confucian philosophy, family values and related influences, political uncertainties, and institutional variety in support of lifelong learning. Further, this paper argues that some factors which positively influence the development of a learning culture in Hong Kong, are absent in the United States, while certain strengths related to learning opportunities in the United States are weaker or absent in Hong Kong.

INTRODUCTION

The approach used to explore lifelong learning in this paper embraces psychological views which consider human life from lifespan perspectives. This approach is taken because it emphasizes significant and manifold possibilities and adaptations that affect human lives. To maximize human potential, and curtail the waste that can ravage lives, learning and development throughout the lifespan deserve our critical attention, especially from parents and teachers. Proper nurturance and growth of children and adults require that key factors associated with human development are appreciated and taken into account. As well, since people do not develop only in families and schools, it is important to recognize and consider sociocultural factors that underlie and influence individual behaviour.

Few would dispute the notion that the early period of socialization and human development is a time when foundations are set, and that these largely determine the course and quality of human life including much of the preferences and aptitudes that set the stage for lifelong learning. However, though much is known with regard to effective activities that could be practised during this period, actual practices most often don't reflect the best methods for producing and supporting development opportunities, socialization practices, and an orientation towards lifelong learning.

Attacks against education in the United States are commonplace, often criticizing school and teacher quality. Further, many pupils and parents in the United States perceive learning to be laborious and not "fun", clearly building a poor foundation for lifelong learning. This perception may be seen as frivolous, contrasting with the very serious attitudes of Chinese pupils and parents (Stevenson & Lee, 1990). Compared to the United States, the rote curriculum and study approaches to learning in Hong Kong, Japan, and other societies in Asia and Europe force young people to study hard under conditions of extreme anxiety as they seek to pass life-determining examinations (Yee, 1989; 1992, Chapter 6). Whether through indulgence or drudgery brought about by poor application of what is known of psychological development, lifelong learning may be lost in both these contexts at precisely the time when it should be taking root.

DEVELOPMENTAL PSYCHOLOGY

In the past, psychologists focused mainly on very early child development in order to study the obvious and remarkable changes in life; however, more common now are approaches that consider human development as a broad lifespan issue, based in part on the realization that people develop and change from birth throughout life. Learning to crawl and walk, recognize close family members and surroundings, speak and understand language, and so forth, are pivotal stages in early maturation. The names and works of developmental psychologists, including Jean Piaget on cognitive development, Mary Ainsworth and many others on attachment, and Laurence Kohlberg on moral reasoning, are familiar to those with a grounding in psychology (see Atkinson, Atkinson, Smith & Bem, 1990, Chapter 3).

Humans experience rapid growth from birth through puberty and the teen-years, a period that requires favourable social conditions in order for the many changes which are taking place to blossom and mature. For example, children are born with what Noam Chomsky (1972) called the language acquisition device (LAD), lasting the first three years. During that period, the child soaks up whatever languages are used within the immediate social environment. Though people can and do learn languages throughout their lives, LAD is an innate process especially designed to help babies, who at that stage lack developed learning skills, to acquire linguistic acuity quickly. We know that language usage within the social environment influences children's linguistic, cognitive and emotional development, and that youngsters can be sadly shortchanged by untoward family conditions which provide meagre and unsavoury surroundings for language growth and more. As youngsters mature towards and into the teens, the brain and central nervous system provide increasing cognitive capability, which receives, digests, and remembers ideas and learnings from home, neighbourhood, and school environments. This is clearly a period when the proclivity and opportunity to embrace lifelong learning is pivotal.

In the United States, adolescence is often a trying, even volatile experience for youth and families as the child matures physiologically towards young adulthood. Although Asians and Europeans pass through the same biological changes, adolescence has not been as troublesome for them as in the U.S. This contrast no doubt comes from sociocultural differences, understanding of which points out the inseparable, complex relationship of nature and nurture as already implied with LAD. Although less obviously than children and adolescents, adults also develop and change significantly. In effect, humans are individuals with biological and personal differences as well as members of sociocultural groups. Outcomes from this psychological and sociocultural complex produce the vast family of mankind and both affect the potential and propensity for lifelong learning.

ERIK ERIKSON'S STAGES OF LIFE

In order to help understand how the human complex develops in a comprehensive, systematic way, Erikson's (1963) developmental theory identifies eight major psychosocial crises that all individuals pass through. The theory argues that how these crises are resolved, or not, largely determines the quality of people's lives. The following paragraphs in this section focus on three of these stages.

Table 1:
Erikson's Stages of Psychosocial Development*

Stages	Pyschosocial Crises	Social Unit of Importance	Favorable Outcomes
1. First year of life	Trust vs. mistrust	parents	Trust & optimism
2. Second year	Autonomy vs. doubt	family members	Sense of control & adequacy
3. Third – fifth year	Initiative vs. guilt	family & relatives	Purpose & direction; ability to initiate
4. Sixth year to puberty	Industry vs. inferiority	neighborhood & school	Competence in social, intellectual & physical skills
5. Adolescence	Identity vs. role confusion	peer groups	Integrated self-image as a unique & worthy person; social roles in formation
6. Early adulthood	Intimacy vs. isolation	family & friends	Ability to form close, lasting relationships; to make career commitments
7. Middle adulthood	Generativity vs. self-absorption	interest & work group & family network	Concern for family, society & future generations
8. The Aging years	Integrity vs. despair	Family network & community	A sense of fulfilment & satisfaction with one's life; willingness to face death

* adapted from Erikson (1963, pp. 222-247)

Table 1 shows that the first psychosocial crisis involves learning to *Trust or Mistrust* close ones and the immediate environment. Through the social atmosphere created by families, and their nurturing patterns, parents give their babies ample reason to feel loved or disliked, warm or cold, secure or fearful, and so forth, all of which creates a sense of trusting or mistrusting life and others. When babies are handled roughly, fed and cleansed irregularly, and spoken to without affection day after day, they learn to mistrust, a strong perception that can last their whole lives. However, for the most part, the universal cuteness of babies and their crying help win parental affection (cf. Ainsworth, Blehar, Walthers & Wall, 1978).

During stage five, adolescents struggle with the psychosocial crisis of *Identity versus Role Confusion*. This occurs in the teen years when questions such as, who am I, what am I going to be, and what is my role in life, become all important. In Hong Kong, and in many other societies, answers to these questions are generally ready-made, easy to understand, and given to young people by their families and society. However, adolescents in the United States are allowed more freedom and flexibility as well as far greater opportunities to be what they want, as compared to adolescents in other societies. As a result, answers to these sorts of questions are not so obvious, and the resulting psychosocial crisis may be more troublesome and painful for them and their families. In effect, indecision is fostered by parental tolerance and an abundance of options. One's academic ability and standing, career interests and options, peer pressures to conform, family support, and needs and problems surface and shape a healthy identity or, alternatively, enhance role confusion. From school, family and other role models, and personal inclinations, attitudes and habits, promoting lifelong learning can take root and expand during the teen years or they can wither and die.

Throughout the developed world, adolescents are thinking ahead to what they will do after secondary schooling — to seek work or participate in higher education. By this time, their families, teachers, and peers have helped to mould their tentative self-concepts — to be good or bad, an achiever, a laggard, a worker, a professional, a parent, or a patriot. Given an individual who has progressed into adolescence, who is academically "adequate" (in Hong Kong this means having done well in the Certificate of Education Examination at age 16, while in the United States it means good grades and above average scores on standardized tests at age 18), who has a supportive and loving family, who can handle peer pressure, and who can look forward to higher education with career options in mind, we can infer that this person has or is obtaining sound identity formation and a healthy self-concept. However, there is an important distinction to be made. Unlike Hong Kong's exam-driven frenzy, the U.S. system allows many youths to seek in-school fulfilment through sports and other extracurricular activities even when their grades are mediocre.

Although adolescents outside the United States tend to be more docile, they do not always escape *Identity versus Role Confusion* concerns intact. As strong sociocultural influences and parental pressures influence behaviour, teenage dependents may seem relatively conformist in societies such as Hong Kong. However, role confusion can erupt explosively, in turn leading to antisocial behaviour. By way of example, the crime rate for Hong Kong adolescents has been rising alarmingly over the past few years, teenage suicides have become increasingly common in East Asia, and recent studies report increased drug use among adolescents in Hong Kong as well as the United States.

During the eighth and last stage of life, *Integrity versus Despair*, the elderly consider their past and develop an overall sense of satisfaction or dissatisfaction with their lives. Since nothing in the past can be modified, what they recall and regard as significant and how they and others interpret their lives provide an overall, deep-seated feeling of integrity and fulfilment or tragic despair and bitterness. Given an older person who is fortunate to have enjoyed a happy, compatible family and group of friends, a noteworthy career that has provided for self-pride and well-being as a retiree, hobbies and interests that stimulate learning, and a general sense of success despite the normal disappointments of life, that person will attain and enjoy integrity during the final stage. As Erikson said, when parents are not afraid of dying, their children will not be afraid of living!

Social-psychological perspectives, such as Erikson's Eight Stages of life, help anticipate and prepare for developmental changes and needs through the lifespan. More specifically, they can be used as a framework for understanding how individuals, as well as groups and the society as a whole, develop or fail to develop attitudes and values, including an orientation towards lifelong learning.

THE CONFUCIAN TRADITION

Hong Kong has a bustling population of 6.3 million, 97% of whom are ethnic Chinese. Although the territory is a mixture of East and West, Hong Kong residents have retained Chinese traditions, especially Confucianism, which upholds education and learnedness among its highest values. Confucian philosophy asserts that knowledge and virtue can be acquired by all who seek them, not just the educated and wealthy. The great sage believed that individuals must learn to become humane through lifelong study, reflection, discipline, and humility. This potential to learn and enhance the self separates human beings from lower creatures who do not have these same abilities. Since Confucianism continues to strongly influence the Chinese societies of East Asia, and has long been incorporated into the cultures of Japan, South Korea, and Vietnam, it may be argued that Confucian ethics have played a role in the recent economic success enjoyed by East Asian communities. Perhaps more importantly, it is abundantly clear that Confucian philosophy plays a critical role in so far as influencing attitudes towards learning (Yee, 1994).

In his Analects (Lau, 1979; 2:4 and 7:20), Confucius admitted that he himself had to work very hard to acquire the knowledge that brought him wisdom. Since so much is to be learned, education must be pursued at an early age, and throughout the lifespan, with hard work and discipline. Figurines of Confucius as a teacher often show him with a stern face, holding a stick to punish lazy and wayward students. In traditional China, a child's training was methodical. Children were first asked to do simple tasks, such as helping to sweep the floor, greeting elders, and responding to simple questions. In time, a well-defined curriculum was developed, including an introduction to the six arts — ritual, music, archery, charioteering, calligraphy, and arithmetic. According to Tu (1993), this curriculum involves physical as well as mental and spiritual discipline and study.

Confucius wrote that, at the age of fifteen, his heart was set on learning. Thus, in Erikson's terms, as an adolescent Confucius marked his identity and role as a lifelong learner — one who could go beyond basic schooling to assume greater responsibility for his own studies and reflection. Thus, according to the ancient classic, *The Great Learning*, written by unknown Confucian scholars and memorized by Chinese youth, the goals of superior learning are to: (1) cultivate one's personal knowledge; (2) help others realize themselves; and (3) strive for moral excellence.

Besides teaching that people have the potential and responsibility to learn and improve themselves morally throughout life, Confucius also placed increasing demands of self-betterment on the most intellectually capable. Arguably, the most significant impact of Confucian educational philosophy on the Chinese has been his definition of the political role of intellectuals and their duty as scholar-officials to society and the ruler. The Confucian ideal of "inner sageliness and outer kingliness" implied that sageliness takes precedence over kingliness and that only a sage is qualified to be a ruler. At the very least, an emperor should try to see wisdom through diligent learning. Confucius hoped that education would cultivate a learned elite that would bring about political reforms to overcome China's problems and result in the ideal society, similar to that which had existed in ancient times (Association for the Study of Confucianism, 1988; Kuang, 1985).

Confucius also wanted moral education to influence the order and harmony of society. As Hall & Ames (1987) wrote, the West Han (202 B.C.- 25 A.D.) scholar-officials exploited this goal by establishing standards of ethical behaviour for the society-at-large. In turn, these became the tools and force of authoritarian misrule that have been the bane of the Chinese ever since (Yee, 1992). The authority of the ruler over the minister, the father over the son, and the husband over the wife were firmly set in the formulation of the "three bonds". Also, five vital relationships were established, then promoted and maintained with moral benevolence: ruler-minister, father-son, elder brother-younger brother, husband-wife, and friend-friend. At the pinnacle, the sage king was the absolute master of and exemplar for society and all below.

Although those ideals have been extremely difficult, if not impossible, to accomplish at the national level, success has been achieved within the family, the most stable and durable social institution of the Chinese (Tu, 1993; Yee, 1992, pp. 181-190). Emphasizing the great importance of the extended and nuclear family as key microcosms of society, Confucianism relates equally to families of all social levels in professing the values of filial responsibility, affection, fraternity, loyalty, and obedience. Irrespective of material advantage, Confucian values can be achieved and maintained whether a family or individual is rich or poor. Yee (1992, p. 185) wrote:

While the family provides vital human functions for all peoples, none can rival the Chinese familial group in its comprehensive handling of basic human activities across the centuries. The Chinese family is perhaps the most self-reliant of world families. Lacking viable state and community

social systems, such as education, religion and social welfare, the Chinese...
have made the most of the family to fulfil basic human needs and cultural
aspirations.

Most importantly, for thousands of years, the Chinese family has sustained and
emphasized broad educational values, including an accent on and proclivity for lifelong learning, and fostered positive attitudes towards learning as it is linked with
academic achievement.

THE FAMILY IN HONG KONG TODAY

Confucian values still direct Hong Kong families, most notedly in terms of parental
concerns for their children's education. Despite Hong Kong's cosmopolitan,
East-West mix of cultures, the people remain quite conservative in terms of social
attitudes and values. Traditional Confucian values have undergone only slow ero-
sion over time, and remain the dominant behavioral influence (Cheng, 1992).
Compared to the United States, Hong Kong's families are cohesive, as the divorce
rate is still very low despite increases in recent years. Attempts by the Hong Kong
Government to influence community values is met with suspicion, while the people make conservative demands on the Government. Conservative values are well
documented, with examples including public rejection of the decriminalization of
homosexuality, demands for greater services for the elderly, and stricter control of
pornography. However, the best examples of Confucianism's influence on the Hong
Kong people is shown in their undiminished belief in the worth of education
throughout the lifespan and the strong faithfulness of young people to their parents
despite Hong Kong's current propensity for increased influence of Western culture
(Rock Solid, 1996).

Hong Kong parents commonly make enormous sacrifices to support the schooling of their youth, whom they inculcate to a degree not seen in the West with the
belief that social mobility and success in life are best achieved through educational
achievement. Familial differences in wealth are seen in school options; the
well-to-do send their offspring to the best schools that they can afford, even abroad,
while the poor have no choice but local public education. The Institute of
International Education reported that 12,018 students from H.K. were studying in
U.S. colleges and universities in 1995-96 (Desruisseaux, 1996). Sizable as that number may seem, it is a drop of 7.1% from the previous year due to the rigorous recruiting by Australian institutions, though this may change given the most recent
outbreak of anti-Asian bigotry in Australia (Chow, 1996).

In keeping with Chinese family values, parents look forward to their offsprings'
future ability to provide for their old age and, unlike the West, regard support for
their children's education as the best investment in social security. In its "Life Styles
Special Report" (1996, p. 37) on family values, the *Far Eastern Economic Review*
reported that readers of 10 Asian nations placed "greater stress on the need for harmony, and respect for authority, than [did] Westerners". Reflecting traditional
respect for old China's scholar-official traditions, many Hong Kong parents have
been pleased in the past to see their children enter the Hong Kong Government

ranks as civil servants. Now the ambitions have changed somewhat, and more parents desire that their children achieve professional status, as in medicine, accounting, engineering, and law.

In terms of Erikson's Eight Stages of Life, therefore, the pragmatic, family-centred Chinese make the most of learning and its fruits throughout the lifespan. Education during the fourth stage (elementary school years), the fifth stage (secondary school years), and onward helps to promote an ongoing continuity of "generativity" and "integrity" for the generations. The link is clear: by doing everything possible to raise their youth with affection and inculcate a disciplined drive for higher levels of educational attainment, Chinese parents not only help their offspring advance and progress in life but secure satisfaction and dignity for their own senior years. Conditions that would bring an older Chinese to "despair" are easy to identify and comprehend.

There is, however, a significant problem underlying much of what may be termed the symbiotic link between education for the young and social security for the old. The Chinese connect learning almost entirely with the status, position, and security it brings, that is to say the extrinsic worth, rather than the intrinsic importance as taught by Confucius. In fact, it is the latter which is more supportive in the longer term for lifelong learning. Similar to hierarchical authority, supposedly based on moral benevolence that in practice became misrule through authoritarian paternalism, lifelong learning and education for self-improvement and humaneness has become linked primarily to status and well-being.

HONG KONG'S TURBULENT HISTORY AND UNCERTAIN FUTURE

The older generation of Hong Kong Chinese, those who lived through World War II, experienced very hard times during childhood and adolescence. Suffering from the war and consequent devastation, people of that generation faced severe economic hardships and even famine. It is not surprising, therefore, that education for most of them was a luxury and often impossible to obtain. In fact, the Japanese occupying force within Hong Kong tried to reduce the territory's population as much as possible, food and other essentials had to be imported, and the harbour was closed throughout the war by U.S. submarines and airplanes. Except for a handful of primary schools which employed the Japanese language, all schools, including the University of Hong Kong, were closed.

Following World War II, the Chinese who survived harboured a burning desire for hard work and education. While working day and night, many completed secondary education through evening and weekend classes as well as on-the-job training. Among this population, the drive for academic credentials, economic success and self-improvement was striking, and continues even today to be a hallmark of Hong Kong society. Through this behaviour it was clear that Confucian values were alive and well.

In Confucian societies, academic status and work merit have been and continue to be the most important criteria for determining employment and advancement. Not surprisingly, a survey of Hong Kong workers taken in the three-month period ending February 1993 found a strong correlation between educational attainment and occupation (Choi, 1993). Of the managers and professionals who were surveyed, 30% (figures rounded to nearest percentage) had completed graduate and professional education, and 57% had completed degree-level education, post-secondary technical training or, at a minimum, middle school education. With regard to clerks, salespeople, and service workers, only 5% had completed post-secondary education. Almost 75% of manual workers, who had the least education, strongly agreed that education was important to personal success. Sharing traditional attitudes towards education, the Hong Kong labourers equated jobs and wages with education and learning. Clearly, the link between education and success, and the appropriateness of this link, continues to be strongly embedded within Hong Kong society. It is relevant to consider future events in the context of these beliefs.

After more than 150 years as a British colony, Hong Kong will return to China's sovereignty at midnight, June 30, 1997. The 12 years since the Sino-British Declaration was signed in 1984 have been filled with often raucous disputes over many matters affecting Hong Kong affairs and preparations for 1997. In that climate, it is clear that many within Hong Kong view the historic turnover with unease. Activities of the past few decades, including Tiananmen Square and the Cultural Revolution, along with broad expectations to which the Hong Kong Chinese have grown accustomed, including political dissent and free speech, have contributed to this uneasiness. In this climate, about 60,000 people have emmigrated annually from Hong Kong since 1984 (Howlett, 1996, p. 396). The number would almost certainly have been higher, but has been buffered by the quotas imposed by Australia, Canada, the United States, and other "desirable" nations. True to expectations, those favoured by "free" societies have been the educated and the skilled; in effect, many of the best candidates and success stories of lifelong learning have emmigrated with their families. According to Yee (1992), Hong Kong has been the classic geographic and psychological "stepping-stone" from and to China for the Chinese people since it was ceded to the British in 1840.

Assessing attitudes within Hong Kong towards 1997, Cheng (1992, pp. 18-20) reported that "Younger and richer people are much more worried about 1997 than those who have no options other than to stay ... those who have the option to emigrate tend to do so in order to secure an 'insurance policy'. Afterwards, they can afford to have a realistic assessment of China's policy towards Hong Kong ... [after Tiananmen] about one-third of the territory's households were planning to emigrate... ." Cheng said that the number of those seeking to move has declined because of "their realistic appraisals of the options and opportunity costs of emigration." As the changeover approaches, however, increased pessimism has been demonstrated by the sharp decline in law and medical school applications, especially by the best students. Graduation after 1997, even from one of Hong Kong's most prestigious institutions, presents a high degree of uncertainty (Cheng, 1996, p. 8). In pursuing education, especially in Hong Kong, where pragmatism is keen, people require purpose and stability so that they know what they study will be useful to their lives. However, polls conducted in March 1997 found that attitudes towards the 1997 turnover are mostly positive among all age groups in Hong Kong, perhaps due to the people's hopes for the best (Mak, 1997).

Although Hong Kong's present circumstances are unique, the value and importance of lifelong learning is no less significant there than elsewhere, and may in fact be more portentous. For example, Hong Kong's future has clear implications for preparatory learning. Those who are unable to speak Mandarin Chinese should consider the study of China's national dialect, which differs greatly from Cantonese, the local Hong Kong dialect. Also, since Hong Kong has retained traditional characters in writing and printed matter, the simplified characters standardized by China will require study. At present, however, Hong Kong's situation has been trying, and much of the attention that would otherwise be directed towards lifelong learning is on hold.

THE UNITED STATES AND COMPARISONS WITH HONG KONG

Education in the United States differs greatly from Hong Kong (and most of the world), as the focus in the United States is predominately on the individual, not the family, and schools bear much more, if not all, of the educational burden. Though families in the United States vary, most play a more benign role overall than is the case in Hong Kong and other societies. In the United States, the traditional two-parent family is in decline, and more and more children are being raised in single-parent families and in poor homes, often verging on or actually in poverty. Budgetary and other institutional challenges faced by the U.S. public school systems are resulting in reduced educational expenditures, and a proposed system of school vouchers will allow more — usually the brighter and richer — students to attend private schools of their choice.

A national survey of 1,514 United States adults conducted towards the end of 1995 by the Kaiser Family Foundation, Harvard University, and *The Washington Post* (Morin & Balz, 1996) found that a majority of those surveyed have lost trust in human nature, the government, institutions in general, and each other. Besides widespread cynicism among adults in the United States, including the belief that life for their children will be worse than for themselves, the survey found that knowledge of basic civics and history was often misinformed and faulty. All of this and more indicates that the United States population may be suffering greater "isolation," "self-absorption," and "despair" in terms of Erikson's Stages 6 through 8 — alarming phenomena if verified through further studies. Whatever fears may be associated with 1997 in Hong Kong, cynicism is not one of them. This difference between the United States and Hong Kong may be linked to stronger family and group ties.

The present climate for financial commitments to education in the United States is not strong. Also, prevailing attitudes towards individual freedom and self-expression appear to be gaining strength, yet these do not materially enhance lifelong learning. There is overwhelming reliance on television for news and entertainment, and naive, uninformed answers to basic questions regarding the United States Government and society generally (for example, most respondents believed that the United States spends more on foreign aid than medicare and most could not name their House representative) suggest that lifelong learning carries low priority among the general population.

Students in the United States are faced with a multitude of choices and options.

Secondary schools, community colleges and universities provide a plethora of courses and discipline options for the large number of students who have not as yet decided what to do with their lives. Parents now indicate that they place less pressure on their children than in the past in so far as commitments to career planning and educational programming are concerned. Thus, student underpreparedness and opportunities to choose courses and change directions help to prolong adolescence in the United States, a luxury that other societies neither offer nor tolerate. While fewer than 10% of Hong Kong's university-age youth are admitted into higher education, more than 50% are accepted in the United States. Nearly all of those admitted into Hong Kong universities complete degrees in contrast to the assorted and individualized outcomes so common in the United States.

Also in contrast to the United States, very few secondary and university students in Hong Kong work part-time during the academic year. In Hong Kong, both parents of families with modest means will work long hours (14 hour workdays are common) so that their children can study full-time. Hong Kong university students can obtain incentive loans from the Government to cover modest living and tuition costs, while in the U.S., college and university students can also avail themselves of bank and government loans. However, interest rates for U.S. student loans are generally higher than is the case in Hong Kong.

It is difficult to generalize with regard to the differences between education in Hong Kong and the United States, and more particularly with regard to lifelong learning, but several issues are clear. In Hong Kong, education is taken seriously and treated with sobriety and dedication because students and parents recognize that failure to be admitted into a university will result in limited career options, leading in turn to reduced family income and a less secure old age. Higher education admission is the *summum bonum* of all the drudgery and exam fervour suffered by most Hong Kong young people, and the academic track leading to the university is obvious even within the lower grades. For the vast majority of those who are not admitted into local universities, or who do not have the means to study abroad, the future is inextricably linked to lower-tier jobs.

FREEDOM AND FLEXIBILITY IN THE UNITED STATES

The individualized, indulgent (as compared to Hong Kong and other societies) nature of education in the United States creates many distinctions at every school level, perhaps the most important being students who sort themselves by, and perhaps for, academic achievement. For students seeking professional careers obtainable only through higher education, such as law and medicine, "identity" develops with little or no "role confusion". These students begin the process of meeting their reference group's expectations early. For example, secondary and university students associate with like-minded peers and take all or more than the required preparatory courses, and in turn their aptitude test scores tend to reflect greater motivation and readiness. For students in the United States who stretch out their search for "identity", high schools and community colleges accommodate needs and interests with the view that these students will make their own best career decisions over time. In other words, the United States system may seem inefficient and lax compared to Hong Kong, but emphasis on individual preferences and providing varied and supportive curriculum menus are consistent with other values in the United States. In the end, this works well for many students. Interestingly, it could be argued that the Hong Kong system is inefficient, because the prevailing university track in secondary schools produces a failure rate of about 82% and there are few satisfactory alternate programs for those who fail to obtain university admission (Yee, 1994, pp. 48-50). Community colleges have not developed in Hong Kong, likely because the bachelor's degree is the basic career-entry card.

For early- or late-blooming students, provisions for lifelong learning in the United States have been consistent with the philosophy of the worth and dignity of the individual. Whether professional studies, job training, craft and hobby interests, literature, creative arts, and so forth, lifelong learning courses and programs are readily available at publicly funded community colleges as well as through private institutions. Terrance Brown, Chief Executive Officer of the Community Colleges of Spokane in Washington State, reinforces much of this perspective as he welcomes students to the Spokane community colleges (Community Colleges of Spokane, 1995, p. 1).

Welcome to Community Colleges of Spokane. Our colleges offer a warm, friendly environment for you to pursue new career opportunities, activities and personal dreams. No matter where you are in life — whether you're a high school graduate, a displaced homemaker, a dislocated worker, a single parent, a professional/ technical student or a college transfer student — our colleges can help you achieve your goals. Our faculty are dedicated to teaching, our classes are small, and our student services staff are ready to assist you. Your success, of course, will depend on your own commitment to learning. The opportunities you'll find here are many, and the rewards are rich and fulfilling.

Recognizing that manual, unskilled jobs will soon be obsolete, the United States Government has worked to help the nation adjust to the challenges of the information age while at the same time improving overall educational quality. During the 1996 U.S. presidential campaign and in his February 1997 State of the Union address, President Clinton urged the adoption of new programs to promote mass education through the 14th year (community college), and on to university for all who are eligible. However, unlike the centralized, government-controlled educational systems of Hong Kong, other Asian societies, and Europe, education in the United States is decentralized, controlled by the 50 states and local school boards. This difference makes for slower and differentiated change throughout the United States. In fact, President Clinton's proposals may not receive support in Congress. By way of contrast, the Hong Kong Education Department can respond quickly to new policies and programs, having done so quite often in the past. However, an important concern with regard to Hong Kong's well financed educational system is that quality is often questionable in general and especially when new curriculum and policies are introduced. (With respect to financing, US$4.57 billion was allocated for

1,296,519 students in 1995 — see Howlett, 1996, pp. 434 & 459.) Regardless, this is not to argue that a decentralized system as in the United States is superior, particularly in the face of excellent evidence from the centralized educational systems of Germany, Switzerland and Singapore.

Table 2:
Key Features of the Educational Systems in the U.S.A. and Hong Kong*

	USA	Hong Kong
Main Purpose	Focus upon the individual. Develop individual to fullest potential. Transmitter of a cultural heritage that is still forming.	Focus upon effective, lawful citizenry. Develop literate, skilled citizenry ready to serve society's needs and to be able to be self-reliant and productive. Helps select future corps of leaders.
Instructional Mode and Style	Learner-centered; stress on understanding, application and ability to integrate learnings. Use of educational psychology and varied teaching aids and methods. Learner is motivated through self-interest and is mostly active.	Teacher-centered; stress on knowing many factual details and logic of disciplines. Use of lectures, homework and rote learning. Extrinsic and motivating force of examinations determining advancement. Learner is mostly passive.
Curricular Orientation	More present-future oriented. Concern for developing whole person -- cognitive, social-emotional, physical. Social interaction/relations seen as tool to promote whole person. Various tracks, such as university prep and vocational, for choice by secondary students.	More past-present oriented. Mastery of academic knowledge and skills given in preparation for traumatic, do-or-die exams. Linear progression in concepts and skills taught. Curricular prestige hierarchy delimits choice; most secondary students taking university prep.
Ideal Secondary School Graduate	Well-rounded, achieving student/person superior in academic studies as evidenced by grades. Has extra-mural hobbies and/or involved in extra-curricular activities, perhaps student leader and/or outstanding in sports.	Outstanding achiever in school, estimation most by teachers. Performs outstandingly in major examinations, especially for entrance to the best universities. Good-natured, relates well with superiors and peers.
Control and Administration	Administered by local communities through elected boards of education and board-appointed administrators. Each of the 50 states constitutionally responsible; not federal government. Strong tradition of democratic process.	Policies and procedures centrally controlled by the government with little discretionary power given to local authorities and schools.

* adapted from Yee (1989)

COMMENTS FOR POLICY MAKERS

In Hong Kong, the family firmly socializes children and adolescents to accept education as an important and immediate goal. Individual life chances are obviously and inextricably linked to education, as are family benefits including social security. In addition, the Confucian orientation towards the duties, discipline and reflection associated with education and learning directly and indirectly promote participation through the lifespan. Is this enough to sow the seeds for effective lifelong learning? Perhaps not. Uncertainties associated with 1997, along with the emphasis on education for extrinsic rather than intrinsic values, may act as a brake to the broader acceptance of lifelong learning at a time when the need has never been greater.

Similarly, but in different ways, imbuing the concept of and support for lifelong learning in the United States is hindered by significant challenges. Most obvious is the issue that education is broadly, and perhaps increasingly, viewed only as an in-school activity, and in that context this paper has described decreasing direct support from the family for education, particularly when contrasted with Hong Kong. In many families within the United States, and in low income single-parent families in particular, there is little initiative to help children and adolescents see the value of education and lifelong learning in particular. In addition to this, a host of educational options, coupled with little reason to make lasting choices and the absence of economic imperatives such as those found in Hong Kong, may lead to what Erikson described as despair.

Lifelong learning is critically important to Hong Kong and the United States, and both societies would be substantially better off if their peoples were more strongly imbued with the educational tools, commitment and philosophical support for learning throughout the lifespan. Erikson's stages create an effective platform for understanding and evaluating needs and drives as these relate to lifelong learning. Hong Kong has the underlying family support and Confucian tradition, while the United States has an institutional mix that provides an incredibly wide range of lifelong learning opportunities.

Most important for policy makers is to recognize the import of lifelong learning, both for individuals and the society as a whole, and to put in place strategies and practices that will support the development of a lifelong learning ethic. In Hong Kong, stability, confidence and greater emphasis on intrinsic values are required. In the United States, more effective family support and broad values that favour decisions made in support of education and lifelong learning are required. Hong Kong and the United States represent two very different societies, yet both are in need of policy support for lifelong learning. Interestingly, many of the strengths in Hong Kong (and in Confucian societies in general) appear to be weaknesses in the United States, and similarly, many of the strengths in the United States appear to be weaknesses in Hong Kong. In any event, every person in both societies has reason *to learn how to learn* and *to learn throughout the lifespan*.

REFERENCES

Ainsworth, M. D. S., Blehar, M. C., Walthers, E. & Wall, S. (1978). *Patterns of attachment: A psychological study of the strange situation*. Hillsdale, NJ: Erlbaum.

Association for the Study of Confucianism, Shanxi Province. (Ed.). (1988). *A compendium of essays on the study of Confucian thought*. Taiyuan, Shanxi, China: Shanxi Renmin Chubanshe.

Atkinson, R. L., Atkinson, R. C., Smith, E. E., & Bem, D. J. (1990). *Introduction to psychology* (10th ed.). San Diego, CA: Harcourt Brace Jovanovich.

Cheng, J. Y. S. (1992). Values and attitudes of the Hong Kong community. In P. C. K. Kwong (Ed.), *Hong Kong trends 1989-92* (pp. 17-46). Hong Kong: Chinese University Press.

Cheng, J. Y. S. (1996). *Professional education and qualifications: Issues in the approach to 1997* (Report of the Contemporary China Research Centre). Hong Kong: City University of Hong Kong.

Choi, P. K. (1995). Education. In S. K. Lau, W. K. Lee, P. S. Wan, & Wong S. L. (Eds.), *Indicators of social development: Hong Kong 1993* (pp. 171-204). Hong Kong: Hong Kong Institute of Asia-Pacific Studies, Chinese University of Hong Kong.

Chomsky, N. (1972). *Language and mind*. New York: Harcourt Brace Jovanovich.

Chow, L. (1996, November 28). White noise: Asians feel the brunt of an anti-immigrant backlash. *Far Eastern Economic Review, 159*(48), 27-28.

Community Colleges of Spokane. (1995). *1995-1997 Catalog*. Spokane, WA: Author.

Desruisseaux, P. (1996, December 6). A record number of foreign students enrolled at U.S. colleges last year. *Chronicle of Higher Education*, A64-A69.

Erikson, E. H. (1963). *Childhood and society* (2nd ed.). New York: Norton.

Hall, D. L. & Ames, R. T. (1987). *Thinking through Confucius*. Albany, NY: State University of New York Press.

Howlett, B. (Ed.). (1996). *Hong Kong 1996*. Hong Kong: Hong Kong Government Publications.

Lau, D. C. (1979). *Confucius: The analects*. [Trans.]. Harmondsworth, England: Penguin.

Life styles special report. (1996, September 12). *Far Eastern Economic Review, (159)*39, 37-47.

Kuang, Y. M. (1985). *A critical biography of Confucius*. Jinan, Shandong: Qilu Shushe.

Mak, L. (1997, March 1). Deng's good points outweigh bad: Poll. *Hong Kong Standard*. (Internet edition.)

Morin, R., & Balz, D. (1996, January 28). Americans losing trust in each other and institutions. *Washington Post*, A1, A6. & A7.

Rock solid (1996, December 5). *Far Eastern Economic Review, 159(49)*, 50-55.

Stevenson, H.W., & Lee, S.Y. (1990). Contexts of achievement. *Monographs of Social Research Child Development*, 55(1-2, Serial No. 221).

Tu, W. M. (1993). *Way, learning and politics: Essays on the Confucian intellectual.* New York: State University of New York Press.

Yee, A. H. (1989). Cross-cultural perspectives on higher education in East Asia: Psychological effects upon Asian students. *Journal of Multilingual and Multicultural Development, 10*(3), 213-232.

Yee, A. H. (1992). *A people misruled: The Chinese stepping-stone* (2nd. ed., Rev.). Singapore: Heinemann Asia.

Yee, A. H. (Ed.). (1994). *East Asian higher education: Traditions and transformations.* Oxford: Pergamon/Elsevier.

Yukiko Sawano

Yukiko Sawano holds degrees from Tokyo University of Foreign Studies (B.A.) and the University of Tokyo (M.Ed.). Currently, she is a Senior Researcher in the Research Department of Lifelong Learning at the National Institute for Educational Research in Japan. Mrs. Sawano has for some time been keenly interested in comparative studies on educational policies and lifelong learning systems, and has written several books in these fields including *Schools in the World: A Comparative Cultural Perspective* (1995), *Styles of Learning: Introduction for Lifelong Learning* (1996), and *Comparative Studies on Lifelong Learning Policies* (1997). In her spare time she enjoys flower arranging, swimming, and snorkeling.

Lifelong Learning:
An Instrument for Improving School Education in Japan?

by Yukiko Sawano

Japan has long been a society that values and practices lifelong learning. Embedded in the daily fabric of Japanese life, lifelong learning has become institutionalized and bureaucratized. This paper argues that, in spite of this emphasis, lifelong learning has not been successful in so far as building a learning ethic, one that prizes learning, teaches creativity, includes everyone, and is seamless. This paper describes the current state of lifelong learning in Japan, and discusses the division between non-formal (social) education and formal schooling, problems associated with the latter, and the potential for a revitalized system of learning. In this new vision for learning, the school, the home, and the community come together as one, not as cooperants with divided areas of responsibility, but rather as a single, harmonious unit.

INTRODUCTION

In order to construct a rich, active and participative society within Japan for the 21st century, it is important to build and develop a lifelong learning society — one where "people can learn at any time in their life stage by freely choosing [from among] the learning opportunities ...." (Monbusho, 1996, p.2).

Since the late 1980's, the term "lifelong learning" (shogai-gakushu, in Japanese) has become increasingly celebrated among citizens in Japan. The expression can be heard and read, quite easily, everyday. In local papers, in government publications, and in commercial journals, lifelong learning and discussions related to it are explored in detail. According to a recent public opinion survey on lifelong learning conducted by the Prime Minister's Office, participation in learning programs of various kinds has increased from 40% in 1990 to 48% in 1992 (figures rounded to the nearest whole number) (Monbusho, 1996, p.10).

Discussions regarding lifelong learning are often quite broad in nature; however, the perspective most closely associated with the term tends to reflect a somewhat narrow, leisure-oriented view. For many Japanese, lifelong learning relates only to those specific activities undertaken for pleasure, mainly by housewives and retired people. In fact, this leisure perspective is borne out in practice as many more adult learners in Japan take courses related to personal health and sports, such as exercise, nutrition, jogging, and swimming, and to hobbies such as music, art, flower arranging, dance, and calligraphy, as compared with courses specific to acquiring professional knowledge and skills as these relate to vocational training (Monbusho, 1996, p. 11).

For some time the Government of Japan has been making extensive efforts to promote a broader and more inclusive picture of lifelong learning within the society, but this struggle has had little success, or at least not as much as had been hoped. The goal of creating a lifelong learning society remains just that, a picture of what could be, rather than what is. Further, the transformation of Japanese society as proposed by the National Council on Educational Reform, an ad hoc organization established as an advisory committee to the Prime Minister from 1984 to 1987, has not yet been fully realized. The goals of this committee included the following:

- recasting the diploma-oriented society (gakureki shakai), where too much emphasis is placed on elementary and secondary school education, and especially on preparatory courses for entrance examinations to upper secondary schools and higher education institutions, into a community where learning at each stage is assessed appropriately;

- providing citizens with a broad range of learning opportunities that respond to the growing demand for the type of education which enriches minds and fulfils lives, a demand that is emerging in concert with higher incomes, increased leisure time, aging and the overall maturation of Japanese society;

- facilitating opportunities for all citizens in Japan to continue learning throughout the lifespan in order to cope with the social, economic and technological changes taking place, including the substantially increased use of higher technology, the explosive growth in information, internationalization, and structural changes taking place in business and industry as these affect society generally.

These same goals have recently been reiterated in the latest White Paper from the Ministry of Education, Science, Sports and Culture of Japan, a document which brings a new urgency to the context with a special section titled "Tasks and Prospects of Lifelong Learning — Increasing Diversity and Level of Knowledge" (Monbusho, 1996).

In the next few pages, this paper describes how mechanisms to disseminate and promote the concept of lifelong learning and to foster the transition of Japan to a lifelong learning society have been established at national and local levels in recent years. It also reflects on the problems which are emerging at this time from the introduction of lifelong learning policies. The paper then turns its focus to elementary and secondary school education, the precursor and a necessary foundation for lifelong learning. It identifies issues specific to elementary and secondary school education in Japan, and discusses how educational qualities and themes associated with lifelong learning policies and philosophy may be effectively used as tools for overcoming some of the negative phenomena associated with school education in Japan. Finally, the paper examines the future for lifelong learning policies, with a specific view towards considering how a lifelong learning ethos could be used to overcome problems associated with elementary and secondary school education in Japan.

The Japanese experience with lifelong learning can be a useful tool for other Asia Pacific economies as they develop and implement broad lifelong learning policies, programs and practices. Of most value will be the Japanese experience with excessive competition in the early learning environment, and what can be done, or avoided, to counter this problem through the use of lifelong learning.

BUREAUCRATIC AND LEGAL MECHANISMS TO PROMOTE LIFELONG LEARNING

In June 1990, the Japanese government enacted a law for the "Development of Mechanisms and Measures for the Promotion of Lifelong Learning" (abbreviated as the "Law for the Promotion of Lifelong Learning"). This legislation identified systems and projects to be implemented at the national and prefecture level which would promote lifelong learning. Specifically, the law prescribed:

- the establishment of Lifelong Learning Councils, at national and prefecture levels, to be comprised of specialists from various fields including the private sector;

- a system for planning, developing and implementing local measures to promote lifelong learning;

- lifelong learning liaison and cooperation schemes for municipalities and prefectures;

- criteria to be used for projects that would deliver learning programs, and surveys to be used for assessing the learning demands and needs of residents at the prefecture level.

In accordance with this new law, the National Council for Lifelong Learning was established in 1990 within the Ministry of Education, Science, Sports and Culture. The Council is charged with facilitating and implementing the new national policies for lifelong learning, and since its beginning a priority has been the establishment of Lifelong Learning Councils. Since that time approximately 85% of the prefectures have established planning systems to coordinate lifelong learning linkages with activities taking place between Prefectural Boards of Education and other local public departments, and as of 1995, 65% of the prefectures had established Lifelong Learning Councils (Monbusho, 1996, p.3). In addition to this, nearly 60% of the municipalities have developed systems which actively promote lifelong learning through a variety of activities including Lifelong Learning Promotion Conferences. The law, bureaucratic in nature though it is, has resulted in a well developed set of strategies for promoting, supporting and programming lifelong learning activities.

National Subsidy for Promoting Lifelong Learning

Recently, the National Government, through the Ministry of Education, Science, Sports and Culture, has been encouraging local governments to implement additional measures which promote lifelong learning. This has been done through the use of subsidies for various "model projects" which are implemented within the prefectures and municipalities. Following are a few examples of model projects which have attracted subsidies. The variety is notable.

Social Education Leaders

This project identifies and qualifies personnel who have rich educational backgrounds to act as instructors for non-formal education (known as social education in Japan) targeted at youth, women, senior citizens and others. Similar activities have been in place since as early as 1972, but these have been subsumed under the lifelong learning project beginning in 1989.

Promoting Volunteer Activities

According to a 1992 report from the National Lifelong Learning Council, voluntary activities are themselves lifelong learning experiences which facilitate personal development and growth for the volunteer and for others in the community. As a result, the Ministry funded this project with the intention of developing a "volunteer environment" within each community, the goal being to create a climate where persons share their experiences and expertise as community volunteers through a variety of activities at the prefecture level. Included for funding are liaison and coordination of volunteer activities in the prefecture, identification of places for voluntary activities to take place, provision of volunteer information and consultation, development of curriculum for the training of volunteers, training of volunteers, and the establishment of Lifelong Learning Volunteer Centres.

Community Circle Activities

This program was started by the Ministry of Education, Science, Sports and Culture in 1992. It subsidizes children's "circle activities". These take place during school holidays, typically in neighbouring communities. Circle activities are designed to develop in younger children an eagerness for learning, and an ability to identify problems and search for creative and innovative solutions. It is thought that these activities will develop a lifelong interest in learning during a critical stage of development. The National Lifelong Learning Council considers it particularly important to enrich out-of-school activities for youth in order to promote lifelong learning.

Promoting Women's Lifelong Learning

In Japan, it is considered to be very important to build a society where women have the opportunity to participate fully. This requires changing the traditional stereotypes where there has been, and continues to be, a high degree of role separation, and developing a climate where women feel comfortable and welcome to participate in any field. In order to build this more inclusive society, the Ministry of Education, Science, Sports and Culture has been facilitating the participation of women in a wide variety of activities according to ability and interests.

Wide Area Project

This is a component part of the broader Local Lifelong Learning Promotion Project, and has as its key aim the promotion of activities that develop a wide, perhaps even global, geographic perspective among the community. Issues and themes of particular interest which may be supported through this project include the maintenance of global ecology, trends in the consumer movement, and international relations.

School Extension Courses

This project opens the doors of the upper secondary schools and the professional training colleges to the people in the community, thereby providing them with opportunities to learn specialized occupational skills and study liberal arts disciplines. The project also encourages these schools and colleges to include current issues, such as aging and AIDS, in many of the courses they offer.

Recurrent Education Promotion

One of the high priority areas for the development of lifelong learning activities is the promotion and implementation of recurrent training and education programs for workers. The Ministry of Education, Science, Sports and Culture has, therefore, created this experimental project to promote systematic and continuing recurrent education that deals expressly with the needs of workers and industry in each community. This program relies on the use of teaching and research facilities at local universities and colleges.

Developing Lifelong Learning Information Systems

This project followed from the Second Report on Educational Reform which was issued in 1986 by the National Council of Educational Reform. The aim of the project is to encourage every prefecture to collect information and develop a computerized data base describing the various lifelong learning activities offered within the district. The data is then shared with the municipalities and its residents in order to encourage greater and more selective participation in lifelong learning activities. By the end of fiscal 1997, all prefectures in Japan will have developed a lifelong learning information system.

In the fiscal year 1995 the national subsidy for these activities and others that fell within the "Local Lifelong Learning Promotion Subsidy" program totalled in excess of $4 billion U.S. (Somucho, 1996). Relative to other economies, this is a substantial investment in a nationally structured, locally implemented, and highly systematic plan to support lifelong learning.

Difficulties with Lifelong Learning Promotion Program

Although there has been a large fiscal investment in lifelong learning within Japan, there have and continue to be a number of problems which have been identified with the structure and the implementation of the programming. According to a 1995 survey on lifelong learning, conducted by the Administrative Inspection Bureau of the Management and Coordination Agency of Japan, there is a broad need to promote lifelong learning policies more systematically and comprehensively within the society (Somucho, 1996).

The Bureau identified specific problems including the fact that local public authorities are often not very eager when it comes to implementing measures which promote lifelong learning (see Somucho, 1996, pp. 6-7). Also, coordination between the public and private sectors when conducting lifelong learning projects is lacking. A third problem relates to the length of time it has taken to reorganize non-formal education and place it into the lifelong learning system context. The fourth problem is that the administration and management of various projects to promote lifelong learning are often incomplete and not comprehensive enough. A fifth problem relates to the fact that the national subsidy is not effective in so far as guiding local authorities as they attempt to promote lifelong learning.

When specific cases are examined, the root cause of many of the problems appears to be related to the very centralized, top-down administration and budgetary system. Local governments are quite typically eager to get whatever funding might be available, often with little regard to the actual feasibility of implementing the related projects. As a consequence, outcomes are often minimal, little more than paper requirements. Meaningful content is lacking, as are uniform measures, and similar programs designed to promote lifelong learning are implemented in radically different manners in different localities across Japan.

As one example, most of the prefectures in Japan are now offering training courses and workshops for volunteers, and creating data banks that list the human resources available to act as volunteer instructors for various lifelong learning activities. However, the volunteers are now complaining that, although they are trained and willing, no one asks them to actually lead or teach any programming. In effect, they don't have any opportunities to put their training into action. Another example relates to the actual databases in certain prefectures. Because data are not systematically recorded, and often not updated, it takes too long to retrieve correct and useful information. In fact, there are some cases where usable information is simply not available at all, though data banks may exist. Clearly, these examples not only don't respond to the needs of the citizens, they may actually frustrate interest in lifelong learning activities.

From personal observations made during recent study visits to various municipalities within Japan, and interviews with officials in those jurisdictions, I have concluded that it is not the amount of money allocated to a program which determines success. In fact, it is the degree of creativity, flexibility and commitment brought to the project by the relevant administrators. Also particularly important for program success is the level of participation of residents in the process when planning, implementing and managing lifelong learning at local levels.

SCHOOL CURRICULUM REFORM IN THE CONTEXT OF LIFELONG LEARNING

In parallel with the national policies designed to move Japan towards a lifelong learning society, elementary and secondary school curricula were modified in order to incorporate lifelong learning principles and theories (Monbusho, 1989a, 1989b, 1989c). It is thought that, whereas in the past school education and lifelong learning were two independent activities, they must in fact be made one in order for both to be successful. Revised courses of study were issued in 1989, and these went into effect in elementary schools in April 1992, in lower secondary schools in April 1993, and in upper secondary schools in April 1994. The content in the courses of study incorporated specific themes and goals, as illustrated per the following précis, the purpose being to prepare citizens who will thrive in the 21st century. Though these statements of content are quite broad in nature, they are implemented through specific curriculum delivery strategies.

Cultivation of well-rounded personalities

In order to encourage the development of young people who possess richness of heart and strength of mind, every aspect of educational activities at all levels should take into account the children's levels of development within the context of the respective subjects.

Emphasize basics and the individual traits of pupils

To place more emphasis on the essential knowledge and skills which are required of every citizen in the nation, and to strengthen educational programs which will enable every child to give full play to his or her individuality, curriculum consistency at all school levels, from kindergarten to upper secondary, and for each subject, is imperative.

Cultivate competency for independent learning

To attach more importance to the nurturing of children's capacity to cope in a positive manner with changes taking place in society, as well as to provide a sound base for fostering children's creativity, the ability and willingness for children to learn independently must be emphasized.

Appreciate Japanese culture and promote international understanding

To put more value on developing in children an attitude of respect for Japanese culture and traditions, as well as increase their understanding of the cultures and histories of other countries, all children should develop the qualities exhibited by Japanese who live within the international community.

In short, the revised courses of study emphasize the importance of developing within children the nature and capacity to survive in a rapidly changing society and enable them with key skills that include problem solving and independent thinking, rather than merely providing rote learning around pre-existing knowledge and skills. The development of the desire to learn independently, and to not only cope with change but also to embrace it, is fundamental for lifelong learners. Children must shift their views on learning from the "must" perspective to the "wanting" perspective.

Modifications to the Educational Environment

Changes in the actual learning environment have been part and parcel of the implementation of the new course of study. Specifically, team teaching in public elementary and lower secondary schools has been introduced, multipurpose space to be used for a variety of learning activities has been established, increased use of computers and computer-based instruction has been added, more developed libraries are in place, and, broadly speaking, content and pedagogy which cultivate children's individual natures and needs have been developed and implemented.

At the same time, there has been a growing awareness of the need for children, particularly young children, to experience life and develop and mature through contact with their families, other human beings, their communities, and the natural world. Given the five and a half day school week in Japan, this has been difficult. But, concern over the fact that Japanese children have been experiencing less playtime and less time in the natural environment than ever before has been unabated. With this in mind, it was decided to increase the time available for children to spend with their families by implementing, since September 1992, a five day school week in Japan once a month. Previous to that, students attended school every Saturday morning. In April 1995 this was taken one step further, and students no longer attend school on the second and fourth Saturdays of each month.

The move to fewer hours per week spent in formal schooling reflects a major change in Japanese education. The goal is to support the development of learning outside the formal school system by providing families with more time to spend together.

Double Schooling

In spite of the move to fewer hours of formal schooling, the results have not been as hoped or expected. In fact, the consequences of fewer hours per week spent in class has, for many students, been a negative experience, as participation in cram schools (juku in Japanese) and private lessons has filled the gap.

According to a 1993 survey conducted by the Ministry of Education, Science, Sports and Culture, 24% of elementary school pupils and 36% of lower secondary school pupils attend private cram schools (Monbusho, 1994b). These students do so in order to supplement their regular schooling in an effort to prepare for entrance examinations. These examinations are often required for entry into the next level of schooling. Compared to a survey conducted eight years earlier, participation in cram schools by elementary students has increased by 7%, while participation by lower secondary schools has increased by 10%.

In addition to the Juku, many students in Japan enrol in a variety of private lessons. Recent surveys document (see Monbusho, 1994b) that 77% of elementary school pupils and 28% of lower secondary school pupils take lessons in such fields as calligraphy, abacus, music, dance, art, foreign languages and sports. These numbers also increased, though less dramatically than participation in Juku, during the past decade. A small number of elementary school students and 5% of the lower secondary school pupils are learning at home with tutors, and 12% of elementary school pupils and 12% of lower secondary school pupils are taking interactive correspondent learning courses at home.

Altogether, 84% of elementary school pupils and 78% of lower secondary school pupils participate in at least one out-of-school learning program (Monbusho, 1994b). For girls, the participation rate in private lessons and correspondence courses is highest, while for boys it is the cram schools. As the children get older, the purpose of cram school attendance changes from preparation and review of school lessons to preparation for entrance examinations.

These same data show that there is a link between parental expectations and attendance at cram schools, and this link appears to be getting stronger (Monbusho, 1994b). Parents who want their children to attend higher education are more likely to enrol them in cram schools, and the "higher" or more "elite" the school, the more likely is attendance at a cram school. In 1985, 34% of the parents who wanted their children to attend universities, or in some cases graduate schools, enroled their children in cram schools. By 1990 this had increased to 43%. By way of comparison, in 1985, 26% of parents who wanted their children to attend a junior college or professional school enroled their children in cram schools. In 1990 this figure had risen to 33%.

Regardless of attendance at cram schools, 61% of parents think there is too much emphasis placed on the use of these schools, and that cram school attendance can and does create a number of problems. The following have been described by parents as concerns, with the number in brackets representing the percentage of respondents (parents) who agreed with the particular concern (Monbusho, 1994b):

- in cram schools there is excessive competition in the form of entrance examinations and this has a negative influence on the development of children (58%);

- children who attend cram schools miss other important experiences related to play, community activities, and general living (52%);

- attendance at cram schools for long hours is bad for the health and physical strength of children (48%);

- career guidance in cram schools puts too much emphasis on children's grades, standard deviations and other hard data, while ignoring aptitude and the will to learn (45%);

- attendance at cram schools creates excessive financial burdens for parents (38%);

- in cram schools the priority is on "studying", while "learning" and school education tend to be cast in a negative light (34%);

- cram schools do not develop within children an interest in learning or the ability to learn on one's own initiative, and thinking skills do not develop (26%);

• children feel uneasy and are confused by the instruction given in cram schools because it is substantively different from that given in regular schools (10.8%).

Regardless of any other considerations, seeing children return home from cram schools at 10 p.m., or even as late as 11 p.m., does not leave a healthy impression.

Behavioural Problems Among School Children

In addition to the problems associated with the keen desire that Japanese exhibit for additional schooling, other problems, including truancy and bullying behaviour, have become increasingly common. The current school system is simply not meeting the needs of many Japanese students, and others are either not attending of their own volition or are being denied entry by the system.

According to a 1993 "School Basic Survey" completed by the Ministry of Education, Science, Sports and Culture, an increasing number of elementary and secondary school students were absent from school for more than 30 days for "economic reasons" (Monbusho, 1994a). As well, the number of students who refused to attend on the basis of the simple fact they "dislike ... schools" is also increasing. In 1994, approximately 71,000 elementary school students and approximately 113,000 lower secondary school students were absent from schools for long time periods, and of these, approximately 22% of the elementary school students and 54% of the secondary school students were non-attenders because they "dislike schools" (Monbusho, 1995a). Though the percentage of students who refuse to attend school is relatively small – 0.18% at the elementary level and 1.32 % at the lower secondary level – the actual number of youth affected is quite meaningful.

In addition to the problem of non-attendance, bullying at schools has become a problem. According to Ministry of Education, Science, Sports and Culture data, 11% of elementary school students and 19% of lower secondary school students have identified bullying and fighting as a problem within the school system (Monbusho, 1995a). This has been and continues to be a key factor when students identify causes at the root of negative feelings related to schooling.

Surprising to some observers, but assumed in Japan, is the custom of treating students who refuse to participate in regular compulsory education as having attended. In this way they actually graduate as if the system had served their needs and they it. In fact, there are non-attenders who, although they are technically on school grounds, spend their entire time in the nurse's room. Others who refuse to attend regular school spend their time in psychological counselling or participating in alternative "free schools." These students are not always captured in official data; however, it is increasingly clear that they complete their education, at least on paper, without ever receiving the benefits of full access to in-school learning opportunities.

A MODEL FOR THE NATION'S EDUCATION IN THE 21ST CENTURY

In July 1996, the Central Council for Education, which is an advisory body to the Minister of Education, Science, Sports and Culture, issued a report entitled "A Model for the Nation's Education in the 21st Century" (Chukyoshin, 1996). The report focused on two key phrases for the reform of education in Japan: "zest for living" and "peace of mind".

The Council argues in the report that in order to overcome the problems noted earlier, as well as others, the school system needs to provide children with the strength to survive in a rapidly changing society. This strength will come through, so the Council believes, cultivating a "zest for living" in children in a relaxed atmosphere where all can keep their "peace of mind".

The Council has described "zest for living" as a broadly inclusive term, encapsulating the following:

- the abilities and qualities to identify problems for oneself, to learn and think for oneself, to make judgements and act independently, and to seek and find better ways of solving problems as they arise;

- a pliant sensitivity that can be moved by beautiful things and the wonders of nature, a spirit that emphasizes justice and fairness and is impressed by acts of rightness while abhorring erroneous behaviour, a spirit that values life and has respect for human rights, and a warm heart that is filled with gentleness and consideration for others, is able to think from the perspective of others and is able to sympathize with them;

- a healthy body and the stamina needed to live a vigorous and active life.

"Zest for living" is considered by the Council to be a fundamental competency of lifelong learning. They argue that it is an indispensable element in creative activity and for opening up new frontiers in the context of increasing internationalization and the growth of an information-intensive society. The report points out that in order to cultivate a "zest for living", it is important that home, school and community work together, in partnership, and keep a balance in their shared commitment to education. It also declares an ambition to enlarge the opportunity for children to experience life and nature. In all of this it is assumed that in-school education must strongly emphasize the cultivation of "zest for living".

Curriculum reform focusing on these new directions has already begun, and from a structural perspective, the five day school week is expected to be fully implemented early in the 21st century. Equally important, however, is the ongoing need to re-develop curriculum content and teaching methods. A slimmer curriculum is a key goal. To facilitate this curriculum revision, it will be necessary to create a closer relationship between schools and the local communities, and to increase the educational role and mandate of the community. The business sector and labour unions are also trying to transform the work place so that parents, and especially fathers, will have more time to participate in caring for and educating their children not only at home but also through school and community activities.

Structure of Partnerships in Education

The ideal partnership between school and non-formal education in Japan has, until recently, been symbolised in a key phrase: "gaku-sha renkei". This implies that the functions of school education and those of social education should be complementary, each demonstrating its own educational utility, and with a high degree of cooperation between the two. More recently, there has been a discussion among the policy-makers to move from "cooperation" to "fusion" or "harmony" (yugo). This implies doing away with barriers that exist between schools and social education facilities, as well as with the local community. All resources, and especially human resources, would be embraced in order to improve the quality of education and learning and meet the lifelong learning needs of everyone in the society.

One of the key mechanisms to harmonize the school, home and community which has been recommended in the National Council of Lifelong Learning's latest report, is through the use of lay human resources (Shogaishin, 1996). By involving community personnel in various education activities, harmony can be achieved. Recently, and in order to allow and encourage those people with specialized knowledge and skills from outside the school to participate directly within the educational arena, a formal "Special Arrangement for Part-time Teachers Without Teaching Certificates" was established. Although still quite new, in 1994 there were a total of 2,328 people teaching through this arrangement, most of them in upper secondary schools (Shogaishin, 1996). Advantages associated with the use of lay teachers, or those without formal teaching qualifications, is the diversity they foster in terms of educational context and content. Individuality is also nurtured, and there are advantages in terms of career guidance, since students get a better first hand understanding of various occupations.

In many prefectures and municipalities, citizens have assumed various roles as instructors in and out of the formal school setting. For example, in Iizuka-shi of Fukuoka prefecture, the Iizuka-shi Board of Education recruits volunteers from the Senior Citizen's University and the Senior Citizen's Graduate School, placing them in elementary and lower secondary schools where there is demand from the schools. The volunteers provide support in a variety of instructional areas, including sports and recreation, as well as crafts, calligraphy and drawing.

In another example, schools in Ichikawa-shi of Chiba prefecture invite well-educated citizens, and social education specialists in particular, to act as community instructors. These community members provide support for specialized courses in disciplines such as environmental studies, social studies, and science, and they host various club activities. They also work to open school facilities to the community, conduct extension courses, and organize camping and hiking outings which help "fuse" the school, home and community into one. In each community there are special committees at the city level for overall planning, and each school has a Community School Committee composed of teachers, other school staff, and representatives from the Parent Teachers Association.

Within Japan, these practices are quite innovative. In order to develop and expand the framework and the programming, as well as stay true to the values and philosophy of this initiative, it will be necessary to avoid dividing the roles of the school, the home and the community. Instead, the three must work together in harmony or fusion. In this regard, a system of vertical administration should be considered. It would also be valuable if all citizens have the potential to participate in the decision making process for the planning of education in and out of school, and in the actual process of education and learning. To flourish, the process as it relates to both the school and the community should be transparent so that all the stakeholders are aware of the problems and become part of the solution.

CONCLUDING REMARKS

The Prime Minister of Japan, Ryutaro Hashimoto, stated in his policy speech at the opening of the Diet's regular session on January 20, 1997, that he will encourage school reforms from the point of view of emphasizing lifelong learning (Hashimoto, 1997a, 1997b). Increased importance will be placed on developing diverse competencies, including creativity and critical thinking, and challenging individuals to become the best they can, rather than, as in the past, emphasizing equality and uniformity. The government is prepared to allocate greater budget support for the promotion of lifelong learning opportunities in order for all Japanese citizens to achieve and enjoy an active, happy and meaningful life.

Regardless of government support, there are many problems within the current educational system and attempts to modify that system have not enjoyed universal success. The top heavy bureaucracy has been particularly ineffective. Change may not come quickly, however, some lessons have been learned. For example, it is necessary to review, and where necessary fully redevelop, traditional value systems and expectations related to teaching and learning and to develop a more flexible administrative and management style.

The current move in Japan to merge the formal school system with the non-formal system, and to create one learning system where the school, the home and the community work together, is a major shift in direction. Coupled with this is a move to a leaner, formal curriculum, the use of more lay teachers and instructors, and emphasis placed on learning to learn and learning for the sake of learning. Taken together, these suggest a very different learning system in Japan, one where the borders in education fall, and learning becomes seamless, enjoyable and lifelong.

REFERENCES

Chukyoshin. (1996). *First report of 15th session of the Central Council for Education: A model for the nation's education in the 21st Century — Zest for living and peace of mind.* [Translation]. Tokyo: Monbusho.

Hashimoto, R. (1997a). http://www.kantei.go.jp/jp/970120shisei.html

Hashimoto, R. (1997b). http://www.mofa.go.jp/f_m/hashimoto/140session.html

Monbusho. (1996). *Japanese Government policies in education, science and culture 1996: Tasks and prospects for a lifelong learning society.* [Translation]. Tokyo: Author.

Monbusho. (1995a). Statistical abstract of education, science and culture, 1995. [Translation]. Tokyo: Author.

Monbusho. (1994a). *Japanese Government policies in education, science and culture 1994: New directions in school education — fostering strength of life.* [Translation]. Tokyo: Author.

Monbusho. (1994b). *Report on the survey of cram schools.* [Translation]. Tokyo: Author.

Monbusho. (1989a). *The course of study for elementary school.* [Translation]. Tokyo: Author.

Monbusho. (1989b). *The course of study for lower secondary school.* [Translation]. Tokyo: Author.

Monbusho. (1989c). *The course of study for upper secondary school.* [Translation]. Tokyo: Author.

Shogaishin. (1996, April). *National council of lifelong learning: Report on the measures to enrich lifelong learning opportunities in the community.* [Translation]. Tokyo: Monbusho.

Somucho. (1996). *Survey on the promotion of lifelong learning for fiscal 1995,* 445. Tokyo: Author.

Grace O. M. Lee

Grace Lee is Assistant Professor in the Department of Public and Social Administration at the City University of Hong Kong. Her current teaching and research interests include public administration, human resource management and labour studies. Before joining the university, she worked in the Labour Department of the Hong Kong Government, and her experience with lifelong learning includes working as a course developer, tutor, and student advisor for part-time degree programs at the Open Learning Institute in Hong Kong. Professor Lee has published widely in a variety of journals, including *International Review of Administrative Sciences, Hong Kong Public Administration*, and *Politics, Administration and Change*. In addition, she is co-authoring books on the Hong Kong civil service and unemployment in China. Professor Lee is a member of the Hong Kong Institute of Human Resource Management, the Hong Kong Public Administration Association, and the Executive Council of the International Employment Relations Association. In her spare time, she enjoys reading and music.

Lifelong Learning in Hong Kong

by Grace O. M. Lee

This paper describes the development of lifelong learning in Hong Kong and, in that context, examines Hong Kong Government policies as they relate to lifelong learning. Survey findings from three studies illustrate the huge demand for continuing education, depict the profile of Hong Kong lifelong learners and identify the strong economic justifications for government investment in lifelong learning. However, the government generally has adopted a laissez-faire policy on the promotion of lifelong learning and the provision of continuing education. In view of the implications of lifelong learning for people and the society, this paper argues that the Hong Kong Government should play a more active role in promoting lifelong learning, particularly with regard to the less educated sector of the community which, for various reasons, is less attracted to the idea. The government should also play a more active role coordinating and monitoring adult and continuing education programs, currently dominated by private providers.

THE CONCEPT

Lifelong learning refers to the "lifelong process of continuous learning and adaptation: it is distinguished from lifelong education which refers to the structures, systems, methods and practices that attempt to enhance lifelong learning" (Candy and Crebert, 1991, p.4). Further, these authors argue that the differences between lifelong learning and lifelong education are based on the philosophical implications of the former and the practical applications of the latter. Knapper and Cropley (1985, p. 20) define lifelong education as "a set of organisational, administrative, methodological and procedural measures which accept the importance of promoting lifelong learning." Lifelong learning is not the spontaneous, day-to-day learning of everyday life but what Tough (1971) called "deliberate" learning and which Knapper and Cropley described as having the following characteristics:

- it is intentional — learners are aware that they are learning;

- it has a definite, specific goal, and it is not aimed at vague generalisations such as developing the mind;

- this goal is the reason why the learning is undertaken, and is not motivated simply by factors like boredom;

• and the learner intends to retain what has been learned for a considerable period of time.

The notion of lifelong learning wasn't acknowledged by the Hong Kong
Government until the 1970s, and the creation of the Open Learning Institute (OLI)
in 1989 was a milestone in the development of one component within the lifelong
learning infrastructure. However, in spite of this acknowledgement, later coupled
with the development of the OLI, the government continues to play a limited role
in the promotion of formal lifelong learning, and continuing education specifically.
An historical account is necessary for a full appreciation of the implications of government policy in this context. This paper includes an overview of the development
of continuing education in Hong Kong, an examination of the learner profile, and a
discussion of the economic implications coupled with recommendations for government policy makers.

DEVELOPMENT OF CONTINUING EDUCATION IN HONG KONG

In the 1950s, the concept of continuing education in the sense of providing educa-
tion beyond the typical school leaving age had only just emerged. At this time, the
Adult Education section of the Department of Education and the Kaifong
(Neighbourhood) Associations organized remedial education for adults, while the
Department of Extramural Studies of the University of Hong Kong (renamed as
School of Professional and Continuing Education in January of 1992) was visible but
quite small in scale. In 1956-57, the Extramural Studies Unit offered only 12 courses
with a total enrolment of 330 students. A decade later, the Extramural Department
(renamed the School of Continuing Studies in 1994) of the Chinese University of
Hong Kong was established. At that time, the two universities were unique in offering relatively higher level, intellectually oriented courses to a small minority of well
educated adults. However, only a year later, Caritas Hong Kong, a religious voluntary
organization, established its Continuing and Adult Education Section (now renamed
as Caritas Adult and Higher Education Service) to provide education for adults.

As the economy grew, the seventies saw a surge in demand for personal interest
and vocational courses. Enrolment at the Hong Kong University Extramural
Department grew from 5,808 in 1971-72 to 22,774 in 1981-82, an increase of 292%.
Similarly, enrolment at the Chinese University Extramural Department during this
same period jumped from 13,422 to 31,852, an increase of 137% (Chung, Ho, Liu,
1994, p. 16). Supporting this growth, the Department of Extramural Studies
(renamed as the School of Continuing Education in 1983) of the Hong Kong Baptist
College was created in 1975.

By 1978 the Hong Kong Government began paying attention to lifelong learning,
recognizing in a White Paper that, in principle, education is a continuing lifelong
process and that the development of educational opportunities for mature students
should be welcomed. A scheme for supporting certain voluntary organizations in
order to encourage them to organize and offer remedial courses, of a type specifically designed to meet the needs of adults lacking a strong, basic-level, formal education, was introduced. However, it was stated explicitly that other private providers

of adult education courses would not be subsidized by the government since mature students generally were expected to meet lifelong learning costs with their own earnings. The thrust of the policy for developing adult focused remedial courses was meant to assist and encourage voluntary organizations to complement and supplement the Hong Kong Education Department's own courses. The idea that adult and tertiary education would develop side by side to an appropriate extent if an open education centre was developed had also been expressed (Government Secretariat, 1981, p. 41).

In 1979, the government formed the Advisory Committee on Diversification. The Committee's task was to recommend appropriate responses to the consequences that were resulting from the quotas which had recently been introduced by the United States and other western countries on Hong Kong textile products. This Committee drew attention to the fact that adult education could be a retraining tool, creating cost effective, accessible, upgrading opportunities for out-of-work textile workers who were unable to enrol in full-time formal education. More broadly, it was noted that adult education could also play a pivotal role in the general upgrading of Hong Kong's labour force. Accordingly, the Committee recommended that the government embark on an in-depth study aimed at developing a clearer definition of the purpose of adult education in Hong Kong, and identify specific strategies for the support and coordination of adult education programming. Also recommended was consideration of the development of a Hong Kong open education centre with flexible entry requirements. This centre would provide education for mature students and emphasize self-learning. In 1981, the government admitted that "the adult and continuing education field was very fragmented and it was difficult to obtain hard facts on which a coordinated policy could be based" (Government Secretariat, 1981, p. 39). Following this, however, the government continued to fail at coordinating the efforts of adult and continuing education providers, and tremendous duplication of activities resulted. The problem of duplication has been particularly serious in hobby, language and secondary education courses provided by government departments and voluntary agencies. During this same time period, the government invited a Panel of Visitors to undertake an overall review of the education system of Hong Kong. The Visiting Panel recommended that:

> *all members of society should have an equal opportunity of realising their interests and aptitudes. Because education is accepted as significant in enabling the individual to remain in touch with the changing social and physical environment and in obtaining status, justice demands that access to education be broadened.* (Government of Hong Kong, 1982, pp. 73-4).

The Centre for Professional and Continuing Education of the Hong Kong Polytechnic (renamed the Hong Kong Polytechnic University in November 1994) and the School of Continuing and Professional Education of the City Polytechnic of Hong Kong (renamed the City University of Hong Kong in November 1994) were created in 1988 and 1991 respectively. During this same period, many professional bodies and commercial ventures entered the continuing education field. To this day, these providers vary in size and breadth of operation. Some are departmental extensions of large tertiary institutes, while others are stand-alone operators employing skeleton staffs. Courses range widely, from interest and leisure classes, through to professional qualifications programming. Duration also varies widely. Awards include certificates of attendance, diplomas and degrees. With only a few exceptions, most of the providers are not under the scrutiny of any academic accreditation or validation body; therefore, the standards and quality are not monitored and there is no assurance offered to the learners. Interestingly, and despite the large number of education providers, opportunities to pursue formal degrees are limited.

The establishment of the Open learning Institute (OLI) in 1989 was a breakthrough in the government's involvement in continuing education which had, until this point in time, been *laissez-faire*. What distinguishes the OLI from other continuing education providers, both in Hong Kong and elsewhere, is its focus on offering degree level courses in a part-time distance learning mode to adults, *without concern for prerequisite academic qualifications*. It has equal status with the other degree granting institutions in Hong Kong and overseas both for the purposes of employment and post-graduate studies. Throughout its first five years, the OLI received diminishing government funding and, in 1993, became self-financing. The OLI operates with its own administrative system and salary structure. There have been demands for further government subsidies to support the OLI, but as of this date the government has clearly indicated its reluctance to subsidize adult learners in this forum.

The OLI recruited its first class of students in late July 1989. More than 63,000 applications were received, and the overwhelming response resulted in long queues even for getting an application form (Watt, 1994, p. 13). The OLI was the first dedicated institute created by the government to offer degree level study for adult learners who had missed the opportunity earlier in their academic careers. Further, although free compulsory primary and lower secondary education had been introduced in 1979, university places were scarce until 1988 when the plans for tertiary education expansion were endorsed by the Executive Council. Prior to 1980, only 3% of the typical tertiary education age group could enjoy degree level education, though this grew slowly during the decade. In 1989, the goal was to increase first year, first degree places from 7% to 18% for the 17 to 20 year old age group by the turn of the century; however, the pent-up demand in 1989 was enormous. The overwhelming response to the OLI reflected the undeniable yearning of the Hong Kong adult population for degree level education, though it is also important to recognize that the timing of the OLI's introduction immediately followed the June 4th mainland China incident, thereby illustrating and amplifying public attitudes towards investing in academic credentials in the face of political uncertainties since higher education qualifications were seen as a major factor affecting emigration potential.

On balance, and even after factoring in the development of the OLI, the government's attitudes and policies towards the development of lifelong learning are still best described as *laissez-faire*. Despite expert recommendations for better coordination, equal opportunities and an open learning centre, the government has not played a central role in the provision or the monitoring of adult or continuing education. Hence, lifelong learning has been left mostly in the hands of private providers, with no assurance of quality, standards or integration of learning opportunities. The establishment of the OLI was an important milestone in the development of the formal side of lifelong learning, offering an alternate venue for degree level studies. With its open entry system and no academic prerequisites, OLI learners study at their own pace, in convenient places, and at convenient times. Furthermore, the quality of OLI graduates is maintained by high standards of academic excellence and the degrees are comparable to those offered by other government recognized Higher Education Institutes (HIEs) (i.e., the university sector). However, it is important to recognize that the government is not committed to funding or subsidizing continuing education; the OLI, and as well the continuing education departments of the degree granting institutions, are required to be self-financing.

By April 1994, about 50,000 adults had enroled in OLI courses. Over 17,000 of them are active students, reading for one of the 21 named undergraduate degree and 13 sub-degree programs. Each semester, approximately 40 courses are presented and this number increases between 10% and 15% annually. The OLI graduated its first group of students in December of 1993, and since that time studies have shown student completion rates have been quite acceptable and that the OLI is successfully penetrating the adult first degree population that it was established to serve (Dhanarajan, Swift, & Hope, 1995, p. 179). One in every 150 Hong Kong adults is an OLI student, the median age of OLI students is 27 to 29, and their median annual income is US$14,000. Although entry is open in terms of previous academic qualification, the majority of students have completed at least 11 years of pre-tertiary schooling. The following section details a more comprehensive analysis of the characteristics and motivations of lifelong learners in Hong Kong.

PROFILE OF LIFELONG LEARNERS IN HONG KONG

Three surveys carried out at approximately the same time provide a rather comprehensive picture of the characteristics and the motivations of Hong Kong lifelong learners enroled in continuing education programs. The surveys differed in scope and in terms of the target participants. A broad based random sample telephone survey, conducted by Chan and Holford (1994), determined participation rates in formal lifelong education, the nature of courses taken, motivations supporting course enrolment, and deterrents associated with lifelong learning. By comparison, Chung et al. (1994) focused on students enroled in continuing education offered by continuing education units of the University of Hong Kong, the Chinese University of Hong Kong, the City University of Hong Kong, the Hong Kong Polytechnic University, and the Baptist University, as well as the student body of the OLI. The third study, by Watt (1994), focused solely on the student population of the OLI.

Chan and Holford's study (1994) surveyed a random group of 325 Hong Kong citizens. The following summary, pulled from Chan and Holford's study, paints a general profile of those engaged in formal lifelong learning activities. (Percentages have been rounded to the nearest whole number.) The majority (51%) of the sample was between 20 and 34 years old. Sixty per cent were married, and of those 87% had children. Three-quarters of the respondents had completed only secondary school education or less, 17% per cent had studied at the post-secondary non-degree level, and 7% at the degree level or above. Approximately one-third of the sample group were not in paid employment. These included housewives, students, unemployed and retired persons. The employed group consisted of blue-collar workers (22%), white-collar workers (23%), and professionals and executives (22%). The overall percentage of respondents who had attended at least one course in the past 12 months was quite high (23%). More females (55%) than males (45%) participated in continuing education, and the participation rate was higher for younger people, especially for those between 20 and 34 years of age. The participation rate for married respondents was 17%, while the rate for single respondents was 32%. Twenty-three per cent took courses that lasted more than 100 hours, the type of study which tends to contribute towards a qualification such as a certificate, a diploma or even a degree. Some 26% of course participants received sponsorships from their employers, mostly in the form of refunds for course fees. As one might expect, the course providers were quite varied. However, of the 139 respondents that studied part-time, only 19% enroled in the continuing education divisions or the part-time programs of the HEIs and the OLI. Many more (36%), enroled in courses that were provided by private organizations. The lifelong learners described motivating factors as including the need for "self-development", the need "to improve job skills", and the desire "to fulfil interest". Monetary rewards, including promotion and salary increases, though important, "did not appear to be the main forces driving Hong Kong people to take part in continuing education" (Chan & Holford, 1994, p. 80). Upgrading academic or professional qualifications was important, and more than one-third of the respondents identified this as a major factor. Deterrents included the lack of time, inconvenient meeting time/place, lack of course information, high cost and the lack of self-confidence.

The study by Chung et al. (1994) included 3,998 students enroled in the continuing education units of the HEIs and the OLI. Both the award-bearing and non-award-bearing students were predominantly female (59%), single (69%) and below the age of 30 (62%). For the purpose of comparison, the characteristics of the labour force as reported in the General Household Survey of 1994 First Quarter were used as benchmarks. In terms of occupational distribution, the fastest growing industries in the economic restructuring process, including finance, insurance, real estate, business services, and community, social and personal services, are over-represented in the continuing education programs. Under-represented occupations include manufacturing, construction, wholesale/retail, restaurant/hotel, and import/export. Workers of different tenure and those planning for occupational shifts are motivated by different forces to enrol in award-bearing continuing education courses. Long tenure workers are more concerned with consumption related factors such as "intellectual pursuit" and "social service". Short tenure workers are more motivated by the perception of job-related benefits such as "applicability to present job" and "helpfulness to job change". Continuing education appears to be meeting adult students' needs and, according to their subjective assessment, is reasonably effective in upgrading knowledge, re-training, and teaching new skills that may bring subsequent labour market benefits that include promotions, job enhancements and career changes.

The study by Watt (1994) surveyed 731 students enroled at the OLI. Unlike the findings from the previous two surveys, where females represent more than half the participants, 56% per cent of the OLI respondents were male. Almost half of them (48%) were in the 26 to 35 age group. Slightly more than a quarter (27%) were 25 years of age or younger, and another quarter (24%) were between 36 and 45 years of age. Sixty per cent of the respondents were single, and only 28% of those who were married had children. Ninety-four percent of the respondents did not have a degree. Most were engaged in clerical, technical and administrative jobs in the tertiary industries. In general, the learners were motivated by "cognitive interest", "professional advancement", "social contact" and "social stimulation". The male learners tended to be more oriented towards "professional advancement" and "emigration considerations". Students undertaking business courses looked for pragmatic "job enhancement" while arts students pursued "cognitive interest". Married learners and those with children were more inclined to be motivated by "emigration considerations".

In summary, the three surveys document striking similarities among lifelong learners in terms of sex, age, marital status, occupations and motivation for learning. The ratio of male to female learners and the fact that a majority of the female learners are employed reflects the fact that female workers have become an increasingly large and important component of the labour force. In a labour market in which there are rapid shifts in demand for higher skills, brought on by economic restructuring, younger female workers who are not as well educated as their male counterparts find it necessary to make up for missed educational opportunities through continuing education. Experienced in the labour market, working adults can identify the education opportunities required to keep themselves abreast of vocational demands in a changing work environment. Continuing education provides the ideal mechanism for working adults to update their knowledge and skills without paying the high opportunity costs associated with quitting their jobs. The over-representation of younger and single workers in continuing education is consistent with standard human capital theory. Young workers invest in continuing education more than older workers because their opportunity costs are lower and the length of time before retirement is longer, allowing for greater opportunity to reap the benefits of the training. Single workers invest more in continuing education because the opportunity costs associated with their time are typically lower than is the case for married workers. Motivation for participation in formal lifelong learning is balanced between the self-actualizing factors of "self-development" and "cognitive interest", and the pragmatic considerations of "job change" and "professional advancement". In terms of occupation, the majority of the learners are engaged in the fast growing tertiary industries. Since there have been large employment shifts from the secondary sector to the tertiary sector, training in the tertiary industries is required in order to equip the workers with newly required skills. It also reflects the fact that blue-collar workers are not keenly interested in attending continuing education, or that "continuing education is not an important part of their culture" (Chan and

Holford, 1994, p. 82). However, workers released from shrinking secondary industries often become and stay unemployed because of the mismatch between the skills they possess and those required by employers (Lee, 1996, p. 118). The government should undertake a more proactive role, encouraging workers in these sunset industries to equip themselves with new skills in anticipation of changes as there are strong economic implications for investing in lifelong learning, both for the individuals involved as well as the broader society.

IMPLICATIONS FOR PEOPLE AND THE SOCIETY

In Hong Kong, as is the case elsewhere, there are strong economic justifications for investing in lifelong learning. Continuing education has a consumption side to it as well as an investment side (Chung et al., 1994, pp. 108-9). Education is purely consumption when it satisfies the needs of the learner without affecting earning capacity over time. Intellectual satisfaction, cultivation of the mind, personal development and higher cultural awareness are some of the consumption benefits associated with education generally, and continuing education specifically. To the extent that continuing education improves the skills and productivity of the learners and therefore enhances their earning capacity, it is an investment in human capital. Human capital theory postulates that skills and knowledge attained through education, as well as monetary capital, are vital to economic growth which promotes general productivity, and are at the same time a form of social investment because society benefits as well as the individual learners (Beder, 1981). Private benefits to the learners are the increased earnings that accrue from their investment in continuing education, while the social benefits of continuing education include not only private benefits which accrue to the individuals, in part because these end up being disbursed through the consumption process, but also include the external benefits which the individuals do not capture or internalize. (Further, there are external consumption benefits and external investment benefits - see Chung et al., 1994, pp. 109-111).

Spillover benefits accruing from education are considerable: an educated person is less likely to be involved in crime, more likely to participate in the democratic process, less likely to become unemployed, and more likely to contribute to the cultural richness of the community. The existence of second chance education produces an appearance of greater equality of opportunity and thus legitimizes the structure of the social systems (Jarvis, 1985, p. 144). Conditions that produce unequal opportunities, such as prejudice and uneven access to resources, should be eliminated. Education is a primary, valid vehicle for upward mobility (Goldthorpe, Lleywellyn & Payne, 1980, p. 232). By improving professional skills and qualifications, citizens can take higher-paid jobs and climb the socioeconomic ladder. Adult and continuing education programming provides a second chance for adults who have been denied or who have declined earlier opportunities for higher education, as well as for those whose need for further education developed later in life.

The second type of external benefits are production related. Lifelong learning promotes productivity and facilitates change in a dynamic society (Knapper and Cropley, 1985, pp. 21-4). Continuous change requires continuous learning - lifelong learning. The most obvious area in which rapid change occurs involves the world of work. Factors such as broad technological progress, the development of new manufacturing techniques, the emergence of new products, and increased knowledge are combining to produce work environments where many job types are ceasing to exist, while others are changing so extensively and rapidly that continually upgrading is *de rigueur*. Changes of this sort and magnitude clearly suggest that it is necessary for all workers, and most importantly those at fairly humble levels, to completely renew basic job qualifications several times during a normal lifetime.

This requirement for continual upgrading is particularly important in the Hong Kong context. As an open economy, Hong Kong competes on the international stage for trade and investments. Much of Hong Kong's past success relates to its adaptability and willingness to embrace change. Operating in competitive international markets, the Hong Kong work force must be very flexible and highly adaptive with regard to the delivery of the products and services it provides. This need for flexibility and speedy adaptation implies a high rate of skill and knowledge obsolescence as well as significant labour turnover in the local work force (Chung et al., 1994, p. 6). Continuing education programs, flexibly organized, implemented and then discontinued in a relatively short period of time, are responsive mechanisms for reacting to the shifting demand for skills generated by rapid economic restructuring. With greater support and direction from the government, continuing education programming in support of lifelong learning can be an effective tool for reducing skill shortages, a key barrier to economic growth, and in reducing dislocation that may lead to structural unemployment as the skills of displaced workers become obsolete (Chung et al., 1994, p. 112).

IMPLICATIONS FOR GOVERNMENT POLICY

In the context of economic justifications for lifelong learning, the Hong Kong Government should review its policies and adopt a more proactive role. Insofar as maintaining stability and promoting general economic prosperity is a prime objective of government policy, educational policy makers must adopt an "education for development" or "education for investment" model as the basis for educational planning. Further, the government must take into account the total needs of the economy, with a view to actively forecasting labour market supply and demand (Psacharopoulous & Woodhall, 1985).

With strong demand for lifelong learning, and continuing education in particular, and little competition from government funded programs, many private institutions have been attracted to the sector. An official estimate of part-time study activity in 1992 identified 750,000 persons taking part (see Chan, 1992), and it was estimated that the volume of trade in continuing education amounted to HK$2.6 billion (see Chan and Holford, 1994, p. 75). In 1993, the non-HEIs placed 2,579 advertisements for students, while overseas educational institutions advertised 2,280 times (Chan and Holford, 1994, p. 53). The market share for private institutions offering continuing education courses is much larger than that managed by the HEIs. However, the lack of government regulation and control on the private education providers compromises quality and raises questions about workers' skills levels. The government should be more active. A good start would be the implementation of standards and regulations to protect consumer rights of lifelong learners while guaranteeing the quality of worker skills.

It is worth highlighting that the least educated adults in Hong Kong are among those who are least likely to take advantage of lifelong learning opportunities. The better educated members of society have successfully demanded more educational opportunities, mostly geared to meeting their own needs. If this pattern continues, the gap between the well educated and the poorly-educated will become even wider (see Advisory Council for Adult and Continuing Education, 1983, p. 277). The notion that continuing education "is a side issue, a peripheral activity, is now out-of-date and should be revised" (Lai, 1967). At the Conference of Continuing Education Administrators in 1967, it was noted that "grown up people of all levels of education should have as much right to receiving continuing education as younger people have a right to primary, secondary or university education" (Lai, 1967). In considering the social benefits and spillover effects of continuing education, it is critically important to create a shift in attitudes, particularly among the less well-educated, to engender the view that lifelong learning is a continuing and critically beneficial process in life. The government is in the best position to take up the role for promoting and organizing a "community lifelong learning campaign".

The government must ensure that continuing education receives its fair share of attention and resources. In recognizing the value and contribution of continuing education, it is essential that the government establish a comprehensive lifelong learning system which is efficient, flexible and effective in responding to public demand. As already demonstrated, a piecemeal approach will result in imbalance and duplication. An advisory council for continuing education to facilitate and coordinate the efficient use of resources and to identify new areas of need and priorities for research, training and accreditation in continuing education would be a first good step (see Tsang, 1994, p. 134). Arrangements for consultation and collaboration should be developed, with an efficient and effective division of labour and coordination among various providers of adult and continuing education in order to improve professionalism and mobilize resources and expertise to the fullest (Swinbourne & Wellings, 1989, p. 9).

The government has a responsibility to ensure, within the resources available, the provision of a balanced range of educational opportunities to meet the needs of the whole population. With the introduction in 1978 of nine-year free and compulsory education and the gradual expansion of the number of subsidized places in Form Four and Five (Upper Secondary) to 82% of the 15-year-old age group, the educational standard has improved. Hence, it is logical for continuing education to grow at the post-secondary and degree level in the coming decades. As envisaged by the University and Polytechnic Grants Committee in its interim report in 1993, there will likely be an upsurge in the demand for continuing professional education in Hong Kong. "The pressure comes partly from employers, seeking a better or more appropriately skilled work force, partly from individuals hoping to enhance their career prospects, and partly from customers dissatisfied with out-of-date services" (University and Polytechnic Grants Council, 1993, pp. 6-7). As well as funding the public and voluntary continuing education institutions, the government should consider other strategies for supporting formal lifelong learning activities. These could include financial subsidies for those who cannot afford to invest in lifelong learning, permitting tax rebates for course fees, and providing incentives for employers to invest in staff development programs. These measures, though targeted at individuals and firms, will benefit the broader society and help insure that Hong Kong maintains its competitive position as a world class manufacturing and trading economy while at the same time responding to the needs of all its citizens.

REFERENCES

Advisory Council for Adult and Continuing Education. (1983). Continuing education from policies to practice. In M. Tight (Ed.), *Opportunities for adult education.* Kent: Biddles Limited.

Beder, H. W. (1981). Adult education should not require support from learner fees. In B. W. Kreitlon (Ed.), *Examining controversies in continuing education.* San Francisco: Jossey-Bass.

Candy, P. C. & Crebert, R. G. (1991). Lifelong learning: An enduring mandate for higher education. *Higher Education Research and Development, 10*(1), 3-17.

Chan, F. T. & Holford, J. (1994). The Hong Kong adult learner: A profile. In N. Lee & A. Lam. (Eds.), *Professional and continuing education in Hong Kong.* Hong Kong: Hong Kong University Press.

Chan, J. (1992). *Community needs, labour demand in Hong Kong: Laissez-faire versus consumer protection.* Paper presented at the International Conference on Continuing Higher Education in Hong Kong: Local Needs and International Networking into 21st Century, Hong Kong.

Chung, Y. P., Ho, L. S., & Liu P. W. (1994). *An economic analysis of continuing education: Costs, benefits, trends and issues.* University and Polytechnics Grants Council: Hong Kong.

Dhanarajan, G., Swift, D. F., & Hope, A. (1995). Planning for self financing at the Open Learning Institute of Hong Kong. In G. Dhanarajan, P. K. Ip, K. S. Yuen, & C. S. Swales. (Eds.), *Economics of distance education: Recent experience.* Hong Kong: Open Learning Institute.

General household survey: Labour force characteristics. (1994). Hong Kong: Government Census and Statistics Department.

Goldthorpe, J. H., Lleywellyn, C. M., Payne, C. (1980). *Social mobility and class structure in modern Britain.* Oxford: Clarendon Press.

Government of Hong Kong. (1982). *A perspective on education in Hong Kong: Report by a visiting panel.* Hong Kong: Government Printer.

Government Secretariat. (1981). *Hong Kong education system.* Hong Kong: Government Printer.

Jarvis, P. (1985). *The sociology of adult and continuing education.* London: Croom Helm.

Knapper, C. K. & Cropley, A. J. (1985). *Lifelong learning and higher education.* New Hampshire: Croom Helm.

Lai, T. C. (1967). *A new force in continuing education.* Paper presented at the Conference of Continuing Education Administrators, Chinese University of Hong Kong, Hong Kong.

Lee, G. O. M. (1996). Unemployment in Hong Kong: Causes and coping strategies. *Labour-Management Cooperation: From Labour Disputes to Cooperation.* Tokyo: Asian Productivity Organization.

Psacharopoulous, G. & Woodhall, M. (1985). *Education for development: An analysis of investment choices.* New York: University Press for the World Bank.

Swinbourne, E. & Wellings, J. (1989). *Government roles in adult education: International perspectives.* Sydney: Grade 88 Inc.

Tough, A. (1971). *The adult's learning projects.* Toronto: Ontario Institute for Studies in Education.

Tsang, P. W. (1994). *Adult education in Hong Kong: A study of the School of Professional and Continuing Education.* Unpublished master's thesis, University of Hong Kong, Hong Kong.

University and Polytechnic Grants Council. (1993). *Interim report on higher education 1991 - 2001.* Hong Kong: Government Printer.

Watt, Y. H. W. (1994). *Motivations of adult learners: A study of students in the Open Learning Institute of Hong Kong, with policy implications.* Unpublished master's thesis, City University of Hong Kong, Hong Kong.

Brian Rice

and John Steckley

Brian Rice is a Mohawk. Though born in the American state of New York, he has lived most of his life in Canada. He holds undergraduate and graduate degrees from Concordia University (Montreal, Canada), as well as a Native Teachers Certificate from McGill University (Montreal, Canada). Currently, Brian is finishing a Ph.D. in Traditional Knowledge at the California Institute of Traditional Studies (U.S.A.) and lecturing in the Native Studies Department at the University of Sudbury (Canada).

John Steckley is a faculty member in the Liberal Arts School at Humber College (Toronto, Canada), where he teaches courses on Native Studies. John holds a B.A. from York University (Toronto, Canada) and an M.A. from Memorial University (St. Johns, Nfld., Canada.). He has published more than 100 articles in academic journals and the popular press, including an article on Jesuit writing in the Huron language which was recognized with an award from the American Ethnohistorical Society. In his leisure time John is a drummer in a rock band.

Lifelong Learning and Cultural Identity:
Canada's Native People

by Brian Rice and John Steckley

Native people within Canada are faced with many challenges, a host of which relate to learning and culture. When should learning take place, who should be taught, what should be learned, who will do the teaching, and how should traditional learning be mixed with contemporary learning? These issues are among the most critical for the cultural survival and continuing contribution of Canada's Native populations to the larger society including its economic well being. This paper describes two elements in traditional Native culture that have been lost for many Natives, and which need to be used as mechanisms for re-establishing traditional links that will make learning for Canada's Natives a lifelong and culturally infused process. Commitment from all members of Native communities, as well as acceptance, support and respect from the dominant culture, are required in order for Natives to re-establish links to what was in the past and needs to be in the future learning through the lifespan.

INTRODUCTION

Many APEC member economies include in their populations aboriginal or indigenous people who are minorities within the larger populations. These people share common problems and, in many cases, are working towards common solutions. Increasingly, lifelong learning may be viewed as a critical solution.

With the lifelong learning context, strategies used by one group can be profitably adopted by others. The Maori in New Zealand, for one example, have broken important ground in revitalizing their minority language with *Kohanga Reo* or "language nests", in which urban Maori pre-schoolers are instructed using the Maori language through a culturally sensitive and community-based program (Fleras 1989). The success of the *Kohanga Reo* inspired the Hawaiian people to develop their similar *Punana Leo* (Kimura 1987). Both of these programs have served as instructive models for people involved in the teaching and revitalization of Canadian Native languages.

This paper will examine problems that Canadian Native people face while implementing educational policies which incorporate various aspects of their cultural traditions. It will be suggested that in order for lifelong learning to be fully and completely embedded within indigenous cultures, as once was the norm, the aboriginal community itself has to embark on a path of traditional lifelong learning. Adults must learn along with the children. Further, it will be argued that this must be done in such a way that allows for self-driven, comprehensive, relatively unstructured and informal, but still dedicated pursuit of learning. Though this may sound somewhat radical and perhaps even unprecedented, the fact is it closely reflects many contemporary notions and characteristics associated with lifelong learning, including those described by Candy and Crebert (1991, p. 7):

> *Lifelong learning is characterised by its unstructured nature, and is based on the philosophy that education should be openly and easily accessible to all at any time of life; it establishes that self-improvement and enrichment are goals that are equally as important as the need to update professional and vocational skills.*

TWO ELEMENTS OF TRADITIONAL NATIVE EDUCATION

Historian J.R. Miller (1966, p. 15) examines the traditional education of Canada's Native people with the succinct but meaningful observation, "Not all societies have schools, but all human communities possess educational systems". Crucial to the arguments to be made in this paper is the significance of two elements of "schoolless", traditional Native education. The first is what Miller terms "a heavy reliance on the use of stories for didactic purposes" (p. 17). Key here is the role of the Elders as story tellers, as lifelong learning facilitators mixing entertainment with object lessons and providing community members of all ages with a solid foundation for their cultural identity.   Jake Thomas, a highly-respected *Cayuga* Native Elder, describes his recollections as a young man when this process was used to impart traditional knowledge. Elders would visit from many of the different communities and would tell stories for hours on end. In fact, these same Elders would sometimes visit each other for months at a time, telling stories and teaching the ceremonies and roles that people of all ages needed to know in order to keep their traditional culture alive and strong.

The second important element of traditional Native education that Miller (p. 17) describes is "the utilization of more formal and ritualized ceremonies to impart rite-of-passage lessons with due solemnity". It is argued in this paper that for effective lifelong learning to take place among indigenous peoples, the use of Elders and others as storytellers as well as more formal rite-of-passage learning experiences must be incorporated into the education process if it is to be truly life long and culturally meaningful for Canada's Native peoples. Perhaps the same may hold true, in appropriately differing forms, for other indigenous people in APEC member economies.

THE OBSTACLE OF ATTITUDE

A major obstacle in the development, or perhaps more appropriately described as the re-development, of lifelong learning is "attitude". Marie Battiste, a Canadian Native *Micmac* scholar, uses the term "cognitive imperialism" to describe the dilemmas faced by Native educators in Canada today.

[Cognitive imperialism is] ... the last stage of imperialism wherein the impe-rialist seeks to whitewash the tribal mind and soul and to create doubt.
(Battiste 1986:37)

In making this comment, Battiste was referring primarily to the effects of resi-dential schools on Native people in Canada. These schools existed from the late nineteenth century until the early 1970s. They were called residential schools because the children were taken away from their parents and their communities, as much as 500 kilometres away, and made to live in residences attached to the schools. They were run by various Christian churches, and, for the most part, were dedicated towards separating Native children from their traditional culture, from their identity. By doing so, Native people came to doubt the viability of their cul-tural traditions in today's post industrial age. Through to this day these questions remain, as Natives query whether or not it is possible to be Native, and at the same time to be a successful member of the larger society.

In the educational context, these doubts continue to make Native people uncer-tain as to whether problems associated with managing their own schools are the result of colonial government interference or merely reflect the fact that their cul-tures, as they once knew them, were not "advanced" enough to acclimate to "mod-ern" life. As a result, Native educators often lack the cultural confidence to be antecedently innovative, and instead are prone to locking themselves into Western academic frameworks while not looking for alternatives that are based on tradition-al ways of knowing. In terms of the central issue of this paper, the residential schools dealt a major blow to traditional learning in general and lifelong learning in particular among Native people by attempting to, and to a large extent succeeding in, separating learning from cultural identity. It is important to add that the resi-dential schools did this with intent, the view being that by teaching Native children in a non-Native context, they would in fact become acculturated within, though not necessarily a part of, the larger society. In effect, they would become non-Natives.

TRADITIONAL CULTURE AND SCIENCE

"Modern" disciplines of study, such as science, can be taught through the medium of traditional culture. Pam Colorado, *Oneida* Native founder of the Indigenous Science Network, has developed a system for integrating traditional star knowledge and the use of contemporary star maps by describing where stars are situated with-in an appropriate cultural context. She teaches this at the Traditional Knowledge Program in the California Institute of Integral Studies. Combining the two cultural traditions helps establish and reinforce Native respect for the knowledge of their ancestors, and assists in the teaching of traditional stories while still providing instruction in a "modern" scientific discipline.

The following illustration describes merging of the traditional along with the modern discipline. In the Iroquois tradition, when the constellation *Ursa Major* reaches the most northerly point within the northern hemisphere during the month of October, it is known as the time of the "Bear and the Three Hunters". When this happens it is said that the three stars that make up the handle of Ursa Major are hunters, and that they shoot the bear. This signal marks the point in the season when deciduous leaves begin to turn red from the blood of the bear and the men then know autumn has arrived and it is time for the hunting season to begin. By incorporating traditional stories within the broader discipline, and not just in Astronomy, but also within all other areas of study, Native students develop an appreciation for and understanding of phenomena within their own cultural context.

In another example, the Fetzner Institute (Kalamazoo, Michigan, U.S.A.) is using Native languages to help symbolise the principles of quantum physics, and in fact the Institute is bringing Western scientists and Native linguists together to help develop and understand different ways of investigating the relationships which exist between all natural things. Increasingly, Native stories, terms and descriptions are being used to express holistic relationships within science that can't be easily or completely communicated with European languages.

THE OBSTACLE OF CULTURE LOSS

The problem of the loss of traditional culture, created by residential schools and other mainstream assimilative forces, remains significant. Though Native educators often assume traditional values and cultural factors still exist in most Native communities and that these can be brought directly into the educational context, this is not always true. However, what does remain, to at least some degree, are rites-of-passage and other life stage activities which can be used to re-create the broad lifelong learning framework for Native people. As a result, the importance of these activities should not be underestimated.

The traditional rite-of-passage known as the Vision Quest (see Appendix A p. 226) is particularly useful for the institutionalization of a traditional lifelong learning framework. Its success as a cultural learning tool is related in part to its versatility and adaptability. Traditionally the Vision Quest was undertaken near the time a young Native man reached puberty. Those especially gifted in receiving visions also engaged in Vision Quests during later periods in life. Today, it is primarily adults that are involved in this rite-of-passage, the purpose no longer being one of linking with adulthood, but instead linking with traditional cultural identity. This transformation of the ritual is strong evidence of its importance and adaptability.

Another aspect of the flexibility of the Vision Quest is its cross-cultural dimension. Traditional lifelong learning within Native cultures sometimes involves being taught by those who, in a broader sense, are one's "own people"; in effect, one Native community is taught by another Native community. Through this type of relationship, Native people who have continued to enjoy an established and largely unbroken Vision Quest process assist those who lost certain elements and may be unable to replicate the entire ceremony. For example, the *Kenienke:haka* or *Mohawks*, a strong Native population living almost exclusively in the southern area of Canada, near urban centres such as Montreal, Quebec, and Brantford, Ontario, have in recent years been able to strengthen their connection with the Vision Quest in part through what they have learned from the more northern, less urban *Anishnabe* or *Ojibwa*, and more specifically from members of the *Midewewin*, an organization dedicated to preserving and promoting the traditions of the Ojibwa, but also willing to help all Native peoples.

LANGUAGE AND LINGUISTIC ELDERS

The connection between the health of a minority language and the vitality of cultural identity is well established. The linguistic element of lifelong learning - some would describe it as the foundation - is challenged by Native attitudes and culture loss. Part of cognitive imperialism relates to the linguistic version of the "either/or" fallacy. This involves concluding that instruction in a Native language reduces one's ability to learn how to cope within the broader society. In other words, it is believed by some that you can't learn the Native language without giving up opportunities to learn, develop and be "successful" on the "outside". It becomes an either/or choice; you can't have both. Within Native communities, this view tends to be accepted by Native people who, through such influences as the residential schools, have lost or who never learned their own language. Not knowing the traditional language, and not benefitting from its cultural contribution in creating a strong sense of purpose and self-identity, makes it more difficult for the Natives who do not speak their own language to appreciate the value in teaching it to their children, even in Native-run schools.

Learning the language, particularly for Native people, is a critical component of the lifelong learning process. Even a modest level of instruction for Native adults in traditional language has been found to develop a strong and deep sense of cultural completeness.

Offering a variety of in-school language classes is one mode of delivery which will help ensure at least some success and consequent access to the broader opportunities associated with lifelong learning and cultural identity. However, this paper argues that more informal and less-structured ways of language learning should, or even must, be utilized. For example, Maria Campbell, a *Metis* writer of some renown and considerable ability, is a technically fluent *Cree* speaker who recently described a long and at first unsuccessful attempt to translate a traditional story. Initially her technique was based on a simple translation, word for word, phrase for phrase. In spite of the technical fit, she was dissatisfied with the English meanings. Finally, she invested much time listening to stories and having discussions with a Metis elder, and through this process came to understand the "deeper meanings". Learning language has to be much more than being able to translate words, particularly for Native groups. The purpose is to learn the culture, to be party to and fused with the lifelong learning cycle. This is most successful through non-formal association with Elders.

But how do you insure that there will always be knowledgeable Elders who can not only teach the language but who truly *know* the language? What's needed is to first overcome a second element of the either/or fallacy. This is the belief that everyone must be a speaker or else the language will die, a not uncommon view within Native communities. Discussions with various Native scholars have suggested that there are several possible solutions, one of which is for Native communities to determine which words everyone should know, and to ensure this learning is strongly supported. At the same time, the community would secure and protect the availability of a critical mass of speakers who are fully conversant in the language, the stories and the traditional culture. This is to some degree rather like the Hindu tradition of ensuring a supply of scholars who knew the holy language of Sanskrit. The Native community would be obliged to ensure that at least some of its members embarked on a lifelong learning mission of language and cultural study. Others could always learn from them, though to a more limited extent.

ELDERS AND RITES OF PASSAGE

Storytelling by Elders has always been a key element in traditional Native education, and it is critical that this be incorporated into any strategy for lifelong learning. However, this is easier said than done. Beatrice Medicine (1992), a *Lakota Sioux* educator, describes how people are often quick off the mark to say "consult the Elders", almost as if they are chanting a mantra. Often unasked is the question regarding how the consultation takes place.

People responsible for the hiring of older Indians as resource people make the mistake of merely putting them in a classroom with young children. The elders want to tell stories as they used to do but children are either too impatient to listen, or perhaps do not understand.

(Vivian Ayoungman as cited by Medicine, 1992, p. 150)

It is important to recognize the total context of the story-telling. Lifelong learning and the cultural framework as a whole are inseparable, and for aboriginal people may well be one and the same. Placing Elders in presentation-to-a-group settings, bound by highly-structured time constraints, seating arrangements and external notions of protocol and hierarchies, deviates completely from the cultural context. Traditionally children and adults alike learned from the Elders in one-on-one, repeated contacts in locations and at times that were mutually agreed upon. Further, what the Elders presented were not just isolated, amusing and interesting stories. They proffered the complete culture and people learned life through seamless, intertwined combinations of parables, allegories, lessons and even poetry, all of which were presented through entertaining and amusing conversations over a long period of time. For example, teaching traditional skills often involved telling stories to children that interwove the origin and history of the skill or the item involved with the more concrete "how to" required for basic skill competency. In today's context, Ojibwa adults being taught how to make a Little Boy Drum, also learn how healing came to their people and of the respect that must be given to the animals, plants, rocks and water that contribute to the making of the drum. Elder Jake Thomas, when he teaches Native people of all ages how to make beads, causes all of his students to become aware of the peace-making role of shell-bead wampum within the history of Cayuga culture. In order for the stories to be successful forms of modern yet traditional lifelong learning, they must serve the full cultural context.

More intense than the teaching of roles, history, skills and crafts is the range of activity associated with various rites-of-passage. Unlike other traditional learning exercises, this one is more strongly influenced by differences among various Native groups as well as spirituality, including the infusion of western-based religious beliefs. Regardless, Miller (1996, p. 16) noted that despite the differences traditionally existing among different Native groups:

the various educational practices of the Aboriginal populations did share a common philosophical or spiritual orientation. For all these peoples, instruction was suffused with their deeply ingrained spirituality, an invariable tendency to relate the material and personal in their lives to the spirits and the unseen.

But what resolve exists between traditional Native spirituality and Western-based Christian religions which have for some time in the past, and continue to, strongly influence many Native communities? For example, the *Micmac, Mohawk, Huron, Metis, Odawa* and *Algonquin* communities have integrated Catholicism as an integral part of what their Elders refer to as traditional life, and this sometimes causes confusion and conflict with regard to religious practices. The answers are not clear; however, what can be said is that there is a strong tradition of Native spiritual leaders who have during the course of their lives been "in both camps", one example being the famous Lakota holy man, Black Elk, who was once a Catholic lay preacher. This suggests that opportunities for a merging of different perspectives do exist.

Regardless, in some Native communities there is considerable conflict between Christian Natives and traditionalists who want to return to the spirituality framework which existed prior to contact with Europeans and Christians, as well as conflict between Christian sects, though this seems to lessen somewhat when the religious leaders are Native rather than non-Native. This is not a simple problem to resolve, but lessons learned from language assimilation or through incorporating science with traditional beliefs may be of some help. This paper argues that by having the entire community take part in broader spiritual, lifelong learning traditions, including rites-of-passage, the issues associated with incorporating or excluding Western spiritual beliefs will resolve themselves as Native people become stronger within their own learning traditions and therefore more able to appropriately affiliate with other views. Elders can and must perform a key role in this process.

At the heart of much of this are the traditional Native rites-of-passage, and more specifically the Vision Quest. Its utility is not just spiritual in nature, but rather it, perhaps more than other elements in the lifelong learning process, can be used as an effective bridge between cultures. The Vision Quest as an alternative form of justice provides a case in point. Just a few years ago, a young *Bella Coola* Native man was increasingly involved with crimes that demonstrated increasing levels of violence. His uncle requested the court to enforce a traditional Native remedy. The judge agreed, and the young man was left on an isolated, west coast island alone, with some food and other supplies. During the course of his several months' stay, he saw visions of the "ugly spirit" he had become, and came to learn how he should change his life. At the end of his stay the man was welcomed back by the Elders, and the entire community acknowledged his "graduation" and re-entry in the community through a "washing" ceremony. (Interestingly, the story was documented in modern fashion through videotape and the ecumenical nature of the washing ceremony symbolized by the song "Amazing Grace" which was selected as background music.)

In a related fashion, Elders visiting Native inmates in prisons have begun holding traditional ceremonies such as the Sweat Lodge and smudging, which is ritual "bathing" in the sacred smoke of sweetgrass, sage or cedar. For Native prisoners who have never had a productive relationship with their culture, this has proven to be a first step towards cultural embracement and traditional lifelong learning. It has also had a demonstrable effect on what the dominant culture refers to as rehabilitation.

IMPLICATIONS FOR LIFELONG LEARNING IN APEC COUNTRIES

What are the implications for lifelong learning with respect to indigenous peoples living in APEC countries? First, this paper documents the need for traditional learning practices of indigenous peoples to be accepted and supported, most importantly because they have validity in the modern context for both the indigenous groups and the larger, dominant cultures. Indigenous people will have difficulties being successful in the larger cultural context without strong links to and a recognition and acceptance of their underlying culture. This requires flexibility on the part of mainstream educational institutions, and an openness to the idea that "modern" takes many forms. It also requires that the indigenous peoples themselves understand and accept learning as a lifelong process for the entire community, an ideology once inherent in the traditional culture and only recently abandoned. For some, doubts will continue with regard to the viability of learning and living within the traditional cultural context while at the same time achieving success and flourishing within the dominant group. For these people, there is a need to appreciate the fact that learning which strengthens identity does not take away from the effective development of skills and knowledge, that learning is much broader than skill acquisition or cultural adaptation, and that traditional learning for indigenous people has always been and should in the future be lifelong. Required is a strategy whereby the community experiences lifelong learning together. The most consequential element of this is learning language. This does not necessarily mean that all members of the community will be fluent speakers, but rather that there will be fluent speakers within all age cohorts. Support for this from the dominant culture is critical, and learning from successful Native language programs within the APEC membership would bring powerful benefits throughout the region.

Elders and the learning they facilitate must be respected, and part of that respect entails having the Elders presenting within their traditional cultural context. Further, it is important that the cultural identity component of learning be linked with applications appropriate for life in today's society. This could include the more prosaic examples of being able to create something, as well as the more radical illustrations associated with being better prepared for various rites-of-passage. This, of course, is only radical in the sense of the culture being preserved, not in the way it is preserved. Muslims before and during their pilgrimage to Mecca, Catholics preparing for confirmation, and Jews getting ready for bar and bat mitzvahs undergo preparatory learning processes without this being thought of as taking something away from their ability to cope within modern society.

In part, the solution may relate to the packaging, or some might say unpackaging, of learning. Formal education tends to focus on stages, a rigid curricula, and grading at predetermined ages. Programs are typically centred around some form of paper promotion (diplomas, degrees, and grades), and teachers are available within established times at centralized institutions. But the lifelong learning that indigenous people must go through to keep their cultural identity strong, an indispensable part of any lifelong learning plan, requires that language learning, elders and their stories, and rites-of-passage be available at times, ages, places and sequences that reflect the needs and life schedules of individuals, not the semester-based plans of institutions. Effective lifelong learning for indigenous peoples must be developed within the traditional cultural context, not apart from it.

Canada's Native people historically had a well-established system of lifelong learning in which there was no separation between "vocational" and "cultural". Instead, all learning was intertwined, braided like a good rope. It was contact with Western culture, particularly in the form of residential schools, that unravelled the rope, making it ineffective. Natives are now reforming the rope, making it strong again by reconnecting cultural identity and lifelong learning. Perhaps in this way Canadian Natives are providing a lesson, not just for themselves, but for indigenous peoples as well as members of dominant cultures throughout the APEC region.

Member economies will be well served to recall that APEC Leaders and Ministers have emphasized the centrality of people to the APEC vision and the APEC agenda, and in particular the promotion of the well-being of *all people* within the region. The well-being of indigenous people can only be delivered in concert with strategies and programs that support the enhancement of cultural well-being, which in turn will almost certainly be an outgrowth of strong, effective and culturally embedded lifelong learning practices and programs.

Appendix A

- The Ojibwa Vision Quest -

There is a great deal of mystery surrounding the Vision Quest. Even Natives suffer from misapprehensions, in part a legacy of residential school ignorance and ethnocentric suspicions. This appendix describes simply and succinctly a traditional *Ojibwa* Vision Quest, starting with a description of the Sweat Lodge.

The Sweat Lodge itself is constructed of 16 overlapping willow poles. It is shaped to resemble the sky world above that covers the earth like a dome. The entrance must face the east as this is where all birth takes place, starting with sunrise. During the course of the day, the sun moves into the western sky, sinking below the horizon only to be reborn again the next day. All life works in this cyclical manner.

A pit is dug inside the centre of the lodge where the grandfathers are received and where they meet mother earth. The grandfathers are stones, the oldest elements in creation. As such, they hold the mysteries of all the ages. Before the grandfathers are brought into the lodge, they are first placed at the bottom of a sacred fire in front of the lodge. Here they are heated until they become white hot. How long the Vision Quest seeker plans to sweat will determine how many stones will be called upon to guide him in the Sweat Lodge. Between the Sweat Lodge and the sacred fire is a pathway of cedar. Once this path is made it may never be crossed.

When the Sweat Lodge and sacred fire are prepared, the Elder calls the participants to the fire. They then throw sacred tobacco into the fire and pray. This is how the people give thanks to the creator. The Elder then tells how the Sweat Lodge came to be, a story which describes how a little boy was sent to the seven grandfather spirits in the star world during a time of great sickness and was given the gift of the Sweat Lodge to bring back to his people for healing. A water drum is placed inside the Sweat Lodge close to the entrance. This drum is called the Little Boy Drum in remembrance of the little boy who brought back the teachings. The participants greet the drum as they enter. It has seven stones that surround the top, representing the seven grandfathers who first gave the little boy the teaching. When the Sweat Lodge is occupied, the Elder sings the ceremonial songs that have been handed down from generation to generation.

The grandfathers are then brought in to the lodge and placed in the pit. The Elder throws water onto the grandfathers, and the steam makes the lodge quite hot. After the initial sweat is completed, each participant goes to a small lodge and begins to meditate. Cedar leaves are placed around these lodges in order to provide protection from any evil spirits that may try to enter during fasting. From this stage on, the participants are alone with their thoughts. Each day, however, the Elder queries each participant about his spiritual experience. That is the only time the participants speak.

The nights are said to have their own special nature. The first is described as the night of doubt, where participants pray but are uncertain about what will happen. Hunger is mitigated by a feeling of excitement. The second night is one of fear, sometimes known as the dark night of the soul. Participants realize that their bodies are beginning to weaken, and they may question their resolve. The third night is the night of the spirit. It is often said that if something meaningful is going to happen, it will occur between the beginning of the spirit night until the fast is finished.

On the fourth day, the sacred fire is lit once again and participants drink cedar tea before entering the Sweat Lodge. After the fast, breaking another sweat is not easy. Participants often feel faint, and those that have had visions during the four days are given tobacco to offer to the grandfather spirits, thanking them for what they have been taught or shown. This might include thanks for being given a name, or discovering one's totem animal.

When the final sweat has been completed the participants leave the lodge. At this stage they are given cedar leaves to put into their shoes in order to have the strength to walk away from the lodge. The final stage of the Vision Quest is the feast. This includes eating and giving gifts to the Elder as well as to others who have assisted the participants in preparing for the quest. This reflects the value of generosity, highly respected by the Ojibwa.

This rite of passage is one of the most important events in Native life. The loss of it is one of the reasons why Native youth and adults have so many difficulties adjusting to the outside society. The Vision Quest is where Natives begin to find themselves in the journey of lifelong learning.

REFERENCES

Battiste, M. (1986). Micmac literacy and cognitive assimilation. In J. Barman, Y. Hebert, & D. McCaskill (Eds.), *Indian education in Canada: Vol. 1 the legacy* (pp. 23-44).

Candy, P. and Crebert, R.G. (1991). Lifelong learning: An enduring mandate for higher education. *Higher Education Research and Development 10*(1), 3-17.

Fleras, A. (1989). Te Kohanga Reo: A Maori renewal program in New Zealand. *Canadian Journal of Native Education 16*(2), 78-85.

Kimura, L. L. & 'Aha Punana Leo. (1987). The Hawaiian language and its revitalization.   In F. Ahenakew & S. Fredeen (Eds.), *Our languages, our survival: Proceedings of the Seventh Native American Languages Issues* (pp. 117-123). Saskatoon: Saskatchewan Indian Languages Institute.

Medicine, Beatrice (1987) My Elders tell me. In J. Barman, Y. Hebert, & D. McCaskill (Eds.), *Indian education in Canada: Vol. 2 the challenge* (pp. 142-152). Vancouver: UBC Press.

Miller, J. R. (1996). *Shingwauk's vision: A history of Native residential schools.* Toronto: University of Toronto Press.

Ma. Celeste T. Gonzales

and Ma. Concepcion V. Pijano

Ma. Celeste Gonzales completed her doctorate in Education at the University of San Francisco. At present, she is the Chair of the Education Department at Ateneo de Manila University. Aside from teaching, she is called upon by other departments in the University as well as other institutions to facilitate workshops in teaching methodologies and curriculum development. When she is not busy teaching or leading workshops, she is at home tending to her garden.

Ma. Concepcion Pijano holds an M. A. in Public Administration from Pace University in New York. She serves as Executive Director to two national institutions: the Federation of Accrediting Agencies of the Philippines and the Philippine Accrediting Association of Schools, Colleges and Universities. She has been with the latter organization for 19 years, assisting schools in their quest for quality. She has logged more than 1,000 school visits and consultancies, and lives out of a suitcase. She is a confirmed workaholic.

Non-formal Education in the Philippines: A Fundamental Step Towards Lifelong Learning

by Ma. Celeste T. Gonzales and Ma. Concepcion V. Pijano

The Philippines formally recognized the importance of education in its 1987 Constitution and, perhaps more importantly, made specific reference to non-formal learning, informal learning and a variety of delivery approaches and learning systems. Clearly, this established a base for and support of lifelong learning within the Philippines. However, regardless of how well meaning the intentions may have been, formal support for lifelong learning does not automatically create an integrated, fully developed system for learning opportunities that are available to all citizens everywhere throughout the lifespan. This paper describes the development of elements of what will, hopefully, in time, become an integrated system of lifelong learning. Specific emphasis is placed on non-formal programs of learning, and these are described in some detail. The paper concludes that there is an imbalance between resources currently expended on formal education when compared with the monies spent on and the potential that exists within the non-formal subsystem. Policy makers are encouraged to redress this.

INTRODUCTION

Philippine society has for some time recognized and clearly institutionalized the paramount importance of education for economic and social development. Specifically, Article XIV of the 1987 Philippine Constitution contains nineteen sections dealing with "Education, Science and Technology, Arts, Culture and Sports". The 1987 Constitution is the first Philippine Constitution containing an entire article on education, advocating the rights of all Filipino citizens to quality education at all levels and making education accessible to all (Villacorta, 1987, p. 50).

Current leaders in education, government, religion, business, non-governmental organizations, and professional associations also posit a lifelong learning orientation. They believe it is important to educate Filipinos not only for academic gains, but also to support economic competitiveness, cross-cultural understanding, social transformation and the development of a national identity. All of this will then bolster the platform from which the Philippines reaches out to the rest of the world, especially the Asia-Pacific Rim community.

According to Cross (1981), lifelong learning is based on the notion that education is a continuing activity taking place throughout the lifespan for everyone who lives with the accelerating pace of change. It involves learning by people of all ages and from all walks of life using the multiple learning resources of society in order to learn whatever they need or want to learn. Three basic concepts about the nature of lifelong learning are implied. First, people should be encouraged to become self-directed learners and active agents of their own education. Second, there are alternative educational sources besides schools and colleges that serve the educational needs of people. Third, these learning resources and experiences are available to all, anytime, and on a full-time or part-time basis. Lifelong learning also "establishes that self-improvement and enrichment are goals that are equally as important as the need to update professional and vocational skills" (Candy & Crebert, 1991, p. 7).

THE PHILIPPINE EDUCATIONAL SYSTEM

The Philippine educational system is composed of two major subsystems, the formal and the non-formal. The formal subsystem consists of sequential academic schooling at several levels. Included are six years of elementary education, four years of secondary education, and a variety of post-secondary programs. The post-secondary levels include one to three years of technical/vocational education or a minimum of four years of tertiary education. The completion of each level is a prerequisite for entry into the next. The formal education subsystem provides students with basic skills of numeracy and functional literacy and grants certifications of proficiency in different academic disciplines. As is the case in most formal subsystems, the three levels of schooling focus for the most part on academic training and scholastic competence.

Non-formal education may be described as any organized and systematic learning conducted largely outside the formal educational subsystem that may or may not provide certification. Definitions aside, the characteristics of non-formal education make it quite different from the formal subsystem in a number of ways. First, non-formal education addresses the needs of those who were not able to participate in the formal subsystem. In this regard, the clientele are quite different. A substantial number dropped out of the formal subsystem, the reasons for this being numerous though mostly centred on poverty. The organization, specific activities and delivery methods associated with non-formal education are designed to meet the express needs of the distinct clientele (see Congressional Commission on Education, 1993). At present, non-formal education in the Philippines has four thrusts:

- family life skills, including health, nutrition, childcare, household management, and family planning;

- vocational skills;

- functional literacy;

- livelihood skills.

Non-formal education is provided separately and apart from the formal school subsystem and does not serve as an entry point to a higher level of formal education. In this regard the two subsystems are separate, and little room for movement between the two is currently available. Non-formal education concentrates on the acquisition of skills necessary for employability and competitiveness in the labour market. The availability of non-formal education expands educational access to more citizens representing a variety of demographic characteristics, socioeconomic origins, and general interests (Department of Education, Culture and Sports, 1994). In effect, the non-formal subsystem makes education available to a very large number of Filipinos who would otherwise not have an opportunity to participate in any educational opportunities.

Given this brief description of the formal and non-formal subsystems of education in the Philippines, it is apparent that a subsystem of lifelong learning would lean heavily on both. Candy and Crebert describe lifelong learning as an overarching umbrella, perhaps best characterised as a context rather than a program or programs, from whose central hub radiates a variety of spokes each of which, perhaps, represents an educational opportunity. To take the metaphor further, in the Filipino context, the formal and non-formal education subsystems, as defined and described here, are major spokes, from which a whole series of other spokes arise. (It is important to note that neither reflect the very significant and important "informal" component of lifelong learning.)

Most interesting and germane to this paper is the fact that "schooling" in the Philippines has been equated almost entirely to the formal subsystem rather than the non-formal, in spite of the size and importance of the latter. The structured period of formal schooling, which involves preparation for adult life and which ends when one receives a diploma, is the primary concern of legislators and educators. The formal diploma, for its part, is the passport to economic and social mobility and, as a result, emphasis and support in terms of resources, policies and programs have always been given to the formal education subsystem notwithstanding recent efforts to promote the visibility and advantages of the non-formal subsystem (Centre for Research and Communications, 1986).

THE DEVELOPMENT OF NON-FORMAL EDUCATION

A review of the development of the educational system in the Philippines from the early 1970s onwards reveals that there have been significant efforts directed towards the development and institutionalization of non-formal education. With the advent of the report by Faure et al. (1972), commissioned by the United Nations Educational, Scientific and Cultural Organization (UNESCO), the non-formal subsystem was accorded more importance and was seen to be a viable alternative to the formal subsystem.

In 1977, the government institutionalized non-formal education through the creation of the Office of the Undersecretary of Non-formal Education under the Ministry of Education, Culture and Sports. This was accomplished through Presidential Decree 1139. The office of the Undersecretary for Non-Formal Education was given responsibility to serve as the coordinating arm for integrating all programs of various government and non-government entities involved in non-formal education in the Philippines. At this time, almost all government agencies participated in the design and delivery of a variety of nationwide training programs, the goal being to upgrade the Filipino human resource base through literacy programming, industry training and upgrading, and value enhancement for development.

In 1979, non-governmental organizations (NGOs), including schools, church organizations, civic groups, and foundations, initiated various non-formal education programs in response to the government's call to help the less fortunate sectors of society. At this time one group of private institutions banded together to form what became the Private Institutions and Schools National Association in Non-Formal Education (PRISNANFE). This organization integrated under one office the efforts of a conglomeration of private schools undertaking non-formal education projects.

In the same year, the Philippine Accrediting Association of Schools, Colleges and Universities (PAASCU) encouraged its member schools to initiate and implement non-formal education programs and projects. Service to the community was included in the criteria for accreditation. An accredited institution was expected to become directly involved in non-formal education and to offer programs "beyond its walls".

In the mid-80's, the Association for Non-Traditional Education in the Philippines (ANTEP) was established through the generosity of the Canadian government and the Association of Canadian Community Colleges (ACCC). Two national organizations, the Catholic Educational Association (CEAP) and the Association of Christian Schools and Colleges (ASC), spearheaded the development of ANTEP.

Later, the Education for All (EFA) movement of UNESCO gave the non-formal education subsystem its greatest boost. It served as a powerful impetus and support for those engaged in non-formal education to meet the basic literacy needs of all children, youth and adults. By acknowledging that the formal subsystem was not able to meet the broad learning requirements of individuals and communities, a variety of educational projects and delivery systems was necessary. EFA stressed the importance of various non-formal learning approaches and methodologies to supplement, complement and enrich formal education. Following the work of EFA it can be said that acceptance, if not support, for non-formal education was institutionalized within the Philippines.

CURRENT DEVELOPMENTS

The importance of non-formal education, as well as informal and indigenous education, was further elevated by recognizing and supporting it in Article XIV, Section 2 (4) of the 1987 Constitution:

The State shall encourage non-formal, informal and indigenous learning systems, as well as self-learning, independent, and out-of-school study programs, particularly those that respond to community needs, and provide adult citizens, the disabled, out-of-school youth with learning in civics, vocational efficiency and other skills.

The non-formal education programs in the country focus on the following thrusts:

- the promotion of literacy programs for the attainment of basic skills that include numeracy and functional literacy and which are basic needs for every individual;

- the development of livelihood skills which manifest in the individual specific competencies that prepare, improve, and enhance employability and economic productivity;

- the expansion of certification and equivalency programs, which are administered by the formal education subsystem, into the non-formal sector.

As described earlier, non-formal educational programs are conducted by both public and private sector organizations. Within the government, the primary agency is the Department of Education, Culture and Sports (DECS), and more specifically the Bureau of Non-Formal Education. Almost all government agencies, including the Departments of Health, Agriculture, Trade and Industry, National Defense, and Social Welfare and Development, as well as the National Manpower and Youth Council (NMYC), have developed and integrated non-formal education into their activities.

In 1994, the Philippine educational system was restructured. Two government entities were created: the Commission on Higher Education (CHED) and the Technical Education and Skills Development Authority (TESDA). The CHED is responsible for both public and private institutions of higher education as well as degree-granting programs in all post-secondary educational institutions. TESDA, on the other hand, was created by merging the NMYC and the Bureau of Technical and Vocational Education. Both CHED and TESDA support and relate to a variety of non-formal educational programs.

Regardless of government support and involvement, the strongest proponents and most active implementors of non-formal education in the Philippines have been and continue to be the private schools, churches, civic organizations and foundations (Congressional Commission on Education, 1993). Their activities range from basic level skills training through to values formation. The delivery systems for many of these activities include seminars and workshops, community assemblies, television and radio broadcast programming, correspondence courses, home visits, self-directed learning modules, and practical work. The curricula designs of the various programs vary from agency to agency and are tailored to the specific needs of the clientele. Variety is the key.

SPECIFIC PROGRAMS

A multiplicity of specific non-formal education initiatives can be grouped within five major sectors. Although non-formal in nature, some have links to the formal education sector.

Literacy Education

Literacy education is spearheaded by the Bureau of Non-Formal Education (BNFE) with its functional literacy program that includes the teaching of reading, writing and arithmetic. Literacy classes are organized by DECS for out-of-school youth and adults in all of the 14 regions of the country. Other BNFE programs include the Magbassa Kita Project and the Female Functional Literacy Program assisted by UNICEF. The Magbassa Kita Project uses the phonosyllabic method for teaching reading. This approach shortens the learning time for basic literacy to just three months. The project has benefitted more than a hundred thousand out-of-school youth and adults in 13 regions of the country. The Female Functional Literacy Program focuses on the seven provinces in the Visayas and Mindanao where illiteracy rates among women are highest.

Livelihood Skills

The Livelihood Skills Development Program of DECS is designed to equip the unemployed and underemployed with vocational and technical skills through short term training programs. Examples of courses offered include dressmaking, electronics, cosmetology, bookkeeping and cooking.

Also involved in skills training is NMYC. It targets clientele in the out-of-school youth group, as well as, like DECS, the unemployed and underemployed. The three key NMYC skills training program groups are Industrial Training, Rural Training and Special Programs. In 1990, 133,473 trainees graduated from these three programs (Congressional Commission on Education, 1993, p. 130).

In skills training, the Dual Training System is used where students receive a combination of in-school and in-workplace programming. For four days per week the trainees receive practical exposure and specialized training in a firm, coupled with theoretical instruction twice a week. This program relies on strong cooperation between schools, industry and government.

Another livelihood skills project of the BNFE, in collaboration with SEAMEO-INNOTECH (South East Asian Ministers of Education - Regional Centre for Educational Innovation and Technology), is the Development of a Learning System for the Improvement of Life (DELSILIFE). This is a community-based education intervention program that seeks to improve the quality of life and develop skills needed locally within the community. Programs are offered in nutrition, literacy and handicrafts.

Certification and Equivalency Programs

Equivalency programs enable students to enter or re-enter the formal school subsystem using a certification system that accredits learning from outside the formal subsystem. As well as supporting re-entry into the formal school subsystem, equivalency programs accredit skills and job experiences for employment purposes.

One of the best known certification and equivalency programs within the Philippines is the Accreditation Equivalency Program (AEP) of DECS. School drop-outs completing this program re-enter the formal school subsystem or gain work in a company through the accreditation of knowledge and skills acquired via a variety of non-formal avenues. This program is based in part on the Philippines Educational Placement Test (PEPT) which is used to assess student proficiencies.

The Continuing Learning Delivery System is one of BNFE's Distance Education programs. It is geared towards developing competencies associated with secondary school curriculum, and evaluating and certifying students as graduates of the secondary level. Subjects are completed in modules and students work independently. Upon completion of the modules, students sit for a comprehensive examination. The BNFE is currently developing a non-formal Alternative Learning System. Classified as an alternative equivalency program, it is designed to run parallel with and be comparable to the formal school subsystem.

With the issuance of Executive Order No. 330 on July 30th, 1996, the newly created Commission on Higher Education has been given a mandate to expand and strengthen tertiary education equivalency and accreditation programs. This is clear recognition that education and the acquisition of expertise and skills are processes that take place within the work environment and that credit should be given for this.

Continuing Education Among Professionals

Recently, there has been increased emphasis and concern related to the need for degree holders to regularly acquire new skills and take part in professional updating programs. It is the Philippines Professional Regulations Commission which formally encourages professionals to keep abreast of developments in their professions. Recently, this has been entrenched by the requirement that all practising professionals must show proof of compliance with new requirements for continuing professional education before they are allowed to renew their licenses (Rosas, 1996, p. 3).

School and University Initiatives

In 1995 the University of the Philippines (UP) established the UP Open University (UPOU), an institutional arm which embodies the philosophy of open learning. Unlike the United Kingdom Open University, the UPOU operates within the system of a conventional university and remains linked to the academic programs of the UP. UPOU reaches out, through the distance and open learning modes to people who are not able to participate in classroom style education. As more programs are offered, the UPOU will be tapping a variety of cooperative agencies nationwide to act as on-site support and learning centres. The UPOU could be the "biggest" campus because it will offer courses throughout the entire country (Doyo, 1995). Distance and open education are gaining acceptance and being promoted within the Philippines.

Accredited institutions which account for 15% of the total number of schools in the country have established a variety of non-formal educational and learning programs and projects that respond to the specific and immediate needs of the communities they serve (Federation of Accrediting Agencies of the Philippines, 1996). These programs focus on a multiplicity of curriculum areas using an assortment of delivery approaches. Included are livelihood skills training, vocational and technical training, course delivery through night programs at high schools for adult learners, instruction in family life skills for men and women, and courses and programs in values formation. These programs and the associated extension services seek to empower learners and improve the quality of life for the individuals and their families. Faculty members from the institutions often act in an advisory capacity for the programs, alongside students and graduates. At the same time, these institutions often support the wider community by making their physical resources available for non-formal education, and they establish ongoing links with non-formal education graduates in order to provide them with upgrading and retraining initiatives. In various ways, therefore, the broader programming associated with non-formal education directly provides and supports greater service to the community.

CONCLUSION

Despite significant progress in the development and delivery of non-formal educational opportunities within the last two decades, there continues to be a shortfall in terms of what has been achieved versus the full potential to enrich the overall system of education. Although the government formally supports non-formal education, and has specifically referred to its importance and value in the constitution, funds for non-formal educational programs continue to be inadequate. DECS-BNFE has openly lamented the disparity between funds allocated to formal and non-formal education (Congressional Commission on Education, 1993). It has been estimated that less than 8% of the intended clientele for non-formal education was accessed in 1990, while the formal education subsystem succeeded in reaching 57% percent of its target clientele. This situation is due largely to the very small budget appropriated for non-formal training in terms of the client size. Lack of funding and other resources hampers the delivery of non-formal education services in the Philippines, and will likely continue to do so into the future. This lack of support or imbalance in funding can be attributed in part to the strong and long-entrenched interests within the formal subsystem, coupled with the relative newness of the non-formal subsystem. Policy makers and politicians need to be encouraged to assess the relative potential of the two subsystems, the formal and the non-formal, and direct funding in such a way as to benefit the largest numbers of learners. In turn, this will have the greatest economic effect and benefits for the Philippines as a whole.

Another problem which has been encountered in the delivery of non-formal education is the lack of coordination and systematic planning amongst the various implementing agencies. Each organization has specific target clientele and activities, but there remains considerable overlap. As a result, there is a continuing need to consciously evaluate the functions and resources of all the deliverers involved with non-formal education in order to minimize overlap and maximize the use of scarce resources. Closer coordination and ongoing communication between officials and leaders in both the public and private sectors, as well as government and NGOs, are required. Systematic linkages are the key to avoiding duplication. This issue assumes greater significance in the context of the restructuring of the educational system and the creation of both the Commission on Higher Education and the Technical Education and Skills Development Authority. There is a need to clarify the roles of each of these agencies in terms of the delivery of non-formal educational services in the country.

It is important to acknowledge that many initiatives related to non-formal education have been implemented within the Philippines during the past few years. However, there remains a need for the educational system broadly, and especially institutions of higher education, to redirect programs and services in an effort to balance these with the larger society's need for lifelong learning opportunities. Higher education institutions need to assume a far greater role in promoting the goals of lifelong learning. Universities and colleges should take the lead by introducing a full range of innovative programming and other academic services. Curricula should embrace and reflect technological, economic, social and cultural issues, and non-traditional delivery methods should be part of every institution's repertoire. In a rapidly changing world, colleges and universities need to cater to the demands of a more diversified clientele and respond to the growing needs of the labour market.

The movement towards non-formal distance education is a timely one. Distance education has the potential to contribute significantly to human resource development by widening access to higher education and reducing costs for students, industry and the government. In the Philippines, a country with more than 7,000 islands, distance education will open windows of opportunity, break down barriers of time and space, and unleash the full potential for non-formal education as a viable alternative to the formal subsystem. This is the opportunity that faces the Philippines as it stands at the threshold of the third millennium, and policy makers need to focus directly and with deliberate reflection on the opportunities presented.

REFERENCES

Candy, P. & Crebert, R.G. (1991). Lifelong learning: An enduring mandate for higher education. *Higher Education Research and Development 10*(1), 3-15.

Centre for Research and Communications. (1986). *The Philippines at the crossroads: Some visions for the nation.* Manila: Author.

Congressional Commission on Education (EDCOM). (1993). *Education and manpower development programs: Vol. 1. Areas of concern in Philippine education, Book one. Making education work.* Quezon City, Philippines: Congressional Oversight Committee on Education.

Constitution of the Republic of the Philippines - 1987. (1987). Manila: Rex Book Store.

Cross, P. (1981). *Adults as learners.* San Francisco: Jossey-Bass.

Department of Education, Culture and Sports. (1994). *Education 2000: The first two years.* Manila: Author.

Doyo, C. P. (1995, July 2). UP's Open University. *The Sunday Inquirer, 10*(18), 7-8.

Faure, E., Herrera, F., Kaddoura, A., Lopes, H., Petrovosky, A., Rahnema, M., & Ward, F. (1972). *Learning to be: The world of education today and tomorrow.* Paris: UNESCO.

Federation of Accrediting Agencies of the Philippines. (1996). *FAAP Directory.* Manila: Philippines.

Rosas, N. L. (1996, October). *Professional regulation of continuing education.* Paper presented at the First National Congress on Continuing Education, Manila, Philippines.

Villacorta, W. V. (1987). Education and the new constitution. In R. J. Bonoan (Ed.), *Higher education for national reconstruction* (pp. 44-52). Manila: National Book Store.

Judy Huang

In 1992, Judy Huang received her doctorate from the University of Georgia (U.S.A.). Currently, she is Head of the Library at the National Open University in Chinese Taipei. Her foremost goal is to make the university's library an integral part of the lifelong learning fabric for people in Chinese Taipei. Dr. Huang's research interests include the use of multimedia in learning, as well as distance education. When she is not directing and developing the library or working on research projects, she devotes her time to family life with her three children and husband.

Distance Education: A Key Strategy for Lifelong Learning in Chinese Taipei

by Judy Huang

In this era of advanced technology and with the explosion of the information age, lifelong learning has become a requisite for full-time employment. In Chinese Taipei, distance education may be the most important vehicle for the delivery of formal, vocationally-oriented lifelong learning. It is open, cost-effective, moderately uncomplicated to establish, and minimizes the bureaucracy typically associated with fixed institutions. Changes in distance education within Chinese Taipei during the past decade have been profound, and include the establishment of the Open University in 1986, the subsequent development of degree programs, the creation of new open universities in Taipei and Kaohsiung, and the development of distance education programs within the community of established and traditional universities. The future for lifelong learning in Chinese Taipei appears bright, in large measure related to the successful implementation of distance education as a tool for broad workforce development. Further, with the aid of distance education, the striking economic development enjoyed by Chinese Taipei during the past thirty years may well be replicated during the course of the next three decades.

INTRODUCTION

In every corner of the globe, in developed and developing economies alike, and in every facet of their daily lives, people are increasingly dependent on information. At the same time, the world's storehouse of information is increasing, at an accelerating rate. Given this dependency on knowledge coupled with the tremendous expansion in the sheer quantity of information, it has become critical for every working adult to accumulate educational capital throughout the lifespan. Not so long ago, workers were trained once; now, workers are trained, re-trained and trained again. As well as the benefits that accrue to individuals who learn throughout the course of their lives, the economic benefits for the society as a whole are enormous. Thus, the nature and value of individual educational development is clearly and openly intertwined with societal benefits accruing from broad economic development. Given the nature of Chinese Taipei society, this symbiotic unfolding is highly significant.

Lifelong learning is inclusive. In this regard it is markedly different for several reasons than its much smaller subset, the school-age learning experience. Lifelong learning includes experiences that range from the very general and theoretical, through to the applied and pragmatic. It also deals with the vocational and the avocational, from birth to death. In effect, it is the total sum of experiences that affect an individual's behaviour and abilities throughout a lifetime. Clearly, the avocational side of lifelong learning, if indeed it can be segregated, does not fit even as an extension within the conventional school setting. Small overlaps aside, they are for the most part quite different sets of experiences, including context, goals, motivations, supporting environments, and learning modes. But what of the ongoing vocational element of lifelong learning? Is it merely an extension of what and how we learned as full-time students in elementary, secondary and so-called tertiary education? In fact, the characteristics associated with lifelong vocational education, and this includes the curricula, the goals, the methods, and the institutions such as they are, must be by design and need considerably different. Simply put, conventional colleges and universities and the associated systems are not adequately equipped to respond to all the vocational training needs of a learning society.

In Chinese Taipei and elsewhere, the number of traditional colleges and universities and the available seats within these schools are inadequate to meet the educational and vocational training needs of adults. However, even if the quantity issue was resolved, the design of traditional college and university schooling is conceptually limited, and has as its primary foundation and method of teaching a focus on younger adults. Older learners are not attracted to and do not learn effectively in this type of environment. As well, conventional colleges and universities seldom teach applied, practical knowledge that relates to on-the-job skills. In no small measure this is a reflection of the limited job experience of most teachers working within this system. More significantly, conventional colleges and universities are limited in location and time, making it impossible for working adults, the rural population, and disadvantaged groups to access these institutions. Adults need an educational system that has the flexibility and diversity, including breadth and depth, to provide advanced education for everyone. The most obvious and effective solution is distance education.

DISTANCE EDUCATION

Distance education has became an important and meaningful element of higher education systems in many developed economies. Perhaps the most well-known example of tertiary level distance education is the United Kingdom's Open University. However, distance education has also caught on in the Netherlands, Canada, Sir Lanka and many other countries. Following are reasons why distance education has become so wide-spread, and is seen by many educators in Chinese Taipei as critical for the ongoing development of a seamless system of lifelong learning in this economy.

Distance education transcends the conventional barriers of location and time. It reflects characteristics of openness and continuity, and compared with fixed institutions can be expanded or contracted with relative ease. Adults find the delivery method to be fitting and relevant, perhaps the best model for acquiring a variety of specialized knowledge and skills at different times for diverse purposes throughout the lifespan. There is no need to leave full-time employment, no need to take large amounts of time away from the family or leisure pursuits, and no need to travel long distances according to fixed schedules. Similarly, the elaborate bureaucracies associated with traditional schooling are minimized and registration is simple, particularly where an open admissions policy is in place.

The number of places in conventional colleges and universities and school systems will always be limited, reflecting in part the fixed capacities of the campus and the faculty. Developmental and operational costs associated with conventional colleges and universities are high. By comparison, distance education has lower start-up costs, and much lower operational costs. With "campus-free" distance education, variable costs, once the system is operational, tend to be flat. That is, beyond a relatively small number of students, the costs per student are the same or slightly less. The increasing use of technology to broaden the scope of distance education has great potential for further reducing costs per student. In Chinese Taipei, the distance education-based National Open University, with its budget of NT$800,000,000, accommodates approximately 30,000 adult students each year. By comparison, the National Taiwan University, one of the larger universities in Chinese Taipei, has an annual budget of $NT3,500,000,000 for its 21,000 students (Ministry of Education, 1996). Though gross numbers of this sort beg some level of refinement, the differential costs remain substantial and manifest.

During the past decade, distance education in Chinese Taipei has gained some measure of acceptance from the public and considerable confidence has been expressed by the government. Research done by Hsieh (1996) on the economics of distance education supports the conclusion that it has had a very positive influence on labour force skills development and economic growth. As a result, distance education has been identified by the government as a key tool on the Chinese Taipei human resource agenda. During the next three decades it is expected that distance education will be one of the fundamental instruments for developing and re-developing vocational and technical skills throughout the economy, thereby keeping the workforce skilled to a level of competitiveness that will build on the already substantial economic development witnessed during the past thirty years. There is no doubt that within Chinese Taipei, distance education is a key strategy for supporting the broader lifelong learning context.

THE DEVELOPMENT OF DISTANCE EDUCATION

To appreciate the role of distance education in Chinese Taipei, it is necessary to at least touch on the recent and broader evolution of the society because the development of distance education interrelates directly and conspicuously with significant social and economic changes. The following section of this paper discusses this development in two parts. First, the relationship between Chinese Taipei society and distance education is examined. Second, the history of specific distance education institutions is detailed.

Chinese Taipei Society and Distance Education

In the following paragraphs, three historical time periods are used to frame the development of distance education as Chinese Taipei society evolved both socially and economically.

From about 1949 to the mid 1960s, Chinese Taipei was recovering from conflict. The strong economic growth seen in the late 1960s was yet to emerge, and the broader society was showing only moderate signs of what was to be an exceptional transformation. During this period, production was tied closely to natural resources, while farming, fishing, forestry and animal husbandry constituted the mainstays of the economy. As a consequence, educational attainment for the majority of the population was limited to elementary and secondary education. During this period the literacy rate hovered at a respectable but not lofty 67% (all percentages are rounded to the nearest whole number), and average annual personal income was around US$2,800. In order to dramatically improve the general welfare of society, the government not only strongly sought to restructure economic production, but also implemented a coherent and broad-based educational system by building new schools for all levels of learners and establishing a specialized educational broadcasting system as well as correspondence schools. The effort to remedy the shortcomings of the school system of the day quite fortuitously laid the foundation for later distance education efforts.

From the middle of the 1960s to the beginning of the 1980s, industry and commerce grew steadily, soon becoming the focal point of society in Chinese Taipei. During this period the government initiated numerous public enterprises, such as the "Ten Major Construction Projects", to strengthen the industrial infrastructure and provide many employment opportunities. This had a major influence on economic well being, and significantly increased the average income level within Chinese Taipei. As well as emphasizing economic development, the government heavily stressed the development of education. In fact, education and economic development were from the outset critically linked in the minds of policy makers. During this period the average level of education increased dramatically, and the literacy rate finally reached 90%. These changes spurred rapid economic growth, while commerce along with heavy and light industry became the most productive sectors of the economy, responsible for approximately 43% of the GNP. The proportion of the population working in the commercial and industrial sectors also increased dramatically, from 22% in 1961 to 41% in 1980. As a spin off to this growth, the need for skilled business managers also increased (Huang, 1993a). On the basis of these developments, educational policy makers upgraded supplementary education programs to create the first distance colleges which were collectively named the "Taiwan Provincial Taipei College of Business". This was not unlike fuelling the fire with more fire since this new institution fostered additional potential for economic development and kindled a strong desire for even more distance education during this period of accelerating change.

From 1980 until the present, all sectors of society in Chinese Taipei have felt the pressures associated with the need to continually restructure for economic progress in the face of demands made by the world marketplace. Although the internal economy remained the key focus for development, broader society, including the government and cultural sectors, entered a period of critical self-examination in order to identify new ways of thinking, new ways of producing and competing, and new value systems that would enhance the overall growth and development within Chinese Taipei. Specifically, more openness and involvement were sought in politics, the economy, and education. As these were attained, the working class and middle class grew, as did their influence. The demand for access to higher education rose steadily in order to meet the needs of an increasingly affluent and questioning society. In concert with the development of the information age and global competition, it became apparent that the higher education institutions of the day, along with the college level distance education program described earlier, were not sufficient to meet the demands or standards now required by a strongly motivated and diverse population. In 1980, the urgent need for increased and open higher education for personal and professional growth resulted in plans developed by the Ministry of Education for a full-scale distance education university. After five years of research, including evaluation of open universities around the world, Chinese Taipei's highest institution of distance education - the National Open University, often referred to simply as the Open University - was established in 1986.

During the past ten years, Chinese Taipei's trade-oriented economy and the development of higher technologies have been significant factors fuelling the demand for higher education including distance education. This expansion of education has proceeded in concert with the many social changes which occurred during the three historical periods. As illustrated in *The Relationship Between the Background of Students at the National Open University and Social Structure in Taiwan* (Huang, 1993b), the relative importance of commerce within different geographical areas of Chinese Taipei was, in fact, critical to promoting greater participation in the National Open University. Also, broadly available new technology and lifestyle-related advertising further motivated people to aggressively seek flexible and diversified educational programming in order to take advantage of the opportunities associated with a modern and developed society.

In short, distance education in its first phase acted as a supplement in order to respond to the shortcomings of traditional or conventional education. But as broad educational consciousness was raised among the people, and the concept and benefits of lifelong learning became clearer, distance education has come to occupy a pivotal position within the educational infrastructure. In fact, it can be argued that the development and delivery of high quality lifelong learning opportunities of many types throughout Chinese Taipei will in the future be most directly related to the further development of distance education facilities. Is distance education the principal panacea for supporting economic growth and encouraging personal development? For Chinese Taipei, the answer may well be yes.

Distance Education Institutions

Distance education, defined as an education form that delivers teaching activities through correspondence or other forms of technology such as television and computers, had its origins more than thirty years ago when the China Correspondence School instructed students through learning packages delivered by correspondence. In 1966, when the Ministry of Education established the Taiwan Provincial

Taipei College of Business, television and radio were incorporated into the delivery methodologies, and face-to-face tutoring was used only as an auxiliary technique. These methods of distance delivery are described within Chinese Taipei as the "Four Links of Instruction for Distance Education." As suggested earlier in this paper, the Taiwan Provincial Taipei College of Business was established to support broad economic development by targeting education at the business and management sector. Though in retrospect the activities of this college may seem limited and almost superficial, its influence both in terms of human resources trained and the development of demand for distance education was considerable.

As Chinese Taipei continued to develop, and the general population gradually came to accept the notion that lifelong learning was directly linked to personal development and economic well being, the desirability of having university level distance education became widely accepted. Hence, the National Open University opened its doors in 1986 with a mandate that included "improving the quality of human resources and broadly raising the national level of culture and education" (see Cheng, 1995). Through 1996, the National Open University has graduated twelve-thousand adult students and countless more have benefited from the wide variety of educational programs broadcast by the university. Over the course of the past decade the university has focused on three broad distance education goals.

The first of these goals has been to deliver high quality education broadly throughout Chinese Taipei. More specifically, this has been an effort to enhance access, particularly for the disenfranchised or disadvantaged, including handicapped adults, adults in rural areas, and women.

The second goal has been to develop degree granting programs. When the National Open University was founded, it was permitted to grant diplomas only. After years of lobbying and negotiating with government and the legislative Yuan, regulations giving the university the right to confer undergraduate degrees were passed in 1994. During recent discussions, it was agreed that the National Open University will soon include a graduate school. The implications for those citizens who are unable to attend a traditional university are significant.

The third goal has been to increase the number of academic departments. The National Open University was originally established with just three academic departments. However, after years of program development work, since for a distance education institution it is not a matter of simply hiring faculty, three more departments have been added. Currently, the six academic departments include humanities, business, social science, living sciences, public administration, and management & information.

PARTICIPATION IN DISTANCE EDUCATION

Distance education in Chinese Taipei has proven to be a popular form of participating in the lifelong learning process. In addition, it is increasingly accepted that more educational opportunities help build prosperity for society in a broad sense, not just for the participants. For these reasons, research has been conducted to determine who participates in distance education, motivations for participating, and changes that are occurring in the distance education population. The following summarizes some of the findings.

According to 1995 survey data collected by the National Open University, the male/female participation ratio is 30/70. Most students (65%) are 25 to 39 years of age. Interestingly, government employees comprise the largest single group (33%) of participants, with participants from the business sectors representing the second largest group (18%). These numbers clearly reflect the mix of programs and courses currently offered. Slightly more than half the students (51%) graduated from high school before entering the National Open University, and a large percentage of them (44%) were college graduates from either junior or senior colleges prior to admission.

Another recent study, based on responses from 1489 questionnaires and titled "Needs Assessment of Adult Students in the National Open University", describes National Open University participants as typically married, middle class, and with incomes slightly below the average (Huang, 1996). These students put a high value on lifelong learning, and consider learning and education useful for increasing their abilities to perform effectively on the job as well as for obtaining promotions. The reasons given for participating specifically in the National Open University's distance education programming include augmenting knowledge and skills, pursuing personal interests, raising personal educational levels, enjoying the social aspects associated with university, and increasing the chances for job promotion. These students expressed considerable satisfaction with their experience at the National Open University, and especially commented on increased self-confidence, the strong feelings of independence, and increased interest in learning.

Comparisons with Chinese Taipei's conventional higher education system are interesting. While the percentage of female students has increased from 43% in 1980 to 51% in 1994 in the conventional higher education system, the percentage of female students has increased from 61% in 1986 to 70% in 1995 at the National Open University. Similarly, in the Open Junior College system female participants represented 79% of the total student body in 1994. Clearly, the distance education approach is more attractive to women as reflected by their higher participation rates. Secondly, and perhaps more interestingly, women's participation in distance higher education is increasing at a faster rate than in the conventional system.

The age of distance education participants has also changed. When the National Open University first enroled students, 34% of the participants were 24 years of age or younger, 27% were 25 to 29 years of age, and 17% were between 35 and 39 years of age. These groups represented the three largest by age and accounted for almost 80% of the student body. By 1991 this distribution had changed considerably. The 25 to 29 years of age group became the largest, representing 26% of total participation, the 30 to 34 years of age group became the second largest, representing 20%, and those under 24 years of age comprised only the fourth largest group. The 1996 figures again show the 25 to 29 and 30 to 34 years of age groups as the two largest, but they are now almost the same size, each representing approximately 23% of the total student body. The percentage of students under the age of 24 continues to decrease. These data suggest a trend for increased participation from older adults and decreased participation from younger adults. Initially, participation in distance education by young adults may have simply been a novel substitute for conventional universities (Huang, 1993a, 1993b, 1996).

Participants with business or trade related jobs, such as sales or international trade, were the largest group of students in 1986, and at this same time government employees were the second largest group. By 1996 these two groups had reversed themselves. During the same period, increased participation rates from the service sector, education, and the military were observed.

Overall, distance education and distance education learners in Chinese Taipei have changed radically during the past three decades, most notably with more women, more older adults, and more non-business sector workers participating. These changes are related at least in part to the new academic departments at the National Open University, particularly those such as health care which attract greater interest on the part of female participants. Other factors that are thought to have greatly influenced the makeup of the participants include the broad acceptance of the importance of learning through the lifespan as well as social change, economic development, the technical revolution, and the arrival of the information age. Given that the National Open University, the centrepiece for distance education in Chinese Taipei, is only ten years old, it is clear that more research needs to be conducted in order to determine how the institution can best respond to its mission and meet the needs of its stakeholders.

DEMAND FOR DISTANCE EDUCATION

The outlook for distance education and its role in Chinese Taipei is quite bright. Ten years ago, the notion of a wide-ranging university level distance education program was a dream. Now it is a reality, along with broad public support for distance education programming. According to a 1995 survey on distance education, 82% of the public who were questioned agreed that "Open University graduates are positively recognized by Chinese Taipei society." As well as the positive views among the general public, the fact that one third of Open University graduates has continued or returned for further education after graduation from the university speaks directly to the benefits received (see Huang, 1995).

A 1995 workforce survey found 17% of employees unable to find jobs appropriate for their training, 6% holding positions for which they were not trained, and 7% underpaid for the roles they performed (Executive Yuan, 1996). These groups, along with the growing portion of the population seeking to more broadly improve its employment options, suggest that the need for lifelong learning, adult education, and distance education in particular will continue to grow. For those who are currently working, distance education provides opportunities for skills upgrading in the areas in which they are currently employed, or to learn entirely new skills in anticipation of changing jobs. Distance education is particularly important for women, in part because within Chinese Taipei society there is a heavy obligation for women to stay at home when they have young children. It is not unusual for these women to be out of the workforce for as long as ten years, and keeping up-to-date through the traditional school system is not feasible. If they are interested in employment after their children become older, these women can take advantage of distance education before they are actually ready to take a job. As well, there is increasing demand from senior citizens, the handicapped, members of the rural population, and those who are interested in pursuing knowledge for its own sake. Clearly the distance education market is diverse and vibrant. To have reached this stage in a mere ten years is astonishing.

POLICY ENVIRONMENT

The success of the distance education program and the Open University has given rise to a variety of policy reviews. These have focused on three prime areas: the issue of open entrance to higher education; the development of additional open universities; and competition in distance education from traditional universities.

Education policies are continuing to emphasize the need to ensure opportunities for all and avoid creating second class citizens for whom access to lifelong learning opportunities are restricted. In this regard, the system of entrance examinations is being questioned. In the past, all applicants to the National Open University were required to pass an entrance examination. On average, approximately 75% were successful, and the remainder were simply turned away. However, a recent decision by the Education Reform Committee has eliminated the entrance examination. Applicants are now required only to complete a registration form. The open entrance policy has certain weaknesses, such as having the potential to negatively affect the quality of courses or overwhelm the institution with large numbers of applicants; however, it has most certainly addressed the issue of access and opportunity. In general, it is felt that by opening access, the educational fabric of the society as a whole will be advantaged, and the economic output of the economy will increase. Thus, every member of society will, in the end, benefit.

Until recently, the National Open University had a monopoly on distance education throughout Chinese Taipei. However, the legislative Yuan recently passed a regulation designed to open the market for the establishment of new open universities. This change will give learners increased access to post-secondary distance education and is also expected to serve the secondary purpose of enhancing quality in education through competition. At this stage, the two largest cities in Chinese Taipei, Taipei and Kaohsiung, are in the process of establishing open universities. Since the National Open University and these two new universities will be competing with each other for students, improvements in student services, the quality of teaching, and the variety of subjects available is expected.

The obvious success of distance education has begun to attract the traditional universities into the distance education field. More of them are now beginning to implement distance education programming, in some cases with government support. Recently, several of these universities have begun experimenting with distance delivery tele-teaching through advanced technology computer systems and satellite communications.

Taken together, the government policies which have influenced open admissions, the creation of new open learning universities, and the involvement of traditional universities in distance delivery, have had the effect of multiplying the number and types of distance learning opportunities as well as increasing the quality of distance learning in Chinese Taipei. If past experience holds true, these opportunities will generate even more demand, which in turn will encourage the government and the institutions to create additional opportunities. The result is more people engaged in lifelong learning, a higher educational level being achieved within the society, increased production and economic growth, and, ultimately, a higher standard of living enjoyed by all.

CHALLENGES

Although the prospects for distance education in Chinese Taipei are justifiably promising, some problems do exist and must be resolved. This will require the cooperation of the institutions, government, administrators, faculty and students. For example, the distance education system spends a large portion of its budget on the development of textbooks and the production of instructional television and radio programs. To date there has been little cooperation among institutions in so far as sharing instructional materials or production costs. Typical of bureaucracies, this waste of money and time is frustrating for the faculty and students. Improvements could be made quite easily by simply coordinating development efforts among distance education institutions with similar needs, both domestically and overseas.

The target population for distance education is adults; however, instructional methods in distance education only rarely incorporate approaches typically believed to be the most appropriate for the teaching of adults. Andragogy, a term popularized by Knowles (1976), is the art and science of helping adults learn. It rests on four assumptions: adult learners are increasingly self-directed; experiential learning techniques have more meaning; learning should be applied; and learning should lead to increased competencies. Distance education has certain limitations, and the assumptions inherent in andragogy are difficult to incorporate. For example, developing and incorporating a learner's self-direction within a distance education program is very challenging. Beyond that, many adult learners and instructors continue to rely on methods that limit independence, critical thinking, and intellectual inquiry. Finally, performance evaluation is restricted by traditional examinations, and question-answer types of homework. More diverse and creative approaches, such as written project reports, are not often seen. If distance education is to fulfil its mission, more effective, adult-based delivery and evaluation tools must be incorporated.

More than 70% of present distance education course participants are "teacher dependent", that is they are most comfortable when they have at least some face-to-face, traditional contact with the teacher (Huang, 1996). It is difficult to reconcile this with adult education and learning autonomy, leading ultimately to self-directed lifelong learning. Self-direction and independence, however, are not easy to achieve for adults in Chinese Taipei, and the problem may have its roots in the educational foundations of the secondary school system and the passive nature of learning therein. The need for independent inquiry and critical thinking skills is growing within the workplace, and distance education programs need to foster and model these behaviours.

Although there is strong recognition of and support for graduates from the Open University, some areas of the economy continue to give preference to graduates from conventional universities. Further, less than half (45%) of the graduates from the National Open University feel that their academic achievements are fully appreciated by their families or their employers (Li, 1996).This suggests that although distance education has made great inroads in Chinese Taipei, the belief that qualifications from the National Open University are second class persists. It is thought, though, that as distance education graduates demonstrate success in all walks of life, greater acceptance will be forthcoming.

Distance education first began as supplemental to the mainstream system of education, as a stop gap or backfiller. It provided some relief to those who needed a second chance, and gave an economic boost to the economy. Notwithstanding its humble and modest origins, distance education in Chinese Taipei is a critical component of today's educational platform, and perhaps the most important element in the lifelong learning infrastructure that will move the society ever forward in its quest for economic growth and an increased standard of living for all its citizens.

REFERENCES

Cheng, Y. Y. (1995). *The positioning of distance education: An introductory view from the R.O.C. experience.* Proceedings of the International Conference of South Africa, University of South Africa, Pretoria, R.S.A.

Executive Yuan. (1996). *Monthly bulletin of manpower statistics of Taiwan.* Taipei: Directorate General of Budget Accounting and Statistics.

Hsieh, M. J. (1996). *Distance education and manpower development in Taiwan.* Taipei: Hen-Hsuen Publishing.

Huang, T. J. (1993a). *The state of distance education in Taiwan.* Proceedings of the 1993 International Symposium on Adult Education. Chien-Young, People's Republic of China.

Huang, T. J. (1993b). *The relationship between the background of students at the National Open University and social structure in Taiwan.* Proceedings of the 1993 Adult and Distance Education Conference, pp. 241-260. National Open University, Taipei.

Huang, T. J. (1995). *Taiwanese need for distance education.* Taipei: The Department of Research and Development at The National Open University.

Knowles, M. S. (1976). *The modern practice of adult education.* New York: Cambridge Books.

Li, L. C. (1996). *Self evaluation and work of NOU graduates.* Taipei: The Department of Research and Development at the National Open University.

Ministry of Education. (1996). *Educational statistics 1996.* Taipei.

Carolyn M. Mann

Carolyn Mann holds an M.B.A. from Wright State University (U.S.A.) and is completing a doctorate at Ohio State University (U.S.A.). She has been involved with prior learning assessment for the past seventeen years. At the present time she is a Professor at Sinclair College in Dayton, Ohio, where she is responsible for the administration and marketing of the college's prior learning assessment program. In 1994 Carolyn was asked to direct the Ohio office of the American Council on Education's Program on Noncollegiate-Sponsored Instruction. She holds responsibilities for the marketing and coordination of corporate training programs for college credit, and is a senior trainer with the Council of Adult and Experiential Learning. Carolyn is an avid reader and a collector of teapots.

Prior Learning Assessment: U.S. Experience Facilitating Lifelong Learning

by Carolyn M. Mann

Traditional lock-step education and training excludes many learners from the lifelong learning continuum, particularly those who are older or who come from disadvantaged groups, and at the same time further entrenches a costly and time consuming method for upgrading skills and qualifications within a workforce. By way of contrast, prior learning assessment is an effective tool for ensuring that duplication in training and education is absent or at least minimized. It is also an excellent resource for adult learners to assess their learning needs, review their commitment to upgrading, and clearly identify the resources that will be required. In addition, faculty who become involved in prior learning assessment activities are strongly challenged to review their methods and approaches to education. This paper argues that of the three main techniques for prior learning assessment, portfolio development and review is the most appropriate. For APEC member economies, with their ever growing needs for an up-to-date and highly skilled human resource base, the advantages of effective and wide spread prior learning assessment programs are substantial.

INTRODUCTION

Linear notions of education as they apply to the development of a workforce are outdated. The days of educating only the young are passé. Growth and development in an environment characterized by rapid change requires people who understand the importance of information, and who use that information to construct knowledge, think creatively and function productively (Cross, 1991).

Employers no longer want workers who simply come to the job on time and do what they are told when they are told. Today, an unskilled low-wage workforce has limited advantages in a global environment. What is required by employers are workers who are thinkers and learners, and for this reason today's workplace increasingly emphasizes lifelong learning. Various reports suggest that highly desired skills include the abilities to read, write, compute, communicate, manage personal issues, adapt, work in groups, influence others and, perhaps most importantly, learn. Managers need to be able to engineer innovation and lead others during times of uncertainty, to find creative solutions to problems that arise from change, and to facilitate their own and their employees' learning in order to keep abreast of current trends and information (see for example Marsick, 1988).

In fact, successful organizations will require individuals to do more than adapt, change and learn new skills. Workers must become self-reflective and critical of what they learn, how they learn, and why they learn. As well, they must assume more responsibility and control over how their learning activities are structured. Marsick (1988) suggests that a new organizational model is emerging, one that demands the following characteristics:

* the integration of personal development and technical or vocational development;

* a focus on group as well as individual learning;

* a concern for critical reflection, for problem setting, as well as for problem solving;

* an emphasis on informal learning;

* an organizational model which functions as a learning system.

The key theme is one of being able to manage and master learning throughout the lifespan.

There is a strong and well documented connection between investment in education and training and its influence on the availability of qualified manpower which, in turn, leads to stronger economic growth and development. In this day and age, with rapid technological change and increased competition of a global nature, learning throughout the lifespan has become a critical component of workforce development. Just as important is the need to ensure that training is not duplicated or unnecessarily repetitive. Economies where training is done once in an effective, appropriate and well documented fashion, have a distinct advantage. Prior learning assessment is a critical tool in the documenting process, and hence a key asset in support of lifelong learning processes.

The ongoing development of APEC's human resource base is not a task to be left strictly to the education and training community nor to the business or industrial communities. It requires the creation of strong, effective links between these communities in order to develop learning packages that respond in a timely and effective fashion to workers' needs throughout the lifespan. Prior learning assessment programs serve as one of these critical links, encouraging adult learners to build on learning from a variety of recognized, non-collegiate experiences and providing them with a means for accessing specialized, higher technical and vocational education.

PRIOR LEARNING ASSESSMENT

In North America, prior learning is the term used to describe learning which has been acquired through non-academic life and work experience, typically in advance of formal contact with a college or university. Prior learning is the learning that adults often want recognized in the form of college credit toward academic degrees or other credentials. As well, prior learning may be used to gain entry into higher level training without first enroling in preparatory or prerequisite courses.

Interest in prior learning assessment was spurred by the acknowledgment some decades ago that learning activities are not planned and delivered solely by educational institutions. Allen Tough's (1967) ground breaking study alerted educators to the depth and breadth of learning activities in which adults typically participate. For example, this study found that 90% of adults are involved in at least one learning activity annually, and the average learner conducts five learning activities per year with an investment averaging 100 hours per learning effort. In addition, 80% of all learning projects are initiated by the learner, not by institutions, and adults are often involved in a variety of learning activities which are not sponsored or directed by higher education. Though these findings may seem somewhat dated in the context of the 90's, a time when we have come to accept much of the lifelong context associated with today's adult learners, the importance of learner-initiated, learner-driven, and non-institutional learning should not be taken for granted.

The variety of learning activities undertaken by adults is endless, and many organizations, whose primary function is something other than education, are directly involved in the business of supplying learning experiences. Business and industry, as well as not-for-profit and governmental agencies, spend billions of dollars annually on training. Cross (1991) states that in the United States only one-third of organized learning opportunities are delivered by institutions of higher education. The remaining two-thirds are provided by a vast array of other "schools" and non-college providers, offering courses for both professional development and personal fulfilment.

Prior learning assessment is a system of evaluating and granting college credits to adults who can articulate and document that they have achieved the objectives of a given course or set of competencies. The rationale supporting prior learning assessment rests on the notions that knowledge is valid regardless of the source and that most learning occurs outside the walls of higher education. The Council for Adult and Experiential Learning's (CAEL) early validation study documented the fact that college-level learning can and does occur outside of a college classroom, and, more importantly, there are valid and reliable ways to evaluate this learning for college credit (see Willingham & Associates, 1976). Numerous colleges and universities have confirmed and supported this finding by helping thousands of adults to receive recognition for college-level learning and continue their studies in order to complete academic degrees.

One of the major misconceptions associated with prior learning assessment is that it is recognition of prior *experience*. In fact, a focus on experience suggests nothing more than time on task and in no way guarantees that learning took place. To merely record that an individual worked as a purchasing agent or as a small business owner for three years documents only the time. The intention of prior learning assessment is to take the process a step further and to explore what the person learned from the experience about purchasing, business ownership or management. What skills and knowledge were acquired? Are the competencies equivalent to competencies achieved in courses offered at colleges and universities?

Academic evaluation of prior learning shifts the focus to the learner and the learning, and away from where the learning occurred or how long it took. While the rationale is simple and easy enough for faculty and administrators to conceptualize, implementation of prior learning assessment raises difficult but interesting questions about teaching and learning. Clearly, learning is not an isolated event. It takes place within a complex context of people, policies, procedures and structures, many of which have developed over a long period of time during which intellectual barriers and vested interests have become ingrained. Prior learning assessment challenges faculty notions of education and questions who should be in control of the learning process. It also brings into question the traditional faculty role of being central to the learning process as well as being the gatekeeper and bearer of all knowledge.

The most basic question regarding prior learning assessment is often asked by potential students as well as by the faculty: *Is the process worth the effort?* An individual who has owned his own business and managed 20 to 30 employees over a ten-year period may be quite knowledgeable in the areas of business ownership, management, finance and marketing. Another individual who has worked in the social services area may have learned about counselling, communications and how to work through a host of agencies in order to assist clients. Clearly, a great deal of learning has taken place, and demonstrable outcomes of these experiences can be articulated and documented. For adults learners, in most cases the benefits accruing from the investment of time in the process are well worth the effort. Adults don't want to replicate learning, and will often not bother with higher education if duplication is required in order to meet the needs of the institution. Thus, when presented with the alternatives of taking a class that repeats what is already known or of documenting skills and competencies, adult learners more often than not choose prior learning assessment.

In addition to granting academic recognition, prior learning assessment helps adult learners set realistic goals and develop educational plans. Students are given the opportunity to reflect on and assess their varying levels of expertise and calculate how these relate to overall degree plans, as well as determine how these plans will influence personal and career development. Self-esteem typically increases as adult learners receive concrete validation of their learning based on prior experiences, often beyond their expectations, and this in turn influences motivation. As well, students gain confidence in their ability as learners, and develop an increased appreciation of the value associated with lifelong learning.

In some circumstances, particularly where credit is given for portions of courses or programs, prior learning assessment enables faculty to make maximum use of what students have already learned and to build on that learning, linking classroom learning to real world experiences. Through this process, faculty gain a better perspective of the types of learning that occur in other organizations. In addition, the mechanisms for assessing prior learning require faculty to reflect on assumptions they hold with regard to teaching and learning, and often encourage them to make changes in course content, delivery and evaluation in order to create learning experiences which are more meaningful to the learners.

Students are attracted to institutions with prior learning assessment programs, and they more often stay to complete their degrees at those institutions and return later to attend other courses in order to update their knowledge and skills. Business and industry are attracted to institutions with prior learning assessment programs because they see these programs as time considerate and responsive to the needs of adult learners, thus employees are more motivated to upgrade, learn on a regular basis, and pursue academic degrees. The process avoids duplication of learning efforts and enables organizations to make better use of their training dollars. In many cases, the relationships that develop between specific businesses and colleges through structured prior learning assessment programs and skill training have spun off other advantages, sometimes in the form of shared technology and courses delivered at work sites. The results tend to be mutually beneficial, an effective foundation for all partnerships.

METHODS

In the United States there are three basic approaches commonly used to award credit for prior learning: tests, evaluation of non-college sponsored training, and assessment of individualized portfolios (see Miller and Daloz, 1987). Testing remains the principal method used by colleges and universities, and a CAEL sponsored survey of educational institutions found that 76% of the responding institutions awarded credit for standardized tests. By contrast, this same survey found that only 42% of responding institutions awarded credit through comprehensive assessment of prior learning from life and work experiences by portfolio assessment (Fugate, 1991).

Tests and Non-College Sponsored Training

Two types of examinations are typically used to evaluate prior learning: standardized examinations, and proficiency/challenge examinations. Standardized tests in a limited number of different subject areas have been developed and marketed by such groups as the Educational Testing Services (ETS) and the American College Testing Services (ACT). The examinations are prepared by a committee of experts, and test results are compared against traditional college courses to develop normative scores. In some prior learning assessment environments, college and university faculty prepare proficiency examinations for their own courses which students can then challenge in order to receive academic credit. These examinations have the advantage of expanding the subject areas available to students, and they also allow individual faculty members to be more directly involved in the preparation of the test and the evaluation of individuals.

As an alternative to standardized tests and faculty developed challenge examinations, the American Council on Education (ACE) has, since 1945, evaluated military training and made recommendations for appropriate college credit. In 1976, ACE expanded this process to include the evaluation of other non-college sponsored, ongoing training programs. These recommendations are published for colleges and universities to consider when awarding college credit. ACE evaluations are conducted by teams of faculty drawn from a variety of institutions. The variables used to ascertain recommended college credits include the intended learning outcomes, the length of training time, the levels of training complexity, and the assessment methods employed to evaluate achievement of learning outcomes.

These are difficulties associated with non-college sponsored training and testing. For example, ACE program evaluations do not have universal utility for students interested in prior learning assessment since not all students have been in the military nor have they all participated in a program evaluated by ACE. The cost of program evaluations by ACE must be covered by the organization whose training is being evaluated, and as a result not all organizations can afford to participate. Prior learning is not always easily categorized into a traditional subject area, and as a result standardized tests may not fit with student learning. Even when prior learning can be related to a specific subject area, such as drafting, there may not be a standardized test or challenge examination available. Testing is in fact a very conventional classroom tool. When used for prior learning assessment it reflects a traditional technique being imposed on a non-traditional learner, the result often creating incongruence between the subject and the learner (Knapp, 1975; Simosko, 1988).

Portfolio Assessment

Neither testing nor non-college sponsored training assessments provide mechanisms for helping adult learners to evaluate their own learning and to develop plans for enhancing or building upon previous knowledge. Many colleges and universities have, however, developed a third approach, a portfolio process which can be used as a basis for awarding credit for non-college learning. While less widely used, Miller & Daloz (1987) describe the portfolio process as offering both methodological and educational advantages over the other two methods. Advising and assisting the learners to identify college-level learning and determining how such learning relates to overall degree plans are crucial components of a portfolio process. In addition, portfolio evaluation provides a more holistic approach for prior learning assessment than is the case with standardized tests and program evaluation. The portfolio process focuses on the identification and articulation of learning as well as the measurement and evaluation of the learning. Standardized examinations and ACE program evaluations, by comparison, focus only on measurement and evaluation of prior learning. Standardized tests and program evaluations may, however, be incorporated into the portfolio process, allowing individuals and institutions to take advantage of the strengths of all three methods.

A portfolio for prior learning assessment is a formal document which details learning acquired through non-college experiences. It is used as the basis for requesting college recognition based on experiential learning. Typically, a portfolio includes the following elements (see Mann, 1993, p. 5):

- a life history or autobiography which profiles the most important events in a person's life;

- a chronological record which provides a year-by-year list of experiences since graduation from high school;

- a goals paper which describes the person's personal, career, and educational goals;

- a narrative, sometimes referred to as a competency, which includes concise statements of life experience and of the learning that resulted from these experiences;

• documents which substantiate a person's learning experiences.

The "portfolio" represents more than a physical document. Perhaps more importantly it reflects the process of identifying, articulating and documenting non-college learning (Knapp, 1975; Simosko, 1988; Willingham, 1976).

The preparation of this portfolio is an exercise in self-evaluation, introspection, analysis, and synthesis. It is an educational experience in itself. It requires you to relate your past learning experiences to your own educational goals, to exhibit critical self-analysis, and to demonstrate your ability to organize documentation in a clear, concise manner. (Mann, 1993, p. 4).

Preparing a prior learning portfolio is not an easy task, nor can it be done quickly. In fact, a learner should not be asked nor expected to do so without careful consideration of the educational value of the process, the commitment required for effective completion, and reflection on how the process directly relates to the achievement of academic goals. The preparation of a portfolio should not be an isolated event, but instead it is most beneficial when integrated into the overall framework of academic goals. Inappropriately, some faculty evaluators may want to recognize prior learning merely as a means to give credit for elective hours, or as a basis to waive requirements for one concentration while expecting learners to take more courses in another area. This type of approach does not honour the basic rationale for prior learning assessment. The development of a portfolio and its subsequent evaluation needs to be a full partner in the individual's educational program, and the process should directly enhance the value of the overall educational experience.

Most institutions that use a portfolio for prior learning assessment provide a *Portfolio Development* workshop or credit course in order to assist students with the process. While developing a portfolio, students are assessing their own learning, most often with the assistance of a faculty member, and in turn they develop a better understanding of how their learning relates to an academic degree. During the process they identify their strengths and weaknesses, and how the college curriculum can help redress weaknesses while capitalizing on strengths.

Portfolio development and assessment is also a learning experience for faculty, requiring them to be actively involved in the entire process. Prior learning assessment can't take place until faculty articulate standards for evaluating prior learning, and colleges and universities must formally define what constitutes college-level learning and publish the criteria and standards for students' use. Shelton and Armistead (1989) argue that the definition of college-level learning will vary according to the mission and educational philosophy of the institution, but that in general it will be learning that typically falls within a domain considered appropriate for higher education, and learners will understand both theory and skill components, recognize appropriate methods of inquiry for the discipline, and be able to apply knowledge beyond a specific context.

CONCLUSIONS

In spite of the research done on prior learning assessment, and the experience of many institutions during the past decade in particular, several issues continue to complicate the process. In particular, prior learning assessment is highly individualistic, non-routine, and will almost certainly continue to be this way in the future. This makes it time-consuming and expensive. Further, not all prior learning relates to an academic setting, nor is it easily categorized as college-level learning. This makes the conversion from life experience to college credit, at times, quite enigmatic. The supervision associated with prior learning ranges from fully independent experiences through to highly strategic, well planned and monitored learning. The former are most difficult to effectively document, while the latter, though potentially easier, are still challenging. To complicate matters, several years often pass before the learner petitions for assessment. This may make documentation difficult to compile.

Regardless of the challenges, the benefits clearly encourage both learners and institutions to participate in prior learning assessment activities, and not just in the United States. Activities related to prior learning assessment have recently been a focus of attention in Australia, Canada, and New Zealand. In differing ways, each of these APEC members has implemented the concept of prior learning assessment to help adults obtain a range of learning experiences and associated credentials (see Cohen & Whitaker, 1994). New Zealand in particular has been heavily involved with the identification of competency and skill standards for various occupations and the awarding of certification based on these.

In the United States and elsewhere, prior learning assessment programs may be one of the most effective tools for providing access opportunities to individuals who have been denied opportunities for further education. Alienated from traditional learning systems, or simply unable to access them because of time, distance, finances, life stage or other factors, the disenfranchised have new hope for recognition of experience through the prior learning assessment context.

Further, and perhaps most importantly from a regional human resource perspective, the demands of industry can no longer tolerate the costs associated with lockstep re-training and upskilling when the need does not exist. For all learners to be forced through the same set of prerequisites and learning activities is terribly costly, for individuals, firms and the society at large, and is a major impediment to lifelong learning. Economic competition and personal development require the individualization that prior learning assessment fosters, and APEC member economies are well advised to consider regional programs for recognition of and accreditation for prior learning.

REFERENCES

Cohen, R. & Whitaker, U. (1994). Assessing learning from experience. In M. Keeton (Ed.), *Perspectives on experiential learning: Prelude to a global conversation about learning* (pp. 35-54). Chicago: International Experiential Learning Conference and CAEL.

Cross, K. P. (1991). The roads to a learning society. In L. Lamdin (Ed.), *Roads to a learning society* (pp. 133-140). Chicago: CAEL.

Fugate, M. (1991). *CAEL's Prior learning assessment survey.* Paper presented at CAEL's International Assembly, San Diego, California.

Knapp, J. (1975). *A guide for assessing prior experience through portfolios* (CAEL Working Paper # 6). Princeton, New Jersey: Educational Testing Service.

Mann, C. M. (1993). *Credit for lifelong learning.* Bloomington, Indiana: Tichenor.

Marsick, V.J. (1987). *Learning in the workplace.* New York: Croom Helm.

Miller, M. R. & Daloz, L.A. (1987). Assessment of prior learning: Good practices assure congruity between work and education. *Equity and Excellence, 24*(3), 30-34.

Shelton, S. E. & Armistead, L. P. (1989). The practice of awarding credit for prior learning in the community college. *Community / Junior College Quarterly, 13,* 23-31.

Simosko, S. (1988). *Assessing learning: A CAEL handbook for faculty.* Columbia, Maryland: CAEL.

Tough, A. M. (1967). *Learning without a teacher: A study of tasks and assistance during adult self-teaching projects.* Toronto: Ontario Institute for Studies in Education.

Willingham, W. W. & Associates. (1976). *The CAEL validation report.* Columbia, Maryland: CAEL.

Willingham, W.W. (1976). Critical issues and basic requirements for assessment. In M. Keeton (Ed.), *Experiential learning, rationale, characteristics, and assessment* (pp. 224-244). San Francisco: Jossey-Bass.

Jiro Yoshio

Jiro Yoshio holds an M.A. from Central Michigan University, and is a professor of technical education at Tokyo Gakugei University. He is a longtime supporter of technical education programs in the Asia-Pacific region, and has written several books on technical education and international cooperation. In the early 1970s, Professor Yoshio was seconded by his government to work at the regional Colombo Plan Staff College, which at that time was located in Singapore. Following from that experience, he conducted in-country technical training programs in such diverse places as Fiji, Papua New Guinea, Pakistan, Sri Lanka and Nepal. Now he is working with SEAMEO VOCTEC, the Southeast Asian Ministers of Education Organization centre in Brunei that specializes in vocational and technical education, where his specialty is the development of multimedia teaching and learning resources for technician education. An ardent self-taught photographer, Professor Yoshio has been taking and exhibiting photographs since the early 1950s.

Thoughts on a Regional Approach for Lifelong Learning

by Jiro Yoshio

Two changes are occurring, almost simultaneously, within many East and Southeast Asian APEC economies. First, economic growth is surging, and along with this there is unprecedented demand for highly educated and well trained technicians along with other skilled labour. This demand should be viewed as an opportunity to improve lifelong learning opportunities for many in the region. The second change is related to the advances made in telecommunications, computing and multimedia technologies, all of which are interrelated and have great potential to affect education in the region. By using the new technologies to meet, on a regional basis, the need for a broad lifelong learning infrastructure, the lives of ordinary citizens throughout the region will become measurably better.

THE CONTEXT

For many East and Southeast Asian APEC economies, changes in the quality of life during the past several decades have been obvious and profound as indicated by identifiable demographic socio-economic standards, educational standards achieved, and levels of industrialization realized. At this same time, the educational infrastructure has changed only slightly; though simple capacity may have expanded and evolved, the basic model and internal workings of the system are little different than was the case thirty years ago. Basic education is delivered in a traditional, expensive and time consuming manner, retraining and upgrading is fragmented, and many developing economies have yet to effectively deal with high rates of illiteracy. In today's context, the importance of lifelong learning is dramatic and increasing. It is imperative, therefore, that greater attention be paid to developing a modern, substantial, exemplary, educational infrastructure, and in particular one that can be shared among APEC members. Lifelong learning needs should be at the core of such a system.

APEC members will, in the 21st century, need to develop educational systems that respond to the personal and professional learning needs of all citizens. In particular, attention must be paid to the evolving demands of technical workers for continual upgrading and re-skilling, at the trades and technologist levels as well as at the science and engineering levels. To broadly increase the learning opportunities for technical professionals within a single APEC member economy is a daunting task; in fact, however, the time has come to assess regional approaches and establish a paradigm that extends beyond single economies. Undoubtedly, as technology changes, the nature of 21st century learning systems will be questioned. This paper argues that, given the technical advances in the past decade, proposals for regional cooperation with regard to lifelong learning, and technical education in particular, using the technology of today, along with what is clearly manifest on the technical horizon, are strongly warranted.

Member economies in the East and Southeast Asian region of APEC are experiencing enormous increases in the demand for highly skilled and well educated technicians, along with other skilled labour, and this trend is expected to continue well into the next century. Industries, many of which are multinational enterprises, face the dilemma of a fast growing demand for industrial and consumer products coupled with the exploding high-tech job market, both of which lead to severely increased competition for highly trained labour. At the same time, there is relatively little increase in the size of the pool. To meet current product demand, while at the same time incorporating technical advances in product design and production, firms must acquire additional staff trained at higher and higher levels. The message is clear: the trained human resource pool is inadequate.

The regular school system within many APEC economies can be described for the most part as isolated and fragmented. Re-training, up-skilling, basic literacy, refresher training and so on, are often available on an ad-hoc basis, but for the most part there is little in the way of systems-wide coordination. At the regional level one can find, without too much trouble, examples of cooperative training, and particularly noteworthy examples, most often one of a kind, do in fact exist. However, the notion of seamless education throughout the lifespan, incorporating a full range of technical, professional developmental opportunities, remains, for most of the workforce in the region, unheard of. A regional, lifelong, shared and mutually supported approach to learning is at this stage an almost mythical goal.

What changes have occurred which suggest the time is ripe for broad regional solutions related to education and lifelong learning? Most importantly, the advancements made in communications' technologies have eliminated the distance and time issues that in the past prevented regional solutions from being considered. In part because time and distance are no longer issues, advanced technology industries now are spreading to many economies where, in the past, only low skill employment existed. Drawn by easy access to labour, often at lower wages, and increased access to developing markets, the multinationals are creating borderless economies. This is changing the face of education and training, making it borderless in the sense that an advanced technology firm operating in Thailand and the Philippines, for example, requires technical training and education for technicians and other skilled workers, and, hopefully, lifelong learning solutions, in both economies. A single solution set will almost always be preferred simply because it will be the least complicated and likely the most cost effective.

With recent advances in digital technology, it is now possible to share the resources of individual countries, as well as their experience and expertise, and offer better learning solutions to workers wherever they are and whenever the need is warranted. With cooperation and support from multilateral organizations such as the Association of Southeast Asian Nations, APEC and others, which have demonstrated specific interest and concern for human resource development, meaningful possibilities exist for developing and providing useful, realistic and broad-based lifelong learning programs to both self-directed people (those who for reasons of self-advancement and personal development interests drive their own learning needs) and industry-oriented people (those whose training needs are driven by the needs of the employer and changing technology). Now the time is ripe to establish an integrated lifelong learning system for multiple economies, especially those which have attracted advanced technology multinational industries.

This paper describes and discusses issues pertinent to the development of viable lifelong learning systems, including the framework for programming, possible technologies to apply, program policies and practices, and finally, significant benefits. Further, the broad lifelong learning paradigm being presented will have implications for all education and training disciplines. By implementing a versatile, multifaceted approach, as suggested in the following pages, industries will create substantial problem-solving expertise, increase potential for human resource and firm mobility, and generally augment stability and opportunities for economic growth within the firm, within specific economies, and regionally.

THE NEED FOR BORDERLESS TRAINING

Throughout the late 1980s and the 1990s, multinational industries moved deftly and quickly into and throughout the Asian sub-region of APEC. As a result, we now see complex industrial products being produced in economies that, in the 1970s and early 1980s, were comprised largely of unskilled labour. As evidence of this, throughout the sub-region, an increasing number of economies produce not only automobiles and computers, but also a host of complex chemical and biological products. Asian manufacturers now assemble product in a number of different economies, but are at the same time being challenged by new and innovative manufacturers and brands that are being produced by home-grown firms in economic environments that were, just a few short years ago, described as being only in the early stages of industrialization. These new firms, not satisfied with single markets, are themselves expanding regionally through a host of joint ventures (Kumagai, 1996).

In order to survive and grow, borderless industrial activities require a well-educated and highly trained human resource base. To at least some degree, segments of the workforce must be mobile, able to train internationally, and willing to work in different cultural contexts. The speed of technological change puts an additional demand on these industries and on the workforce. The current environment for automobile manufacturing in Thailand illustrates the complex relationships between manufacturing, competition, international alliances and the need for a technically skilled workforce (Fairclough, 1996).

Regardless of an economy's level of industrialization, all routinely use and rely on technical platforms that include sophisticated computer applications, satellite communications, and aeronautics. As well, each East and Southeast Asian economy has a basic labour pool that includes highly specialized communications professionals. Complex interfaces connect all segments of the society, and these are the characteristics that bind and support the potential for broader, regional lifelong learning strategies implemented in part through distance education strategies.

Throughout the region, various schools and training institutions offer technical education that includes vocational, industrial, engineering and science education. Many of these schools are independently successful, providing students with access to broad and fundamental knowledge as well as basic skill sets. However, as noted earlier, integration within the region is almost totally absent, and, in fact, integration within a single economy is often lacking. Few of these schools and institutions offer high-level, advanced technology training, and those that do cannot come close to meeting current demand.

In the past, relatively low levels of human resource output associated with these schools and training institutions were a closer match with the minimalistic needs of industry, and in that setting many firms hired workers capable of executing only specific, basic level job skills. In some cases, industries expect to play a role in educating and training their new employees for high-level, advanced technology applications within the industry, and in order to do this certain of the larger firms operate their own training schools. Others, many of which are regional, multinational industries in the sub-region, have taken advantage of bilateral and multilateral Overseas Development Assistance (ODA) schemes to assist with human resource training. Japan in particular has provided ODA funding as a tool for both assisting the multinationals and at the same time developing human resource pools that increase the living standards and employment opportunities for many individuals. The U.S.A, Canada and many European nations have contributed in a similar manner. (It is worth noting, however, that in the ODA context there have been some constraints including content, duration, and number and selection of participants for training courses.)

In the future, however, ODA assistance will not be able to provide the appropriate level of support for several reasons. These include the reduction in ODA funding from a number of economies, the increased requirements for training given the expansion of industry, and the higher levels of training required for advanced technology solutions. Further, in the future there will be increased emphasis on the manpower needs of small- and medium-sized enterprises (SMEs), an area where training needs are modest, narrow and specialized, and where new human resource solutions will be required. In fact, no firms will be practically adept, sufficiently large, or comprehensive enough to adequately train technicians in the diverse skill sets required for technical production in the 21st century. In addition, even if industries, at least temporarily, were able to adequately train new technicians, there is growing concern about the need to retrain older workers. Highly specialized training solutions, reductions in ODA funding, the inability of large organizations to train in every specialty and the need to bring relevant training to the doors of SMEs has created a problem in need of a regional solution.

Now that advanced technology industries are distributed throughout the region, as compared with earlier approaches where similar industries tended to locate side by side, technician education and training must also be broadened. Not only do firms lack the required size and human resource requirements to provide full training solutions, many economies are similarly unable to respond to the variety, depth and changing needs associated with technical education. Technicians must commit to continuous skill updating, and lifelong learning opportunities must be available to all who want them, with as few restrictions as possible concerning nationality or training location. Further, training programs themselves must be updated frequently to keep pace with industrial innovation. The result is an urgent need for borderless education and training programs; international cooperation will be required.

CURRENT LIFELONG LEARNING

For purposes of comparison and contrast, it is useful to briefly examine some of the approaches and issues associated with vocationally-oriented lifelong learning in Japan. From these, implications can be drawn for the sub-region under discussion.

By way of example, consider a Japanese dust control technician in an IC chip manufacturing facility. For a worker of this sort, and many others, there will be training strategies associated with two broad vocational training goals. The first goal is to stay current in the job and prepare for changes that are technology or market driven. The second goal would be to expand and enhance skill sets in order to enhance job opportunities. The first goal is met through what is known as vocationally-oriented or company-oriented learning programs, and the second through self-directed learning programs.

With vocationally-oriented programs, technicians are typically eligible to receive a host of in-service training courses and programs. Using the IC dust control technician example, a technician would be required to have up-to-date knowledge and skills related to a broad range of technical areas including static electricity and air quality circulation measurement and control. The content of most training courses would be directly related to the technician's job. However, other courses, broader in nature, would also be available. Most of these company-oriented programs and courses would be competency-based, with clearly stated, highly specific, and quantifiably measurable objectives. In the Japanese context, no fees would be charged, and the training would be delivered during regular working hours.

Problems associated with this approach include credit transfer, or rather the lack of it. In-house training does not for the most part result in acknowledged, transferable training credits. In part this is not surprising since the firm is not providing the training in order for the technician to gain employment elsewhere, and the firm is therefore reluctant to see great value in awarding recognizable credits. However, even within the company there are drawbacks. If, for instance, the technician does not have a university degree, an ODA based foreign assignment would not be permitted on the basis of in-service training alone because no broadly recognizable credit is given and recognized credentials are *de rigueur* for overseas postings. Because there is no system of equating courses and programs between companies, if a worker moves from one employer to another, comparisons cannot be made. As a result, needless, repetitive training almost certainly takes place, As well, some courses are publicly funded and all workers, regardless of employer, may have access to them; however, the credit and recognition issue remains firmly entrenched. Workers would be strongly advantaged if all training was coordinated, systematized and evaluated by external accrediting agencies in order for training to be transparent and portable.

Self-directed programs are somewhat different. With self-directed training, broader needs are being addressed, so, for example, the technician may want to improve basic language skills, master computer technology, learn a foreign language, or become proficient in a particular hobby. Many of these options are widely available via radio, on television, through the church, in the community centre, or at a traditional school. Often, technical high schools offer computer literacy courses free of charge. Notable is the fact that in most of these courses there are no prerequisites, so the learner self-selects the course content and level according to personal interest and self-assessment, from primary levels through to the professional tier. Fees for the courses range from nil to very expensive, according to the nature of the course and materials involved. The term or length of courses varies according to the complexity of the discipline. Recently, the development of the Internet has broadened these opportunities. For the most part, however, difficulties with accreditation remain firmly entrenched.

The advantages of the Japanese system include the flexibility associated with the parallel opportunities for vocationally-oriented and self-directed study. As a building block for lifelong learning, this system brings a measure of strength because it provides for and encourages self-direction while at the same time including specific vocational training alongside learning for self-interests both within and outside of the vocational context. Regional strategies for lifelong learning should incorporate these strengths.

PROGRAMMING CHARACTERISTICS

For an effective, broad-based, sub-regional, international approach to technical training, a rational, well developed structure is required. The programming should include capacity for vocational and non-vocational learning, access should be universal, and an open-door policy with no prerequisites followed. Standardized courses and topics within a logical and efficient framework should be based on distance learning principles. Although some degree of flexibility will be required, a high degree of uniformity brings continuity and stability. Learning programs with no established framework or no consistent approach are subject to fragmentation and disunity.

Competency-Based Education

Given the need for integration, consistency, applied focus, transferability, credit recognition, regional access, multiple delivery modes, and different cultural contexts, a competency-based approach for training is demanded. Organized by modules, competency-based education (CBE) learning units are self-contained, learner-driven, instructional packages. Learners pace themselves according to their own needs and abilities. A module covers either a single element of subject matter or a group of content elements forming a discreet unit of subject matter or area of skill development. Each module has a clearly defined objective (see Meyer, 1988).

A CBE approach shifts learning from a teacher-centred focus to one which is student-centred. Once this shift is made, timing, modules, place and goals are driven by the student, not the system. Assessment of all learning is based on the demonstration of objectively verifiable knowledge and skill sets. CBE works well with mature students, precisely those for whom the traditional school process is least appropriate (see Joyner, 1995).

Vocational training should for the most part be accommodated while the learner is on-the-job, similar to the Japanese vocational-oriented programming described earlier, even when delivered from a distance. The firm and the learners profit from this training, and the flexibility in terms of content selection, timing, duration of study, place of study, and study strategies attract and benefit both (see Gahlot, 1995). Large programs are sub-divided into small programs, and in turn these are divided into ever smaller units, down to the level at which specific outcomes testing is suitable.

Topics for the vocational components must be identified and vetted by industry in order to be specifically suited to industrial needs. Introductory areas of study would be broad in nature, covering areas such as information technology and computer applications. These would be followed by more specialized programming such as 3D animation, flexible manufacturing techniques, and multimedia applications.

Industry Cooperation

As suggested earlier, the rate of technological change does not provide enough time for school-based education, particularly with the attendant curriculum development, teacher training, government approvals, political decisions, registration, and other bureaucratic processes, to supply the required human resource base. Further, many companies cannot provide adequate training because they lack the resources, particularly SMEs. Now, when firms with similar manpower requirements are spread across a region instead of being concentrated in one or two areas, these factors merge to support the notion of shared, regional training.

Many firms have specialized training packages, often developed at great expense, for specific skill sets. It is wasteful and non-productive for these to be duplicated again and again by multiple firms as well as by publicly supported schools, often in outmoded formats. However, few firms have shown a willingness to support cooperative training ventures among themselves in the past, so is there a difference in today's environment? The argument presented here is that firms are becoming increasingly diversified and many more are now investing in each other. Their needs have merged, and the financial health of one benefits the others. These factors suggest that the time is ripe for multinational training organizations to work hand in hand with SMEs and for large multinationals to deliver training regionally. Not quite arms-length organizations, these educational entrepreneurs would provide a fast-paced, integrated, modern curricula with regionally transferrable credits to meet the needs of both industry and formal education. They could purchase at least some training materials in generic form from existing organizations, and might well receive initial funding from international organizations as well as through ODA programs.

Technology

Recent improvements in digital technologies have literally changed the face of telecommunications and computing. Only a few years ago, with analog equipment, all facets of communications technology were by comparison quite limited. Now, the issue of data quantity is for most functions resolved, as are speed and quality. High speed, digital satellite communications and fibre optics make it possible to send and receive large volumes of data inexpensively and very, very quickly. Inexpensive computers permit learners to link to data streams, and multimedia applications allow us to format and present information in interesting and meaningful ways. During the course of the next ten years, as we learn to harness and apply the technologies, change will be enormous. However, in the meantime, it is clear that there are three primary areas with great potential to affect education: telecommunications technology, computers and multimedia applications. These three technologies will for the first time permit practical, on-line, synchronous distance education. Borders, distance and time have become secondary.

Less than ten years ago, producing multimedia self-learning courseware was exorbitantly expensive, and only a few of the largest colleges, universities and private training institutions could afford to invest in the development of interactive guides, films and limited computer applications to support the teaching and learning process. The material that was produced tended to be static, inflexible, and rarely updated. Much of it was designed simply to replace teachers. Now, multimedia applications can be created directly by teachers who are willing to invest a relatively modest amount of time learning how to patch material together using a variety of software programs and hardware. In fact, the ease with which this can be done has changed dramatically during the last two to three years. Programming tools have become increasingly user-friendly, and soon little formal training of any type will be required.

The Internet, though it has been in service in various forms, mostly in the west, for more than a decade, is only now being widely adopted in Asia as the *de facto* standard for inexpensive, fast, regional communications. It brings within the reach of any computer literate individual, databases that far exceed what any library can provide, and it does so very often in an entertaining and highly educational manner. The potential for interactivity is an added bonus. For development of course materials, the Internet and World Wide Web are rich sources for finding and extracting materials, much of it at no cost. In many respects, it is quite surprising that outmoded curriculum materials, standard textbooks for example, continue to be valued. This is perhaps a reflection more of administrators and bureaucrats than of true worth and need. Soon, standard books on most subjects will be widely available free of charge since all it takes is one author to simply "post" material to the Web.

Combining learning materials into useful sequences and forms (multimedia teaching and learning resources - MMT/Ls) will, however, continue to bring a strong value added ingredient to the overall system. Whereas, in the past, assembly of information was a major component in the curriculum development process, data is now abundant, easy to reach, and most often free. It is the packaging that creates the added dimension, and the best packagers will be highly sought after. In turn, and to a larger degree, the skill of developers will be influenced by available software. Basic tools such as HTML and VRML for the Web are being eclipsed by Java and composite authoring programs such as Macromedia's Director. Given the rapid rates of development and change, it is difficult to even imagine the course authoring tools that will be available in the year 2000!

At this stage the issue of technology is for all intents and purposes resolved, though it will be increasingly refined over the years. Putting materials into a distance education design takes place almost spontaneously. The cost of teacher-centred learning is too high for universal replication in much of the APEC region, and learner-centred approaches are proving to be more attractive not to mention far more cost-effective. It may be that we are seeing the last generation that will want to sit in front of a teacher rather than manage their own education. By studying at work or at home, vocationally-directed and self-directed learners will be highly motivated because of the accessibility of the technology and the mobility and interactivity of the programs. All programs will be easily adaptable, flexible and economically viable. Learning and productivity will increase dramatically.

There are some drawbacks frustrating the wide-spread use of computers, though these are no longer as problematic as some might suggest. For example, the expense of computers has dropped dramatically during the past three years, in spite of the fact that manufacturers have managed to ply a market skimming strategy particularly in developed economies. By regularly introducing newer and faster platforms with more features, they have managed to keep prices and margins relatively high. However, it is difficult to imagine how much more computing power is in fact required for basic education. True, faster computers and more sophisticated computers will drive high-level manufacturing and production, but the issue of computing power for basic level technician training and upgrading is resolved. At this stage, a basic computer system costs little more than an expensive overhead projector or film equipment, and reliability is no longer the issue it once was.

Basic, multiple station computer sites can be installed even in remote locations to serve widely disparate needs. Teachers, or better still, facilitators, can be trained to use these basic sites with minimal instruction and even develop software that best suits specific situations. If networks are not available, the use of CD-ROMs can serve as a cost-effective solution.

A key part of the solution set will be to create development and consulting centres where courseware would be created, networks maintained and credentialling facilitated. These centres would not require large numbers of staff, nor would the costs be high. The consequences would, however, be impressive. By combining basic, computer-related technologies with a competency-based modular system and distance delivery, exciting, integrated, consistent, regional lifelong learning programs can be created.

POLICY & PRACTICES

Establishing efficient and effective lifelong learning programming is clearly essential if APEC economies are to foster human resource development and bring the benefits of increased economic development to all members of their respective societies. Lifelong learning to satisfy both individual needs as well as the demands of industry will only be successfully implemented through the collaborative and collective efforts of APEC member economies. Some APEC member economies have begun to develop integrated lifelong learning programs, but as noted earlier these are for the most part fragmented and inconsistent. To make the best use of existing technology, human resources, and information, the development and implementation of specific policies and practices supported by politicians, governments, the private sector, UNESCO, ILO, NGOs and much of the current educational infrastructure, are needed. This framework should not clash with the basic notion of a lifelong learning system that is self-directed.

Official Support

In Japan, for example, the Ministry of Education and Culture is legally responsible for championing "Lifelong Learning Promotion". Within this legal foundation, the Ministry supports a full range of lifelong learning activities at public halls, libraries, museums, and other institutions. The Ministry also supervises specific programs for the education and training of the leaders of lifelong learning projects. Based on other legal prescriptions, "Human Resource Development Promotion" for example, the Ministry of Labor provides financial support for individual lifelong learning activities as well as those developed and implemented by industries.

In its ODA programming, the government of Japan recognizes the importance of lifelong learning, and technical upgrading in particular, within the context of available and developing technology as well as best practice delivery techniques. Distance study, for example, is used for a variety of projects such as the telecommunications technician training widely offered to developing economies within APEC. Japanese industry is also "formally" involved through examples provided earlier in the paper as well as through government supported research and study on lifelong learning.

Government supported, official policies, as well as a formal commitment and direct involvement from industry, provides the basis for a strong lifelong learning ethic in Japan, and the value of having this foundation should not be underestimated. In Japan, this approach has over the years been institutionalized and is now a fully accepted and articulated element of Japanese life. Action, not words, is needed at the individual economy level within APEC if a regional strategy is to work.

Self-Directed Study

There have in the past been tendencies for lifelong learning to be narrowly defined, focusing on specific elements such as continuing vocational training for workers, promotion of immigrant literacy, and retraining of the unemployed and women (Maehara, 1994). In this age, however, lifelong learning policy and practice perspectives must include self-directed learning of all sorts, as described earlier in this paper, and the broader learning context, rather than a simple industrial focus.

Somewhat paradoxically, it can be argued that in many learning contexts it is more beneficial to promote self-directed interdisciplinary study and the creative examination of connecting technologies, and that this often leads to more new product development and applications than do more lock-step vocationally-oriented courses. Recognition of this potential contradiction should encourage policy makers to concentrate on constructing support systems and sound foundations for broad, comprehensive lifelong learning strategies.

Accreditation

Lifelong learning programming must be developed within the context of a fully articulated, transferable and accountable system. It is too costly and time consuming to train and re-train the same workers simply because the system does not recognize learning from different sources. Up-dating courses in particular lack cohesion and transferability, and these are going to be the basis for much of the lifelong learning activities in the Asia Pacific region.

In a regional context, the difficulties associated with technical training and upgrading accreditation may seem to be so monumental as to be unassailable. However, we simply cannot afford to accept that view. The well-being of the people in the region should provide the impetus required to resolve this issue, regardless of strong and vested self-interests that will need to be set aside. Governments in particular need to understand that the broader purpose must be served, whatever short term expense this may involve. The system must be accountable, fair, objective and broad-based. Learners deserve accreditation and this will in turn have a huge influence on motivation as it relates to vocational upgrading.

Openness and Overseeing

The notion of having an open and transparent systems approach to lifelong learning has many advantages. If resources and data are widely available, and protective measures such as copyright and confidentiality minimized, greater gains will be realized for the region. By sharing learning assets, much of which will occur naturally through the Web, borderless communities of curriculum and course developers will create educational and economic gain for all the players, not just the developed economies or wealthier elements in any one society. If all the participants in lifelong learning programs allow free dissemination of all learning materials, the most disadvantaged members of our societies will profit immeasurably.

An agreed-upon international organization could act as an arbiter for dispute resolution and to create and support a system which would consolidate many of the practices and learning programs which are currently operating in isolation. With a regional perspective, this organization would be a clearing house responsible for collecting and distributing training materials and standards. Furthermore, it could oversee and resolve all issues related to copyright. As a leader in research and development, the organization would survey instructional methodology, establish a consistent evaluation system, manage distance delivery technology, train and arrange for technical support, and refine curricula.

BENEFITS AND CHALLENGE

The benefits associated with a comprehensive, integrated, regional system of lifelong learning development and implementation are considerable; the challenges, daunting as they might be, pale in comparison. For this reason, it is important that self interests be set aside.

It is important to recognize that there are two, broad but related beneficiaries. First, the people of the region will be most affected. The opportunity to learn, regularly and consistently with high quality learning materials at a convenient place and time throughout the lifespan under a CBE distance education structure with full, transferable accreditation, would on a national, let alone a regional scale, be unprecedented. Perhaps most importantly, such a system will have its greatest affect on the most disenfranchised members of the region. The system will, in effect, begin to regionally and on a broad scale re-address the growing gap between the educated and the under-educated, between the rich and the poor.

Industry, and hence the economy as a whole, will be the second beneficiary. An updated workforce, access to a larger highly-trained labour pool, and improved production standards and therefore cost performance will be tangible rewards. For this reason, it makes sense for industry to participate, and even contribute in terms of making current training materials broadly available. For some firms, the opportunity to participate directly or indirectly in the delivery of regional training by being course providers or sponsors will be an added incentive.

Who will be the losers? In effect, the only losers in a visionary program as described in these pages will be those who benefit from monopolies on education or those who operate industrial manufacturing concerns with ill educated labour paid at low wages, who in effect take advantage of restrictive educational opportunities and prevent broader economic well being. The challenge for APEC economies will be to ignore entrenched powers and seize this 21st century opportunity.

REFERENCES

Fairclough, G. (1996, November 14). Learning curve. *Far Eastern Economic Review,* *159*(46), 34.

Gahlot, P. (1995). Flexible modular distance learning for updating and upgrading technical teachers in TVET institutions. *CPSC Quarterly, 22*(4), 10-21. Manila: Colombo Plan Staff College.

Joyner, C. (1995). The DACUM technique and competency-based education. In J. D. Dennison (Ed.), *Challenge and opportunity* (pp. 243-255). Vancouver: University of British Columbia Press.

Kumagai, C. (1996). *Industrial production of Japanese manufacturers in South East Asia.* Tokyo: Open University.

Maehara, Y. (1994). Patterns of lifelong education in Japan. *International Review of Education, 40*(3-5), 333-338.

Meyer, R. (1988). *Modules from design to implementation.* Manila: Colombo Plan Staff College.

Arief S. Sadiman

and Rafael Rahardjo

Arief Sadiman holds a Master of Science degree in Instructional Technology from Syracuse University, New York, and a Ph.D. in Educational Technology from the Institute of Teachers' Training of Jakarta. Currently, Dr. Arief is Director of the Centre for Communications Technology for Education and Culture at the Ministry of Education and Culture in Indonesia. His responsibilities include the development of the Open Junior Secondary School system, managing the Indonesian Distance Learning Network, and working on the establishment of the SEAMEO Regional Centre for Open Learning. Dr. Arief co-authored, with Rafael Rahardjo and David Seligman, a monograph on SMP Terbuka which was published by UNESCO/UNDP. During his spare time he enjoys listening to music and drawing.

Rafael Rahardjo holds a Master of Science in Instructional Technology from Syracuse University. Retired since 1987, Drs. Rahardjo now works as a consultant on instructional development and training. Along with Dr. Arief and David Seligman, he was co-author of a monograph on SMP Terbuka published by UNESCO/UNDP. Travelling, badminton, and table tennis are among his hobbies.

Contribution of SMP Terbuka Toward Lifelong Learning in Indonesia

by Arief S. Sadiman and Rafael Rahardjo

The Open Junior Secondary School, or "SMP Terbuka", was developed as a pilot project intended to run from 1979 to 1984 and provide junior secondary school education through distance education delivery to students who might otherwise not have the opportunity to receive education beyond primary school. It is fast becoming a key component of the educational infrastructure, and will most certainly be a critical ingredient in the development of an overall system of lifelong learning in Indonesia. Originally operating in only five schools in five provinces, SMP Terbuka was first designed to help meet the shortfall predicted in the school building program. This original mandate was extended to 1989 at which time it was expected that the government would be able to provide the required additional school buildings and facilities. However, the pilot was so successful that SMP Terbuka has become an integral part of the government's plans to address the learning needs of approximately 6.2 million school age children by the year 2004/2005. SMP Terbuka has been charged with the education of 2.25 million of these children.

INTRODUCTION

Although different in structure, the Open Junior Secondary School SMP Terbuka is part of the formal educational system in Indonesia, and uses the same Junior Secondary School (SMP) curricula and assessment criteria in its programs as is used in standard programming. In the SMP Terbuka system, students convene for independent study in clusters of learning groups called "Tempat Kegiatan Belajar" (TKB), formed within the boundaries of the base school. This paper describes the development, structure and growth of the Open Junior Secondary School SMP Terbuka in Indonesia.

The approach of SMP Terbuka differs from that of its regular counterparts in that it handles the learning process of its students through distance and independent learning. It operates on the theory that for a desired learning behaviour to occur (result), certain strategies have to be applied (treatment) to a specific audience with certain characteristics (condition). This approach builds on the premise that when different treatments are applied to students in different conditions, equally successful results may occur.

SMP Terbuka is based on this last approach. It is for disadvantaged children (different conditions), who learn independently from printed modules, the main media for instruction, and with limited face to face teacher interaction (different treatment). This type of treatment is intended to yield the same or very similar results (same results).

Table 1

CONDITION	TREATMENT	RESULT
same	same	same
same	different	different
different	same	different
different	different	same

At the present time in Indonesia, large numbers of primary school students, particularly those faced with geographic and socioeconomic constraints, are currently deprived of educational opportunities. SMP Terbuka makes further education accessible to these students.

As Rumble (1986) points out, the significant advantages of distance education include reaching a large number of individuals who for a variety of reasons would not be able to attend classroom-based activities and providing flexible easy to use learning materials relatively cheaply given sufficient students in the system for economies of scale to be enjoyed. He further argues, however, that cost-effectiveness is not always an end in and of itself. Distance education may be the only practical way of reaching some target groups, and the cost of doing so may be a secondary consideration. This is the case in Indonesia.

OVERVIEW OF OPERATIONS

SMP Terbuka utilizes the same national curriculum as do the regular SMPs. In order to provide a reference and standard for the design and development of independent learning materials, this base curriculum has been elaborated into Basic Patterns of Learning and Teaching named "Pola Dasar Kegiatan Belajar Mengajar" (PDKBM). This has been further broken down into Basic Media Program Outlines, "Garis Besar Isi Program Media" (GBIPM).

The national curriculum, since the initiation of SMP Terbuka, has undergone several changes. Hence, materials and support programs for SMP Terbuka have been adjusted accordingly. For example, the first SMP Terbuka modules were based on the 1975 SMP curriculum and written by trained lecturers of the Institutes of Teacher's Education and Training (IKIP). Successive SMP curriculum changes took place in 1984 and in 1994. Pilot testing of module were conducted in Kalianda, one of the pilot schools located in Lampung, South Sumatra in January of 1992. With the introduction of the 1994 curriculum, revised learning materials, including radio and audio cassette modules, have been available since the 1994/95 school year.

The quarter semester system, adopted in 1994/95, requires four subjects for the Local School Final Examination (EBTA), and an additional six subjects for the State

Final Examination (EBTANAS). The first four include:

• Religion with five electives - Islam, Christian/Protestant, Catholic, Hindu, and Buddhism;

• Health and Sports;

• Arts and craftsmanship;

• Local content - local language, culture, arts, home industries and vocational skills.

Graduates of any recognized primary school, including the Islamic "Madrasah Ibtidaiyah" (MI), the Small Elementary School (SD Kecil) and the Community Elementary (SD Pamong), between the ages of 11 and 18, are eligible for admission to SMP Terbuka. Within the context of UBE, priority is given to school-age children between 13 and 15 in order to meet the projected demand for a technically trained workforce in the era of increased global competition. Students learn through specially structured distance learning packages utilizing self-instructional modules and small group learning. This is supplemented by radio broadcasts, cassettes, and slide and video programs. Unlike students in a regular SMP, students in SMP Terbuka spend most of their learning time in independent study at their TKB, supervised and guided by "Guru Pamong" (Teacher Aides). They are, however, required to attend weekly face-to-face interactions with their "Guru Bina" (Subject Teachers) to discuss their progress and address any problems that have arisen from their independent work. Graduates of this program receive the same certificate as graduates of the regular school stream, for they learn from the same curriculum and, most importantly, participate in the same national examination.

ADMINISTRATION

SMP Terbuka is part of the formal Indonesian school system, and its positioning within the system is illustrated in Figure 1.

The management of SMP Terbuka operates through a Directorate of General Secondary Education which is comprised of two task forces. The Development Task Force, based at the Center for Communication Technology for Education and Culture, or Pustekkom, is concerned with the development and production of masters for common learning materials as well as supporting media. The Management Task Force, based at Dikmenum, is concerned with the overall implementation and operation of the system.

In order for the whole system to operate smoothly, linkages have been established with appropriate agencies in other Ministries, such as the Ministry of Information (MOI), the Ministry of Religious Affairs (MORA), and the Ministry of Home Affairs (MOHA).

At the central level, Pustekkom is required to establish linkages with the National Radio Station, the Radio Republik Indonesia (RRI). The National Television Network, Telvisi Republik Indonesia, arranges for air time, program scheduling, and the actual transmission. These two entities are under the jurisdiction of the MOI. Liaison with printing firms is carried out by Dikmenum annually, through a competitive bid-

Figure 1: Formal School Structure of National Education System

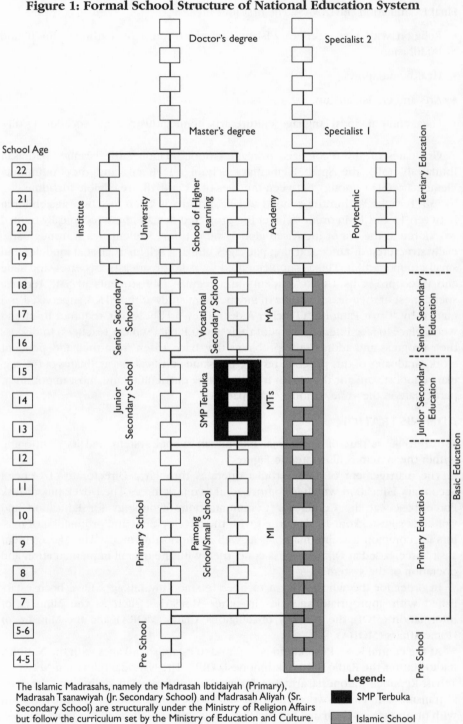

The Islamic Madrasahs, namely the Madrasah Ibtidaiyah (Primary), Madrasah Tsanawiyah (Jr. Secondary School) and Madrasah Aliyah (Sr. Secondary School) are structurally under the Ministry of Religion Affairs but follow the curriculum set by the Ministry of Education and Culture.

Legend:
- SMP Terbuka
- Islamic School

ding process, for delivery of printed modules.

At the provincial level, SMP Terbuka is managed by a group responsible for the logistics, monitoring and distribution infrastructures. This group is referred to as the Local Technical Team, the Tim Teknis Daerah, which is located at and operates under the coordination of the District Office of the Ministry of Education and Culture (MOEC), or Kantor Wilayah Kabupaten Pedidikan dan Kebudayaan (Kandep Dikbud). The Tim Teknis Daerah distributes the learning materials, equipment and other related resources to recipient schools through the Unit Bantuan Belajar Siswa (UBB) which is under the sub-district office of the MOEC, or Kantor Wilayah Kecamatan Pendidkan dan Kebudayaan (Kancam Dikbud). When dealing with primary education issues, Kanwil Dikbud consults with the Provincial Education Service (Dinas P and K), a constituent body of MOHA under the Governor. This is because primary schools in Indonesia are academically under the MOEC, but administratively under the MOHA. The Islamic schools administratively and from the Islamic discipline perspective report to MORA. At the school level, the administrative and managerial responsibilities are in hands of the Principal of the base school who is assisted by the Vice-Principal and the subject teachers. These relationships are detailed in Figure 2.

DEVELOPMENT AND GROWTH

Conceived in 1976, SMP Terbuka was not simply an attempt at political expediency. In fact, great effort has been made to stay true to the basic educational foundation and educational standards. In part, this is why the same national examination is required of all students, both those in the regular system and those who graduate through SMP Terbuka.

The SMP Terbuka system was designed to be dynamically responsive to development needs as well as compensatory in nature (Sadiman, Seligman, Rahardjo, 1995). As a result of the elementary schools construction project undertaken by Presidential mandate, called the Inpres School Project, which is part of the Primary Education Universalization drive, the Government of Indonesia projected explosive growth in the number of elementary school graduates from 1980 onward. SMP Terbuka was originally conceived and developed to address the educational needs of this group. Its main target was disadvantaged school-age children between the ages of 11 and 18, particularly those prevented by geographic or socioeconomic barriers from attending the regular SMP. With the introduction of the Universal Nine Year Basic Education (UBE) in 1994, entry priority is given to graduates 13 through 15 years of age of any recognized elementary school.

Originally experimental and small in scale, SMP Terbuka has always operated by making optimal, non-intrusive use of available resources. As early as 1985, studies indicated that it was a viable and acceptable alternative for students because it:

- made optimal use of local learning resources;

- overcame geographical and socioeconomic constraints making education more widely available;

Figure 2: SMP Terbuka Operational Linkages

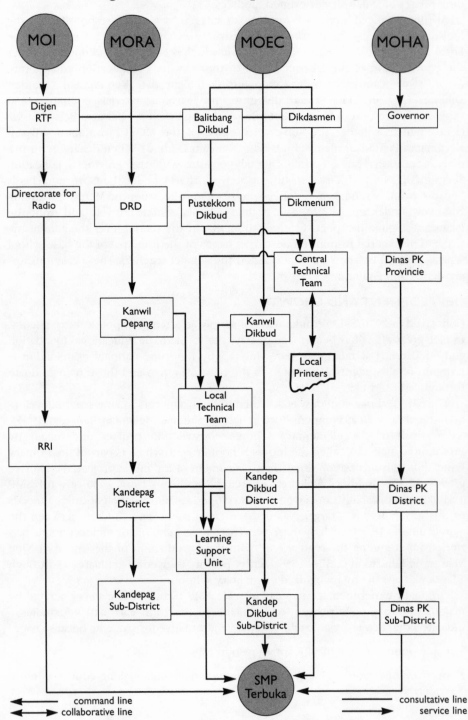

- helped cope with the shortage of classrooms and teachers;

- developed students' independent learning habits, a critical characteristic associated with lifelong learning opportunities;

- served students with different social and learning characteristics, thereby being inclusive rather than exclusive;

- helped cultivate the concept that learning can be ubiquitous and does not necessarily have to be confined to a school building (flexible learning); and

- operated at a fraction of the cost of the regular school system, thereby optimizing existing resources.

Most importantly, however, it had by this stage proven itself as a system that was based on and incorporated a sound theoretical foundation which produced skilled graduates every bit as capable as those studying in the more formal system. From an original base of 5 locations in just 5 provinces, it now operates with 956 locations in 27 provinces. Initially, this growth was relatively slow.

1990/91	15 locations in 9 provinces
1991/92	20 locations in 14 provinces
1992/93	25 locations in 19 provinces
1993/94	34 locations in 25 provinces

However, with the introduction of UBE, mandated by the President on National Education Day, May 2, 1994, the development accelerated.

1994/95	59 locations in 26 provinces (10,620 students enroled)
1995/96	356 locations in 27 provinces (64,080 students enroled)
1996/97	956 locations in 27 provinces (172,082 students enroled)

It is projected that by the end of the decade, there will be 3,270 SMP Terbuka locations with a total enrolment of 410,500 students. This number will increase dramatically as SMP Terbuka prepares to deal with 2.25 million students, its share of the 6.2 million students targeted by the UBE for the school year 2004/2005.

HUMAN RESOURCE DEVELOPMENT

In reference to a World Bank study in 1993, Wardiman (1994) states that economic success in eight economies, including the three newly industrialized economies of Indonesia, Malaysia and Thailand, is largely due to the effective development of physical and human capital and, more specifically, to the sharpened focus of human resource development towards vocational and technical education. In Indonesia, as in most developing economies, one of the most critical policy areas is ensuring that human resource development practices are aimed at building a skilled, flexible and technically capable workforce. This drive towards greater economic development and a technically capable workforce is focused first and foremost on primary and secondary school education levels. Clearly, this platform must exist before broader, higher education can take place. As Wardiman further points out, a survey of Asia described in *The Economist* (Asia Survey, 1993) notes that the successes enjoyed by East Asian countries in terms of strong economic development are directly attributed to the focus of educational resources on primary and secondary education rather than higher education, for it is this approach that has the greatest influence on the productivity of the mass of the workforce. In the case of Indonesia, it is this large scale workforce that will provide the economy with a comparative advantage, at least temporarily, in light manufacturing. The article further states that this approach to the development of an educational infrastructure will do more than anything else to promote income equality, consumer spending power, and broad support for high growth and pro-business policies. SMP Terbuka has excelled in the preparation of a technology-literate workforce.

SMP TERBUKA AS A PLATFORM FOR LIFELONG LEARNING

The Declaration of Human Rights, Article 26 stipulates that "the proper goal of education is not to preserve a system but to enrich the lives of more people by providing more education of quality, more effectively, more quickly and at a cost the country can bear. Everyone has the right to education. Education shall be free, at least in the elementary and fundamental stages. Elementary education shall be compulsory. Technical and professional education shall be made generally available and higher education shall be equally accessible to all on the basis of merit." An educational system is but a means, not an end in itself. The accomplishments of SMP Terbuka in the realm of economic development must be understood to be part of broader strategic measures for the achievement of national development goals, one of which is to provide more lifelong learning opportunities of all kinds throughout the lifespan.

If, as Bishop (1989) contends, future trends in education include a move toward a more flexible, open and lifelong system of educational opportunities, other APEC economies may draw from the experience of SMP Terbuka. The evidence is abundant, the lessons are clear, and the results are substantial. Bishop (1989) also describes a number of specific pedagogical characteristics which he believes are linked to the future of learning and which are clearly represented by the SMP Terbuka system. For example, Bishop suggests learning opportunities must, in the future, be more flexible, diversified, and offer multiple entry points. The establishment of SMP Terbuka was based on just such a conceptual framework in the sense that it is dynamically responsive to an existing environment, local conditions and prevailing political climate (Sadiman, Seligman, Rahardjo, 1995). In addition, Bishop suggests the education systems of the future must be lifelong, or linked with lifelong learning opportunities. Presently, SMP Terbuka focuses on junior secondary school; however, it represents an educational philosophy and infrastructure which can support a host of lifelong learning opportunities, including basic literacy, upgrading, retraining and even craft and hobby pursuits. The essence of SMP Terbuka is flexibility, independent learning, and opportunity.

It is also suggested by Bishop (1989) that the world of education must link with the world of work, and it must not be limited in time (the school stage) nor confined in space (the school building). SMP Terbuka is a system which, given the fact it doesn't have a fixed structure, can link directly with the world of work, now and in the future. It is not confined to buildings, nor is it limited to a certain time or stage in life. SMP Terbuka is positioned to provide equal learning opportunities for all people, irrespective of age, sex, previous educational achievement, or place of residence or income.

These properties strongly support the need for a paradigm shift with respect to our approaches towards learning. These changes will reflect the nature of the system described by Mukhopadhyay (1995) when he wrote of the need to move from conventional approaches to a more open system, utilizing distance delivery. Tied to this need are the opportunities which are now evolving from rapid developments in a host of computer-based learning technologies.

As Mason (1994) states, advancements in digitized interactive media and communications technologies are characterized by the very real potential to increase access to education and training, provide equality of opportunity between the educationally rich areas and the disadvantaged, furnish lifelong learning opportunities which are independent of time and place (networks, not buildings are the educational future), facilitate sharing of scarce resources, and prompt interactivity. Digitized interactive media, Internet communication networks and teleconferencing systems, for instance, offer innumerable alternative strategies for solving educational problems which require more flexibility, accessibility, and promptness of information irrespective of time and distance.

In fact, new technology in learning has been shown to provide cognitive benefits as well as to assist with the affective and motivational aspects of learning. SMP Terbuka currently achieves these goals; however, the notion of employing new technologies, hand-in-hand with the SMP Terbuka system, suggests a monumental opportunity to expand the influence and outcomes, perhaps even beyond the most optimistic visions that were proposed when the system was first introduced.

The SMP Terbuka experience has demonstrated that such learning can occur anywhere and that young children can be habituated to learn independently. As school-age children benefit from this reform, our attention should turn to the adult learners, making the dream of lifelong learning a reality.

REFERENCES

Asia Survey. (1993, October 30). *The Economist, 392*(7835).

Bishop, G. (1989). *Alternative strategies for education.* London: McMillan, Ltd.

Mason, R. (1994). *Using communications media in open and flexible learning.* London: Kogan Page.

Mukhopadhyay, M. (1995). *Shifting paradigms in open and distance education.* A paper presented before the IDLN First International Symposium: Networking into the 21st Century, Jakarta.

Rumble, G. (1992). *The management of the distance learning system.* Paris: UNESCO, International Institute for Educational Planning.

Sadiman, A. S., Seligman, D., & Rahardjo, R. (1995). *SMP Terbuka - The Open Junior Secondary School system: An Indonesian case study* (INS/88/028). Jakarta: UNDP-UNESCO.

UNESCO (1995). SMP Tebuka - *The Open Junior Secondary School: An Indonesian case study.* Jakarta: UNDP-UNESCO INS/88/028.

Wardiman, D. (1994). *Human resources and education policy in Indonesia.* Jakarta: Ministry of Education and Culture.

World Bank. (1993). *The east Asian miracle: Economic growth and public policy.* London: Oxford University Press.

Min Sun Pak

Dr. Min Sun Pak completed his Bachelor of Science (Engineering) at the Korean Military Academy in Seoul, and his Ph.D. in Information Sciences at the University of North Texas. Currently he is Assistant Professor and Director of Faculty and Scholarly Affairs in the Computer Science Department at Kwangwoon University in Seoul. Dr. Pak's specialty is expert systems and hypertext markup language, and he recently published an article in a North Texas research journal on commercial loans analysis and expert systems. He has a specific interest in lifelong learning, and has developed computer training programs for students who are not able to attend university as regular students. Dr. Pak enjoys the outdoors, and his hobbies include mountaineering.

Two Wheels for Lifelong Learning in Korea: Credit Banking & Multimedia Technology

by Min Sun Pak

For several centuries, lifelong learning was a traditional paradigm of education in Korea. However, for almost five decades the educational establishment has focused students' energies almost solely on the preparation for writing college entrance examinations. As a result, the lifelong learning paradigm has been lost. Now, there is a new opportunity for lifelong learning in Korea. Recent commitments by policy makers to broaden access and the creation of a Bureau of Lifelong Learning suggest that the time is ripe for progressive educational change. Such change could effectively include a system of computerized academic credit banking, designed to take accreditation out of the hands of elitist universities and colleges, along with the use of technology and multimedia applications specifically in order to ensure the widespread distance delivery of learning opportunities. The goal would be a re-vitalized lifelong learning paradigm that over time will reunite vocational and non-vocational learning.

THE LOST PARADIGM

"Life is too short to finish learning." "Getting older occurs at a faster rate than does learning." "Learning from the younger generation is not shameful." These are translations of venerable Korean proverbs, and each demonstrates and emphasizes the importance and value of learning, and the fact that in Korea learning has in a traditional sense been thought to be a lifelong process. This lifelong paradigm has until recently been one of the most important and enduring characteristics of the education system, both formal and informal, in Korea.

Traditionally, learning in Korea was comprehensive in nature. The learning that took place at home worked in concert with what was learned in school, if there was a school. Formal learning and informal learning meshed. Knowledge and skills were important elements of learning, but just as important were values such as loyalty, honesty, integrity and truthfulness. All of these were a conscious part of the overall learning framework, much of which was learned at home. With three generations of Koreans occupying the conventional household, children and grandchildren were inculcated, usually by the grandparents, with such values as loyalty to the country, devotion to parents, service to the community, etiquette, wisdom, diligence, frugality, and, most importantly, a love for learning. Teaching the need for discipline, a key element in Korean society, was for the most part a specific role and responsibility of grandparents.

Since the mid 1940s, dramatic changes have occurred in Korean society, one of the most important and far reaching being the development of new approaches and new values associated with the formal system of education. On the one hand it can be argued that educational opportunities improved, at least in the sense of number of places, the variety of opportunities, and level of studies available; however, what has been lost is much of the lifelong perspective along with the integration of the formal and the informal. The growth of formal education through the 1950s and the 1960s brought with it a divorce from the informal side, coupled with a very strong emphasis on the notion that education is first and foremost a means to an end as opposed to an end in and of itself. In particular, a system devolved which in its present state has a narrow and single-minded purpose: the writing of college entrance examinations.

In Korea, opportunities for participation in higher education are strictly limited, and access into colleges and universities is controlled through the use of entrance examinations. More than half the eligible population is prevented from attending undergraduate studies simply because the number of places available does not reflect the demand. Parents find themselves caught in a system where the only realistic opportunity appears to be for their sons and daughters to focus solely on preparatory studies for writing the college entrance tests, knowing that half will not be successful. For those who succeed, entry into university is the reward. For those who don't, the consequences are far ranging and significant. Regardless of success or failure, the costs associated with losing a system where the formal blends with the informal and where learning is valued for its own sake cannot be estimated. Korean society has lost the lifelong paradigm.

To fully appreciate this system, and the associated implications, it is important to acknowledge the fact that in Korea graduation from university is not simply an academic honour. It reflects admission to a particular position in society, and influences marriage prospects, job opportunities and even friendships. Most companies strongly differentiate between those jobs which require a university degree, regardless of qualifications or skills, and those that do not. The result is that a not so invisible barrier has been created, preventing those below from achieving their potential, and cushioning and protecting those above, regardless of ability. Social status, as determined by university graduation, has become more important than competence.

NEW DIRECTIONS

Recently there has been broad recognition of and increasing concern within Korean society for the problems associated with the emphasis on entrance tests for accessing higher education as well as the effects of limiting the number of places available. In the first instance, the educational system has evolved into one where the entire focus for learning is unidirectional, and as a result it is neither broad nor integrative. There is one goal, and students focus only on that goal. The needs of modern-day industry in Korea are substantial. Required in the workforce are a vast array of independent thinking and problem solving skills, but instead, for many years of study, the developmental emphasis is on passing a single entrance exam. Increased technical sophistication and global competition have further ripened the required skill set, but each year in Korea has been one where students have if anything simply become more focused on that one exam. With regard to the limitation of the number of university seats available, the effect has been one of polarization and neglect. Those who pass the test are successful, and those who do not are effectively isolated from the opportunities associated with university admission. Can a society effectively compete in a global marketplace and at the same time limit advanced educational opportunities by as much as fifty percent? In the information age, the answer is most assuredly "no".

In 1995 the Korean government initiated plans to re-develop the educational system, implementing both a more open approach and one that will support the basic premises inherent in lifelong learning (see the Education Innovation Committee, 1995). In this initiative, special attention will be paid to providing ongoing opportunities for people to upgrade their technical and vocational skills on a continuing basis. As well, the new plans call for ensuring that educational facilities and opportunities, including broader access, will be available to all citizens without restrictions that in the past have typically been associated with time and place.

The terminology "open learning" and "lifelong learning", which are at the heart of the new policies, include a variety of interrelated concepts and practices. For example, open learning, described by Johnson (1990) as emphasizing the opportunity for learners to undertake further education, regardless of age, locale, or previous experience, is critical to the new plan since it is expected that entry restrictions for higher education will be reduced or possibly eliminated, and older citizens, not just those who are at the traditional post-secondary age, will have access. Adult education, as one component of lifelong learning, and described by Lengrand (1991) as education continued throughout [or later in] life, will be newly emphasized, as will recurrent education, defined by Ironside (1991) as the discontinuous, periodic participation in educational programs [throughout life]. Similarly, Candy and Crebert's (1991) characterization of lifelong learning as being unstructured by nature, and based on the philosophy that education should be openly and easily accessible to all, at all times of life, is apropos to the new approach being developed and implemented in Korea.

Enlarging the scope of learning opportunities in all ways is the cornerstone of the new program. Without continuous learning, no worker will have job security in the environment of today, characterized as it is by an exponential growth of knowledge, rapidly developing technology, and fierce global competition. Today's shortened product life cycle and the voracious demands made by consumers for newer and better products, combine to make business tougher and more aggressive than ever before for every Asia Pacific economy. A continually upgraded workforce is at the heart of a successful business and industrial sector.

In order to implement the new program, the Korean government recently established the Bureau of Lifelong Learning. This agency operates under the aegis of the Ministry of Education, and in order to fulfil its tasks has assumed some of the responsibilities formerly under the control of the Bureau of International and Social Education. In the past, the term "social education" was used to describe the limited programs of instruction offered to students who were unsuccessful in the university entrance examination. As a result, the term and the associated bureaucracy became tainted, and were not able in the new climate to convey the full context of lifelong learning. For these reasons, a new bureau with a new vision was required.

EDUCATIONAL DEMOCRATIZATION

The emphasis on and influence of greater access to post-secondary education in Korea should not be underestimated. Since the completion of the 4th National Economic Development Plan at the end of the 1970s, there has been a strong commitment to what in Korea may be referred to as economic democracy: the right of all citizens to benefit equally with regard to the opportunities arising from the economic gains being experienced by the society as a whole. Political democracy, described here as government initiated by the people, has been a source of struggle through the 1980s, but is now a firmly established resolution.

Regardless of the changes in the economic and political climates, a large percentage of the Korean population, totalling some twenty million, continue to suffer from disparate access to the more than considerable benefits accruing from an undergraduate university education. This has led to social separation, played a significant role in determining life chances, and been a governor restricting economic growth by limiting the skills of the workforce. Through the development and introduction of the new lifelong learning policy by the government and the Bureau of Lifelong Learning, Koreans expect to enjoy what may be termed "educational democracy" by the end of the current decade.

In a society distinguished by educational democracy, everyone has freedom to access the educational establishment. Regardless of age, gender, family connections, social status, religious affiliation or geographic location, all members of the society may apply for educational access and may reasonably expect to be admitted. The influence of this measure is difficult to conceive of unless you have experienced the absence of educational democracy. Broad economic and political changes aside, the development of open access to lifelong learning opportunities in Korea for all citizens may well induce a quiet but momentous social revolution, one which results in overall ability rather than a single examination being the factor that most influences life chances, a circumstance enjoyed by other societies but to date foreign to Koreans.

RECOVERING THE ESSENCE OF EDUCATION

Continuous technological change and increased global competition, referred to earlier in this paper, have created the necessity to retrain and upgrade the skills and knowledge of all workers on a frequent basis. Only a lifelong learning paradigm encourages the re-skilling that is necessary in today's economy. The move back to a society which prizes learning for the sake of learning and makes learning opportunities widely available will go a long way to satisfy the demands arising from technical and economic forces. To keep your job in a changing environment, you will need to be frequently re-trained. To get a promotion you will need to develop new skills. To become re-employed if your job has become outdated or unnecessary, you will need fresh expertise. However, what of the non-vocational side of lifelong learning? According to traditional Korean ideology, the real essence of education is bound up with gaining maturity, wisdom, self-improvement and enrichment, and simply appreciating the joy of learning. To date, that essence has been lost or set aside in the competition to succeed with the post-secondary entrance examinations. Will the development of an open access educational system, and lifelong learning opportunities for all, encourage educational recovery with regard to the essence or the non-vocational side of learning? This is an important question, and one that deserves considerable consideration on the part of policy makers and educational theorists.

Korean society, in the first half of this century and earlier, was traditionally bound together by its system of education where the norms, values, beliefs and mores were learned as part of an informal process through the lifespan. The society was stronger and more productive because of the common threads taught to all. A lifelong learning system that focuses *only* on the vocational side of education will not do justice to the informal side of learning, the side where throughout learning the people become a society. However, it can be argued that a stronger vocational side, one where access is open, broad abilities are emphasized, and a lifelong perspective advocated, can provide the foundation for the development of the non-vocational side.

That foundation will rest in part on having people experience the broader values and benefits associated with education. For example, as described earlier, on-going vocational education can lead to greater job stability, increased job enhancement, more opportunities for on-the-job promotions and overall greater economic well-being. This will sow the seeds for the re-birth of learning for the sake of learning, providing of course that the promises associated with vocational learning are in fact delivered. In this regard, it is important that Korean policy makers work to avoid the sorts of problems that have become associated with vocational education, a number of which are apparent in systems where open access has been the norm.

Two problems typically associated with vocational education include: (a) requiring all learners to learn the same curricula in the same way, and not adequately, if at all, taking into account experiences that are not accredited university experiences; and (b) not embracing technology to maximize educational benefits. In order to create the most productive environment for open access and lifelong learning in Korea, and one that will encourage the re-birth of the essence of education, the inclusion of non-vocational alongside vocational, this paper argues for the utilization of a computerized academic credit banking system as well as the incorporation of multimedia technology as a foundation for virtually all educational activities.

COMPUTERIZED ACADEMIC CREDIT BANKING SYSTEM

Systems and bureaucracies quickly become entrenched, taking on a life of their own and often neglecting the needs of those for whom they were originally established. Nowhere is this more apparent than with traditional educational bureaucracies, and requirements for all students to take the same courses, regardless of whether or not they already have the skills. Students should be allowed, or perhaps even required, to record lifetime learning, noting courses taken, seminars completed, job tasks demonstrated, and skills achieved, and courses should be increasingly competency-based, allowing students to work specifically on the development of the skills or competencies they lack, while simply demonstrating those they already possess.

Along with these changes, and in part to initiate some, a computerized academic credit banking system (CACBS) should be established. The CACBS would allow students to register and accumulate academic credits into an academic account following strict but objective accreditation guidelines. Certificates, diplomas, licenses and even degrees would be conferred at such time as the accumulated academic credits satisfy appropriate graduation or accreditation criteria. The CACBS would allow students to take credits from a variety of educational institutions without traditional limitations such as time or type of institution, and the computerized nature would allow for a broad-based, interactive system that in time could be expanded, at least regionally, within the Asia Pacific area. Within Korea the benefits for firms as well as for individuals would be considerable, and a scheme of this nature would help respond to demands for greater regional labour mobility, a goal voiced by various organizations including the Asia Pacific Economic Cooperation Forum.

In the current environment, there are many vested interests associated with the maintenance of individual institutions, particularly colleges and universities, each of which has its own standards for admission, coursework and graduation. In today's environment, the issue of whether students attend college to get an education or get a degree is critical. For many students, particularly in the age of the entrance examination, attendance at university is for the sole purpose of getting the degree. If standards for degree attainment were consistent, yet flexible, transparent and widely available, students attending university under the new access policy would be encouraged to select institutions on the basis of the learning provided. Further, students would not be locked into an institution for the entire degree program, and required to go through additional courses and irrelevant material simply because the individual institution with its monopoly has become the locus for all learning decisions.

The development of a CACBS in Korea will not be easy. To date, the recognition of academic credits between universities and colleges is not a common practice. As monopoly-like institutions, they simply don't have to cooperate given that the demand for seats in higher education during the course of the past fifty years has far outstripped supply. Universities and colleges have become accustomed to their privileged status, a result of the bottleneck established by government policies. Competition, and the good things it often brings to systems economic and otherwise, are absent. Although educational reform has been recommended almost biennially within Korea, usually in the name of an educational review or policy direction, little has changed. The opportunities associated with the development of the Bureau of Lifelong Learning auger for great potential, but only if the universities and colleges can be forced to more freely compete and students are allowed choices and awarded credit based on objective, open criteria.

Gradual implementation of CACBS is suggested, especially with regard to the identification of institutions for initial development and participation. In order to signal the importance and value of the system, it would be best to begin with national post-secondary institutions, focusing on mutual accreditation for academic credits among universities and colleges. The second stage would be the inclusion of educational and training institutions affiliated with universities or colleges. These would include specialized institutes. Third into the mix would be not-for-profit, municipal government schools as well as community organizations. This recognition would begin the notion of formally bringing the vocational and non-vocational sides of lifelong learning into the same paradigm. The fourth and final group would be private institutions operating on a for-profit basis.

The benefits associated with a CACBS are considerable, particularly in Korea where the problems identified with the under-supply of post-secondary educational opportunities and the isolated and elitist institutions are considerable. For this reason, the development of objective and strictly consistent standards must be emphasized. These should be a government priority and a government responsibility, perhaps associated with the new Bureau of Lifelong Learning.

MULTIMEDIA TECHNOLOGY FOR LIFELONG LEARNING

A truly open, highly accessible and relevant system of vocational and non-vocational learning will only be achieved if it incorporates distance delivery and a learner-centred philosophy. In the first instance, though Korea is not a particularly large country, still the population is spread across a geographic area that makes access to the large cities for the purpose of attending fixed-place, educational institutions improbable for a substantial portion of the population. Distance delivery can resolve the issue, and will in effect do much to make access equitable.

Second, in order to respond to the total demand at times which suit the learner, and to ensure that technical education in particular reflects the technology of the day, education cannot continue in all its forms to be teacher- and institution-centred. The availability of educational opportunities only when the teacher is ready will not achieve the goals described in this paper. What is required is the effective use of new technology, including distance education and interactive multimedia technologies to deliver learning opportunities throughout the country and perhaps throughout Asia Pacific regions.

Multimedia technology is still very much in its infancy, but even at this stage it is clear there is a revolution afoot in education. No longer are students dependent on teachers, and no longer do institutions have a monopoly on learning. Certification continues to be a holy grail, but it too will soon be transformed. In fact, traditional learning as experienced by today's adults may already be an artifact, tenaciously clinging to life only because it is what we have come to know best and because it creates conventional jobs for many who have benefited from the system. Regardless, multimedia technology, including access to the Internet and the World Wide Web, will give young and old the broadest opportunities and the best learning anywhere and anytime. It will transform the way in which we live by connecting people with more information more quickly and in a more usable fashion than any of us are likely able to imagine. The challenge for Korea is twofold: blend its new found commitment to access and open education with a system that ensures institutions compete to meet the needs of students; and, at the same time, put resources into developing multimedia learning applications and distance education technology.

In an important first step, the Government of Korea plans to install fibre optic cable into every home by the year 2015 as part of its commitment to ensure broad access to the information superhighway. High-performance connections between homes, schools, workplaces, libraries, and community centres will be a major step towards fulfilling the obligation to bring accessible and lifelong learning to the people, for the democratization of education if you will, as well as for creating a venue that will once again bring the vocational and non-vocational elements of learning together in order to create a single platform. The challenges may be intimidating, but the rewards are clearly unparalleled. For Korea, the opportunities associated with lifelong learning may be the most socially important and meaningful of the 21st century.

REFERENCES

Candy P. C. & Crebert, R. G. (1991). Lifelong learning: An enduring mandate for higher education. *Higher Education Research and Development 10*(1), 3-15.

Education Innovation Committee. (1995). *Education innovation plan.* Seoul: The Ministry of Education Of Korea.

Ironside, D.J. (1991). Concepts and definitions. In C. J. Timus (Ed.), *Lifelong education for adults: An international handbook.* Oxford: Pergamon.

Johnson, R. (1990). Open learning: Policy and practice. *Commissioned Report No. 4.* Canberra: National Board of Employment, Education and Training.

Lengrand, P. (1991). Lifelong education: Growth of the concept. In C.J. Timus (Ed.), *Lifelong education for adults: An international handbook.* Oxford: Pergamon.

Alice Lee

Alice Lee holds a Bachelor of Science degree from McGill University and a Master of Business Administration degree from the University of Toronto. She has extensive experience in the public sector with Canada's Department of Finance, Health Canada, and Industry Canada. She has also worked for the World Bank as a public health consultant in Washington, and has project experience in parts of Africa including Tanzania and Guinea. Currently, Alice is a consultant in the private sector. She enjoys outdoor sports, learning about different cultures, and has a lifelong interest in cooking.

Lifelong Learning, Workforce Development and Economic Success

by Alice Lee

From Singapore's "Total Business Centre", designed to attract international busi-ness investment to help support plans for intensive and ongoing workforce re-training, to Canada's CANARIE project, designed to link the efforts of government, industry, and education in a coordinated response to workforce development needs, APEC member economies have developed different approach-es for responding to the evolution of information technology and the need for lifelong learning. This paper describes the environment within the APEC region that is creating pressure for workforce development and lifelong learning, dis-cusses examples of various infrastructure activities intended to support the for-mation of a learning society, and identifies key strategies common to the development of a lifelong learning culture.

INTRODUCTION

Lifelong learning is a broad, conceptual term which is used to describe the process of continuous learning, personal enrichment and extension of knowledge that takes place over the course of the human lifespan. Learning, as the prime sub-component, presupposes a process of self-directed, though perhaps economically driven, explo-ration and discovery of knowledge, skills and abilities. Included in the lifelong learn-ing concept are formal, non-formal, and informal experiences, such as schooling, on-the-job training, learning by doing, and all other everyday forms of experience. In effect, to live is to learn.

Dramatic advances in technology, spiralling economic competition, and increas-ing global trade are changing the world at a dizzying pace. Linked to these changes is the need for increased and ongoing self-directed and self-driven learning in order for people and systems to respond and adapt to the changing world. The key chal-lenge facing all societies is to develop and implement effective ways for citizens to maximize their learning potential throughout the lifespan.

This paper argues that lifelong learning is critical to the success of APEC and its member economies and details ventures which verify that there is a host of new learning initiatives underway which are marked by innovation, variety and distinc-tiveness from the traditional educational establishment. Further, this paper exploits the view that lifelong learning for the 21st century requires a strong, policy-sup-ported, information technology (IT) infrastructure. Concrete examples of how selected APEC members, and particularly Canada, are developing such structures are described.

APEC AND THE ENVIRONMENT

APEC is an eighteen member economic forum with a population exceeding two billion. The members are geographically distant, culturally distinct and economically different. The region as a whole is characterized by strong and continuing economic growth (see Economic Committee, 1996), and all APEC members embrace the notion that human capital formation and investment in people are key determinants in achieving sustainable economic growth. Within East Asia, the average annual economic growth has been particularly strong and is predicted to average more than 8% during 1997 (Economic Committee, 1996, p. 4). Although the broad APEC market has tremendous growth potential, it is important to note that the region faces enormous productivity and technology variances resulting in significant measure from the fact that APEC members reflect a broad range of economic development stages.

The globalization of economic activity is related to several factors, including free market policies, increasing cross-ownership, escalating labour mobility, and the freer flow of capital. Economies are being linked without regard to national boundaries, if not by design then by market factors. Further, technological advances have, during the past decade in particular, combined with broad economic integration to speed the development of the global economy. The result is increased and increasing competition. In order to survive, and indeed profit, in the global economy, workers in the new order need to be educated, re-educated and educated again. A carefully designed and comprehensive program of learning opportunities, which encompasses a developed structure for learning at all levels in all places at all times throughout the lifespan, has become crucial in order to prepare the workforce of the future.

Skills and knowledge are the basis for higher wage employment and economic competitiveness. The combination of technological advances and the processes associated with the ever widening integration of the global economy have made it necessary for workers to acquire new skills throughout the lifespan. Innovation, freer trade, and technology are driving educational change, while changes in employment opportunities and living standards are byproducts. Particularly within the Asian APEC economies, newly industrialized and industrializing members are moving, or desperately trying to move, from low technology, labour intensive production into more technologically advanced activities.

The overall environment is characterised by three key opportunities and challenges:

- there continues to be an unrelenting need to upgrade the quality of skills within the workforce in order to maintain international competitiveness;

- there will be unprecedented investment in infrastructure and advanced information technology including telecommunications within the region (Asian members will spend in excess of US$1 trillion on infrastructure during the next decade - see *APEC: Opening Doors for Canadian Business)*;

- there are significant risks associated with the fact that rapid development and advances are increasing the gap between the rich and poor, and that certain disadvantaged groups may be increasingly marginalized and unable to compete in the new environment.

Learning and education are central to both the opportunities and the challenges.

PRESSURES TO UPGRADE THE WORKFORCE

The shift from a low skilled labour market orientation towards highly skilled knowledge workers is growing at a dramatic rate in many economies. Hong Kong and Chinese Taipei are examples of this trend. Three decades earlier, these economies were characterized by low level technical production and manufacturing. Now, Hong Kong has established itself as a centre for business and finance, developing plants and production activities in the P.R.C. During this same period Chinese Taipei has generated an enviable reputation in the field of information technology, both in manufacturing and in research and development.

In effect, the escalating race throughout the region to the higher end of the production and service delivery continuum is requiring a new workforce, one that is highly trained, flexible and not only open to re-training throughout the lifespan but actually seeks it out and embraces it. A further consequence of the demand for a workforce that embodies greater effectiveness and more efficient use of resources is the search for alternatives to the existing educational structures, programs and delivery methods. What is needed, and needed now, are learning alternatives that provide quicker and more targeted skills and knowledge development within the workforce, and all this at an increasingly higher level of technical sophistication.

The 21st century will see rising demand from employers for highly skilled employees, and unless the educational qualifications of the labour force are upgraded as fast as the shift in demand for labour, inequality and disparities will widen. In effect, the argument made here is that a lifelong learning system can be the solution for inequality within an economy and perhaps within the region. Conversely, without an effective lifelong learning system, the distance between the have and have-not members of the societies will not only widen, but may in fact become so distant as to become irrecoverable.

Acquiring and maintaining a competitive advantage is directly linked to the knowledge and skills of employees. Ongoing learning is the key to organizational versatility, adaptability and overall effectiveness. Three factors become extremely important in a highly competitive environment:

- quality, because consumers, particularly as they grow wealthier, tend to invest in products that provide the greatest value;

- productivity, because, to remain productive, producers must provide goods and services that parallel demand, on time and at a favourable cost;

- innovation, because the creative application of resources makes producers more responsive to consumer needs.

The relationship between the development of human capital and economic growth is especially well illustrated within the East Asian region. Specifically, there is strong evidence of this link in Hong Kong and Chinese Taipei, as described earlier, in Japan, Korea, and Singapore, and to a lesser extent and more recently in Malaysia and Thailand. The transition from labour intensive industries to knowledge-based ones in less than a generation can be attributed in substantial measure to education and training, along with hard work. System-wide planning and certain cultural traits have also supported this transition.

Not surprisingly, the diversity of comparative advantages in Asia has been reflected in the structure of exports from this region. The least developed economies were more dependent on exports of primary products and low-end manufacturing. However, as economies developed, exports shifted to include more finished products. At this same time, many of these economies, including Singapore and Chinese Taipei, faced increased labour and materials costs, and were forced to re-examine tactics for growth and competitiveness. Large investments in infrastructure, such as research institutes, allowed them to become generators and exporters of knowledge-based products and services, as in the examples of Singapore and Chinese Taipei. Within the past decade these economies have invested beyond their borders, shifting labour intensive manufacturing into southeast Asia and the P.R.C.

Perhaps most pertinent in the overall context of this discussion is the fact that the system of education and training implemented and developed in the fast-growing Asian economies during the past few decades has been significant but at the same time quite traditional. Included has been an emphasis on in-school learning, differentiated vocational and academic streams, and a highly competitive environment. Mass education has not meant similar opportunities for all. Rather, educational structures have produced the type of workers in more or less suitable quantities for the current stage of economic development and regional competition. Now, there is a need for a new paradigm. Lifelong learning is not simply more learning, nor is it simply learning at a higher level. Lifelong learning incorporates the development of a learning culture, something that schools and educational systems have in the past failed to achieve. What we are seeing now is the evolution of new learning paradigms.

NEW APPROACHES TO WORKFORCE LEARNING

This section of the paper details several Asian examples of new and widely differing approaches which are being set in motion in order to construct and develop much needed lifelong learning communities.

Singapore

The labour shortages of the mid-1970s in Singapore led to the development of technology intensive manufacturing industries. Concurrently, there was a renewed emphasis on technical education and training as well as expanded incentives for more research and development. In the 1980s, the government determined to develop knowledge intensive industries which, in turn, led to the current focus on IT, aerospace technology, pharmaceutical products, and computer aided design and computer aided manufacturing (CAD/CAM).

With its high labour costs, Singapore focused on a "Total Business Centre" strategy, whereby tax reductions and exemptions were given to foreign companies that established comprehensive operations within the economy. Another strategy was to continually upgrade the skills of the workforce, the Institute for Technical Education and the polytechnics being the driving force for much of this, along with increasing R&D incentives. Singapore expects to gain competitive advantage by becoming an electronic society, but the workforce issue must be continually addressed. In what may turn out to be a simple yet extremely effective strategy, Singapore is developing a product known as the Students' Multimedia Integrated Learning Environment, or SMILE (Smile ..., 1996). Launched in early 1996, this effort integrates the expertise Singapore wants to develop and become known for, with an applied solution that will be used to develop the workforce needed to support the product. The end has become the means.

Rather than relying purely on the traditional education system to drive this initiative, it is driven by collaboration between Informatics Holdings Limited and Singapore's National Computer Board's Information Technology Institute. In Singapore, the notion of involving business and industry in workforce training has always been very strong. In this case, however, it is taken to a new level. Business and industry is not simply going to be the curriculum focus, it is going to be much of the development and delivery mechanism as well. This is quite a departure when compared with educational systems where the private sector may be involved, or at least appear to be involved, in curriculum decisions but the delivery continues to remain almost entirely in teacher-centred educational institutions. Singapore intends to turn the paradigm around and become a leader in the development and export of IT-enhanced learning technology. Given Singapore's previous record of successes in planned development, APEC members would be well advised to pay close attention to this initiative.

Chinese Taipei

In little more than a decade Chinese Taipei has established itself as a leading centre for higher technology research and development, and for IT training. It did this through several strategies, key among them was the development of the Hsinchu Science-Based Industrial Park (SIPA) in 1980. Since the time of its establishment, this enclave has developed a world-wide reputation as an IT research and learning community, and has attracted a host of high profile companies that includes Acer Computer, United Microelectronics Corp., and Texas Instruments-Acer Inc. State-of-the-art infrastructure, a host of government incentives, R&D grants, and close proximity to air and sea ports, made Hsinchu a success in so far as attracting higher technology companies.

More importantly, at Hsinchu it has been the synergy of companies and personnel on site that have, in turn, attracted more human resources in order to build the learning community. Success begets success. From the earliest stages, every effort was made to incorporate technical training alongside the research and development activities, and as of this date, for example, more than 1,000 US-trained engineers have been attracted to the park because of the working and learning opportunities it provides (Spotlight on Success, 1996).The private sector, government and not-for-profit foundations, along with innovative universities and research institutes, have formed creative research, training and production relationships at Hsinchu that support integrated lifelong learning (see Hatton, 1995, pp. 73-76).At this stage, the human resource base at Hsinchu is the foundation for one of the most successful IT learning communities in the world. Working and learning have become synonymous.

Currently, Chinese Taipei is developing a new site along similar lines in the south near Kaoshiung.Though in the early stages of development, this is planned implementation of the broader concept which is designed to turn Chinese Taipei into an island of intelligent industrial parks. Clearly, lifelong learning is an inherent part of the design, and a component which feeds on itself to build further success.

Malaysia

Malaysia is chasing some of the region's more developed economies with its economic development plan titled *Vision 2020* (see Ahmad Sarji Abudl Hamid, 1993). The goal of this plan is to position Malaysia as a developed economy through productivity-led growth by the year 2020.

One element in the overall plan, to be developed over the course of the next two decades, is the formation of a Multimedia Super Corridor (MSC).The MSC pictures Malaysia as an island of excellence in technology, infrastructure, legislation and policies. Leading to this will be the formation of an electronic government, universities, research and development centres, tele-medicine centres, and high speed road and rail links.The government has created the Multimedia Development Corporation to manage and market the Multimedia Super Corridor.This plan and the success to date contrasts with economies where merely maintaining current roads appears to be stretching resources to their limits.

In order to upgrade skills development and management training, Malaysia currently has 60,000 students studying at colleges and universities overseas as it re-develops its education and training at home. As well, Malaysia is partnering with world centres of excellence in a variety of technical areas and Smart Cities. A new Multimedia University, scheduled for completion in the fall of 1997, will be geared to meet the specific needs of the information technology industry.

Underlying *Vision 2020* and the MSC is the development of the workforce and a concomitant lifelong learning ethic in the context of technical and vocational education within Malaysia. In fact, it could be said that *Vision 2020* and the MSC are simply the carrots which are designed to draw resources which will support ongoing workforce development.Whatever the case, it is clear that Malaysia is committed to the creation of a learning culture, and the goals do not focus on today's needs but rather they anticipate the future and are actively positioning the economy and the workforce. Contrast this with economies where there is no agreement on a national plan, let alone the activities to implement it.

CONVERGENCE, EDUCATION AND CANADA

Advancements in communications technology are leading to a convergence of computers, telephones, televisions, fax machines, video cameras, and satellites. This is affecting the way people around the world work, shop, bank, communicate and entertain. The influence of new technology on education has at this stage been more rhetoric than action, but this will soon change. New technologies when applied to learning will vastly improve access to resources and information, provide differential responses to specific learning needs, and better share scarce resources. Technology may also directly affect our internal capability to receive, digest and use knowledge.

In education, there is much detailed speculation about the influence of technology, specifically on distance education, as well as the influence of new learning technologies on the traditional teaching and learning model. The Internet and World Wide Web, in particular, appear to present opportunities that will challenge the very nature of education, or learning, and forever alter an establishment that has long enjoyed a monopoly on much of the learning environment. Very soon, the *information consumer* will have the potential to force a shift away from the classroom setting and into a *virtual learning environment*. Learners will soon demand learning opportunities regardless of where and who they are, and the competition will be notable.

Critical to the development of effective lifelong learning opportunities in a world of convergence is the establishment and maintenance of a "climate" or infrastructure for advanced information technology and telecommunications. Technology is a powerful engine for driving the development of new learning opportunities, but it is critical that the proper foundation and environment be established at a national level. With regard to education in Canada, the information highway is a work in progress. It promises, but has not yet delivered, a means for providing more practical, more varied, less expensive and enormously better learning opportunities. Canada continues to be concerned with the development of an infrastructure to support the information highway and specific strategies are being developed in recognition of the fact that a well developed infrastructure will facilitate better long term access to learning opportunities.

In this regard, the Canadian Jobs and Growth Agenda has been developed in order to increase productivity by encouraging growth. It focuses on three areas: youth, technology, and trade. In turn, these reflect lifelong learning, technology and APEC. In effect, the Jobs and Growth Agenda is a national plan to create an infrastructure for lifelong learning that will support the development of a comprehensive, competitive, highly skilled workforce beyond 2010. In this plan certain initiatives are being implemented which will exploit and develop the lifelong learning foundation. What follows is a brief summary of four examples.

Information Highway Advisory Council

The Canadian Information Highway Advisory Council was established in 1994 by John Manley, Canada's Minister of Industry. Broadly speaking, its purpose is to create jobs through innovation and investment, reinforce Canadian identity, and ensure *universal access* to the Internet and other information technology at reasonable cost. The operating principles under which the Council functions include lifelong learning as a key design element in Canada's information highway (Information Highway Advisory Council, 1996).

The Council debates a variety of public policy issues that have the potential to affect how innovation, investment and access to communications technology in Canada will occur. These include how fast information networks should be built, the balance between competition and regulation, control of communication networks, standards, federal and provincial coordination, control or censorship of information, privacy, consumer awareness, and the potential for affecting government activities. On a broad scale, the Information Highway Advisory Council is developing policy related to the development of the technology that will support the growth of a lifelong learning culture. The Council has stated that "if Canadians are to compete effectively on the global Information Highway, they need to embrace learning ..." (Information Highway Advisory Council, 1996, p. 2). Perhaps better than any other policy body in Canada, the Council reflects a concerted effort on the part of the Canadian Government to develop national policy and structure directly related to lifelong learning opportunities in the broadest context.

Canadian Network for the Advancement of Research, Industry and Education

In Canada, beyond the work of the Information Highway Advisory Council, the need for the development of an IT infrastructure which will further support the evolution of a lifelong learning environment has led to the creation of partnerships that include government, business, educators, and researchers. One of the key initiatives undertaken to foster the growth of these partnerships has been the formation of the Canadian Network for the Advancement of Research, Industry and Education (CANARIE). This is a not-for-profit organization with 140 members from industry and the research and education communities.

CANARIE's mission is to accelerate the emergence of Canada's Information Society (CANARIE, 1996). This includes the facilitation and development of Canada's communications structure and the development within Canada of next-generation advanced IT network products and applications. Unlike many other forms of government support, CANARIE's Technology and Applications Development (TAD) specifically targets for-profit corporations. Financial support from CANARIE for research and development projects can be as high as 50% of eligible project costs, though the average is approximately 30%. Emphasis is placed on projects which will likely lead to commercial success, and which involve more than one for-profit contractor. CANARIE shares in the commercial success of funded ventures through royalty agreements. In effect, CANARIE is an independent, though government funded body which supports private sector IT research projects and development activities that have demonstrable likelihood for commercial success. In this way, CANARIE is a policy implementation body designed to promote the development of in-Canada tools that will support the development of critical IT applications.

SchoolNet

The objective of the SchoolNet Program is to broadly enhance educational opportunities in Canadian schools by linking them electronically and making national and international resources available to all users. From the public's perspective, it is one of the most transparent examples of Canada's attempts to build a lifelong learning technology-based infrastructure.

In Canada, education is a provincial responsibility and the SchoolNet project, therefore, involves provincial and territorial governments, elementary and secondary schools, post-secondary institutions, and private industry. Currently, there are more than forty public and private sector partners involved with SchoolNet. Ultimately, this program is expected to provide the infrastructure for student and teacher interaction without regard to location or time. For students groomed in this system, it could provide the basis for individualized learning throughout the lifespan.

By 1998, SchoolNet is expected to link 6.5 million elementary and secondary students through 16,500 schools and 3,400 libraries. Rural students will have access to the same resources as those in urban areas, a major development in educational opportunities within an economy marked by large rural expanses and, in some cases, hundred of kilometres separating communities. In addition, the SchoolNet Community Access Project will provide up to 1,000 rural communities with access to the information highway, including the 400 aboriginal schools which fall under federal jurisdiction. Completion of this project will position Canada as the first country in the world to connect all of its schools to the information highway.

Health Iway

The Canadian Health Iway is a technical framework designed to provide network-based health services across the country. For Canada, this is a critical issue. Canada's geography is such that the delivery of health care to all its citizens is difficult, particularly in the case of those who live in northern and rural areas. This is exacerbated by the fact that people in Canada are living longer, as is the case with many other APEC economies, and the cohort of older citizens is growing larger both in terms of actual numbers and as a percentage of the total population. The so-called "baby boomer" generation, which is the bubble cohort born in the wake of World War II, is adding to the dynamic. Almost three decades ago, Canada committed itself to a government funded national health care system. Now, in the context of the issues just noted, that system may be in jeopardy. Technology and lifelong learning have the potential to provide a partial solution.

With Health Iway there is a strong technical emphasis. The program is based on network architecture; sender, receiver, and carrier capabilities; operational hardware and software; user training and support services; health information technology; and telecommunication products. However, more important is the relationship to education and lifelong learning in particular. Lifelong learning, as described in the introduction to this paper, is a broad conceptual term that includes all learning relevant for personal and professional benefits. In the past, health care was primarily a matter for specialists, individuals did relatively little to manage their own care and the costs reflected this. In the future, there will be increasing need for individuals to manage their own health, both when they are healthy and when they are not. Health Iway is a tool for developing and supporting this. It will provide continual learning opportunities through health education services, health databases, and screening tools, all of which are integral elements for Canada's lifelong learning network in the 21st century.

EQUITY AND DISPARITIES

Noted earlier in this paper is the potential for reinforcing existing workforce inequalities and, potentially, making them larger. This is an issue facing all economies that are focusing on workforce-upgrading as they attempt to stimulate economic growth and prepare for increasing regional if not global competition.

In newly developing economies, this issue of increasing disparities may be most obvious and of greatest concern. Here, many rural groups have yet to step on even the first rung of industrialization, and the poor in some of the world's largest and most congested cities are eking out a living at best. These people continue to live at a subsistence level, or in some cases below it. Access to education is marginal or nonexistent, jobs are not available, and direct economic support is infrequent or absent. As the workforce shifts up the skill ladder, these groups become increasingly unlikely to benefit from any economic successes which may be developed and enjoyed at the personal level. Their only opportunities are likely to arise from direct government support, programming that is often too little and too late, and a route that does not typically generate self-sufficiency.

A second layer, those who through innovative programs, perseverance or mere happenstance have managed to get to the first rung of employment, are those most likely to fall off the ladder as the workforce is compelled to adjust to a changing and increasingly skilled work environment. If permitted to happen, there is the potential to lose much of the development success that has been gained in the last three decades. In this context, women as well as ethnic minorities may be the first to fall off the ladder given an environment without commitment and innovative policies and programs that ensure these groups do not become re-marginalized.

The third group at risk include those who are currently employed, but in job areas where the skills are such that developmental opportunities are unlikely to be generated. This can occur for a number of reasons. For example, skilled workers in industries where the entire workforce is outdated are unlikely candidates for re-training. Similarly, older workers and those who are less flexible, such as workers who have social and cultural ties with extended families, are also less likely to be targeted for re-training opportunities. Although this may benefit young, single workers, the overall effect on the society can be extraordinarily problematic. In a similar vein, the shift in labour markets from "blue collar" to "white collar" workers presents analogous issues. Blue collar workers when compared with white collar workers are, quite simply, less likely to be seen as candidates for up-skilling and re-training.

For many APEC members there is also the continual threat of much needed expertise leaving the economy. This is prompted by supply and demand differentials which are related to varying growth rates in different parts of the economy. Economies intent on ensuring a smooth transition to lifelong learning need to address this issue, likely through carefully thought out policy initiatives.

Ideally, an effective learning environment will address the imbalance in terms of learning needs as these exist within different strata and communities. The goal must be an inclusive learning society where there are opportunities and hope for all. Without this inclusiveness there will be ongoing instabilities and significant risk for economic losses. Parallels can and are being drawn at the regional level. As a result, the need for APEC and other organizations to share development perspectives and resources is critical.

STRATEGIES FOR THE ROAD AHEAD

The road to lifelong learning, workforce development and economic success is one and the same, but there are many different paths. Though it is difficult to imagine a society in the 21st century enjoying the benefits of economic growth without a comprehensive, inclusive system of lifelong learning, it is also clear that APEC member economies will achieve this in different ways. There do appear, however, to be several key tools or strategies that are proving to be successful for the development of lifelong learning, a competitive workforce and economic success across the region.

Partnership and Participation

The establishment of partnerships between government, business, and learning institutions appears to be fundamental to the development of planned infrastructure and programming in support of lifelong learning. The examples in Singapore, Chinese Taipei, Malaysia and Canada, detailed earlier in this paper, support the premise that public and private sector partnerships, as well as partnerships solely within the private sector, provide the synergy and complementarity required to develop innovative, large scale technical solutions and opportunities. Clearly, whatever government can do to benefit the development and growth of partnerships in education and learning will benefit the development of effective systems. As well as bringing different expertise to the task, partnerships, more importantly, break down artificial barriers between disciplines.

Technology as a Tool

The use of technology, and information technology in particular, is a critical tool for the development of lifelong learning opportunities. Traditional approaches to learning, particularly those which are teacher-centred and institution-driven, are not going to meet the training, re-training and personal development needs of the 21st century. The scale of learning needs for the 21st century is going to drive the development of applied educational technology.

An analogy may be drawn with the development of computer systems. From the late 1940s to the early 1980s, a period of 35 years, computer technology was impressive in so far as its ability to deal with specific tasks, most of those large in scale and of a routine nature. But day-to-day life was not obviously and immediately affected by this technology. Now, with the advent of the personal computer, the real revolution in computer technology has begun. With education and learning it may be the same. Large educational institutions are now attempting to harness the power and applications associated with various technologies including the Internet and World Wide Web, and to a certain extent some have accomplished this, albeit in a coarse manner. However, the effect on the general population remains limited. When the technology associated with learning infiltrates everyone's workplace and home, the real revolution will have begun.

Infrastructure versus Programming

There is a need for both infrastructure development and for operative programming in order to optimize the development of lifelong learning systems. The comparison is nicely illustrated by comparing two companies, one which always implemented ideas in the first month and then spent the next two years developing the infrastructure, fine tuning and correcting the problems, while the other always spent two years developing structure and preparing for the opportunity followed by a one month implementation. In the first instance the tendency for error is extreme and costly. In the second example the market opportunities are lost and the environment so radically changed that the plan is outdated before it is implemented. Infrastructure development must be combined with operational programming in order to take advantage of the combined opportunities afforded by a sound platform alongside practical experience and feedback.

Concluding Comment

The development of a skilled human resource base is critical, a necessary tool for economic success in the next century. Building capacity, partnerships and a learning society is a goal common to all APEC members. Effective use of technology will ensure that success.

In the new global economy, where knowledge is the key resource, the quality of a nation's human resources is critical to ensuring competitiveness. ... The key to prosperity in the knowledge economy is for workers to make intelligent use of information. Learning must span all our working lives. Technology will make that possible.

(Information Highway Advisory Council, 1996)

REFERENCES

Ahmad Sarji Abudl Hamid. (1993). *Malaysia's vision 2020: Understanding the concept, implications and challenges.* Kuala Lumpur: Pelanduk Publications.

APEC: Opening doors for Canadian business. Ottawa: Department of Foreign Affairs and International Trade.

CANARIE. (1996). *1996 TAD FAQ.* http://www.canarie.ca/eng/tad/96/tadfaq96.html

Economic Committee. (1996). *1996 APEC economic outlook.* Singapore: Asia Pacific Economic Cooperation Secretariat.

Hatton, M. J. (Ed.). (1995). *Exemplary training models in industrial technology.* Ottawa: Association of Canadian Community Colleges.

Information Highway Advisory Council. (1996). *Executive summary.* http://info.ic.gc.ca/info-highway/final.report/eng/exsum.html

SMILE - The Learning and Education Environment in the Information Age. (1996, January 31). Singapore: Formatics Holdings Limited.

Chuan Lee

Dr. Chuan Lee is Vice President and Professor of Graduate Studies at Ming Chuan University in Chinese Taipei. He specializes in Management Science, and also acts as managing director for several foundations and enterprises within the community. In the past, Dr. Lee has been on the faculty of Tamkang and the Chinese Culture University Graduate Institutes, and has been a visiting lecturer at Westminster College, University of Oxford. Dr. Lee's educational background includes an undergraduate degree from the Chinese Culture University, an M.S. degree in Management from the State University of New York at Binghamton, and a Ph.D. from the University of Southern California in Post-secondary and Higher Education. His publications include a textbook on management, a book titled *Development of Higher Education in China*, and various research and journal articles including *Post-secondary Vocational Education in the Republic of China: A Model*, *The Changing Face of Technological and Vocational Education in the Republic of China on Taiwan*, and *Implementation of Total Quality Management in Higher Education*. In his free time, Dr. Lee enjoys spending time with his family and pursuing his interest in research on oriental herbal medicines.

From Supplemental Education to Lifelong Learning in Chinese Taipei

by Chuan Lee

Although lifelong learning has become accepted in other economies, it remains a relatively new and as yet unestablished concept in Chinese Taipei. This is in spite of the significant and urgent need to develop an effective, broad and inclusive system of lifelong learning. Currently adult education programming in Chinese Taipei focuses on supplemental education, social education, open colleges and an open university. At present, only 5% of the adult population of Chinese Taipei participate. The Ministry of Education has been implementing policies and structures since 1990, at the direction of the President of Chinese Taipei, to strengthen lifelong learning. Regardless, much remains to be done and it cannot be said that Chinese Taipei is well on the road to creating a lifelong learning society. Obstacles to lifelong learning include limited access to programming, an emphasis on formal, degree granting higher education at the expense of other options, and the lack of a single lifelong learning authority.

INTRODUCTION

During the past twenty years, Chinese Taipei has revolutionized its workforce and become a high-technology, information-based society. The result is that more and more of the working population is dedicated to the communications industries. Within the past fifteen years, revolutionary changes have taken place in computer and electronic technology, resulting in a surging demand for an up-to-date, highly trained workforce. Although the number of training opportunities has increased dramatically during this period, supply does not come close to meeting demand.

In a recent work, James Martin (1996, p. 7) observed that "we must grow human potential as fast as we grow technological potential". In this regard, Chinese Taipei has fallen short of the mark. To address this shortcoming, Chinese Taipei needs to rapidly develop and deploy a national action plan for lifelong learning. To properly examine the current context in Chinese Taipei, and to identify areas specifically in need of development, a portrait of lifelong learning is appropriate.

Lifelong learning includes both formal and non-formal education, and it integrates all educational levels and structures, regardless of time, space, content or learning styles (Davis, Wood, & Smith, 1986). Lifelong learning incorporates a variety of learning methods and strategies, ranging from self-guided study through to formal education. Developed and developing economies have in the latter part of this century relied on formal education in order to respond to most learning needs. However, in the society of the future, all members of society will require not only formal schooling but also a plan for and access to lifelong learning. Societies will become learning communities, providing a host of continuous opportunities throughout the lifespan.

This new approach to learning and education reflects a fresh commitment towards the development of human resource potential. Investment in this potential through lifelong learning requires that strategic choices be made at the national, regional and community levels in order to establish relevant and efficient systems for lifelong learning. Key, practical elements in the development of a lifelong learning system include:

- completion of a needs analysis for individuals, groups and the society at large;

- clarification of structural roles and relationships, particularly between the formal and informal systems;

- identification of all the stakeholders and their respective roles (such as government, educational institutions, the private sector, volunteer organizations, and individuals);

- creation of collaborative networks and partnerships amongst the stakeholders;

- provision of information on lifelong learning throughout the society and at every level, coupled with incentives to participate;

- institutionalization of a common vision of lifelong learning and commitment to this vision as evidenced by the establishment of a single, appropriately resourced coordinating body.

Against the background of this framework of elements, there is work to be done within Chinese Taipei.

CURRENT STATUS OF LIFELONG LEARNING IN CHINESE TAIPEI

The concept of lifelong learning was discussed within the international community as early as the 1970s, and has been ardently promoted by the United Nations Educational, Scientific and Cultural Organization (UNESCO) (see Faure, et al., 1972). Lifelong learning in Chinese Taipei, however, remains a relatively new and as yet unfocused topic. Even at this stage the Ministry of Education (MOE) has yet to assign a specific division to integrate and coordinate lifelong learning resources in Chinese Taipei. Currently, the Social Education Division of the MOE is responsible for adult education in Chinese Taipei, and the adult education system as a whole is regulated by various divisions within the MOE.

"Supplemental Education", the label used for formal adult education in Chinese Taipei, includes adult programming in the elementary, junior and senior high schools, and in the junior colleges. In 1995, supplemental education accounted for 27,334 students studying in 342 schools at the elementary school level, 24,610 students studying in 224 schools at the middle school level, 7,532 students studying in 8 schools at the senior high school level, 211,325 students studying at the vocational high school level, and 33,762 students studying in the 8 junior colleges which offer college-level supplemental education to the general public (Executive Yuan, 1995). Given the population of Chinese Taipei, it is clear that this type of education is not widely and commonly accessed by adult learners, nor is it a primary focus of the major educational providers.

Also a component part of the existing lifelong learning structure in Chinese Taipei is the non-formal adult education system, identified by the MOE as "Social Education". Organizations providing social education include cultural, artistic and scientific organizations. As a result, libraries, museums, theatres, memorial halls, and sports facilities are governed by the social education regulations and provide a variety of lifelong learning opportunities to the general public. In 1995, there were 13 national, 58 provincial, and 353 county and local government social education organizations.

In addition to these organizations and programs, Chinese Taipei offers adult education through distance learning. This is organized through a well-designed Open University and four Open Junior Colleges. As of 1994, there were more than 140,000 and 200,000 graduates from the Open University and Open Junior Colleges, respectively. With the notable exception of the Open University, there has been no formal administrative bureau or independent fund to coordinate and promote adult education (Hwang, 1995).

Regardless of the type or venue for supplemental education offered within Chinese Taipei, the effect has been to provide a second chance for those who did not or were not able to take advantage of educational opportunities during their youth. In effect, supplemental and, to a lesser extent, adult education provides a second chance. For most citizens, the opportunity to build on their education is the only means for improving their standard of living.

Given the number of persons in Chinese Taipei who fall in the illiterate or poorly educated categories, it is astonishing that there has been so little demand for supplemental education. Two reasons may explain this. First, it is a commonly accepted notion in Chinese Taipei that a one-time educational experience during youth should be sufficient for the rest of one's life. Second, for many years no government ministry successfully promoted supplemental education. Currently, Chinese Taipei enrols approximately 5,300,000 students, of which 94% are in the formal education system and only 6% are learning through the Supplemental Schools or the Open University system (Ministry of Education, 1995). Only 5% of all adults are enroled in any form of adult education.

If Chinese Taipei expects to address the long-term educational needs of its population, particularly in the highly competitive communications industries, then both the educational structures and the attitudes of the people must be recast. A fully integrated lifelong learning system will be a necessity for Chinese Taipei in the 21st century.

SUPPLEMENTAL EDUCATION AND LIFELONG EDUCATION

As described earlier in this paper, the potential pool of lifelong learners in Chinese

Taipei is enormous. According to a MOE survey of people over the age of 60, there are more than 1.3 million illiterate and nearly 5.3 million adults with education at or below the elementary school level (Ministry of Education, 1992). In addition, nearly 8.3 million persons, or 57% of the total adult population, never study or even bother to read magazines (Ministry of Internal Affairs, 1992). These data are astonishing, indicating as they do that more than half of the total adult population of Chinese Taipei is either incapable of or not interested in acquiring new information. Given the population base and the current status of lifelong learning, the task of addressing learning throughout the lifespan in Chinese Taipei is indeed daunting.

This problem is compounded by the fact that Chinese Taipei has tied its economic fortunes to the production of information technology. Clearly, the 21st century will bring higher levels of competition, and the need for a well trained workforce who will take it upon themselves to continually update their knowledge and skills. Even those professionals who hold degrees or diplomas cannot afford to be complacent. The fact is that one-time education is no longer sufficient for a lifetime of work. Continuous learning will become synonymous with continuous improvement.

Further to this issue, the lack of technical knowledge and expertise, or the simple inability to use this knowledge or apply these skills, is creating a new definition of "illiterate". It can now be applied to professionally trained, technical personnel who fail to maintain currency in their fields. The notion of continuous learning is necessary not only for the survival of the individual, but also for the survival of businesses and corporations. In fact, it could be argued that the very survival of the Chinese Taipei economy is at stake. It is also important to recognize that the education being described here goes beyond simple acquisition of new vocabulary and general working skills. A highly technical and information-based society needs a level of sophistication that far exceeds what was acceptable only a few years ago.

At present, the adult education system in Chinese Taipei, as is the case in many other economies, has emphasized and become dependent on the formal school system to fulfil the educational and training needs of its adult population. This reflects the prevailing belief of the people in Chinese Taipei that a school-based education, and the resulting diploma or degree, is the only appropriate path to securing a good job and promotions. Although alternate channels for achieving professional certification coupled with a variety of learning venues are available, broad acceptance of these "alternate" credentials by potential employers is uncommon. As a result, endorsement by the general population continues to be marginal. Achievement is linked to successful graduation from formal schooling and, as a result, the pursuit of a higher degree through traditional channels continues to be over-emphasized. This situation leads to tremendous competition among school goers.

All schools at all levels evaluate prospective students according to entrance exam scores, and admit them accordingly. Students who do not pass the entrance exam are discouraged from seeking out alternative forms of training. Instead, they tend to enrol in "cram schools" in order to re-try the entrance exams for the formal educational system. It is difficult to promote lifelong learning in the context of these attitudes. However, if Chinese Taipei does not develop new systems and new values, the society will be ill-prepared to face the economic challenges of the 21st century.

GOVERNMENT INITIATIVES

During the 7th National Education Conference in 1994, the MOE specifically stated that lifelong learning will be key to the future development of education in Chinese Taipei. At the same time, President Teng-hui Lee delivered an important speech on education, stating,

> *The ideal of lifelong learning is to ensure the needs of education at every level of growth. In order to construct a learning society, we have to remove the idea of solely seeking a higher degree and try our best to get our people back to school to be re-educated.*   (Ministry of Education, 1994)

The same year, during the Teachers' Day banquet, President Lee again emphasized this point and urged the development of a lifelong learning system and perspective. In this speech, President Lee brought the private sector into the equation. He said,

> *Due to the rapid changes in modern society, everyone needs to be re-educated and re-trained all the time. Our society should be able to provide a variety of opportunities for learning and training. In addition to the formal education, schools should also strengthen both adult education and continuing education. Private organizations should also play a key role in the area of social education and offer related educational services to the general public so that we can make our society more suitable for lifelong learning and every person has access to educational opportunities.*
> (Ministry of Education, 1994)

Subsequently, the MOE announced a "White Paper" on Education in Chinese Taipei and stated that the major goal of future development in Chinese Taipei education would be to establish a sound lifelong learning system while developing a learner-friendly society.

Demonstrating its commitment towards a lifelong learning system, the MOE drafted an "Adult Education Law". In order to further promote the formation of a society of lifelong learners, the MOE initiated a "5-Year Plan to Develop and Improve Adult Education". Initial investment during the first year of the five year plan was in the order of NT$240 million. However, it is expected that the total government investment in this effort will top NT$3.5 billion dollars by early in the new millennium.

Traditionally, and as noted earlier in this paper, adult education has been limited to formal, in-school educational programming. However, with support from the government, programming via radio and television broadcasting systems has recently allowed more people to benefit from adult education curricula. At the same time, a variety of new delivery and learning methods are being deployed, including seminar series, conferences, self-study programs, consultant and advisor systems, home study applications, and practical training programs. With the increasing variety of delivery methods, more opportunities in more forms will be available for people to pursue lifelong learning options.

Through the present five-year plan, it is expected that more independent, non-profit, educational organizations will be formed. Some of these, such as the Adult Education Center at the Taiwan Normal University, will be attached to universities. Others, such as the Adult Education Resource Centers located in various cities, will be government directed, either locally or nationally. Still others, such as the Adult Continuing Education Centers in vocational high schools, will be locally directed. Together, these institutions will have a significant effect on the quantity, quality and variety of lifelong learning programs available in Chinese Taipei.

Further expansion of the lifelong learning concept can be seen in the newly developed senior citizens' educational programming, a host of women's learning activities, leisure education training, self-improvement activities, and professional development and skills training workshops. Assuming these initiatives are successful, it is expected that lifelong learning activities will drive a new and fast expanding trend in personal and professional development through a host of channels in Chinese Taipei.

COMPARISONS WITH OTHER ECONOMIES

At this time there remain two key differences in terms of lifelong learning in Chinese Taipei compared with other developing economies. First, in Chinese Taipei, private organizations remain virtually untapped as sources of lifelong learning programming and expertise. One of the requirements associated with an effective system of lifelong learning is the need to make learning more available, broader in nature, and more practical. Joint ventures with private organizations are an effective and efficient method for broadening the scope of learning programs and ensuring a fast and efficient response to market demands. However, to date there have been only a few private organizations within Chinese Taipei that have focused on the provision of lifelong learning programming. In order to cultivate an effective system of lifelong learning, there needs to be greater private sector involvement within Chinese Taipei. The government cannot do it all.

The second key difference relates to the fact that colleges and universities in Chinese Taipei do not contribute in a significant manner to the provision of lifelong learning. By nature, colleges and universities tend to be exclusive rather than inclusive, and nowhere is this more obvious than in Chinese Taipei. In many other economies, colleges and universities have played a role, albeit more often than not a small one, in continuing education programming. This has not only expanded the services and programming functions of the colleges and universities that do this, but it has also had a significant effect on the population by opening the doors of higher education more widely than would otherwise have been the case. Currently, adult education in Chinese Taipei colleges and universities is underdeveloped. Even though the colleges and universities promote the concept of adult education, the actual programming is minimal and often weak, reflecting restrictions of tradition, funding and structure.

Observing other lifelong education systems, we can see that lifelong learning strongly influenced by community-based initiatives and universities is becoming the norm. In Japan, though the formal school system does not support adult education, there are many learning activities provided by private organizations and supported by both the government and the community at large. Virtually every community has at least one organization dedicated to promoting adult education activities and coordinating with the local libraries, museums, social education facilities and job training centers to form an integrated local learning network. In fact, promotion of lifelong learning by private organizations has become the hallmark of Japanese lifelong education (see Hwang, 1994, p. 366-368).

Private sector organizations in Europe and the United States are also known for playing a more active role in the provision of lifelong learning than is the case in Chinese Taipei. Further, colleges and universities in these jurisdictions commonly promote a host of lifelong learning activities through adult and continuing education programming. This reflects recent trends and sharp changes in the structure and philosophy associated with the traditional university.

The British Open University is thought to be a new style of university, specifically structured to suit the needs of adult learners. Similar off-campus degree programs offered in other European countries and in the United States of America are designed to provide programming without the boundaries associated with time, location, and form. The off-campus degree approach not only promotes transferability, but also acts as a credit transfer mechanism, counting and recognizing credits from other universities as well as crediting previous learning and work experiences. The number of students completing programs through the non-traditional universities is increasing.

Universities have a unique status in most societies. They are seen as repositories of knowledge and culture, centers of research, and are equipped with highly trained personnel who have a particular focus on research. Justifiably, they are respected as the highest rung on the educational ladder. However, faced with the very different needs of the next century, colleges and universities in Chinese Taipei must re-evaluate their functions and responsibilities. These institutions must broaden their contribution to the society in order for more people to benefit from a wider variety of adult educational programs. It must be the responsibility of colleges and universities in Chinese Taipei to provide access to lifelong learners sooner rather than later.

FUTURE DEVELOPMENTS

The emphasis on formal education in Chinese Taipei needs to be addressed. Currently, the system is uni-directional, lacks flexibility, and does not come close to meeting the professional and personal needs of a society in transition. A true learning society must achieve a balance between formal and non-formal educational opportunities, and provide the diverse educational programming needed to satisfy the range of societal and individual needs. This is the immediate challenge.

Inspired by the lifelong learning ideal, the MOE is currently launching an educational reform which is designed to overcome the constraints of traditional education in Chinese Taipei. Specifically, the MOE is working toward ameliorating the current exam system, a system marked by its life-determining focus, and at the same time developing a host of new learning paths conspicuous for their variety and flexibility. The goal is to provide learning opportunities at every stage in life. As long as a person wishes to learn, opportunities will be present. In particular, those who need a "second chance" will find it easy to identify and attend a learning program specific to individual interests and needs.

As Chinese Taipei moves towards the implementation of a learning society, colleges and universities face a decision point. Though the MOE continues to encourage these institutions to promote and offer adult education programming, traditional university values continue to pose a significant barrier. On the positive side, continuing education has been adopted by the colleges and universities, and many have established "Schools of Adult Education" along with modified entrance requirements. In some cases these modifications include changing the examination methods, modifying approaches for admission, and taking life experience into account. This has provided citizens in Chinese Taipei with an alternative for acquiring diplomas and degrees. However, it is not enough, and supply does not come close to meeting demand. If the universities are not willing or able to modify their programming to a much greater extent, the MOE may create adult education alternatives that will bypass the colleges and universities (Chang, 1996).

Chinese Taipei's lifelong learning development target is to provide a range of programming for 40% of the adult population by the year 2010. To achieve this, adult education programming offered through colleges and universities must make use of a variety of new media, including cable television, the Internet, CD ROM, and other distance learning modes. Currently there are more than 3.6 million households in Chinese Taipei with cable television, representing more than 50% of the population (Cheng, 1995). For this reason it is the most obvious media to initiate widespread university-based continuing education programming. Though this is just one element of a comprehensive lifelong learning system, it would be a significant start for Chinese Taipei.

In order to encourage private philanthropic organizations to participate in lifelong learning promotion and programming, Chinese Taipei has launched several community projects that focus on the delivery of adult education programming. These efforts have taken the form of encouraging private philanthropic organizations to host community activities. However, though specific initiatives have been successful, there are not enough educational foundations and other similar organizations registered with the MOE in order to have a substantial influence on programming. To date, the solution for this problem is not obvious. Anticipating that private companies will take up the slack with regard to the provision of lifelong learning activities may also be problematic. These organizations tend to focus on specific areas, such as high-level technical training, leaving the large sectors, such as adult basic education, unserviced.

In Chinese Taipei, there are many learning centers within large metropolitan areas which provide a variety of short courses aimed at adults. However, these do not address the needs of the rural population or those who live in smaller centres. To partially address this issue, the MOE is planning to convert six Social Education Centers, located in Taipei, Kaoshiung, Hsin Chu, Chang Hwa, Tainan, and Taitung, into centers specially designed for the promotion and delivery of adult education. The MOE is also implementing a special project, "Establishing a Social Education

Network and Counselling System Project", which will convert libraries into local adult education centres (R.O.C., 1994). This will allow learners island-wide to access educational learning channels directly through their local libraries. These local adult education centres would be resourced by the six regional centres noted above.

CONCLUSION

While Chinese Taipei has at last begun the lifelong learning journey, the road remains long. While the MOE has made progress in so far as providing information on lifelong learning at the community level, and encouraged participation, the results have yet to be significant.

Needs analysis, at the individual, local and national levels, has yet to be completed, and efforts with regard to the development of partnerships and collaborations have been sluggish. Corporate and business involvement in lifelong learning is virtually non-existent, and all these issues may be attributed to the lack of a single, focused, comprehensive strategy. Until such a strategy is convincingly implemented Chinese Taipei may be losing ground to other economies with regard to the development of a lifelong learning society.

Clearly, the nature of work, both now and in the foreseeable future, requires constant retraining, upgrading and ongoing learning. Knowledge has, indeed, become the most valuable asset for individuals and for the society. To establish a lifelong learning society, the people of Chinese Taipei must alter their traditional views of education and learning, and accept that learning throughout the lifespan is a necessity for everyone.

REFERENCES

Chang, J. C. (1996, April 8). Degrees to be granted through university extension programs beginning after this summer break. *China Times*. p. 1

Cheng, L. Y. (1995). *Study of the general public's demand for cable TV and local news*. Unpublished thesis, Graduate Institute of Journalism, Cheng Chih University, Taipei.

Davis, E., Wood, J.M., & Smith, B.W. (1986). *Recurrent education: A revived agenda*. London: Croom Helm.

Executive Yuan. (1995). *Introduction to the Republic of China administrative organization*. Taipei: Government Information Office.

Faure, E., Herrera, F., Kaddoura, A., Lopes, H., Petrovosky, A., Rahnema, M., Ward, F. (1972). *Learning to be: The world of education today and tomorrow*. Paris: UNESCO.

Hwang, F. S. (1995). The current status and future development of adult education in Taiwan area. *Adult Education, 8*, 18.

Hwang, T. L. (1994). *New concepts in adult education*. Tokyo: Psychology Publisher.

Martin, J. (1996). *Cybercorp: The new business revolution*. New York, NY: AMACOM

Ministry of Education. (1992). *The educational statistics of the Republic of China*. Taipei: Government Information Office.

Ministry of Education. (1994). *Proceedings of the 7th R.O.C. conference on education - June 22-25, 1994*. Taipei: Government Information Office..

Ministry of Education. (1995). *The educational statistics of the Republic of China*. Taipei: Government Information Office.

Ministry of Internal Affairs. (1992). 1991 *Survey of Taiwan national living standards*. Taipei: Government Information Office.

Atsushi Makino

Atsushi Makino completed his university studies, including his Ph.D., at Nagoya University where he is an Associate Professor in the Graduate School of International Development and the School of Education. Currently, he is the project leader for two major developmental activities which focus on lifelong learning. The first, funded by the Kamiya Gakuen Foundation, examines the "Local Lifelong Learning Plan and the Role of Postsecondary Education" in Japan. The second, supported by Japan's Ministry of Education, Science and Culture, has as its goal the construction of a centre for local and regional lifelong learning development in the Graduate School of Education at Nagoya University. In addition to his work in Japan, Dr. Makino has directed research on agricultural technology and educational reform in the Anhui Province of the People's Republic of China, taught at the Shanghai Teacher's College, and been a visiting professor at the Ontario Institute for Studies in Education in Toronto, Canada. He has written more than 90 articles and monographs, including *Education in Contemporary China* and *The Development and Characteristics of Educational Thought in a Modern China - A Study on Tao Xing-zhi's "Life Education" Thought*. Dr. Makino especially enjoys reading, seeing the latest movies and spending time with his children.

Recent Developments in Japan's Lifelong Learning Society

by Atsushi Makino

Japan's recent history has emphasized the development of a strong workforce in support of economic growth, coupled with a population marked by homogeneous values, beliefs and a passionate commitment to the nation. However, all this is changing. The internationalization of the country, the development of an aging society, the coming of the information age at the expense of the industrial age, and changes in the traditional lifelong employment system are influencing the educational establishment and providing the impetus for the development of a lifelong learning system. Reports issuing from the Ad Hoc Council for Educational Reform (Rinji Kyoiku Shingikai or Rinkyoshin) in the late 1980s helped move lifelong learning from the conceptual to the policy stage, following which the Central Committee for Education (Chuo Kyoiku Shingikai or Chukyoshin) detailed recommendations in its "Basic Maintenance for Lifetime Learning Report". In turn, this formed the basis for the "Lifelong Learning Promotion Act" which was passed on July 1st, 1990. Although this law has moved Japanese society closer to a broader system of education and learning through the lifespan, the increased centralization of power and the expanding influence of the Ministry of Education have given rise to concerns which are described in this paper.

THE CONSTRUCTION OF A LIFELONG LEARNING SOCIETY

Lifelong learning is a concept which has become one of the most important keys for understanding modern Japanese society. In fact, commitment has been made within Japan for the development of a comprehensive, integrated lifelong learning society in which each person's vocational and personal development will be influenced by an open-ended, indeterminate, lifelong educational process. All of this will be orchestrated by the state.

In this process, not only will categories, such as school-centred education and social education (non-formal education) become minor, but they will also be reorganized and actualized through a self-development and self-recruiting system which will void traditionally accepted divisions and roles, thereby making the entire concept of education open and amorphous. The degree to which lifelong learning is affecting the basic nature and structure of Japanese society cannot be overestimated. This paper surveys the development of lifelong learning in Japan by examining recent trends, government sponsored reports, and legislation.

AN EVOLVING SOCIETY

It is highly improbable that anything as significant as a comprehensive lifelong learning system would develop in any society, let alone Japanese society, unless there were significant changes occurring at fundamental levels. This section of the paper discusses the most notable of these.

Structural Changes

There have been three structural changes within Japanese society which strongly factor into the development of lifelong learning policy. These include internationalization, the coming of the information age, and the maturation or aging of Japanese society.

It has been said that Japan twice experienced internationalization during its process of economic development. First, as a resource-poor nation, Japan chose to become an industrial centre of world importance in order to develop its economy. The importation of raw materials and the transformation of these materials into products for export to overseas markets was the basis for economic development. To this end, the ability to manufacture these products required giving priority to raising the quality and standard of the labour force. Basic education was expanded as well as the availability of technical studies at post-secondary institutions. This effort allowed the Japanese economy, over time, to produce a wide variety of high quality, affordable goods as "made in Japan". In the end, Japanese businesses captured a large share of the world's markets.

The second phase of Japan's internationalization occurred when the Japanese currency, the yen, became one of the strongest currencies in the world. Japanese capital was used for foreign investments and the purchase of overseas real estate in particular. This was also the period of the "bubble economy" in Japan, which, fuelled by inflated real estate values, did not last very long. Japan was called an "economic giant", and many Japanese manufacturers moved production overseas. At this same time, labourers flowed into Japan from Brazil and various Asian countries, as domestic labour had become scarce and expensive.

Currently, Japan is facing a third type of internationalization. This is resulting from the large number of Japanese going overseas and the large number of people moving to Japan. Of course, the nature of this third stage is different from the previous two. While Japanese goods and money were going overseas during the first two waves of internationalization, Japanese society was still comprised of one people sharing the same consciousness and values. This homogeneous, uniform society through its education system trained a homogeneous and uniformly moulded labour force in order to make the first internationalization phase possible. However, when large numbers of offshore people began arriving in Japan, the situation changed dramatically. The newcomers supplied the labour to do the "3-D" work, that which is difficult, dirty and dangerous. This influx brought different values and cultures to Japan; hence, the homogeneity and uniformity of Japanese society was disturbed. This is the basic motif which illustrates the nature of today's internationalization in Japan.

The evolution to an information-oriented society suggests Japan's industrial structure has undergone a turnabout, from manufacturing industries as the economic centre, to an information-based economy, with the computer industry playing the central role. The old industrial framework had two major features that differed substantially from the new network system. First, the pyramid shaped industrial society was based on a strict management control system and quality control system in which distinctions between various levels in the organization were very clearly defined. The information based society, on the other hand, needs to be operated laterally, between equals, and is by nature oriented toward individualism. Emphasis is on efficiency not hierarchy. Second, whereas the industrial society's political structure was centralized, the information society's structures are highly decentralized or come under smaller "sovereignty areas". These factors, when combined with the new wave of internationalization already described, will disturb what has been a uniformly homogeneous Japanese society. Potentially, they will create a danger in so far as national unity is concerned, as economic development and national unity become somewhat contradictory concepts.

The issue of the aging society will also have profound effects on Japanese society. This maturation will see more people achieving higher, academically boosted careers and more leisure time. Indeed, the aging of Japanese society will have the strongest influence on the societal fabric. By the year 2025 more than 27% of the population will be 65 years of age or older, and by the year 2050 more than 32% of the population will be 65 years of age or older (Asahi Shimbun, January 21, 1997). A super-aging society, in which one in four people will be seniors, is on the near horizon. This maturing of society, by virtue of the aging of its members, should necessarily lead the Japanese toward different social values, and the generally higher level of education will improve the ability of people to make better decisions about how they conduct their daily lives.

In summary, Japan is changing from being a "hard society" in which people are united under the same values and awareness as a nation to becoming a "soft society" in which individual values are respected, and heterogeneous people can coexist while not necessarily holding the same cultural perspectives and personal views.

Changes in the Employment Environment

Lifelong employment and seniority, which have been the centrepieces of the Japanese employment system, are rapidly disappearing as evidenced by the fact that the number of full time employees is decreasing while the number of part-time and contractual employees is increasing (Economic Planning Agency, 1985). This change is the result of several factors. For example, the manufacturing sector, which requires highly skilled and knowledgeable workers, has sent many of them overseas, and the growth of the "network society" and the computer industry has put enormous pressure on the labour pool. Hence, there is an increasing need to retrain senior workers in order to cover for the shortage of younger workers. Large enterprises based in Japan have been re-making sections of their operations into small, independent companies, and also new is the fact that many small venture companies come and go within the Japanese economy.

In this new kind of industrial structure, skills and knowledge are not stored inside companies. Instead, it is the technicians and engineers themselves who are the repositories. Moreover, many businesses do not need to permanently retain employees with specific skill and knowledge sets, a situation which leads to headhunting becoming the norm and where white collar workers can quickly find themselves in part-time jobs or even blue collar work. In addition to these changes in the economic landscape, seniors and housewives are entering the working world in large numbers. Thus, a new picture of the labour market has emerged: workers will change their jobs many times throughout their lives and the learning of new skills and abilities becomes a lifelong endeavour. For Japan, this is a radical departure.

Traditionally, individual employees have enjoyed guaranteed lifelong employment and a guaranteed seniority system. Now, however, employees will have to continuously develop themselves while working under fear of losing their jobs. Within the labour market, individualization will be promoted. Necessarily then, there is a need for the maintenance and expansion of educational and training opportunities for workers. Also required is a national policy to inform and unite the nation within this new context.

Retraining and development will not be part of the public education system. Rather, individuals will assume responsibility for their own development at their own expense. The new post-industrial era carries with it the principle that its beneficiaries, the workers, should pay to develop their own skills over the course of their working lives and that national awareness of this fact must be raised. This concept is at the core of the lifelong learning policies coming to the fore today.

The Dismantling of Schools

How, then, have the new working ability and skill development scheme and the new national unity concept been planned, and what kind of structure will they emulate? The best way to answer these questions is to study educational reform and school reorganization.

A report on educational reform and the dismantling of schools was produced by the Japan Association of Corporate Executives (Keizai Doyukai) in April 1995, and it has since had a strong influence on society. The title, though long, is illuminating: *From School to Community-based Learning Centres: Schools, Families, and Communities Being Aware of their Educational Responsibilities, and Each Giving of its Wisdom and Power to Create New Places to Learn and Grow*.

In the report, the authors identified some of the problems endemic to the school system. Included were bullying, truancy and how the schools have traditionally assumed responsibility for everything from academic instruction to life guidance and discipline. Schools assumed these tasks because of the demands made on parents by the Japanese economy. However, with the current changes taking place in industry, the traditional role fulfilled by the schools will no longer be necessary. The report recommends that the Japanese family, which now has much more free time, along with the community, reclaim responsibilities from the schools, and that all three, the school, the family and the community, should take part in raising children as a combined community based "school".

The boldest reform plan argues that, at school, only language, mathematics and moral education (basic tenets and national awareness of Japan) should be the guaranteed subjects. Other subjects, life guidance, special events and extra-curricular activities should be taken out of the schools and returned to the families and communities, the idea being that parents who now have more spare time can teach and discipline their children as well as take them on family trips to gain a broader perspective of society. The community would provide volunteer activities, clubs, sports and so on, to be organized by local companies. This would give children the opportunity to develop individual identities and abilities.

This argument shows an important turning point in the Japanese view of schools and education. Historically, the Japanese education system was built alongside and in support of the formation of the modern industrial society and nation state, to uniformly train each citizen to be a dedicated worker. The education system, in fact, closely paralleled the manufacturing system. The Japanese manufacturing system, based on Taylor's ideas from earlier in this century, divided the manufacturing process into many steps. Added to this was Ford's assembly line model and conveyor concept. Additionally, overlaid on top of these is the Japanese Total Quality Control (TQC) System. The first two systems made modern manufacturing extremely simple and mass production possible; however, the quality of individual workers was brought into question. In the Japanese TQC system, it is assumed that the quality of labour requires constant improvement in an ongoing effort to improve the quality of the finished product. The system has a very strong labour control aspect. Needless to say, in this type of environment, employee education and loyalty to the work group and company were essential. It was TQC which underpinned the lifelong employment and seniority systems. All told, the analogies with the school system are powerful.

Elementary and junior high school education were assigned the role of inculcating the TQC system. In theory, across all Japanese schools, the quality of the children's education is the same. Effort and desire were viewed as the variables, so if a child had a poor academic record, the reason had to be that he or she was simply not putting forth the effort. The result is a system where children are always competing with each other for grades, or within groups, or against other groups or even other classes in the same school. Hence, the awareness of group identity is strong. Through the school curriculum too, the children are indoctrinated with national awareness and inculcated with national values. This system was the basic mechanism by which national unity and economic success was achieved.

Regardless of what one thinks about this system, economic trends as described earlier in this paper now suggest that the social structure, especially the industrial component, which needed this strong group oriented social acclimatization, must go through a dismantling process. New ways of achieving economic development and national consciousness within an individualized society must be pursued.

In summary, the "Lifelong Learning System" now being promoted in Japan really means constructing a lifelong working ability and skills development system, or, in short, the industrialization of education, based on the principle that the direct beneficiaries should pay for part of it. As well, state unity, formerly realized by a strong group ethic, will be transformed into one which is achieved through direct loyalty or consciousness coming from the individual.

THE EARLY HISTORY OF LIFELONG LEARNING POLICY IN JAPAN

Starting in the early 1970's, advisory organs of the Ministry of Education issued several reports. For example, in 1971, the Central Council for Education (Chuo Kyoiku Shingikai or Chukyoshin), in the introductory preamble to its report titled *About the Basic Policy for Total School System Expansion and Maintenance in the Future*, argued that, from the perspective of lifelong education, the entire educational system needed to be redesigned. Also, in the same year, the Social Education Council (Shakai Kyoiku Shingikai or Shakyoshin) produced a report titled *The Way Social Education Should Deal With Rapid Social Structure Changes*. In it, the Council stated that home based education, school education, and social education have lost their close, organic relationship, and too great a burden and too many expectations have been placed on the school's role. Furthermore, they noted that there is a great inefficiency and overlap, and argued that any concept of education should be reviewed from the point of view of developing lifelong education. From the outset, then, the concept of lifelong education was placed at the centre of reorganizing the entire educational system. Ten years later, in 1981, the Central Council for Education published *Concerning Lifelong Education*, advising that lifelong education is an idea whose purpose is to help people continue learning throughout the lifespan.

There are two important points to consider here. One involves the use of the terms "lifelong education" and "lifelong learning". According to the Ministry of Education, the maintenance and programming of learning opportunities is referred to as "lifelong education", while from the process or the learner's side it is "lifelong learning". In the report, the Ministry of Education emphasized that this is an equal relationship. However, since "lifelong education" is the fundamental notion on which the system rests, lifelong education (the programming) must necessarily determine the direction of lifelong learning (the learner's experience). Therefore, "education" is foremost to "learning", and the system of lifelong education is as a result led by the state as opposed to being driven by the learners. This has turned out to be a critical distinction.

The second point relates to the notion that prescribed social education functions will rely on private educational providers. This reinforced the principle that direct beneficiaries should pay for part of the costs. Moreover, modifying the philosophical perspective to one of voluntary learning and putting the emphasis on personal benefit opened the door for the introduction of market principles. Needless to say, this shift also lightened the government's financial burden.

From these perspectives, a framework for a state-led lifelong learning system has been created. The principal player is the state and the ethic of the "power to self-educate" suggests that the will for learning and the attitudes and abilities to achieve this will develop within the nation (Central Council for Education, 1983).

LIFELONG LEARNING AND THE AD HOC COUNCIL FOR EDUCATIONAL REFORM

It was under the stewardship of the Ad Hoc Council for Educational Reform (Rinji Kyoiku Shingikai or Rinkyoshin) that the notion of lifelong learning went from concept to policy. The Council was convened between 1984 and 1987 by the Nakasone Diet as an advisory organ reporting directly to the Diet and not to the Ministry of Education. In this way the broader government administration stepped into an area normally represented by the Ministry of Education. This section of the paper reviews examples of the Council's reports in order to detail the conceptual development of lifelong learning.

The First Report (June 29, 1985)

In this, the Council's first report (Ad Hoc Council for Educational Reform, 1985), a move toward a lifelong learning system is scarcely mentioned. However, the reasons school based education had so many problems were identified, including the negative influence of the entrenched careerism in academe. A move toward a lifelong learning system of some sort was offered as one of the potential solutions for the negative phenomena in the school system. This report focused primarily on the issue of how to deal with an aging society.

Discussion Summary No. 3 (January 22, 1986)

This summary reflects the preliminary ideas discussed prior to the writing of the second report (Ad Hoc Council for Educational Reform, 1986a). Included are three important themes. First, there was recognition given to the existence of problems in the current education system. Included were the notions of the school-centred society, the uniformity of values, the collapse of communities, and the changes in family structure (for example, the effect of having fewer children in the nuclear family). These were documented and it was agreed that, when taken together, they created problems in the schools. Second, there were documented problems arising from changes in the industrial structure, internationalization and the move toward an information oriented society. Third, there was the weakening of state unity. This led to the notion of creating a lifelong learning system, but the supports for such a system were not clearly identified.

The Second Report (April 23, 1986)

Following from Discussion Summary No. 3, the second report criticized the school based education system in even stronger terms (Ad Hoc Council for Educational Reform, 1986b). It also described the weakening of social unity in the face of the "mass society", a condition which refers to the ways in which groups of individuals associate differently after the traditional society has lost its centripetal, unifying force. Japanese society, as described earlier, is about to undergo a metamorphosis, becoming an internationalized, information oriented, mature society. To support this society, education must fulfil two somewhat contradictory functions. On the one hand it must inculcate certain common values in order to unite the society, and on the other hand it must embrace the multiplicity of values required to impart scientific, technological and other types of knowledge. Hence the report's proclamation that Japan must move toward a lifelong learning system.

The necessity for moving towards a lifelong learning system was supported by three explicit points. First, education has been divided into home education, school education and social education. These categories have been viewed by many as separate entities, each applying to a different age group, when the fact has been that they have been interactive and overlap. All are required in order to produce a rounded citizen. Second, a change in attitude with regard to the infamous "entrance exam war" is required. Japanese society must accept that education is not just for youth; learning throughout the lifespan is needed. Third, many people within the society must acquire new knowledge and technical skills on an ongoing basis in order to keep pace with rapid advances in science and technology. As it turned out, these points played a major role in determining the characteristics of the proposed lifelong learning system. Coupled with this analysis was a description of the need to develop a fair system for evaluating lifelong working ability and skill.

Discussion Summary No. 4 (January 24, 1987)

In this summary, focus was placed on "multiple evaluation" and "systemic flexibility", and the writers criticized the "single-track school system" as being unsuitable for the evolving Japanese society (Ad Hoc Council for Educational Reform, 1987a). They suggested that a multiple evaluation system was required, along with a "public" qualification system which would recognize qualifications gained through work experience. These reforms were notable within the context of the traditional Japanese style employment system — lifelong employment and seniority-based — and gave recognition to the fact that the old system would have to be dismantled.

The Third Report (April 2, 1987)

In this report, "multiple evaluation" was highlighted in the first section of the first chapter (Ad Hoc Council for Educational Reform, 1987b). There, the direction of evaluation was described as "horizontal", meaning across companies or across occupational groupings. Reference was also made to parallel standards, an approach that would entrench a fundamentally new employment system based on an open job qualification system. Further, a relationship between off-the-job training and the private education sector was identified, as well as recognition of the importance of vocational training in high schools.

The Fourth (Final) Report (August 7, 1987)

In this report, the discussions to date, as a whole, were summarized and the direction of the educational reform package was firmly set in place (Ad Hoc Council for Educational Reform, 1987c).

Summary

The ideas of the Ad Hoc Council for Educational Reform regarding the establishment of a lifelong learning system noted that steps needed to be taken to deal with the coming of the internationalized, information oriented, and maturing Japanese society. First, it was concluded that highly talented people, those who will focus on high-end scientific and technical careers, would be trained in the first instance within the school system. Second, many of the responsibilities which heretofore had been in the realm of the school system would be distributed over the broader society, including the family and the community. As well, the promotion of a "dual track" high school education system would increase the number of options taught and hence mobilize people who exhibit different talents early on in their development. Following formal in-school training, labour training or skills and vocational updating would become lifelong working ability development and be driven by individual initiative. Third, in order to maintain core societal values under a state directed system within this new social structure, there would be an emphasis on "moral education" in elementary and junior high schools. Also necessary is the establishment of evaluation standards within the lifelong working ability and skill development system.

LIFELONG LEARNING AND THE CENTRAL COUNCIL FOR EDUCATION

The 14th Central Council for Education, the advisory organ of the Ministry of Education, was formed on April 24, 1989. It was established under direction from the then Education Minister Nishioka in order to reform the education system. On June 13, at the 167th General Meeting, the Council appointed a *Lifelong Learning Sub-Committee*. In total, eight sub-committee meetings as well as three on-site inspections followed. At the 169th General Meeting on October 31 of that same year, the sub-committee submitted a *Progress Report on Our Discussions* (Lifelong Learning Sub-committee, the Central Council for Education, 1989), and, later, on January 30, 1990, the Council submitted a report titled *Basic Maintenance for Lifelong Learning* (Central Council for Education, 1990) to Education Minister Ishibashi.

Education and Learning

Background information in the Council's report detailed the necessity for moving toward a lifelong learning system. Included were the now familiar arguments that had been identified by the Ad Hoc Council for Education Reform: Japanese society was experiencing major change, including the maturation of the community coupled with increased disposable income and more free time; the influence of internationalization and information technology; criticism of what was a highly academic career oriented society; and the need to construct a social system in which people could learn over a lifetime and be evaluated fairly along the way.

The report borrowed a statement from the report of the 12th Central Council for Education report: "lifelong learning is based on each individual's will to learn" (Central Council for Education, 1981). In this case, the pre-condition for learning is within each individual. However, it was also expressed that lifelong education would cultivate the desire and ability to learn as well as maintain social education functions. Implied in this view is the notion that "learning" is held in a secondary context to the body of "education". This view supported, albeit vaguely, a rationale for dismantling some of the basic premises of education. The report described lifelong learning as intentional and organized learning activities which take place at school or in society and include such things as sports, cultural activities, hobbies, recreational activities and volunteer activities. The result was the state, through its educational bureaucracy, intervening in and attempting to control the entire body of learning, including many elements normally considered personal and private.

Intervention in Education

The view that learning should be a secondary context of education led to it becoming a responsibility of local governments. As a result, the lifetime learning promotion centres (tentative name), the core of the lifelong learning system, were to be built in each community. These centres were expected to offer lifelong learning information as well as maintain counselling services for learning; map and track the demand for learning opportunities; plan and develop learning programs; liaise and cooperate with government agencies as well as entrust some operations to the private sector; train leaders and advisors for lifelong learning programming; evaluate the progress towards a lifelong learning system; make courses available to the community; and liaise and cooperate with a "university of the air".

This approach and these activities have raised questions related to certain pieces of legislation including Article 10 of the Fundamental Law of Education and Article 5 of the Social Education Act. Article 10 warns of too much intervention by the educational bureaucracy in the content of education, while Article 5 limits what education boards of local government can do in the realm of social education. Specifically, Article 5 restricts education boards to building facilities, encouraging citizens to initiate and run their own activities, and providing advice if requested.

Education and the Free Market

In the report it was suggested that state control needs to be strengthened; however, it also argued that education should be open to the free market. This latter point was based on the notion, introduced earlier, that beneficiaries should pay for at least part of their learning, and that this would be most effectively fixed through the involvement of the private sector.

Concrete methods for involving the private sector in lifelong learning activities included relying on it first and foremost for the development of education, sports, and cultural facilities — a "lifelong learning activity priority community". It was argued that within each district these facilities should be concentrated in a single centre thereby providing a broad scope of high quality learning opportunities. In order to harness the power of the private sector, it was suggested that a special taxation system and favourable financing opportunities should be considered.

Regardless of private sector involvement, the report left the door open for the central administration to intervene. It also stated that the administration would support private education through incentives, should this become necessary. More generally, the administrative role included cooperating with private educational businesses in order to train lifelong learning leaders as well as to promote the formation of groups which would work as overseers to maintain the quality of lifelong learning programs being delivered by the private sector.

General Administration

An effective lifelong learning system requires strong organizational support as well as effective communication and coordination among various administrative bodies, including, and perhaps most importantly, the citizens for whom the system is to provide benefits. Specifically, there is a need for strong vertical relationships. At the top of the bureaucracy is the Ministry of Education, clearly identified in the report. However, nowhere in the report is mention made of how the citizens will have direct input.

This is a strange omission, as one would think there must be some form of organization established at the local level. Clearly, the special tax system and favourable financing, mentioned earlier, are not within the purview of the local administrators. As well, if the central authority has increasing control over the content of programs, there seems to be little or no opportunity for local influence. Overall, it appears that the local education administration is losing its independence, and the general direction appears to be one of moving towards increasing centralized control.

The Abandonment of Public Job Training

The development of the lifelong learning system is not simply a matter of moving away from a school-based education system or even the reorganization of the education system. It goes beyond that, and includes transforming the industrial structure. In effect, it is a massive reorganization of the national system.

The report discusses "working ability and skill development", where the further development and education of workers would be through off-the-job training. In other words, working ability development would become part and parcel of the private education sector, and individuals would assume the risks and responsibilities for their own learning. The roots of this development can be traced to the educational diversification policy of the 1960's, which did not succeed due to its failure to forecast the demand for certain skills, as well as the difficulties encountered when attempting to train people whose abilities were assessed at too early an age.

The Repositioning of Schools

The report indicates that the role of school based education, in kindergarten, elementary school and junior high school, is to train students such that they develop the desire and ability for self-driven learning. Also, universities, junior and vocational colleges, and high schools would be required to provide various learning opportunities to the people within the community. High schools are located in the centre of this system, and the nationwide goal of a dual track approach within the high schools supports this role.

THE LIFELONG LEARNING PROMOTION ACT

The Lifelong Learning Promotion Act is officially titled "The law to maintain the system to promote lifelong learning". Based on an April 1990 draft from the Ministry of Education, and with subsequent changes following consultation with other ministries, the law was passed by the Diet and enacted on July 1, 1990. The purpose of the law was to legally establish the recommendations from the Central Council for Education report (Central Council for Education, 1990). Following are key issues related to this law.

Beyond the Framework of Current Education Acts

The first aspect of this law that requires comment is the fact that, although it is designed to promote "lifelong learning", there is no definition of lifelong learning within the document. Nor is there any stated doctrine underscoring the establishment of the law or, for that matter, any reference to the outline from the Ministry of Education completed in the preceding April.

When the sub-committee on lifelong learning of the Central Council for Education submitted its interim report in October 1989 (Lifelong Sub-committee, the Central Council for Education, 1989), the Ministry of Education was considering the creation of a "Fundamental Act" which would include a definition and doctrinal information about "lifelong learning". However, it was concluded that it would be too difficult to define lifelong learning and encode it as a law, in part because of the broad nature of the concept including as it does a variety of institutions and fields such as schools, social education, culture, and sports. Because definitions and doctrinal facts are not included in the law, many government ministries and agencies are not able to clearly define what lifelong learning is and is not, nor can they determine with certainty how the concept relates to other policies (Nihon Kyoiku Shimbun, May 12, 1990).

There were other important modifications, including the exclusion of the Ministry of Labour and the Ministry of Health and Welfare from the law. Also, the Ministry of Home Affairs was given some powers to check approval standards. Many other ministries disagreed with the notion of the Ministry of Education, and now also the Ministry of International Trade and Industry, stepping into their administrative territory through the law. In fact, the Ministry of Posts and Telecommunications openly criticized the Ministry of Education claiming that it was trying to expand its power in an adventuristic fashion under the guise of the lifelong learning concept (Yomiuri Shimbun, May 11, 1990).

Looking at the issue from a different angle, because the Ministry of Education did not, in the end, include a definition of lifelong learning or enunciate its doctrine, it allowed the lifelong learning law to be constructed and interpreted very differently from existing education laws. Practically speaking, lifelong learning is not education in the traditional sense; therefore, it could not be integrated with the current education laws or even the constitution. This fact opened the door for the Ministry of Education to go beyond the boundaries of so-called general education administration. As well, it allowed the Ministry of International Trade and Industry to become involved with educational policy at the national level. There is also some suggestion of other factors at work in that the initial date for the enforcement of the law was July 1, 1990, which was to all appearances deliberately rushed. It can be posited that a connection existed between the choice of this date and the fact that on the very same date there was to be an American assessment of Japan's efforts to open its markets under the "structural impediments initiative".

Education Administration Subsumed by the General Administration

As discussed earlier, the lifelong learning act was planned outside the framework of current education laws. However, it was not constructed to be completely different from them. As the concept of lifelong learning comes under the control of General Administration, the system growing out of the lifelong learning law will be formed within it and will, technically speaking, place present educational laws on a lower plane. Hence, the educational administration will lose its autonomy and relative independence, and through the lifelong learning policy system be gradually subsumed by General Administration.

At the national government level, it was decided that a Lifelong Learning Council would be established in the Ministry of Education to study and discuss items regarding lifelong learning, social education and school education. Also, the council could propose the results of its deliberations and discussions to the Minister of Education and to the chiefs of other administrative bodies, as well as request cooperation from them, if necessary. In fact, this has created an opportunity for the Ministry of Education to step lightly into other administrative areas.

Transforming the Educational Role at the Local Level

In the lifelong learning council system, the prefectural level council is directly linked to the Ministry of Education's council, and a "top down" system is formed. Moreover, under this law, as described earlier, the role of the local governments is very different from what it was under Article 5 of the Social Education Act.

In Article 3 of the Lifelong Learning Promotion Act the Prefectural Education Board's responsibilities include: collecting and providing information regarding learning and cultural activity opportunities; investigating and studying the demand for learning and evaluating the results of learning; developing learning methods and programs appropriate to the needs of the community; providing training to leaders and advisors including support and advice to local educational and cultural organizations; administering social education classes and providing other learning opportunities. In effect, the local education board duties in these areas, as stipulated in Article 5 of the Social Education Act, were shifted up to the prefectural level. Under this new law, local bodies are no longer responsible for educational administration; therefore, they are prevented from participating in the lifelong learning council system. The effect is to deny local autonomy or self-government.

Education and the Private Sector

In the Lifelong Learning Promotion Act, the "lifelong learning activity priority community" is described as the basic vehicle for promoting lifelong learning within the community and for involving the private sector. The first paragraph of Article 5 of this law describes prefectures as responsible for preparing the groundwork that will provide opportunities for private sector participation, noting that they may apply for approval for any given project from the Ministry of Education or from the Ministry of International Trade and Industry.

It is also clearly stated that private sector organizations participating in lifelong learning activities will receive favourable treatment with regard to financing and taxation. However, this last promise may be questionable in light of certain restrictions, such as stipulations related to public expenditures, noted in Article 89 of the constitution.

The entry of the private sector into the educational market is also encouraged through each area's Chamber of Commerce and Industry. Once again, however, the Ministry of Education and the Ministry of International Trade and Industry hold final power of approval. Moreover, to set approval standards these ministries have to consult with the Minister of Home Affairs and other chiefs of related administrative organizations (see Article 6, Paragraph 2 of the Lifelong Learning Promotion Act). Plainly, the framework of the lifelong learning law consists of subsuming the present educational administration under general administration and introducing the private sector in a complementary manner.

REFLECTIONS ON THE PROCESS AND GOAL

The process of developing a conceptual framework for lifelong learning and bringing this to fruition through policy and legislation has included considerable reorganization along with increasing centralization of responsibilities, expanding the powers of the Ministry of Education, and introducing the private sector into the environment. At best, results have been mixed. Specifically, the role of the Ministry of Education has broadened into areas of general administration, and the concept of education has expanded to include learning more generally, a change which flies in the face of Article 10 of the Fundamentals of Education Act that limits the role of central education administration and guarantees the relative autonomy and freedom of local education administration from the power of central and local general administrations.

The current foundation for a lifelong learning system has been constructed in an atmosphere of crisis management under the cloud of a new economic and social system. While it's true that Japanese society is facing a critical challenge to its traditional social order, and the government is creating new structures to deal with momentous issues, Japan needs to pay extremely close attention to how our lifelong learning system is being developed, and most specifically to the links with and relationships between the labyrinths of general administration. Local autonomy and the individual needs of the people must be recognized and incorporated into any model.

Regardless, what is clear is the fact that Japan must radically redesign its educational and learning system, a process that is well underway. Lifelong learning in Japan will become a fact, and some good progress has been made. To expect perfection may be too quixotic, but, given the importance of the activity, prudence is warranted. For other Asia Pacific economies, the lifelong learning lessons being experienced in Japan may be a useful reference.

REFERENCES

Ad Hoc Council for Educational Reform (Rinji Kyoiku Shingikai or Rinkyoshin). (1985, June 29). *Dai Ichiji Toshin* (the First Report) (Original Report). Tokyo: Rinji Kyoiku Shingikai.

Ad Hoc Council for Educational Reform (Rinji Kyoiku Shingikai). (1986a, January 22). *Shingi Keika no Gaiyo-Sono San* (Discussion summary No. 3) (Original Report). Tokyo: Rinji Kyoiku Shingikai.

Ad Hoc Council for Educational Reform (Rinji Kyoiku Shingikai). (1986b, April 23). *Dai Niji Toshin* (the Second Report) (Original Report). Tokyo: Rinji Kyoiku Shingikai, Tokyo.

Ad Hoc Council for Educational Reform (Rinji Kyoiku Shingikai). (1987a, January 24). *Shingi Keika no Gaiyo-Sono Yon* (Discussion summary No. 4) (Original Report). Tokyo: Rinji Kyoiku Shingikai.

Ad Hoc Council for Educational Reform (Rinji Kyoiku Shingikai). (1987b, April 2). *Dai Sanji Toshin* (the Third Report) (Original Report). Tokyo: Rinji Kyoiku Shingikai.

Ad Hoc Council for Educational Reform (Rinji Kyoiku Shingikai). (1987c, August 7). *Dai Yonji Toshin* (the Fourth Report [Final Report]) (Original Report). Tokyo: Rinij Kyoiku Shingikai.

Asahi Shinbun. (January 21, 1997).

Central Council for Education (Chuo Kyoiku Shingikai or Chukyoshin). (1971). *Kongo niokeru Gakko Kyoiku no Sogotekina Kakuju Seibi no tameno Kihonteki Shisaku ni tsuite* (About the basic policy for total school system expansion and maintenance in the near future) (Original report). Tokyo: Chuo Kyoiku Shingikai.

Central Council for Education (Chuo Kyoiku Shingikai). (1981). *Shogai Kyoiku ni tsuite* (Concerning lifelong education) (Original Report). Tokyo: Chuo Kyoiku Shingikai.

Central Council for Education (Chuo Kyoiku Shingikai). (1983). *Kyouiku Naiyotou Shoiinnkai Shingi Keika Hokoku* (Discussion report of sub-committee on school curriculum, Central Council for Education) (Original Report). Tokyo: Chuo Kyoiku Shingikai.

Central Council for Education (Chuo Kyoiku Shingikai). (1990, January 30). *Shogai Gakushu no Kiban Seibi ni tsuite* (Basic maintenance for lifelong learning) (Original Report). Tokyo: Chuo Kyoiku Shingikai.

Economic Planning Agency (Keizai Kikaku-cho), (1985). *Nijuisseiki no Sarariiman Shakai* (The Society of Salaried Workers in 21st Century). Tokyo: Toyo Keizai Shimpo-sha.

Japan Association of Corporate Executives (Keizai Doyukai), (1995). *Gakko kara "Gakko" he: Gakko mo Katei mo Chiiki mo Mizukara no Yakuwari to Sekinin wo Jikakushi, Chie to Chikara wo Dashiai, Atarashii Manabino Ba wo Tsukuro* (From school to community-based learning centres; schools, families, and communities being aware of their educational responsibilities, and each giving of its wisdom and power to create new places to learn and grow) (Original paper). Tokyo: Keizai Doyukai.

Kyoiku Kihon Ho (Fundamental Law of Education). March 31, 1947.

Lifelong Learning Sub-committee, Central Council for Education (Shogai Gakushu ni kansuru Shoiinkai, Chuo Kyoiku Shingikai). (1989, October 31). *Shingi Keika Hokoku* (Progress report on our discussions) (Original Report). Tokyo: Chuo Kyoiku Shingikai.

Nihon Kyoiku Shimbun. (May 12, 1990).

Shakai Kyoiku Ho (Social Education Act). June 10, 1949.

Shogai Gakushu no Shinko no tameno Shisaku no Suishin Taiseitou no Seibi ni kansuru Horitsu (Lifelong Learning Promotion Act). July 1, 1990.

Social Education Council (Shakai Kyoiku Shingikai or Shakyoshin). (1971). *Kyugekina Shakai Kozo no Henka ni Taishosuru Shakai Kyoiku no Arikata ni tsuite* (The way social education should deal with rapid social structure changes) (Original Report). Tokyo: Shakai Kyoiku Shingikai.

Yomiuri Shimbun. (May 11, 1990).

Huiping Wu

and Qilian Ye

On completion of her undergraduate studies at East China Normal University in Shanghai, Huiping Wu worked at the Division of Comparative Studies, Shanghai Institute for Studies in Higher Education. Her primary areas of interest include administration in education, strategic planning, and international comparative higher education. She has published numerous articles and papers, including *Faculty Development in China* (1996), *Fee-paying Public Universities and Private Institutions* (1995), and *British Educational Law-making and Its Implementation* (1993). Ms. Wu is currently completing a Ph.D. in the Department of Theory and Policy Studies in Education at the University of Toronto. In her spare time, she enjoys travelling and dancing.

Qilian Ye is a graduate of Beijing Normal University and is currently Associate Professor and Director of the Division of International Cooperation, National Academy of Education Administration in Beijing. His published works include *The Adjusting Role of Competition and Personnel Market in Higher Education* (1988), *Short Term Effects and Its Strategies in the Course of University Management* (1988), and *A Practical Handbook: Evaluation of School Teachers* (1993). When he is not researching and writing, Mr. Ye enjoys reading and is an amateur photographer.

Lifelong Learning in the People's Republic of China

by Huiping Wu and Qilian Ye

Lifelong learning is relatively new in the People's Republic of China. The notion was first introduced with the translation of the UNESCO report, "Learning To Be: The World of Education Today and Tomorrow", and since that time the importance of lifelong learning, both for economic development and personal enrichment, has been obvious. In addition, the size of the population, its geographic dimensions and large rural areas, and the current economic transition from a planned economy to a market-oriented economy has accented the value of lifelong learning. In 1993, guidelines for educational reform proposed the evolution of the current system of adult education into a lifelong learning system, and in 1995 legislation was passed to establish and improve upon a system of lifelong learning. During the 1990s, a host of institutions, many of them private or semi-private, developed. In spite of progress to date, there are many challenges facing the full implementation of a lifelong learning system. Among these are the current government focus on public school system reform, including higher education, and the lack of financial support. Regardless, the outlook is positive, driven by demand and shaped by the people.

INTRODUCTION

The concept of lifelong learning was first introduced to the People's Republic of China (PRC) in the late 1970's, following the translation of *Learning To Be: The World Of Education Today And Tomorrow* (Faure, et al., 1972), a report issued by the United Nations Educational, Scientific and Cultural Organization (UNESCO) International Commission on the Development of Education. Since then, the attention and practice of lifelong learning have been centred on the field of adult education in the PRC. Although formal adult education programming has existed in the PRC for more than forty years and has provided a sound foundation for various types of programming and learning, the idea of lifelong learning as a systematic, comprehensive, structural and behavioural mode remains relatively new and still tentative.

Regardless of the late start with lifelong learning, significant achievements have recently been made in appreciating the concept and in implementing lifelong learning. In fact, lifelong learning is initiated and motivated more by the society at large, rather than as a "top-down" policy. It is believed by many educators and officials, however, that the implementation of lifelong learning practices will become one of the key strategies in the PRC's ongoing educational reform and that it will play an important role in the twenty-first century as technology, social conditions, and international cooperation combine to create unique educational opportunities.

To date, there have been relatively few broad-based, formal discussions regarding the application of lifelong learning in the PRC, since it has been practised for only a few years and has not been identified as a priority in the national education development policy. This paper presents readers with an overview of lifelong learning in the Chinese context, through a discussion of the conceptual understanding, initiatives and potential, policies and practices, as well as existing problems. By examining what has been done in the PRC, the paper also attempts to analyze possible trends in lifelong learning and provide recommendations for its future evolution.

THE CONCEPTUAL DEVELOPMENT OF LIFELONG LEARNING

Learning To Be: The World of Education Today and Tomorrow (Faure, et al., 1972) was introduced at the beginning of a period of broad educational reforms in the PRC, when education was recognized as being of vital importance for the realization of the modernizations: agriculture, industry, national defense, and science and technology. Consequently, the concept of lifelong learning was widely accepted within the educational establishment. At a minimum, educators felt a duty to articulate the theoretical possibilities of an innovative scheme that could dramatically stimulate the long term goals of Chinese education. In the PRC, lifelong learning is understood to be linked with the need for individual accomplishment, economic and social development, and educational equality. Also, in its ideal sense, lifelong learning should encompass the whole of society and engage each member in learning experiences that last for a lifetime.

Lifelong learning is a philosophical concept that explores the importance of education as it relates to individual accomplishments, motivation for self and societal improvement, and the expansion of conventional leisure activities. It will not be necessary to develop specific educational models for lifelong learning, as it is not formal schooling in the traditional sense, but embraces all modes of formal and informal learning throughout life. By adopting these principles, educators in the PRC are beginning to extend lifelong learning in order to improve the quality of life for all citizens, from the youth to the elderly.

The implementation of lifelong learning is thought to be a necessity in a changing labour market, in accordance with recent rapid cultural, scientific, and technological progress. People generally understand that their early years of traditional formal schooling are no longer adequate to cope with constant economic and social change. Lifelong learning has to date been strongly embraced as it relates to skills training and industrial competition; however, at the same time, the Chinese government is attempting to expand education initiatives in the public and private, formal and non-formal, academic and vocational areas of both professional skills updating and personal interest development in order to meet the different levels and requirements for economic and social enhancement and a healthy society. Although there continues to be some pressure to educate workers primarily for short term gains, there is increasing recognition that lifelong learning perpetuates a long term, overall increased quality of life. The emphasis, at all levels, therefore, is on broad adaptability and continuing flexibility.

Lifelong learning is also important for the achievement of social democracy and equity. It is stated in both the constitution of the People's Republic of China and Education Law that Chinese citizens are entitled to equal educational opportunities, regardless of their race, gender, occupation, religion, or economic status (*Education Law*, 1995). The institutionalization of lifelong learning in the PRC will help accomplish this objective by providing continuing education opportunities for those who did not complete their formal schooling for various reasons. Indeed, a comprehensive commitment to lifelong learning could encourage large numbers of people who have previously been excluded from further education to participate.

Overall, lifelong learning in the PRC is evolving, albeit slowly, from an adult education system which was established in parallel with the formal school system more than forty years ago. Programming has included theoretical and practical training in a variety of fields and delivery systems. Included are literacy classes, general education, junior specialized training, senior specialized training, correspondence and television broadcasting programs at both the secondary and university levels, workers' universities, agricultural universities, and programs for upgrading of cadres and other management personnel. Lifelong learning is expanding the range of adult education programming in terms of purposes, age groups, content, and delivery methodologies. Beyond the widely accepted adult liberal education and vocational training programs which are required for a productive workforce, the lifelong learning paradigm is bringing personal interest, and recreational and leisure activities to the context.

SOCIAL INITIATIVES AND POTENTIAL

During the past fifteen years, the PRC has been undergoing a fundamental change, one marked by a shift from a planned economic system to a market-oriented economic system. This process has profoundly affected educational development and the education system as a whole. In concert with this change, the demand for lifelong learning has increased dramatically.

In response to the pressures arising from this economic and social change, the PRC has adapted well, applying modern techniques to age-old problems as they pertain to education and learning. Increased enthusiasm for lifelong learning among individuals, enterprises, and even entire communities has resulted from these pressures, particularly as they relate to economic change, rapid developments in science and technology, increased emphasis on individual achievement, and the overall need for educational expansion. Although the size of the population presents novel challenges, these have been confronted with a deep sense of urgency and responsibility.

Since 1978, when the economic reforms began, the market-oriented system has grown and developed within the PRC. This has been a significant and fundamental change, which has in turn brought about a vast need for personnel who understand market-oriented economics from a variety of perspectives. However, given the size of the PRC, existing formal school and adult education systems have been unable to meet this demand, especially in the areas of business management, trade and finance, engineering, and legal services. This pressure for skilled personnel will likely remain unabated as continuing changes provide increased demand for personnel. In an effort to address this problem, a number of education and training institutions of various types and levels have been established.

Rapid developments in science and technology have also fuelled demand for lifelong learning. In particular, the introduction of newer technologies and production methods in developed countries has acted as a catalyst to promote much of the economic transformation in the PRC. As developed economies move to higher level production systems, more low and intermediate level production moves into the PRC. As a result, it is now apparent that all workers require a variety of skills and broad expertise which can be applied to many jobs, rather than the single set of skills that has been a trademark in the past.

The PRC has recently faced changes of unprecedented magnitude in its traditional industries (including, for example, textile production, mining, and heavy industry), and a large number of the workers in these so-called "sun-set" industries have been forced to change careers or take early retirement. In order for these industries to take advantage of market opportunities, or in some cases merely survive, their workforces must be upgraded to work at higher knowledge levels particularly with new technology. Many must also be cross-trained, developing skills that allow them to work beyond one narrow focus. Characteristics of the required learning in this environment have been described as high, new and fast. "High" refers to the higher level of learning and the higher qualification requirements; "new" refers to the new knowledge content and skill acquisition; and "fast" refers to learning concepts and skills more quickly and with higher efficiency levels. Although the economic transformation and technological advances have been major influencers affecting the need and desire for lifelong learning, it is recognized that industrial needs alone should not be the only or even the primary rationale for the development of a learning society.

While economic development has had a great impact in so far as satisfying material needs within the society, many Chinese citizens view learning later in the lifespan as a mechanism for meeting spiritual and cultural needs. In fact, regardless of the need for new working skills in the context of changing and higher technology, people are paying more and more attention to their personal needs and quality of life issues.

A noticeable push for lifelong learning in the PRC is coming from the growing population of senior citizens. More than ever before, the PRC is becoming a society with a large cohort of older citizens. According to a recent study, the portion of the population 65 years of age or older will by the end of this century have reached 130 million and account for 10% of the population (Xiang, 1996, p. 29). As the material life for this group improves, there will be increasing demand for a higher "quality of life", including lifelong learning opportunities.

Recently, special institutions for senior learners have emerged in Shanghai,

Beijing and a few other cities, and it is estimated that within the PRC there are now more than 5,000 "Senior's Universities" (Xiang, 1996, p. 8). Neither part of the regular school system nor the adult education system, these are private or semi-private institutions sponsored by social organizations. Their programs are quite diversified, and include artistic and leisure pursuits such as drawing, calligraphy, flower planting, *qi gong* (deep breathing exercises), *tai ji* (Chinese traditional shadow boxing), cuisine, foreign languages, music, dancing, and health care. This is a brave new departure for learning within the PRC, and it embodies the meaning and spirit of lifelong learning, well distanced from the formal school system and even the traditions of adult education as they are known in the PRC. It is a system which is driven solely by self-motivation, and the learning is for internal satisfaction as compared with learning that is driven by external needs. This type of programming contributes greatly to Chinese society and cultural development.

A further factor which will greatly support the development of lifelong learning opportunities relates to the nature of the educational system itself. Limiting factors confronting the PRC include its large population, a shortage of natural resources, and one of the lowest GNPs in the world, all of which have seriously hindered improvement in education. According to recent data, the PRC has approximately 200 million learners enroled (not including students in adult education) in its school systems, accounting for 25% of the world's student population. The total educational expenditure is 50 billion Yuan ($6.25US billion). This figure represents only 40 Yuan ($5US) per student per year (Xiang, 1996, p. 4). Given this fiscal environment, 30% of primary school graduates (grade six), 60% of junior middle school graduates (grade nine), and 75% of senior high school graduates (grade twelve) cannot be accommodated at the next level of education (Xiang, 1996, p. 14). The implementation and application of lifelong learning could be the key to solving this problem, and for this reason alone has monumental implications for the PRC.

POLICIES AND PRACTICE DURING THE REFORM DECADE

A review and analysis of policies and legislation since the beginning of educational reforms in 1985 suggests that lifelong learning will become one of the most important strategies for educational innovation in the PRC. And although lifelong learning was not clearly defined in *Decisions On Educational Reform And Development* (1987), the emphasis it places on subsequent reform and the evolution of adult general and vocational education clearly provides a form and foundation for the development of lifelong learning in the PRC.

The notion of lifelong learning was first formally described and proposed by the Chinese government in the 1993 *Programs For Educational Reform and Development*. This publication is considered to be the primary guiding document for recent Chinese educational reforms. Article 10 addresses the evolution of adult in-school education towards a system of lifelong learning by asserting that adult education should be used as the basis for developing a new type of education, one which sees the evolution of the traditional school education system into a system of lifelong learning. Further, the paper argues that this new learning should play a key role in improving the overall quality of life for Chinese citizens, as well as promoting economic and social development (*Programs for Educational Reform and Development*, 1993). Thus, adult education in the PRC is seen as the foundation for lifelong learning and will be used as the basis for the development of lifelong learning policies, programs and practices.

In 1995, lifelong learning was defined and formally sanctioned through legislation, specifically in the PRC's Educational Law, which was passed on March 18th of that year. In Act 2 of the first chapter, the law states: "In meeting the needs of developing a socialist market economy and of social progress, the state shall promote a coordinated development of education of various types, and levels, carry forward educational reform and establish and improve a system of lifelong education" (*Education Law*, 1995). In Act 19 of the second chapter, the Law declares that "the state shall encourage the development of adult education in a variety of forms so that citizens may receive appropriate education in politics, economics, culture, science, technology, professional or vocational knowledge and lifelong education". Act 41 of Chapter Five specifies that "the state shall encourage schools and other educational institutions as well as social organizations to take measures in creating conditions for citizens to receive life-long education". (The distinction between lifelong learning and lifelong education is not, at this stage, made within the legislation, policy discussions or applications. And although this might be bothersome in some contexts, the overall benefits even without this distinction, cannot be overstated. Formally and practically, the PRC is clearly on the path to lifelong learning.)

Given this legislation and the direct references to a lifelong system, it is clear that an explicit and coordinated plan incorporating policies, programs and practices is necessary for what will be a time of major educational expansion and development. In light of this, goals have been established for the application of lifelong learning. These include reforms in the area of educational administration, a commitment to the implementation of compulsory education, a need to strengthen secondary vocational education, and greater emphasis to be placed on adult education.

At present, the most important educational reform in the PRC is the system-wide reform pertaining to educational administration. The public school system, which in the past has been fully government funded, has evolved into one where public institutions continue to be the major players, while private and semi-private institutions are developing their role as supplementary players. This has been necessary in order to help meet the increasing demand for basic education.

In parallel with the public school system, adult education institutions have in the past been sponsored for the most part by local governments, communities, and large industrial enterprises and companies. These institutions continue to be thought of as a component of the public system, separate and quite different from the newly-opened private and semi-private institutions which are sponsored by individuals and various social organizations and which require learners to pay full tuition fees. Regardless, private institutions are developing within the adult education field, the seeds of lifelong learning are beginning to take broad root and the resultant variety of institutions characterizes the formation of a newly developed and more fully diversified system. Although the size of the PRC and the characteristics of a diversified system may appear to be unwieldy, the restructuring as described will in the long run be more effective in terms of meeting local educational needs and broader programming as required by a developing economy.

According to recent data (Xiang, 1996, pp. 8-9), by the end of 1993 no less than 16 private or semi-private universities and colleges had been sanctioned by the State Education Commission, and 800 private institutions were registered with local education bureaus. These latter institutions offer higher level continuing education, including foreign languages, professional training, and general interest courses. (Most of the registrants in these institutions are either university graduates or undergraduates.) At the secondary level, 30,000 private and semi-private institutions had been opened. These offer general knowledge courses and skills training. Interestingly, more than 5,000 institutions for senior learners emerged at the same time. The total number of private and semi-private institutions reached 60,000, including those offering formal primary and secondary school education. These numbers suggest that private and semi-private institutions are becoming major players practising and supporting lifelong learning programming. Overall, it is clear that the shift in policies and programming has made it possible for many more people to be involved in learning programs.

The nine-year compulsory education program has been strengthened in order to establish a firm basis for lifelong learning. In an economy with a population of 1.2 billion, the universal provision of educational opportunity has always been a significant challenge; however, it is a basic requirement which must be met if the goal of "lifelong learning opportunities for all" is to be realized. In this regard, the *Compulsory Education Law*, issued in 1986, has been a key strategy. It confirms the importance of education and the State's commitment to provide basic skills and knowledge to the population as a whole.

Data indicate that in 1949 approximately 80% of the population in the PRC was illiterate. However, during the period from 1949 through 1982, more than 140 million individuals acquired the tools of basic literacy through various forms of full- and part-time study involving day schools, night schools, correspondence courses, and literacy classes sponsored by local governments (Zhou, 1989, p. 27). At this time, more than halfway through the 1990's, the elimination of illiteracy continues to be a major priority. On average, more than 4 million Chinese develop basic literacy tools each year, and enrolment in the nine-year compulsory education program has reached 98% of the school age cohort (*Educational Statistics Yearbook of China*, 1996, p.125). It is expected that the PRC will achieve full participation in the nine year compulsory education program by the end of the century. This emphasis on basic literacy has paid major dividends and establishes the potential for lifelong learning.

Vocational education is a key component for a lifelong learning foundation in the PRC. In the past, primary education focused on general learning. Now, vocational education has been added to the junior, middle, and senior secondary school levels in order to address the balance between theory and practice, especially important to middle schools in rural areas. In 1991, slightly more than 50% of those enroled in senior secondary level were receiving vocational education training, reflecting since 1980 an increase of more than 600% (Guo, 1996, p. 154).

At the same time, in order to develop a readiness for lifelong learning, and for assuming responsibility for one's own learning, training in problem solving, and self-directed study and research techniques has been added to the curriculum at all levels. The exploration of personal interests and individual talents is also encouraged, as are leisure education activities. In this context, adult education programming is playing a major role.

To meet needs associated with economic development and technological change, 1987's *Decisions on Adult Education Reform* prescribed the need for in-service technical training and updating. Since then, great strides have been made in the area of in-service training programs. For example, from 1987 through 1991, 110 million persons participated in in-service training. Of these, 89 million enroled in skill development or technical training programs, while the remainder received training in management and administration. The number of persons taking advantage of in-service training has increased so rapidly that they now account for almost 60% of the total increase of 10.3 million learners between 1986 and 1991 (Guo, 1996, p. 156).

Overall program diversification is strongly encouraged, especially in the adult higher education system. Therefore, and in order to meet the growing demand for qualified personnel trained to professional levels, adult higher education has become an important component of the higher education system, particularly since 1979. According to 1994 data (*Educational Statistics Yearbook of China*, 1996, p. 125), there were more than 2.35 million persons enroled in adult higher education institutions, an increase of nearly half a million in just one year. In support of this, there are 1,172 full-time and part-time adult institutions of higher learning including 46 broadcast universities, 703 workers' universities, 4 agricultural universities, 170 management institutes, 245 institutes of education and management, and 4 correspondence colleges. All of these offer formal degrees or certificates issued by the State Education Commission. In addition, 836 universities and colleges from the public education system offer a variety of night or correspondence programs for adult higher learning, as do approximately 400 institutions newly established by the private and semi-private sectors. Also, State regulated self-study exam agencies are located in all provinces. The self-study exams are divided into 110 specialities with more than a thousand subjects, and, through to the end of 1992, 120,000 of 5 million participants had completed the entire program and obtained a degree or certificate. Given their flexibility and numbers, these self-study agencies will become increasingly important as lifelong learning grows and develops. As of 1993, adult higher education enrolment exceeded 1.4 million, equivalent to 65% of the total enrolment of regular full-time colleges and universities; the number of graduates from adult higher education reached 517,700, representing slightly more than 80% of the total graduate population (Ji, 1994, p. 298).

ONGOING PROBLEMS & POTENTIAL ENTHUSIASM

In light of the foregoing, it is clear that lifelong learning has taken firm root and has become ingrained within the educational system in the PRC. Not only are policies in place, but programming and practices are evident and widespread. The influence is not confined to economic-based concerns, but rather the social aspects are considered just as important. Regardless of this, problems, including a shortfall in financial resources, decreasing support from certain levels of government, an imbalance in the development of programs from region to region, and the absence of a dominant strategic plan to establish a systematic structure for lifelong learning, exist.

Financial challenges are strongly influencing and disrupting the educational system in the PRC. At this time, particularly in light of the economic climate, the rate of technological change and increased social demands, the central government is not able to fully and adequately support the system. Ensuring funding for lifelong learning is crucial, yet the present circumstances make this challenge appear almost insurmountable. New and novel approaches for supporting education are obviously required. Most institutions having lifelong learning programming as their major focus, including seniors' universities and various continuing education programs, are private or semi-private. They have strong ideological support from social organizations and communities, but their fiscal survival relies primarily on tuition fees with some additional support from local businesses and other organizations. Most of these institutions will, consequently, be limited in terms of their ability to grow, evolve and adapt. They lack the potential for further accomplishment since they are not able to establish stronger and long term financial support.

It is important to note that in comparison with the many detailed policies relating to the reform of regular degree and certificate educational programs, there is a decided lack of concrete measures or strategies for medium to long term improvements in lifelong learning policies, programs and practices. The momentum exists, but the detailed plan and support is, for the most part, absent. Lifelong learning has been formalized in the 1995 *Education Law*, and as such has been accepted and, to a degree, institutionalized. However, lifelong learning is for the most part thought to be a personal need rather than a broad, economic and social trend for which the government should provide strong, effective and increased policy support and direction. Although the number of private and semi-private institutions that deliver lifelong learning is increasing rapidly, they lack official support and are faced by a future that suggests diminishing financial investment. There is broad sense of the potential value associated with lifelong learning, but the allocation of funds in what is a very complex system remains problematic.

Underfunded though they may be, lifelong learning opportunities are available in the coastal areas and in the big cities where economic development is more advanced. By contrast, however, in the larger rural and less developed territories, the elimination of illiteracy is still regarded as the main task. What may not be fully recognized is the role lifelong learning can play, through alternative delivery mechanisms for example, in the attack on illiteracy. Regardless, the basic literacy issue remains unsolved for large areas of the PRC, and until attitudes change and new priorities are recognized, the ideal of lifelong learning will be difficult to realize on a system wide basis.

The national priority continues to be public school system reform; thus, the conceptually broader notion of lifelong learning and a non-traditional system of continuing education has yet to be fully endorsed. The need to develop continuing education programming is attributed to economic forces within the job market, rather than as a response to worker defined goals. There is a trend, nevertheless, to support more initiatives that arise from and reflect the individual perspective, including programming for seniors.

A related issue which undermines the potential for lifelong learning relates to the learning environment and teaching methodologies. Most institutions delivering what may be described as lifelong learning programming have limited funding, and as a result the teaching facilities are sparse. There is no opportunity to make use of advanced teaching and learning technologies, and this is reinforced by the reliance on teachers from the regular school system. The training these teachers have received is traditional, conservative and classroom based. The opportunity for innovation is stifled since the growth is being directed, albeit without intention, by proponents of the formal system. In fact, many of the programs bear a striking resemblance to full-time, formal school programs, not recognizing the distinctiveness of a lifelong learning philosophy and adult education practices.

FUTURE PERSPECTIVES AND RECOMMENDATIONS

Parallel systems of formal general education and adult education have existed in the PRC for the past four decades. Lifelong learning, by contrast, has only been recently introduced. Though encouraged, institutions delivering lifelong learning programming are not financially supported by the government within the context of the current economic circumstances. As a result, it is not surprising to see considerable debate arising in educational circles as to whether lifelong learning should be separate from or integrated within the formal educational system.

In spite of the challenges, considerable progress has been made with regard to support for and the implementation of lifelong learning policies, programs and practices. The increasing number of local and community based lifelong learning initiatives and the strong demand from the population at large are features which strongly predicate future success. It is unreasonable, however, to suggest that the hurdles facing lifelong learning will be overcome in the short term, in part because they are intimately connected with a challenging economic environment and a variety of national development priorities. However, moderate growth in lifelong learning programming coupled with strong quality improvements in the design and delivery are feasible and structurally possible.

Within the context of the unique characteristics of the PRC and current stages of economic and educational reform, adult professional and vocational education and the related in-service training should be the main focus of lifelong learning development for the next ten years. The PRC remains in a transitional period from the former planned system to a market system, and during this phase the unemployment rate will continue to rise as changes sweep through major industries, some of which will be radically changed while others will simply disappear. Professional and vocational training for persons affected by these changes will be extremely important and most urgent. Major cities, including Beijing and Shanghai, have recently established "Workers' Employment Centres" and "Re-employment Guidance Centres" sponsored by the municipal governments. These are intended to help people who have lost their jobs to obtain new employment. However, there is much more to be done on a nation-wide job training basis for the next few years, and in this regard the central government should take a more active role.

Though it is necessary and important to provide short-term solutions in response to job loss, it is also essential to adapt to the economic and social realities of the future. This involves longer term strategies. In fact, in-service training, skills upgrading, and management development are not only for those people who face unemployment, but also for those who wish to develop their careers. During the next few decades, the need for skills training will be varied and significant, fuelled by technological development and job losses, as well as the upgrading and career development market. Given the number of workers in the PRC, the sheer size of the market for this training will be immense.

Within the Chinese context, private and semi-private institutions should take more responsibility for promoting and implementing lifelong learning. There are two reasons for this. First, it is not possible for the government to control and fully support both the formal school system and non-formal programming. Government priorities are focused on the basic school system and the nine-year compulsory education program, as well as reform in higher education. It is not practical to expect stronger support, let alone effective, directive development for lifelong learning from the government. Second, the newly established private and semi-private sectors are more diversified and prone to having greater potential for educational innovation. This will serve the individual needs of learners better, though comparatively speaking, these institutions have had only a few years' experience, and this with very limited numbers. Further, these institutions are more flexible, more customer responsive, and quicker to respond to new programming needs. They focus more on general interest programs, and tend to stay away from formal programming with its stricter academic and professional standards. The problem of training teachers for lifelong learning programming remains unaddressed, but this can be overcome in time, particularly if these institutions reduce their reliance on teachers trained and developed within the formal system. It is expected that a *Private Education Law*, to be issued in late 1997, will provide support and encouragement for the private and semi-private sectors.

Although the distinction between the formal system of schooling and the broader efforts of private and semi-private lifelong learning institutions as described in this paper will continue to exist, efforts should be made to maximize the benefits of all existing facilities and services. This is particularly important given the funding challenges that face community-based learning programs. Public institutions should voluntarily make their facilities and services available to the community. These include libraries, computer labs, gymnasia, and classrooms. By doing this, public institutions could play a major role in the development of lifelong learning opportunities.

Increasingly, the media needs to be a mechanism for marketing lifelong learning, and all types of lifelong learning should be promoted and delivered through broadcast media with the assistance of broadcast universities and correspondence schools. Compared with the features of formal school education, programs and patterns of lifelong learning are much more flexible and dynamic. Public media, such as television and radio, has the capacity to be the stimulus for distributing learning opportunities widely throughout society, particularly in the PRC where there are large geographic areas to cover with few available services.

Above and beyond the mechanics and rhetoric associated with lifelong learning, there is a strong, sincere and overriding drive for educational development in the PRC. Pressure for change and opportunities, from the society at the grass roots level, is profound, and lifelong learning has emerged as a major force, under difficult circumstances, supporting rapid economic and social development as well as individual fulfilment. Although there has not been a systematic investigation of lifelong learning, nor the development of a formalized structure, it is recognized as the primary tool for facilitating economic and social development in the PRC. As an old saying goes, "never too old to learn". In fact, learning is becoming an exciting lifelong undertaking in the PRC.

REFERENCES

Decisions on adult education reform. (1987). Beijing: People's Education Press.

Education Law. (1995). Beijing: People's Education Press.

Educational statistics yearbook of China. (1996). Beijing: People's Education Press.

Faure, E., Herrera, F., Kaddoura, A., Lopes, H., Petrovosky, A., Rahnema, M., Ward, F. (1972). *Learning to be: The world of education today and tomorrow.* Paris: UNESCO.

Guo, Q. (1996). *Collection on educational legislations, policies, regulations and reports.* Beijing: Beijing Institute Of Broadcasting Publishing House.

Ji, M. (1994). *Higher education reform and development in China.* Beijing: Higher Education Press.

Programs for educational reform and development. (1993). Beijing: People's Education Press.

Xiang, B. (1996). *Studies on educational institutions sponsored by social organizations in China.* Shanghai: Shanghai Academy of Science.

Zhou, B. (1989). *China's education for the 21st century.* Beijing: Higher Education Press.

Michael J. Hatton

Michael Hatton holds a B.A. from McMaster University, an M.S.Ed. from Niagara University, an M.B.A. from York University, and a Ph.D. from the University of Toronto. He is Director of the School of Media Studies at Humber College, Canada's largest college-level media school, and an Associate Member of the graduate faculty of the University of Toronto where he teaches a graduate course in higher education and serves on thesis committees. His research interests include international development and training, organizational behaviour, and corporate governance. His recent publications include *Corporations and Directors: Comparing the Profit and Not-for-Profit Sectors, Cost-Benefit Analysis and Industrial Training* (co-author), and *Exemplary Training Models in Industrial Technology* (editor). In his spare time he enjoys canoeing and is an avid bird watcher with a modest life list.

A Pure Theory of Lifelong Learning[1]

by Michael J. Hatton

Lifelong learning presupposes the development of a learning society, one where active, ongoing learning of a higher order will be broadly embraced. As this learning ethic develops, the demand for increased educational opportunities of all types will be unprecedented. Tiebout's "Pure Theory of Local Expenditures", a seminal paper in finance, has direct application for understanding consumer interests and pressures, the role of the central versus local governments, and the effects of consumer mobility and knowledge. Using his theory as a framework, this paper discusses the emergence of the learning society, coupled with communications technologies and freer trade, and the effects these will have on the formation and delivery of education and educational infrastructure including the blend of public and private sector participation.

TOWARDS A LEARNING SOCIETY

Regardless of whether there is reasonable rational importance for more to be said about lifelong learning, it must be concluded that much more, indeed very much more, will continue to be said. The term has become thematic and evocative; it is raised, praised, discussed, even worshiped, and occasionally, but not for long, discarded, almost every day in the popular press, government documents and academic journals. It has taken on the characteristics of a nondenominational paean, and the proper responses to it are important shibboleths of interest groups and political orientations. It is recognized by most people as a concept of political importance and a factor influencing the political saleability of government roles and levels of expenditures. There is now and will in the future be no avoiding the taking of positions for and against concrete propositions pertaining to lifelong learning and public expenditures.

As with other *truths*, the adoption of lifelong learning into our lives and vocabularies comes with some perils, not the least of which is definitional. What does lifelong learning mean? To whom? When? Clearly, as with many other educational or

---

[1]Pure thought, pure reasoning and pure theory are closely related notions. Aristotle, or the intellectual tradition that bears his name, argued the claim that we can formulate laws of nature by pure thought and that it is not necessary to resort to observation. Immanuel Kant meant by pure reason not much more than we do by "science". Pure theory (of lifelong learning) here means only that the reality of its subject is assumed and can be discretely appreciated, even though it cannot be, nor ever has been, isolated from the contexts in which it has been claimed to exist.

near-educational terms, semantics has not to date been a principal consideration. (After all, as some might say, "this is education, not chemistry.") But surely this should not restrict us from the practice of clearly defining what we mean; rather, it should foster the practice.

In order to better appreciate the difficulties associated with vocabulary in the field of education, let's start with *education* itself. Often, education is used to refer to any experience. Within the experiential framework, education is anything and everything either directly or indirectly enjoyed through the process of living. Seeing the sun, walking in the rain, winning a lottery, making a friend, or listening to a teacher is, within this meaning, education of one sort or another. Or, at the very least, living carries the potential for education. At another time or in another paper, education may be used to refer to business conducted in schools, colleges and universities. Then again, it may be the institutions, or the industry itself. Readers seem proficient at making the adjustment even when, or perhaps because, the term carries potential for such wide variation.

When we move to the subject of *adult education*, or any specialization in education, saying just what we mean and meaning just what we say, should, perhaps, be a less challenging task. Whatever we mean by education, adult education may mean all teaching and learning not directed at children; it may mean adult learning activities not conducted in universities, colleges or professional schools. Adult education may refer to a specific classification of institutions for teaching and learning. Another time it may refer to public policies, or even a cultural climate.

Interestingly, many who address the topic of lifelong learning really mean adult education and perhaps little more. Retraining, upgrading, or further education for those who are past the typical school-leaving age in a society are, for the most part, adult education programs. Irrespective of whether these programs are offered in a community hall, a renovated high school, a mosque or a Toyota factory, it is education for adults, and most often nothing more. Lifelong adult education, or education for adults through the lifespan, merely signifies multiple experiences.

The distinction between education and learning is meaningful in this context. The former may be broadly or narrowly interpreted as a process or as a set of institutions, while the latter is more a product than a process. However, the production of the product is ongoing, and for this reason learning is often confused with process. The very nature of learning and its relationship to life implies that we learn as we live. Lifelong education is a lifespan process, most often associated with institutions. Learning, and lifelong learning especially, are much broader product-oriented concepts. They encompass stock that comes from living or life itself. In this regard, formal education, non-formal education, social and recreational activities and just plain living all play a process role leading to the product of lifelong learning. In effect, lifelong education is the business, and lifelong learning is the product, we expect, of what goes on in that business. To stop learning is to stop living. Ch'i Pai-shih's seal (see Lai, 1973, p. 172), *I shall learn as long as I breathe*, is tautological. It is also a secular metaphysical statement. It expresses an attitude toward life that is in accord with the learning imperatives of an economy that serves the end of more and better consumption.

Lifelong learning has become prominent because factors associated with the development of the information society, including increased competition in the manufacturing and service sectors of our economies and more aggressive and freer trade, have created a need for learning (the products) to be inculcated within all societies more often and more aggressively. More people need to learn more at a higher level in order for economies to grow and remain competitive in the next century (see *Education and the Wealth of Nations*, 1997). Strongly embedded is the notion that more learning of different and various types throughout the lifespan will lead to a better and stronger society overall.

All of this has led to discussions of a "learning society", a paradigm where more active learning of a higher order, much of it related though not exclusively to vocational skill training, will be broadly embraced as a learning ethic throughout the world. This is the notional essence of lifelong learning. Worth emphasising is the fact that although the new learning paradigm has a vocational emphasis when discussed in most papers, it is meant to be far more inclusive. Living becomes an open metaphor for learning.

But what makes these notions different today, when in point of fact education and learning customarily have been portrayed as cure-alls for societal ills? First, there are the drivers of freer trade, higher technology and increased competition. Second, there are opportunities on the near horizon, available through newer communications technologies, that will allow far greater access to educational providers without regard to distance or time, and with a very different cost structure. In short, the need or perceived need for increased educational opportunities, and the resultant learning, is creating unprecedented demand, and supply is likely to be more broadly available with delivery strongly influenced by technology. Thus we move towards a learning society.

TIEBOUT'S THEORY AND THE LEARNING SOCIETY

Education has been typecast as an example of a public good (see Musgrave, 1939; Samuelson, 1954; Tiebout, 1956). Public goods are those where collective consumption takes place, and the enjoyment or consumption by one person does not reduce the enjoyment or consumption by another. Defense and public broadcasting are two common examples. It has been argued that, with public goods, market-type systems fail to deliver the appropriate amount. Voters will be unwilling to reveal their true consumption preferences, and, by understating these, will hope to enjoy the benefits while evading the price.

Charles Tiebout (1956) in his *Pure Theory of Local Expenditures* argued that even if the market does fail with regard to public goods delivered at the central government level, and this remains an opinion under debate, such a failure does not necessarily occur at the local level, at least under certain conditions. Tiebout acknowledged Samuelson's conceptualization of the citizen/taxpayer as consumer. He then gave us a model of local governments as competitive suppliers of goods and services and as tax collectors. Citizens, or consumers/taxpayers, exert pressure on local governments and politicians in part by moving out or moving into jurisdictions. (For this we credit him with the notion of taxpayers "voting with their feet".)

A better way to express epithetically and concisely the serious thinking of Tiebout about ends and means might be: to some extent, politicians and governments must do what their neighbours do, when what their neighbours' politicians and governments do is smarter, more efficient, and more agreeable to their constituents.

Unlike national defense and public radio, education does not necessarily require central government intervention. Indeed, Tiebout points out that there are many public goods which are not delivered by a central government. Fire protection, police services and medical care, as well as education, are not typically associated with a centralized government structure, except perhaps in the smallest of economies where there is little size differential between central and local governments. In fact, within local governments the total dollar value of expenditures is often larger than central government expenditures, particularly if defense is excluded. Also interesting is the fact that local governments vary considerably in terms of the consumption opportunities they provide. For many local governments, education is one of if not the largest single categories of expenditures.

Tiebout's model makes several assumptions, the most important for the purpose of this discussion include: (a) full consumer mobility with no employment-based restrictions; (b) full consumer knowledge of different goods and services available in different communities; and (c) a very large number of communities from which the consumer is free to select. At the time in which Tiebout wrote, the necessity for these assumptions is what made the model a *pure theory*. However, these assumptions, in the face of changes that may be taking place faster than the effects can be reasonably assimilated, may be outdated, and the focal application to education and lifelong learning may only now be appreciated.

When workers must walk to work because they lack basic transportation, the number of choices (freedom) they experience in their lives is limited. When workers get bicycles, choice (freedom) expands dramatically. With the establishment of a basic public transport system, choice (freedom) increases again and even more dramatically. For some, the arrival of personal access to automobiles signals the definitive freedom. However, in all these contexts, a basic structural element remains intact: the worker/consumer must go to the job, the goods, and the services. In the educational context, the consumer goes to the school, to the college or to the university. Learning remains linked to a limited number of fixed-place educational institutions, and while today's consumer experiences some freedom, there is much more to be had.

It is the development of an information society that will result in much greater consumer freedom, a degree of freedom that will seriously challenge central governments, in many ways, for reasons illustrated by Tiebout's theory. Tiebout pointed out, perhaps indirectly, that central governments play a lesser role in the provision of goods and services than might be widely appreciated, and that this is good. The needs of consumers vary, they are not cut from the same cloth, and indeed the variation is extreme. From this comes the notion that the more goods and services provided by the central government, the fewer the choices, and therefore there is less freedom available to the consumer. The more access the consumer has to different bundles of goods and services offered by local governments, the more choices, and hence freedom, enjoyed by the consumer.

The information society, one where electronic communication on an unprecedented scale will provide global access to information and services, is at the doorstep. National barriers, including trade tariffs, which have inhibited freedom in the past, will fall. Some barriers will fall slower than others, but they will fall, everywhere, and sooner rather than later. Regardless, in this decade central governments have continued in various ways to control electronic communications, and some are developing grand schemes to build new barriers in an attempt to prevent the consumer from becoming freer. But the fact remains, as the information society emerges consumers will increasingly experience Tiebout's key assumptions as realities, and education and learning, process and product, will be at the heart of much of this.

Consumer mobility, Tiebout's first assumption, will soon be defined very differently. What matters is not so much the physical ability of the consumer to move, but rather the ability of the consumer to reach out electronically for the purpose of consumption, public and otherwise. Increasingly consumers are doing so without regard to national boundaries. The second assumption, full consumer knowledge, is aided and abetted through the same means. Not only is the consumer increasingly aware of options, but the ability to sift through choices and opportunities is being nourished through electronic channels. The third assumption, having a large number of communities from which the consumer is free to select, is addressed through electronic means and the increasing inability of governments to direct consumer mobility. Access to a world of communities and commodities, including education, is at the doorstep.

The role of central governments is being challenged quite broadly as consumers question, often in a micro sense, what value they deliver. Witness the recent order emerging in Asia and Europe as the strong centrally directed Union of Soviet Socialist Republics disappeared almost overnight. Who can argue that there will *always* be a United Kingdom? Or a united Canada or a united U.S.A.? Though discussions of this sort are quite sensitive, it should be said, and said without equivocation, that evidence suggests an evolutionary tendency towards greater power and autonomy vested within smaller communities which deliver discrete packages of benefits to their members. Directly or indirectly, the question is being asked with more frequency, "what do central governments provide, and at what cost?" Where central governments cost more (usually in the form of taxes) and deliver or are perceived to deliver less, their value will be challenged, and increasingly so as consumers have access to other suppliers. The question of what value large, central governments bring to education generally, and lifelong learning in particular, and at what cost is a natural outcome of the broader discussion.

LOCAL GOVERNMENTS AND THEIR INSTITUTIONS

Local governments in most economies are most directly responsible for delivering, though not necessarily structuring, education. However, there are two key issues to examine, the first being the potential for competition *between* local governments including their institutions, and the second being the potential for increasing competition between local governments and the private sector, particularly in light of borderless economies. This section of the paper examines the first of these.

When a consumer elects to live in one community, rather than another community, some degree of competition is involved. Communities need to offer not only an attractive grouping of goods and services, but must do so in an efficient manner. Assuming reasonable mobility, consumers will elect to live and pay taxes in the community which delivers the preferred goods and services at the lowest cost. Accordingly, there will be efficiencies related to community size, and communities will attempt to attract or deflect new residents in an effort to reach the optimal size.

Local governments and the communities they represent act much like corporations, and indeed some are. The primary goal of a corporation is to survive, while the secondary goal is to grow and increase autonomy. In this context, autonomy is the ability to act upon and influence different issues and enterprises, and is directly related to available resources including the size of the budget. Central governments are most powerful within their jurisdictions because they make laws. However, outside their jurisdictions they are competitors with other governments. Some are more powerful than others, just as some local governments are more powerful than others, but a central government on the regional or world stage is rarely sovereign; it must compete. Local governments compete in a similar manner, but the premise developed here is that they are about to do so in greater numbers and in more ways than ever before.

Competition between local governments is keen and well illustrated within and between Canada and the United States. Suburban tax districts compete with core areas in large cities. Each offers different choices in lifestyle and different tax burdens. Each carves out a niche, presenting the best of what it has to offer. Rural communities in particular actively intervene in the market process to recruit from certain occupational groups, doctors being an obvious case, in order to provide the grouping of goods and services that makes for a desirable community. Small and rural communities also have difficulty maintaining a post-secondary educational infrastructure. Post-secondary educational opportunities, in a large or small community, attract potential residents, particularly those with children. By comparison, older residents have less interest in paying for a fully developed educational infrastructure.

Local governments may purchase services rather than developing infrastructure. The fact is, local governments are increasingly subject to the reality that consumers have increased mobility. If a community is not providing goods and services which are preferred, and at a competitive price, people will move. Competition is increasingly keen. In this respect it is interesting to note recent cross-border recruiting between the United States and Canada. Toronto area nursing schools in particular have become targets for U.S. recruiters. Local governments in parts of Arizona, California and Florida actively recruit nurses, clearly determined to purchase the product rather than develop the educational infrastructure. Why? Tiebout would have us conclude that this approach is more cost effective and that the purchase of services, rather than the development of that component of an educational infrastructure, is part of the unique bundle of goods and services offered by these communities. In the case of retirement communities in the southern U.S., it makes sense for them to buy graduates rather than build schools.

The notion of purchasing already-trained professionals is in some ways no different than purchasing any other commodity such as electricity, water and waste disposal service from a neighbouring jurisdiction. There is one way, however, in which it can be quite different. Local governments in Arizona are not paying Toronto for nurses, a commodity which has cost Toronto and Ontario taxpayers dearly. During their training, the nurses were heavily subsidized both by the city and province. Now they are moving to another jurisdiction before any benefits accrue to the public that subsidized the training. Actual costs and benefits are not easily quantifiable, but in a broad context it is clear that local governments in Arizona are paying a price well below cost for this resource.

Students from one jurisdiction (taxation area) receiving benefits in another has sometimes been addressed through differential tuition fees. The student who studies in New York, but who resides or has resided in Florida, pays out-of-state tuition fees. Similarly, the student who lives in British Columbia and who wishes to study in Arizona will pay a premium. The rationale for this is twofold. First, it is assumed that neither the student nor the student's parents have paid taxes to support the development of the educational infrastructure, and it is also probable that on graduation the student will return home or move elsewhere. In the past, this scheme worked reasonably well, and in those jurisdictions where tuition differentials didn't reflect actual costs it may be that other benefits accrued. In the information society, all of this will be questioned for a variety of reasons, not the least of which is the fact that students may not find it necessary to travel to Toronto, or any other city, in order to make use of the educational resources hosted by that city.

But what of the locally-funded public institutions themselves? These are, or may be considered, extensions of local governments. They are subsidized in whole or in part, directly or indirectly, by regional or local governments rather than central government. Schools, colleges and universities are included in this grouping, and the issues at hand relate directly to lifelong learning.

Locally-funded public institutions have been sheltered from the open market system to varying degrees by geography, trade barriers, public subsidies and, in some cases, monopoly or near-monopoly privileges. Schools, colleges and universities have for the most part played to a home-grown market. Quite recently, local institutions, particularly those which are in the education business, have begun to realize that the consumer is about to be faced with many more opportunities and choices than ever before. Interactive multimedia programming will bring the best educational opportunities from around the world to the consumer's doorstep. How will local schools, particularly those at the post-secondary level, respond?

Many colleges and universities are attempting to acquire a foothold in what is thought to be a quickly evolving and open market for higher education where distance will lose its meaning. At this stage, these institutions are for the most part designing courses and programs for electronic delivery, typically via the internet and world wide web. Arguments which support the early development of electronic course offerings, even before the environment is fully understood or the technology completely developed, are based on territorial imperatives and market axioms. Generally, colleges and universities see the potential for other institutions to poach students, and the development of electronically delivered programs is in most cases a defensive rather than an offensive competitive manoeuvre. The market axiom is that it is much easier to hold or protect market share than steal market share. Hence, the belief is that the first institutions into the market will have an edge.

That having been said, it is difficult to appreciate just how challenging the competitive environment is going to be for publicly-funded educational institutions. To begin with, in an electronically-based information society, students will be able to access a wide range of institutions. Why study at a local college if it becomes possible to enrol at Stanford, the University of Hong Kong, or the National University of Singapore? This is not to suggest that all or even many first-tier institutions will open enrolment since most of the prestige that accrues to the top institutions comes from their ability to exclude. Regardless, all it will take is for a few of the foremost institutions to open enrolment in order to generate a very different competitive environment for local institutions.

In this climate, smaller local institutions may be best advised to focus on the unique strengths they bring to the community and community education, rather than try to compete in the electronic environment with larger well-known institutions. Observation, however, suggests that hard environmental analysis is not widely adopted by smaller local institutions. For the most part these institutions have little experience in a competitive market, and minimal knowledge of marginal costs and market influences. Currently, some are underpricing products and services in order to buy market share with a view to convincing the local community of their institutional importance through large enrolments regardless of where students come from. These institutions may feel that if they lose local students to other institutions, the community will question the necessity for any local support. In the United States, where public community colleges are supported by local tax dollars and governed by locally selected or elected boards, the challenges will be the greatest.

Returning to Tiebout's model, it is clear that market pressures will be exerted on local governments and hence on locally-funded public institutions. Questions will be asked as to why communities should support local schools if higher education in particular can be delivered more effectively and efficiently from elsewhere. Similarly, it will be asked why local taxpayers are supporting local colleges if a significant portion of the benefit is being consumed by others. The national and regional imperatives of "buying locally" will be set aside, if in fact they ever truly existed. In this environment, smaller, second- and third-tier colleges are in danger of becoming anachronisms, particularly if they attempt to challenge first-tier institutions in the international marketplace.

PRIVATE SECTOR COMPETITION

As regulatory walls fall, trade and competition becomes freer, and consumer mobility increases, local governments will be pressured to behave more like rational consumers rather than monopoly producers. They will seek to purchase goods and services on behalf of taxpayers from a wider variety of suppliers, and under Tiebout's model this will lead to dramatically increased options for consumers. For a time, some local governments will be able to act like and compete with private producers, supplying goods and services in which they have a competitive position to other governments and directly to consumers in order to boost revenues and affect the tax base. However, the degree to which local governments will be able to effectively compete in the longer term is likely to be limited. In time, governments at all levels will do less, more effectively. The private sector will do more, more efficiently.

The private sector, then, will crowd the marketplace on a broader, regional and perhaps even global scale pushing government-provided goods and services aside. Consumers generally will question why taxes are paid to any government for collective consumption when those same services can be purchased more inexpensively in the quantity and of the quality demanded by individual consumers. In effect, consumers will question why they would consume precisely what their neighbours consume when they are able to buy directly and get exactly what they prefer, or not buy at all. Generally, the freer and electronically enhanced marketplace will be a far more personalized consumption environment for consumers.

Education broadly, and post-secondary education particularly, is one of the services collectively consumed by taxpayers which will be dramatically altered by market forces including communications technologies and freer trade. Currently, there is an interesting variety within different economies in so far as public and private consumption of post-secondary education is concerned. In East Asia, Hong Kong, Singapore and Malaysia for example, the most prestigious post-secondary institutions are publicly supported colleges and universities. In the United States, the reverse is true. There, the most prestigious colleges and universities are private. In Canada, there are relatively few private institutions. Though most universities and some colleges in Canada hold their own charters, they are almost entirely publicly-funded. The degree of government support along with government legislation has dissuaded private sector competition. The private versus public mix, as well as different status levels, will affect the ways in which these institutions adapt to the more competitive environment.

In the current environment, external providers of services, including education, have been restricted from entry by geography and, in some cases, by law. However, in the case of education, which is a knowledge-based product, governments, central and local, will have great difficulty preventing the entry of local, regional, national and even international providers as the information society takes hold. Earlier in this paper mention was made of education being a public good, one where consumer preferences are difficult to determine and, hence, where there is rationale for government intervention. The environment of the next decade will likely provide ample evidence to contradict this belief.

Education is a superior good. As such, when disposable income increases, peoples' expenditures on education, particularly for their children, increase at a disproportionately faster rate. Education is a commodity that can be provided through a market system, and this is the way in which higher education is currently delivered throughout much of the world, Canada being an exception. Consumers will pay for access to education and training in the private sector, even when it may be available in part through publicly-financed programming, particularly when the demand exceeds the supply available from publicly-supported institutions. Similarly, the private sector demonstrates much greater propensity to fund on-the-job and off-the-job training when the public sector is not providing it. Arguments that the market fails when private firms engage in worker training have been contradicted (see *Schools brief: Investing in people*, pp. 85-86).

The sum of this discussion posits that private sector delivery of education in particular will increase dramatically as technology evolves, trade becomes freer, and the learning society develops. Consumers who want to learn will find ways of doing so, both internal and external to the traditional educational establishment. Students will increasingly cross national boundaries both to avoid particular systems as well as to attend specific opportunities. As the demand for learning opportunities increases dramatically within the context of the learning society, no government and no set of publicly sponsored institutions will be able to adequately respond. Consumers will, in the end, demand greater choice and the right to make their own consumption decisions, and governments will be right when they decide to put these decisions in the hands of consumers.

TIEBOUT'S THEORY AND LIFELONG LEARNING

Tiebout's theory, about which much has been written (see for example, Ellickson, 1970; Hamilton, 1975; Bucovetsky, 1982; Yinger, 1982), has been hotly debated within its conceptual framework. In these pages, it has been argued that in a global economy Tiebout's theory will become increasingly practical under the influences of freer trade, technological evolution, and the arrival of the learning society. Central governments and, more importantly, local governments will be less inclined to produce and deliver goods and services and more inclined to either purchase on behalf of consumers or, better still, leave the consumption decision entirely in the hands of consumers. Governments and the private sector will be increasingly swayed by more mobile consumers who can reach out electronically in order to broaden consumption decisions.

In many economies collective consumption at the local government level far exceeds that which takes place at the central government level. In addition, costs associated with education are often the single largest consumption element at the local government level. Under Tiebout's model, local governments provide a variety of consumption options related to education. Full consumer mobility, extensive consumer knowledge and a large number of communities make the model consumer reactive. To date, these variables and the model have been pure or conceptual only. However, the development of a lifelong learning ethic will create demand, which when coupled with technology and freer trade, will result in the private sector playing a greatly increased role in the delivery of education to meet the quantitative and qualitative demand for lifelong learning. The effect will be to reduce the role of local governments in one of the largest consumption decisions, and hence the degree to which each can distinguish itself. This will further increase pressure for local governments to compete with each other and move Tiebout's model closer to reality.

The future of publicly-funded educational institutions, particularly those with a focus on higher education, in an era characterised by an entrenched lifelong learning ethic, is interesting to consider. First, there will be more institutions, many of them private, and a variety of programming of all types and all levels will be demanded and made available. This will not only result in increased competition and have taxpayers questioning why the public sector shouldn't be less involved, or not at all, but it will also query the broader role of continuing and higher education. Currently, much of what higher education does is to exclude. Through exclusion institutions limit entry into occupations and social status, and are mostly graded on this ability to exclude. The most exclusive institutions of them, and those that want to be exclusive, may not join the lifelong learning path. Instead, some may continue to be what they are, schools for the few rather than schools for the many. Continuing in this track, they run the risk that in a lifelong learning environment more students will discover earlier that, "Four years was enough of Harvard. I still had a lot to learn, but had been given the liberating notion that now I could teach myself" (John Updike, quoted in Simpson, 1988, p. 121). Community colleges and other publicly-funded "access" institutions have been described as inclusive, but in reality are simply less exclusive. In a freer environment they will face vigorous and dynamic challenges. Will they carve out new niches? Can they become entrepreneurial? Will they manage to be inclusive and competitive?

The Scottish statesman Henry Brougham said that, "Education makes a people easy to lead, but difficult to drive; easy to govern, but impossible to enslave" (Vitullo-Martin & Moskin, 1994, p. 99). Perhaps he was confusing education with learning? Ultimately, in a society characterised by lifelong learning, knowledgeable and mobile consumers will shake and shape educational institutions, and those which have been sheltered from the marketplace will be challenged as never before.

REFERENCES

Bucovetsky, S. (1982, February). Inequality in the local public sector. *Journal of Political Economy, 90*, 128-145.

Education and the wealth of nations. (1997, March 29). *The Economist, 342*(8010), 15-16.

Ellickson, B. (1970). *Metropolitan residential location and the public sector.* Unpublished doctoral dissertation, Massachusetts Institute of Technology, Boston.

Hamilton, B. (1975, June). Zoning and property taxation in a system of local governments. *Urban Studies, 12,* 205-211.

Lai, T. C. (1973). *Ch'i Pai Shih.* Hong Kong: Swindon.

Musgrave, R. (1939, February). The voluntary exchange theory of public economy. *Quarterly Journal of Economics, LII*, 213-217.

Samuelson, P. (1954, November). The pure theory of public expenditures. *Review of Economics and Statistics, XXXVI*(4), 387-389.

Schools brief: Investing in people. (1994, March 26th). *The Economist, 330*(7856), 85-86.

Simpson, J. (1988). *Simpson's contemporary quotations.* New York: Houghton Mifflin.

Tiebout, C. M. (1956, October). A pure theory of local expenditures. *Journal of Political Economy, 64*, 416-424.

Vitullo-Martin, J. & Moskin, J. (1994). *Executive's book of quotations.* New York: Oxford University Press.

Yinger, J. (1982, October). Capitalization and the theory of local public finance. *Journal of Political Economy, 90*, 917-943.